Wireless Java™ Programming with Java™ 2 Micro Edition

Yu Feng and Jun Zhu

201 West 103rd St., Indianapolis, Indiana, 46290 USA

Wireless Java™ Programming with Java™ 2 Micro Edition

International Standard Book Number: 0-672-32135-1

Library of Congress Catalog Card Number: 2001086072

Printed in the United States of America

First Printing: June 2001

04   03   02   01   4   3   2   1

Trademarks

Warning and Disclaimer

EXECUTIVE EDITOR
Michael Stephens

ACQUISITIONS EDITOR
Carol Ackerman

DEVELOPMENT EDITOR
Tiffany Taylor

MANAGING EDITOR
Matt Purcell

PROJECT EDITOR
Christina Smith

COPY EDITOR
Kim Cofer

INDEXER
Eric Schroeder

PROOFREADER
Benjamin Berg

TECHNICAL EDITOR
David Fox

TEAM COORDINATOR
Lynne Williams

INTERIOR DESIGNER
Anne Jones

COVER DESIGNER
Aren Howell

Contents at a Glance

Contents

3 Java Wireless Programming Basics 33

About the Authors

Yu Feng is currently an independent consultant specializing in Java technologies such as J2ME, J2EE and object-oriented software development. His J2ME application "MotoShop" won the Grand Prize in the Motorola J2ME Virtual Developer Contest in August 2000.

Before authoring this book, Yu Feng was the chief architect at iNetProfit, Inc., located in Austin, Texas for two years. Prior to iNetProfit, he was a Java and database consultant. Yu Feng has a master's degree in computer science from the University of Texas in Austin and B.S. degree in physics from Peking University.

Dr. Jun Zhu is a research scientist. He has been working with Java technology since 1996. His work is focused on advanced image processing and data mining technology. Dr. Zhu has a Ph.D. in biomedical science and a master's degree in computer science from SUNY at Albany and a bachelor of engineering degree in electrical engineering from Tsinghua University.

Dedication

To Dongling, for her love and support.

To my parents, for their encouragement and inspiration.

—Yu Feng

Dedicated to my wife and my parents.

—Jun Zhu

Acknowledgements

We would like to thank all the fine professionals at Sams for their efforts helping us put this book together. The book would not be possible without Carol Ackerman, Christina Smith, Kim Cofer, and Katie Robinson.

Special thanks to Tiffany Taylor for enduring our not-so-great English and doing such a wonderful job of reviewing and editing this book.

Special thanks to David Fox for adding so much value to this book with his technical insights and perspectives.

We would also like to thank Michael Stephens for giving us the exciting opportunity to write this book. It has been fun and we really enjoyed it.

Tell Us What You Think!

As the reader of this book, *you* are our most important critic and commentator. We value your opinion and want to know what we're doing right, what we could do better, what areas you'd like to see us publish in, and any other words of wisdom you're willing to pass our way.

As an executive editor for Sams Publishing, I welcome your comments. You can fax, e-mail, or write me directly to let me know what you did or didn't like about this book—as well as what we can do to make our books stronger.

Please note that I cannot help you with technical problems related to the topic of this book, and that due to the high volume of mail I receive, I might not be able to reply to every message.

When you write, please be sure to include this book's title and authors' names as well as your name and phone or fax number. I will carefully review your comments and share them with the authors and editors who worked on the book.

Fax: 317-581-4770

E-mail: feedback@samspublishing.com

Mail: Michael Stephens
           Executive Editor
           Sams Publishing
           201 West 103rd Street
           Indianapolis, IN 46290 USA

Introduction

The use of wireless devices such as cellular phones and two-way pagers has undergone tremendous growth over the past few years. According to a recent study, there will be one billion wireless subscribers worldwide by 2004. As the wireless market matures, people will demand more advanced reliable applications. Sun and a group of wireless industry leaders such as Motorola, Nokia, and Palm defined a new set of standards called Java 2 Micro Edition (J2ME) to help develop and deploy the next generation wireless applications that can change the way people live and the way they do business.

J2ME was first introduced at the JavaOne Conference in 1999. It is the edition of the Java 2 platform targeted at consumer electronics and embedded devices. In J2ME, the Connected Limited Device Configuration (CLDC) and the Mobile Information Device Profile (MIDP) are specifically designed for the wireless devices.

The purpose of this book is to help you to understand the concepts of J2ME technology, specifically the CLDC and MIDP, and to teach you how to develop wireless applications using J2ME's CLDC and MIDP. We try to reach this goal by progressively guiding you through all the key aspects of application programming in J2ME MIDP with easy-to-understand examples.

Audience

Since Sun's recent release of J2ME, J2ME technology has generated huge interest among the developer community. More than 500 companies signed up to work with J2ME. Major wireless players such as Motorola, Research in Motion, Palm, and LG Telecom have already begun supporting J2ME on their wireless devices. More and more people are realizing the exciting opportunities in application development by leveraging J2ME technology.

This book is applicable to application developers who have some previous experience with Java and who want to jump-start their wireless application development efforts using J2ME technology.

We assume you at least understand the syntax and basic concepts of Java technology. If you have written some Java programs using J2SE or J2EE, it will help you go through this book and focus more on J2ME-specific parts. If you are not familiar with Java, there are a lot of tutorials and books that teach how to write programs in Java. We don't assume you have any knowledge of the J2ME technology or any experience in application development for wireless devices. Throughout this book, we assume readers are motivated to build the next generation wireless application by leveraging the J2ME technology.

The goal of this book is simple: to help developers understand J2ME MIDP and be able to write applications quickly. We are also developers who write applications for various platforms and are fully aware of the issues and challenges that developers face in their development process. So we focus on what is practical and useful to the application developers. This book comes with practical sample programs that can be applied in real-world development.

The Structure of This Book

This book is organized into three parts.

The first part of this book introduces you to the basic concepts and environments of CLDC and MIDP in J2ME. It has four chapters.

The second part of this book teaches you how to develop applications for wireless devices using J2ME MIDP. It has eight chapters.

The third part contains appendixes with resources and more information about some of the topics covered in this book.

Part I: Getting Started

Chapter 1, "Introduction to Wireless Application Development," gives a brief overview of wireless application development, compares the J2ME technology with the WAP and i-Mode technologies, and explains why J2ME is ideal for developing more sophisticated applications for wireless devices.

Chapter 2, "Java for Wireless Devices," begins by explaining the architecture of the Java 2 platform and where J2ME fits in the architecture. It then takes a look at the building blocks of J2ME, including the configurations and profiles. At the end, it takes you through the steps to set up the two J2ME MIDP programming environments: Sun's Wireless Toolkit and Motorola's CodeWarrior for Java (MotoSDK).

Chapter 3, "Java Wireless Programming Basics," explains the basics of J2ME MIDP application (MIDlet), its life cycle, and the concepts of Application Management Software. It also discusses the Java class libraries of CLDC and MIDP, the limitations of CLDC and KVM, and the internationalization and cross-device development issues using CLDC/MIDP class libraries. In this chapter, the first MIDlet example, HelloWorld, is shown to demonstrate the basics of J2ME MIDP programming.

Chapter 4, "Packaging and Deploying Java Wireless Applications," discusses the packaging and deployment of J2ME MIDP applications. It gives detailed explanations on the concepts of a MIDlet suite, manifest, application descriptor, and the Over-the-Air (OTA) MIDlet deployment. It also shows you how to streamline the packaging and deploying processes using the IDE provided by Sun's Wireless Toolkit and Forte for Java.

Part II: Developing Wireless Applications Using Java

Chapter 5, "Central Components of the UI for Wireless Devices," discusses the two central components of UI programming in a MIDlet: the `Displayable` class and the event-handling model.

Chapter 6, "Using High-Level APIs in UI Development," focuses on the MIDP GUI programming using the high-level GUI components such as `Screen`, `List`, `Textbox`, `Alert`, `Form`, and `Item`. It also discusses the high-level event-handling model including `Command` events and `ItemStateChanged` events. A sample MIDlet application, `MobileScheduler`, is used throughout the chapter to demonstrate how to use these high-level GUI components.

Chapter 7, "Using Low-Level APIs in UI Development," focuses on MIDP GUI programming using the low-level GUI API classes such as `Canvas` and `Graphics`. It also discusses the low-level event-handling methods such as `keyPressed()`, `PointerDragged()`, `paint()`, and so on. To demonstrate how to use these low-level GUI APIs, a schedule viewer with low-level GUI components is added to the `MobileScheduler` sample program in this chapter.

Chapter 8, "Persistent Storage," discusses how to use MIDP's persistent storage— `RecordStore`—with your MIDlet applications. To demonstrate how to use the `RecordStore` class to store and retrieve your data locally, enhanced functionality with persistent storage is added to the `MobileScheduler` sample program in this chapter.

Chapter 9, "Basic Network Programming in J2ME MIDP," explains the basics of network programming with J2ME MIDP and the concept of the Generic Connection framework. It also gives sample MIDlets to demonstrate how to use different types of communication such as sockets, datagrams, and http with your applications.

Chapter 10, "Using XML in Wireless Applications," presents three small footprint XML parsers that are suitable for MIDlet applications: TinyXML, NanoXML, and Ælfred. XML plays an important part in developing enterprise wireless applications. Examples of how to use the different parsing interfaces (event-based and tree-based) from these parsers are given in this chapter as well.

Chapter 11, "A Complete Example: MotoShop," dissects an intelligent comparison shopping application: `MotoShop`, the grand prize winner of Motorola's J2ME Virtual Developer Contest. It explains the different components in full detail including the GUI, networking, XML handling, and Java servlet on the server side.

Chapter 12, "Data Synchronization for Wireless Applications," introduces SyncML, an XML-based data synchronization standard. It demonstrates how to effectively take advantage of this standard to synchronize data with other wireless applications and Internet data portals by adding a data synchronization component to the `MobileScheduler`.

Part III: Appendixes

Appendix A, "CLDC Class Libraries," illustrates the class hierarchy of the CLDC library.

Appendix B, "MIDP Class Libraries," illustrates the class hierarchy of the MIDP library.

In Appendix C, "Resource Links," you will find a list of useful links that are related to J2ME.

Appendix D, "NTT DoCoMo's Java for i-Mode," gives a basic overview of how to go about developing J2ME applications for the NTT DoCoMo's Java enabled phones.

Web Site

You can download the source code for the examples presented in this book from www.samspublishing.com. When you reach that page, enter this book's ISBN number (0672321351) in the search box to access information about the book and a Source Code link. In addition, we set up a companion Web site for this book at http://www.webyu.com/bookj2me/ that contains the source code files and links to other Web sites where you can find useful wireless programming resources. You can also ask questions about this book or J2ME programming through the form we provide at the sites.

Getting Started

Introduction to Wireless Application Development

CHAPTER

1

IN THIS CHAPTER

Introduction

For the last couple of years, the wireless industry has been experiencing tremendous growth. According to a recent study, the total number of wireless subscribers reached 200 million worldwide in the year 2000, and will reach around 1 billion by late 2003. This is a pretty big number compared to the PC installed base of around 350 million worldwide in early 2000. This growth is only going to be enhanced by the 3G wireless broadband network deployment. The third-generation wireless system (3G) is the next-generation packet-based wireless network with greater bandwidth (384K–2Mbps, compared to 2G's 19.2Kbps). The increasing bandwidth will not only provide higher call volume, but also make high-quality audio/video data services possible. Europe and Japan are starting to deploy the 3G network this year. U.S. companies will begin deploying 3G around 2003. New 3G systems will trigger an explosion in wireless Internet and data applications.

Wireless devices are becoming more and more intelligent and powerful and are providing a new notion of communication that we could once only imagine. These connected and intelligent devices are becoming increasingly important in our distributed computing environment.

Today, people enjoy the convenience of accessing real-time information such as news, stock quotes, and weather on the Internet right from their cell phones or PDAs. Most of these wireless applications are powered by technologies such as Wireless Application Protocol (WAP) and i-Mode. As the wireless industry becomes more mature with the increasing bandwidth of wireless networks and the increasing processing power of wireless devices, people will no longer be satisfied only with surfing the Internet from their cell phones. They will demand more interactive and personalized wireless applications that can significantly improve their lifestyles and greatly simplify the way they conduct business.

Java 2 Micro Edition (J2ME) is the solution to these challenges. This chapter first talks about existing wireless applications based on WAP and their limitations. It then introduces the J2ME technology and talks about how J2ME will help you develop the next generation of wireless applications.

WAP and i-Mode

WAP and i-Mode are the two dominant technologies that allow users to access to the Internet from their cell phones. WAP technology has been widely adopted by wireless carriers in Europe and the U.S., whereas i-Mode is very popular in Asia.

The History of WAP

Phone.com (now Open Wave), a merged venture with Software.com, first introduced WAP in 1995. WAP is an open standard that enables easy delivery of information and services to mobile users.

WAP was intended to address the need to access the Internet from handheld devices such as cellular phones and PDAs. It defines a set of standard components that enable communication between mobile terminals and network servers, including the WAP programming model, WAP communication protocol, Wireless Markup Language (WML), WMLScript scripting language, and micro-browser. WAP has received wide support in the wireless industry. Currently, several million subscribers worldwide use WAP-enabled cell phones to access the Internet.

WML is a markup language similar to HTML. WMLScript is a scripting language that extends the computational capabilities of WML. A micro-browser that resides on wireless devices can interpret WML and WMLScript and present content to users. Users have been using WAP to shop, get weather information, trade stocks, and more.

You can find more information about WAP at `http://www.wapforum.com`.

The History of i-Mode

i-Mode was first introduced by the Japanese company NTT DoCoMo. This technology competes with WAP. It offers a similar mechanism to allow users to access the Internet from their wireless devices over a packet-switched network. As of December 2000, about 16 million people use i-Mode–enabled cell phones to access the Internet. The majority of i-Mode users are in Japan and other Asian countries.

i-Mode comes with its own markup language, compact HTML (cHTML), which is in part a subset of ordinary HTML plus some of NTT's proprietary tags or characters such as symbols for joy, kisses, love, sadness, telephone, Shinkansen train, and so on. Because cHTML is a subset of HTML, i-Mode pages can also be viewed by using a regular Web browser. i-Mode phones come with a mini-browser that allows users to access Web content written with cHTML.

You can find more information about i-Mode at `http://www.nttdocomo.com/i/index.html`.

Limitations

Both the WAP technology and the i-Mode technology are comparable to HTML and Web browsers on desktop computers. They provide the platform for delivering information content to wireless devices.

However, WAP and i-Mode are limited in some ways, including lack of security, poor user interfaces, and the requirement of constant airtime for standalone or offline operations. As the wireless industry matures, users demand more secure wireless applications for mobile commerce transactions, more interactive applications such as video games, and more sophisticated applications for client/server enterprise applications.

Java 2 Micro Edition is designed to meet these challenges.

Java 2 Micro Edition

After introducing the Java 2 Standard Edition (J2SE) and the Java 2 Enterprise Edition (J2EE), Sun recently added the Java 2 Micro Edition to the Java 2 platform. J2ME is designed to specifically target consumer devices and electronic appliances, including wireless devices such as cell phones and Palm PDAs.

J2ME provides several benefits for wireless application development.

Platform Independence

Wireless devices vary from each other in shape and functionality. Most of the existing on-device applications for wireless devices were developed using the proprietary system libraries provided by the manufacturer. The programming languages range from C, C++, and Visual Basic to proprietary scripting languages. Applications written for one device will not execute on other devices.

J2ME extends the original "Write Once, Run Anywhere" design philosophy to the wireless world. Wireless applications developed using Java can be run on different devices from different vendors. It greatly improves the program's portability.

Simple Programming Language

Java technology can save development time and cost and thus considerably improve productivity. This factor is particularly critical in today's fast-paced, highly competitive market.

Rich Network Functionality

Wireless applications by nature are network oriented and provide the user with constant communication to the outside world anywhere, anytime. Java is designed with network capabilities in mind; it provides a rich set of network libraries that makes writing network programs much easier.

Built-in Security Model

Java provides several levels of security, from class loader and bytecode verifier to Security Manager, which can protect client systems from untrustworthy programs. Java also provides extended security APIs for securely transforming content over the Web. This approach allows safer transactions for mobile commerce applications and financial applications.

Dynamic Application Deployment

Most of the existing applications on wireless devices are built-in, fixed-feature applications. It is very difficult to upgrade and install new applications without getting the manufacturer involved. J2ME provides a dynamic deployment mechanism that allows applications to be downloaded and installed onto devices over the wireless network. This mechanism is similar to executing a Java applet from your Web browser. This dynamic application deployment not only provides a cost-effective way for vendors and developers to distribute software products, but it also allows users to download applications on demand and personalize their on-device applications dynamically.

Distributed Computing

Java is especially popular when the Internet is the main platform for an application. Java is the de facto first choice for building Web applications. Applications developed using J2ME can be easily integrated with J2EE, which provides backend support to deliver enterprise wireless applications. Wireless applications by nature are thin client. The strong XML support in Java makes client/server or transaction-based applications feasible on the wireless devices.

Graphical User Interface

Just like the user interface support in J2SE, J2ME comes with a rich set of user interface and event handling class libraries that make the most of the limited display space on wireless devices. This user interface support makes sophisticated video games and complex entertainment applications feasible on wireless devices.

Developer Community

The good news for wireless device manufacturers is that by opening their development platform to the Java community, they have gained access to 2.5 million Java talents.

J2ME is designed to support a variety of small devices. To support this wide range of devices, J2ME defines different sets of class libraries and runtime environments for various categories of devices with similar capabilities. For example, wireless devices such as cell phones and two-way pagers are categorized as a group called Mobile Information Devices (MID). This book is intended to be a programming guide for developing wireless applications for this group of devices.

The Future

Even though J2ME brings all these benefits to wireless application development, it is not going to replace the WAP and i-Mode technologies. They are complementary technologies, very much like the Web browsing technology that coexists with desktop Java applications. In the future, the WAP and i-Mode technologies will continue to enjoy their successes in content delivery. As the technologies evolve, we will see increasingly rich media content delivered to wireless devices.

J2ME for wireless applications is still in its infancy. But it will play an increasingly important role in wireless application development as the technology matures. Integration with other existing Java technologies such as J2EE, Java Messaging Service, Remote Message Interface (RMI), and Jini will enable Java developers to take full advantage of Java in the wireless world.

More and more wireless vendors are beginning to support or already support J2ME on their wireless devices. These vendors include Motorola, Research in Motion, NTT DoCoMo, LG Telecom, Nokia, Ericsson, and others. Application development for these wireless devices will be in great demand for the next couple years.

Summary

This chapter briefly discussed existing wireless technologies such as WAP and i-Mode, and explained their limitations. It also introduced J2ME, and explained why it is a good fit for developing more sophisticated wireless applications. In the following chapters, you will learn how to use J2ME's class libraries to develop applications for wireless devices.

Java for Wireless Devices

IN THIS CHAPTER

Overview

The Java 2 Micro Edition (J2ME) is a new member of the Java 2 platform, added a little more than a year ago. It enables a new generation of applications for consumer electronics and embedded devices. J2ME's Connected Limited Device Configuration (CLDC) and Mobile Information Device Profile (MIDP) provide a portable and extensible platform for developing wireless applications for small mobile devices, mainly cellular phones and two-way pagers.

This chapter looks at the big picture of the Java 2 platform, how J2ME fits in the picture, and the building blocks of J2ME.

Sun's J2ME Wireless Toolkit and Metrowerks' CodeWarrior for Java are the two primary programming environments used in this book. The original Motorola Software Development Kit (MotoSDK) for J2ME is now part of CodeWarrior for Java. At the end of the chapter, the section "Setting Up the Development Environment" steps you through the installation process to set up these two development environments.

The Big Picture

Over the last six years, Java has grown into a complete and mature object-oriented development platform for applications in a vast and heterogeneous computing environment. These applications range from enterprise-level server applications to traditional desktop applications, and all the way to embedded applications for small devices.

The current release of the Java 2 platform is defined in three editions, with each edition targeting a particular group of applications. These three Java editions are

- **Java 2 Enterprise Edition (J2EE)**—Designed for heavyweight and scalable business server applications.
- **Java 2 Standard Edition (J2SE)**—Designed for traditional and well-established desktop applications.
- **Java 2 Micro Edition (J2ME)**—Designed for the new generation of applications that target consumer electronics and embedded devices.

Figure 2.1 illustrates the three editions of the current release of the Java 2 platform.

Each Java edition comes with its own virtual machines that are specifically optimized for supporting its target applications. HotSpot VM is a highly tuned Java virtual machine for boosting the performance of server-side applications of J2EE.

JVM is the traditional Java virtual machine optimized for executing desktop applications of J2SE. The HotSpot VM is fully compatible with J2SE as well.

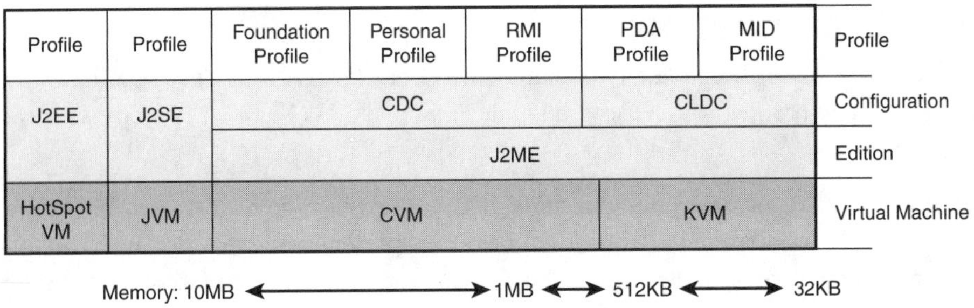

Profile	Profile	Foundation Profile	Personal Profile	RMI Profile	PDA Profile	MID Profile	Profile
J2EE	J2SE	CDC			CLDC		Configuration
		J2ME					Edition
HotSpot VM	JVM	CVM			KVM		Virtual Machine

Memory: 10MB ⟷ 1MB ⟷ 512KB ⟷ 32KB

FIGURE 2.1

The Java 2 platform.

The two Java virtual machines that are designed for J2ME are the C Virtual Machine (CVM) and the K Virtual Machine (KVM). They are very compact in size and require much fewer system resources than the HotSpot VM and the JVM.

The next section discusses in greater detail the various building blocks of J2ME and how it is optimized for the various consumer devices.

What Is J2ME?

J2ME is a lean Java platform targeted specifically at applications running on small devices such as mobile phones, PDAs, Internet screenphones, digital television set-top boxes, automotive entertainment and navigation systems, network switches, home automation components, and so on.

To support the wide variety of device types, J2ME adopts a modular and scalable architecture. As shown in Figure 2.1, J2ME defines three layers of software built upon the native operating system of the device:

- **Java Virtual Machine Layer**—This layer is an implementation of a Java virtual machine that is customized for a particular device's host operating system and supports a particular J2ME configuration. As shown in Figure 2.1, the virtual machines for J2ME are CVM and KVM.

- **Configuration Layer**—A J2ME configuration defines class libraries for a "horizontal" category or grouping of devices based on similar requirements for a total memory budget and processing power. As shown in Figure 2.1, the Connected Device Configuration (CDC) and CLDC are the two configurations identified in J2ME. You'll find more information on CDC and CLDC in the next section.

- **Profile Layer**—Built on top of a specific configuration, a J2ME profile defines class libraries to address the specific demands of a certain vertical market segment. As shown in Figure 2.1, the PDAP, MIDP, Foundation Profile, and Personal Profile are a few example profiles identified in J2ME.

2

JAVA FOR WIRELESS DEVICES

J2ME's Configurations

Configurations and profiles are the two main building blocks in J2ME. The overall purpose of configurations and profiles is to have virtual machines and class libraries optimized for each group of target devices.

The configurations define the minimum set of Java virtual machine features and Java class libraries available on a particular category of devices representing a particular horizontal market. In a way, a configuration defines the lowest common denominator of Java platform features and libraries that developers can assume to be available on all devices. The class libraries defined in a configuration will be available on all devices of the same category.

Currently, two configurations are identified in J2ME: the Connected Device Configuration (CDC) and the Connected Limited Device Configuration (CLDC). These two configurations target two categories of devices with similar total memory budgets and processing power.

CDC devices can be described as *shared*, *fixed*, *connected information devices*. These devices typically have a large range of user interface capabilities, memory budgets in the range of 2 to 16 megabytes, a 32-bit or better CPU, and persistent, high-bandwidth network connections, most often using TCP/IP.

Typical examples of CDC devices include TV set-top boxes, Internet TVs, Internet-enabled screenphones, high-end communicators, and automobile entertainment/navigation systems.

CLDC devices can be described as *personal*, *mobile*, *connected information devices*. These devices typically have very simple user interfaces (compared to desktop computer systems), memory budgets in the range of 128 kilobytes to 1 megabyte, a 16-bit or 32-bit CPU, and low-bandwidth, intermittent networks, which generally don't use TCP/IP.

Typical examples of CLDC devices include low-end cell phones, two-way pagers, and Palm OS handhelds.

Two types of classes are defined in the configuration level: classes inherited from J2SE and classes designed specifically for the needs of small-footprint devices. The classes inherited from J2SE are precisely the same or a subset of the corresponding classes, such as the `java.lang`, `java.io`, and `java.util` packages. Figure 2.2 illustrates the relationships between J2SE, CDC, and CLDC class libraries. As you can see in the figure, the inherited classes in CLDC are upward compatible with those in CDC, and the inherited classes in CDC are upward compatible with J2SE. You can find more information about the class libraries in CLDC in Appendix A, "CLDC Class Libraries."

The non-inherited, configuration-specific classes are not upward compatible with J2SE. In CLDC, these classes belong to the Generic Connection framework; they are defined in the `javax.microedition.io` package. We will discuss the Generic Connection framework further in Chapter 9, "Basic Network Programming in J2ME MIDP."

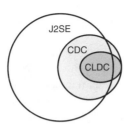

FIGURE 2.2
The relationships between J2SE, CDC, and CLDC class libraries.

J2ME's Virtual Machines

The configurations also specify the features of their underlying Java virtual machines. In the current architecture, the CDC and CLDC each come with their own optimized virtual machine.

The underlying virtual machine for CDC is the C Virtual Machine (CVM), which is a full-featured, small-footprint Java 2 Blue Print virtual machine specifically designed for high-end consumer devices. The CVM has a static footprint of 256KB. The ROMized footprint of CDC is about 1 MB.

> **NOTE**
>
> Both CVM and KVM support the `JavaCodeCompact` utility (also known as the class *pre-linker*, *preloader*, or *ROMizer*). This utility allows Java classes to be linked directly in the virtual machine, reducing VM startup time considerably. For example, when KVM and CLDC are preloaded to the ROM on devices, the CLDC classes are linked directly in the KVM to improve performance. This process is called being *ROMized*.

The underlying virtual machine for CLDC is the K Virtual Machine (KVM), which is a very small, yet very functional, Java virtual machine specifically designed for resource-constrained devices. The *K* in KVM stands for *kilo*. It was so named because its memory budget is measured in kilobytes (whereas desktop systems' are measured in megabytes). KVM is suitable for 16/32-bit RISC/CISC microprocessors with a total memory budget of no more than a few hundred kilobytes (potentially around 128 kilobytes). The current KVM has a static footprint in the range of 40 kilobytes to 80 kilobytes.

J2ME's Profiles

Based on the configuration, a profile defines additional sets of APIs and features for a particular vertical market, device category, or industry. The class libraries in a profile allow developers to access device-specific functionality such as the graphical user interface, network communications, persistent storage, and so on. Generally, the class libraries defined in one profile are not compatible with other profiles.

Several profiles have been defined or are in the process of being defined. As of this writing, the following profiles built on CDC have been released to the public: Foundation profile and RMI profile. So far, only one profile built on CLDC has been released to the public: the MID profile (MIDP). An expert group led by Palm is actively working on the PDA profile (PDAP) based on CLDC. The Personal profile based on CDC is also a profile in the release pipeline. (See Appendix C, "Resource Links," for links to these profiles.)

Briefly, these profiles (also shown in Figure 2.1) are as follows:

- The Foundation profile in CDC is intended to be used by devices requiring a complete implementation of the Java virtual machine up to and including the entire Java 2 Platform, Standard Edition API.

- The RMI profile is a CDC profile that defines the minimal subset of the J2SE 1.3 RMI API.

- The Personal profile is a CDC profile that is extended from Sun's PersonalJava environment. It provides compatibility with applications developed for versions 1.1.x and 1.2.x of the PersonalJava Application Environment Specification.

- PDAP is a CLDC profile that provides user interface and data storage APIs for small, resource-limited handheld devices. At this point, PDAP is mainly designed for the handheld devices powered by the Palm OS, such as Palm Pilots and Visors.

- MIDP is a CLDC profile that provides the user interface, persistence storage, networking, and application model APIs for wireless devices such as low-end cell phones and two-way pagers. Because our book is primarily focused on wireless programming using MIDP and CLDC, we will only talk about these two specifications throughout the book.

It is possible for a single device to have more than one profile. Some of these profiles will be device specific, whereas others will be more application specific. For example, most CDC profiles (such as the RMI profile and the Personal profile) are built on top of the Foundation profile. Applications written for these two profiles will not function without the Foundation profile and CDC.

J2ME for Wireless Devices

J2ME makes a new generation of wireless applications, such as multi-user Internet games, mobile commerce, and enterprise client/server applications, possible on cell phones and two-way pagers. MIDP, CLDC, and KVM form the foundation for developing wireless Java applications. Let's first take a look at how these three components work together to provide the platform for wireless applications.

MIDP/CLDC/KVM

Figure 2.3 illustrates the overall architecture of the J2ME platform for wireless applications.

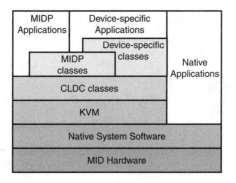

FIGURE 2.3

MIDP architecture.

The architecture can be categorized into five layers. From the bottom up, they are as follows:

- **MID hardware layer**—Refers to cell phones (for example, Motorola's iDEN 3000) or two-way pagers (for example, RIM Blackberry 950).
- **Native system software layer**—Contains the native operating system and system libraries provided by the device manufacturer.
- **KVM layer**—Provides the runtime environment for Java applications.
- **CLDC layer**—Provides core Java APIs for wireless applications.
- **MIDP layer**—Provides the GUI libraries, persistent storage libraries, networking libraries, and timer classes.

In addition to the MIDP class libraries, manufacturers can also provide their own device-specific class libraries to allow developers to take advantage of native functionality, such as telephony, sharing data with native applications (for example, built-in calendar and address book), and querying device information (for example, battery life, signal strength, and so on). Using these vendor-specific classes will greatly enhance the capabilities of your wireless applications, but because they are beyond MIDP scope, applications developed using these classes are not portable across different MIDP devices.

Hardware Requirements

Wireless devices have to meet certain criteria to be able to support J2ME. To run the KVM efficiently with the CLDC libraries, devices must have at least:

- 160KB to 512KB of total memory budget available for the Java platform.
- A 16-bit or 32-bit processor with 25MHz speed.
- Low power consumption, often operating with battery power.
- Connectivity to some kind of network, often with a wireless, intermittent connection and with limited (often 9600bps or less) bandwidth.
- 128 kilobytes of non-volatile memory available for the Java virtual machine and CLDC libraries.
- 32 kilobytes of volatile memory available for the Java runtime and object memory.

The MIDP impose the following requirements on hardware:

Display:

- Screen-size: 96×54
- Display depth: 1 bit
- Pixel shape (aspect ratio): approximately 1:1

Input:

- One or more of the following user-input mechanisms: one-handed keyboard, two-handed keyboard, or touch screen.

Memory:

- 128 kilobytes of non-volatile memory for MIDP components.
- 8 kilobytes of non-volatile memory for application-created persistent data.
- 32 kilobytes of volatile memory for Java runtime (for example, the Java heap).

Networking:

- Two-way, wireless, possibly intermittent, with limited bandwidth.

Wireless Devices

Currently, several device vendors or network carriers are supporting J2ME on their devices. These vendors include

- **LG Telecom** (based in Korea)—Began deploying the J2ME-enabled wireless handset i-Book in October, 2000. The i-Book handset mainly offers entertainment applications targeted at a young customer base in Korea. (A link to LG Telecom's developer site can be found in Appendix C.)

    Figure 2.4 shows a SpaceInvaders game running on the i-Book emulator.

- **NTT DoCoMo**—The largest wireless carrier in Japan. Released two J2ME-enabled handset models (the P503i, manufactured by Panasonic, and the F503i, manufactured by Fujitsu) of their popular i-mode service in February, 2001. Based on J2ME technology, the 503i phones are designed to offer customers online banking, stock trading, and video game capabilities. (A link to NTT DoCoMo's J2ME developer site can be found in Appendix C.)

    Figure 2.5 shows a Mine game application running on DoCoMo's P503i model. Figure 2.6 shows a Mine game running on DoCoMo's F503i model.

- **Motorola**—Released its J2ME-enabled iDEN 3000 cell phones in April, 2001. Motorola also plans to support J2ME on all its future wireless devices including a variety of cell phones, pagers, and personal organizers. (A link to Motorola's developer site can be found in Appendix C.)

    Figure 2.7 shows a Calendar application running on Motorola's iDEN 3000 handset.

- **Research in Motion (RIM)**—A leading designer, manufacturer, and marketer of wireless solutions for the mobile communications market. The company is putting Java technology on its wireless handsets. Future releases of its Blackberry pagers will all support J2ME. (A link to RIM's developer site can be found in Appendix C.)

    Figure 2.8 shows a Java application running on RIM's Blackberry 950.

However, the J2ME implementations from NTT DoCoMo and LG Telecom are not standard; they do not comply with MIDP 1.0 specifications. The class libraries you will find in NTT DoCoMo and LG Telecom's J2ME are their own vendor-specific classes built on top of the CLDC layer, which means standard MIDP applications won't run on their devices. This non-standard implementation is partly due to the fact that LG Telecom and NTT started their MIDP-layer implementation effort before the MIDP specification was finalized.

FIGURE 2.4

SpaceInvaders on an i-Book emulator.

Currently, the J2ME implementations from Motorola and RIM are the only two implementations compliant with the MIDP 1.0 specifications.

FIGURE 2.5

A Mine game on NTT DoCoMo's P503i emulator.

JavaPhone Versus MIDP

If you have heard of or used Sun's JavaPhone API, you may wonder about the difference
between the JavaPhone API and MIDP. The JavaPhone API is an extension to PersonalJava,
defining a set of class libraries that are designed for high-end wireless devices such as Nokia's
9210 Communicator and Ericsson's R380 Communicator. MIDP is really designed for low-end
cell phones and pagers that are limited in memory, processing power, and display capabilities.

FIGURE 2.6

A Mine game on NTT DoCoMo's F503i emulator.

The EPOC operation system shipped by Symbian includes both the JavaPhone API and the PersonalJava runtime environment. In future releases, PersonalJava will be integrated into the Personal profile built on top of the Foundation Profile and the CDC. The JavaPhone API will be supported through the Personal profile.

FIGURE 2.7
A Calendar application running on Motorola's iDEN 3000 emulator.

FIGURE 2.8

A Java application running on a RIM Blackberry 950 emulator.

Setting Up the Development Environment

The Java 2 Platform, Micro Edition, Wireless Toolkit (J2MEWTK) provides the development environment for developing Java applications specifically targeting MIDP devices. The Toolkit comes with four components: a byte-code preverifier, a MIDP device emulator, a basic IDE, and an integrated component with Sun's Forte for Java.

In this book, we will be using the J2ME Wireless Toolkit heavily to compile and execute our sample applications. Besides the J2ME Wireless Toolkit, Motorola's Software Development Kit for J2ME (MotoSDK) is used to compile and execute all the sample applications in Chapter 9. The current release of MotoSDK is tightly integrated with Metrowerks' CodeWarrior for Java.

Both the J2ME Wireless Toolkit and the CodeWarrior for Java allow you to use the command line to compile and start your applications without going through the IDE's GUI. As a matter of fact, most of the examples listed in this book are executed from the command line. The next two sections guide you through the basic process of installing the J2ME Wireless Toolkit and the CodeWarrior for Java. In Chapter 4, "Packaging and Deploying Java Wireless Applications," you will find a section that talks about how to use J2ME Wireless Toolkit's KToolbar IDE and Forte for Java to set up a project and streamline the compilation and packaging processes of your Java wireless applications.

Installing the J2ME Wireless Toolkit for Windows

The J2ME Wireless Toolkit is available for two platforms: one for Sun Solaris and the other one for Microsoft Windows. Here we will only go through the Windows installation. The installation on Solaris is similar. More information can be found in the documentation that comes with the package.

The Windows version of the Toolkit requires a minimum of 64MB memory and 15MB disk space. Here are the steps of the installation process:

1. Download and install Java 2 Standard Edition (J2SE SDK) Version 1.3 or higher.

   JDK1.3 is required for J2MEWTK to function properly. Before installing the J2MEWTK, you need first to have downloaded and installed JDK1.3. JDK1.3 can be downloaded at `http://java.sun.com/j2se/1.3/download-windows.html`.

2. Optionally, download and install Forte for Java.

   As mentioned before, the J2MEWTK can be run standalone or can be run as an integrated component with Forte for Java. If you plan to use it with Forte for Java, you need to install Forte first. Forte for Java Release 2.0 can be downloaded from `http://www.sun.com/forte/ffj/buy.html`. During installation, select J2SE V1.3 or higher as the Java environment. The minimum system requirements for Forte for Java are 300MHz Intel Pentium II CPU, 128MB of memory, and 30MB of disk space. We recommend Forte for Java if you haven't decided on a Java IDE yet.

3. Download and install the J2ME Wireless Toolkit installation package.

   You can download the J2ME Wireless Toolkit installation package at `http://java.sun.com/products/j2mewtoolkit/download.html`. After you finish the download and save the package on your hard drive, start the installation by executing the downloaded file: `j2me_wireless_toolkit-1_0-1.exe`.

   You will see an installation screen like Figure 2.9.

   If you plan to integrate the Toolkit with Forte for Java, select the Integrated option; otherwise, select the Stand Alone option.

4. Once the installation is complete, you should test it to make sure everything is installed properly.

At the DOS prompt, go to the directory `[J2MEWTK_DIR]\apps\example\bin`, where `[J2MEWTK_DIR]` is the installation directory of the Toolkit. The command looks like this on our machine:

`C:\>cd \J2MEWTK\apps\example\bin`

You should see a command batch file named `run.bat`. Execute this command:

`C:\>run.bat`

If the installation was successful, you should see the startup screen of the sample MIDP applications that come with the J2ME Wireless Toolkit, as shown in Figure 2.10.

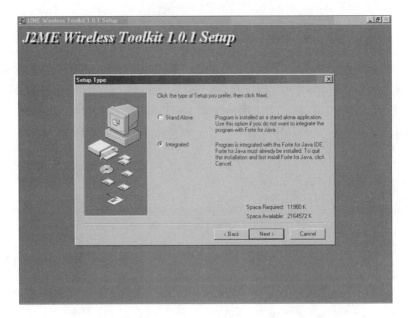

FIGURE 2.9

J2ME Wireless Toolkit installation page.

Once you go through all the steps, the installation is complete. All the related documents are installed under the directory `[J2MEWTK_DIR]\doc`. You should look through the User Guide and Customization Guide before you begin using the Toolkit. All the sample programs are installed under `[J2MEWTK_DIR]\apps`.

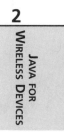

FIGURE 2.10

The startup screen for the J2ME WTK's examples.

Installing MotoSDK for Windows

MotoSDK comes with three components: a bytecode preverifier, a J2ME emulator that is specifically designed for Motorola's wireless handsets, and a configuration editor that allows you create or modify device profiles.

The current release of MotoSDK is no longer a standalone package. It is tightly integrated with Metrowerks' CodeWarrior for Java 6.0. In order to install MotoSDK, you have to download and install Metrowerks' CodeWarrior for Java. However, the examples shown in Chapter 9 are run with command-line scripts and don't require CodeWarrior's IDE. You can find more information about Metrowerks' CodeWarrior at http://www.metrowerks.com.

The Windows version of CodeWarrior for Java 6.0 requires a minimum system of Intel Pentium 100MHz CPU, 64MB of memory, Windows NT Workstation 4.0 (Service Pack 3) or Windows 98, approximately 150MB of free disk space for minimum install, and 450MB for full install.

Here are the steps of the installation process:

1. Download and install Java 2 Standard Edition (J2SE SDK) Version 1.3 or higher.

   Before installing the CodeWarrior for Java 6.0, you need to first download and install JDK1.3. You can download the package at `http://java.sun.com/j2se/1.3/download-windows.html`.

2. Download and install the CodeWarrior for Java 6.0 installation package.

   You can download the CodeWarrior for Java installation package at `http://www0.motorola.com/developers/wireless/technologies/j2me.html`. After you finish the download and save the package on your hard drive, unzip the package `cwjava6evl.zip` to a temporary directory, and execute the installation program `setup.exe` from the temporary directory.

3. Follow the prompts provided by the program to complete the installation.

4. Test your installation.

   At the DOS prompt, go to the directory `[CODEWARRIOR_DIR]\Java_Support\MotoSDK\scripts`, where `[CODEWARRIOR_DIR]` is the installation directory of CodeWarrior for Java. The command looks like this on our computer:

   `C:\>cd \applications\CodeWarrior\Java_Support\MotoSDK\scripts`

   You should be able to find and execute the batch file `runMotoiDEN.bat` in that directory:

   `C:\applications\CodeWarrior\Java_Support\MotoSDK\scripts>runMotoiDEN.bat`

   If the installation was successful, you should see a screen like Figure 2.11, which shows the Bounce example that comes with the MotoSDK. (This program displays four squares of different sizes that bounce around on the screen.)

All the documentation that comes with the MotoSDK is installed under the directory `[CODEWARRIOR_DIR]\Java_Support\MotoSDK\docs`. You should look through the User Guide before you begin using this package. All the sample code is under the directory `[CODEWARRIOR_DIR]\Java_Support\MotoSDK\demo\midlets`. You should also take a look at documents under the directory `[CODEWARRIOR_DIR]\CodeWarrior Manuals\HTML` to get an idea of how to use the tool, especially the document `J2ME_Supplement.chm` that talks about how to use the tool to develop J2ME MIDP applications.

Several other third-party IDEs for J2ME application development such as JBuilder and Zucotto's WHITEboard are also available. You can find links to these packages in Appendix C.

FIGURE 2.11
The Bounce sample program of MotoSDK.

Summary

This chapter briefly discussed the overall architecture of the Java 2 Platform and its three editions, and explained where Java 2 Micro Edition fits in this architecture. It then described the building blocks of J2ME: the configurations and profiles. Because this book is focused on CLDC and MIDP, this chapter explained the details about how CLDC/KVM/MIDP provides the development platform for wireless programming. Finally, it showed you step by step how to set up and test two development environments: Sun's Wireless Toolkit and Metrowerks' CodeWarrior for Java.

Java Wireless Programming Basics

IN THIS CHAPTER

Overview

If you are coming to J2ME from the J2SE or J2EE world, you will find that J2ME programming is not difficult at all. Most of the differences between J2ME and J2SE are due to the fact that the J2ME devices are usually resource limited. This limitation is especially true for the group of devices this book focuses on: the wireless devices (in this book, the term *wireless devices* is used interchangeably with the term Mobile Information Device Profile [MIDP] devices.)

This chapter gives you an overview of the basics of application development with J2ME MIDP, shows you what Java classes are available on the MIDP devices, and also shows you how to write a MIDlet program for use on a MIDP device.

The Java runtime environment on the MIDP devices usually comes with a K Virtual Machine (KVM), Connected Limited Device Configuration (CLDC) libraries, MIDP libraries, and the Application Management Software. The Java libraries in CLDC and MIDP provide the foundation for application programming for wireless devices.

The CLDC Libraries

The CLDC libraries provide device-independent and high-level system and network libraries. Two categories of classes are defined in CLDC: the classes that are a subset of J2SE and the classes that are associated with the CLDC's Generic Connection framework.

The Subset of J2SE

The CLDC classes in the first category are a subset of J2SE libraries. They are defined in the `java.lang`, `java.util`, and `java.io` packages. These fundamental system and data type classes are upward compatible with J2SE and J2EE. For upward compatibility and portability, each class in this category has the same class name and package name as either a J2SE class that it is identical to or a subset of the corresponding J2SE class. These classes also do not add any public or protected methods or fields that are not available in the corresponding J2SE classes. The semantics of these classes and their methods are not changed.

CLDC-Specific Classes

The classes in the second category are defined in the `javax.microedition.io.*` package. These classes are CLDC specific and are not upward compatible with the J2SE libraries. They are a high-level generalization of the networking-related classes in the `java.io` and `java.net` packages.

These classes provide an abstract network communication framework for the J2ME devices. This framework is formally referred to as the *Generic Connection framework*. Most of the classes in the Generic Connection framework are interfaces representing different types of communications such as socket, datagram, serial, and http. It is up to the device manufacturers and network carriers to implement either a full set or a subset of these connection interfaces based on the capacity of their devices and networks.

For your convenience, we have listed all the CLDC classes and interfaces in Appendix A, "CLDC Class Libraries."

The Basic Data Types

The CLDC supports only a subset of the primitive data types of J2SE. These primitive data types are `byte`, `short`, `int`, `long`, `char`, and `boolean`. The `float` and `double` data types are not supported for two reasons: The majority of the CLDC target devices do not have hardware floating-point support, and the cost of supporting floating-point in software is too high.

CLDC also defines a *type wrapper* class for every primitive data type:

```
java.lang.Boolean
java.lang.Byte
java.lang.Character
java.lang.Integer
java.lang.Long
java.lang.Short
```

These type wrapper classes are defined in Java because Java contains many subsystems that can work only with objects. In these cases, you can create an object based on the wrapper class that encapsulates a primitive data type.

The MIDP Libraries

Whereas the CLDC libraries provide device-independent functionality, the MIDP libraries provide device-specific functionality. This functionality includes on-device application management, low-level and high-level graphical user interfaces, persistent storage, and extended network capability.

Application Management Classes

The classes associated with on-device application management are defined in the `javax.microedition.midlet` package.

All MIDP applications must extend the `MIDlet` class in this package and implement its three abstract methods: `startApp()`, `pauseApp()`, and `destroyApp()`.

GUI Classes

The Abstract Windowing Toolkit (AWT) in J2SE is designed for desktop applications. It is too memory intensive for resource-constrained wireless devices. The MIDP takes a different approach to define its graphical user interface libraries and event handling. Two sets of APIs are defined in the GUI package: a high-level API that focuses on cross-device portability, and a low-level API that focuses on device-dependent graphic elements and low-level input events.

The classes associated with the GUI and event handling are defined in the `javax.microedition.lcdui` package.

The `Screen` class is the superclass for all user interface components of the high-level API. These UI components include `Alert`, `Form`, `List`, `TextBox`, and so on.

The `Canvas` class and `Graphics` class are the two main classes in the low-level API. Game applications will most likely make heavy use of the GUI classes in the low-level API.

Chapters 5, 6, and 7 cover these APIs in more detail.

Persistent Storage Classes

MIDP applications sometimes need to store persistent data on a device. The classes defined in the `javax.microedition.rms` package offer a persistent storage mechanism called `RecordStore` that allows applications to add, delete, and update data records to the persistent storage on a device.

The MIDP's `RecordStore` is discussed in Chapter 8, "Persistent Storage."

Network Classes

The Generic Connection framework defined in the CLDC contains a set of connection interfaces, but CLDC doesn't implement the actual protocols behind the connection interfaces. The implementations are left to the MIDP.

Among all the connection interfaces, the `HttpConnection` interface is mandatory for all MIDP implementations. As a result, http communication is guaranteed to be available on all MIDP devices.

The implemented classes of these interfaces can be found in the `javax.microedition.io` package.

The Generic Connection framework and its related classes are discussed further in Chapter 9, "Basic Network Programming in J2ME MIDP."

For your convenience, we have all the classes and interfaces in MIDP listed in Appendix B, "MIDP Class Libraries."

MIDlet

An application on a MIDP device is called a *MIDlet*. A MIDlet is very much like a Java applet. It does not have a `main()` method; instead, a MIDlet must extend the `javax.microedition.midlet.MIDlet` class and implement its three abstract methods: `startApp()`, `pauseApp()`, and `destroyApp()`. A MIDlet also has to define a public no-argument constructor.

The following is the definition of the `javax.microedition.midlet.MIDlet` class:

```
public abstract class MIDlet extends Object {
  protected MIDlet()
  protected abstract void startApp() throws MIDletStateChangeException
  protected abstract void pauseApp()
  protected abstract void destroyApp(boolean unconditional)
    throws MIDletStateChangeException
  public final String getAppProperty(String key)
  public final void notifyDestroyed()
  public final void notifyPaused()
  public final String getAppProperty(String key)
  public final void resumeRequest()
}
```

The `MIDlet` class defines methods that can be invoked by the Application Management Software (AMS) to start and stop a MIDlet application.

MIDlet's Life Cycle

A MIDlet's execution includes three valid states: Active, Paused, and Destroyed. The transitions between the different states are controlled by the AMS through the `startApp()`, `pauseApp()`, and `destroyApp()` methods implemented by the MIDlet. Figure 3.1 illustrates the transitions between the three possible states through calling these three methods.

When a MIDlet is ready to be executed, the AMS first creates an instance of the MIDlet by using its public no-argument constructor. The MIDlet enters the Paused state.

Then the AMS invokes `startApp()` method. The MIDlet enters the Active state, acquires resources it needs, and begins to perform its services. In this state, the MIDlet is running and holding the resources it needs.

When the AMS has determined that it no longer needs the MIDlet to be active and perform its services, it invokes the `pauseApp()` method. The MIDlet is stopped to enter the Paused state. When in this state, the MIDlet must release any resources it has acquired and become inactive. The MIDlet can re-enter the Active state when the AMS calls its `startApp()` method.

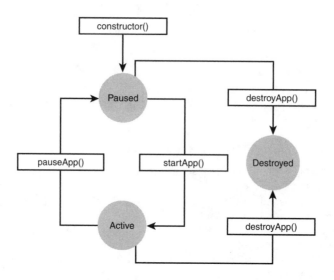

FIGURE 3.1

MIDlet's life cycle.

Finally, when AMS has decided that it no longer needs the MIDlet or it wants to make room for a higher priority program in memory, it signals the MIDlet that it is a candidate to be destroyed by calling the destroyApp() method. The MIDlet enters the Destroyed state. In this state, the MIDlet should clean itself up by releasing all the resources and saving any persistent data, and then terminate.

When the MIDlet is in the middle of an important process, it can request not to enter the Destroyed state by throwing a MIDletStateChangeException. However, this request may or may not be granted by the AMS. The boolean variable unconditional in the signature of the destroyApp() method governs whether this request is a valid response. If the unconditional flag is set to true, the request will be ignored. If the unconditional flag is set to false, the request may be honored. If the request is granted, the destroyApp() method will be called again at a later time.

If the MIDlet itself wants to enter the Paused state or the Destroyed state, it can call the notifyPause() method or the notifyDestroy() method, respectively. Both methods notify AMS that the MIDlet has entered the Paused state or the Destroyed state. In this case, AMS will not call the pauseApp() method or the destroyApp() method. The MIDlet should have performed clean-up actions before notifying the AMS.

MIDlets can only enter the Active state from the Paused state, but they can enter the Destroyed state from both the Paused state and the Active state. MIDlets can enter the Paused state either from the Active state or when activated initially by the AMS.

Application Management Software

The term Application Management Software has been mentioned several times in the previous sections. It is basically a software application that comes with the MIDP implementation that controls the installation, execution, and removal of MIDlets. Sometimes the AMS is also referred to as the *MIDlet Management Software* or the *Java Application Manager*.

The actual implementation of the AMS may vary from device to device, but the basic services it must provide are the same:

- AMS provides ways for users to install and uninstall MIDlets from their wireless devices, either through a serial cable connected to a PC, or remotely via the Internet.

- AMS provides an execution environment for a MIDlet. After a MIDlet is initialized, the AMS makes system resources such as CLDC classes, MIDP classes, and the KVM available to the MIDlet. It also makes all the classes, resource files, and application descriptor files available to the MIDlet at runtime.

- AMS gracefully handles all the errors that occur during the installation and execution of applications without crashing the system.

First Example: "Hello World"

So far, we have discussed the basics of CLDC and MIDP. This section takes a look at your first MIDlet example: HelloWorld. This program performs a trivial task: It displays a test message of *Hello World* on a cell phone screen. Listing 3.1 shows the source code of this MIDlet application.

LISTING 3.1   HelloWorld.java

```java
// include the MIDlet super class
import javax.microedition.midlet.MIDlet;
// include the GUI libraries of MIDP
import javax.microedition.lcdui.*;

/*
 * 1. All MIDlet applications must extend the MIDlet class.
 * 2. CommandListener is the event-handling interface of the
 * high-level GUI API. More details can be found in the
 * Chapter 5 and 6.
 */
public class HelloWorld extends MIDlet implements CommandListener{
  // define the GUI components of HelloWorld
  private Display display;
```

3

JAVA WIRELESS PROGRAMMING BASICS

LISTING 3.1 Continued

```
private TextBox mainScreen = null;
private Command exit;

// define the no-argument constructor
public HelloWorld() {
  display = Display.getDisplay(this);
  mainScreen = new TextBox("HelloWorld", "Hello World", 512,0);
  exit = new Command("exit", Command.EXIT, 2)
  mainScreen.addCommand(exit);
  /*
   * register the MIDlet itself as an event listener
   * of the mainScreen.
   */
  mainScreen.setCommandListener(this);
}

// implement the startApp() method
public void startApp() {
  display.setCurrent(mainScreen);
}

// implement the pauseApp() method
public void pauseApp() {
}

// implement the destroyApp() method
public void destroyApp(boolean unconditional) {
}

/*
 * implement the event handling method defined in
 * the CommandListener interface.
 */
public void commandAction(Command c, Displayable s) {
   // if the EXIT button is clicked, exit the program
   if(c == exit) {
     destroyApp(false);
     notifyDestroyed();
   }
 }
}
```

In this example, `HelloWorld` extends `javax.microedition.midlet.MIDlet` and implements its `startApp()`, `pauseApp()`, and `destroyApp()` methods. It declares three private member variables:

```
private Display display;
private TextBox mainScreen = null;
private Command exit
```

They are initialized in the constructor. A `Display` object represents the manager of the display and input devices of the system. There is exactly one instance of `Display` per MIDlet. The `HelloWorld` MIDlet gets a reference to that instance by calling the `getDisplay()` method. The `TextBox` object `mainScreen` allows the user to enter and edit text. In the `startApp()` method, the MIDlet makes the `mainScreen` visible on the display by calling

```
display.setCurrent(mainScreen)
```

The `Command` object `exitCommand` is attached to the `mainScreen`. The MIDlet registers itself as `mainScreen`'s `CommandListener` by calling

```
mainScreen.setCommandListener(this);
```

When the user pushes the `EXIT` button on the left-hand side of the screen, the event is delegated to the MIDlet. The MIDlet implements the `commandAction()` method in the `CommandListener` interface to handle the event. In the `commandAction()` method, the MIDlet application notifies the AMS to enter the Destroyed state by calling the `notifyDestroyed()` method.

The `pauseApp()` and `destroyApp()` methods are often used to release and clean up resources such as network connections and save data to the persistent storage. Because our example doesn't include any resources that need to be released, these two methods are left empty.

In this chapter and most of the other chapters, Sun's J2ME Wireless Toolkit for Windows (J2MEWTK) is used to compile, preverify, and run the sample programs. Sun's J2MEWTK comes with the reference implementations of KVM, CLDC, and MIDP, along with a wireless device emulator.

To run the `HelloWorld` MIDlet, you will need to install both JDK1.3 and J2MEWTK on your PC. On my laptop (with Windows 2000 installed), the JDK1.3 is installed in the directory `c:\JDK1.3` and the J2MEWTK is installed in the directory `c:\J2MEWTK`. I also have an environment variable `%SUNJ2MEHOME%` set to the J2MEWTK's installation directory. The following command sets the environment variable `SUNJ2MEHOME`:

```
C:\>set SUNJ2MEHOME=c:\J2MEWTK
```

Sun recommends JDK1.3 for building J2ME applications. But you should be able to use the JDK 1.2.2 to perform the same task as well.

Compilation

First, you need to compile the `HelloWorld` Java program. The following command will take care of that:

```
C:\>c:\jdk1.3\bin\javac
     -g:none
     -bootclasspath %SUNJ2MEHOME%\lib\midpapi.zip
     -classpath %SUNJ2MEHOME%\lib\kvem.jar
     HelloWorld.java
```

Because you are using a J2SE compiler to compile your J2ME program, the option `-bootclasspath` has to be used to override J2SE's bootstrap class files with your MIDP class files. The `%SUNJ2MEHOME%\lib\midpapi.zip` package contains all the CLDC and MIDP libraries.

Just placing the MIDP class files in the compiler's class path will not work because the J2SE compiler automatically searches the J2SE core classes first, regardless of what's in the class path. As a result, the compiler will check your class files against the J2SE's core classes and methods instead of the ones in J2ME's CLDC and MIDP libraries. This process will eventually lead to runtime errors in your MIDlets.

The `-g:none` option will turn off all the debugging information to keep the size of your class files down.

Preverification

Before the MIDlet can be executed, it has to go through a process referred to as *preverification*. Traditionally in J2SE, the verification process is performed at runtime by the Java Virtual Machine (JVM). But due to the resource constraints on wireless devices, the class verification of KVM is performed partially off-device and partially on-device to improve runtime performance. The off-device verification process is referred to as *preverification*.

Figure 3.2 illustrates the new class verification process in KVM.

The preverifier inserts the so-called *stack map* attributes into the class files to help the in-device verifier quickly scan through the bytecodes without costly operations. These attributes in the preverified class files are automatically ignored by the JVM's verifier to guarantee upward compatibility with J2SE.

The preverified class files containing the extra attributes are approximately 5% bigger than the original, unmodified class files.

The following is the preverifier's command-line syntax:

```
preverify -check -classpath <CLASSPATH> -d <DEST_DIR> <SRC_DIR>
```

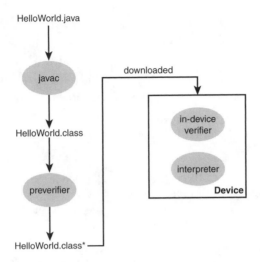

FIGURE 3.2

Class verification process in KVM.

<CLASSPATH> is the location of all classes, *<DEST_DIR>* is the directory in which the preverified classes are stored, and *<SRC_DIR>* is the directory in which the unverified classes are stored. The option `-check` checks against the use of floating-point and finalize methods in the classes.

Here is the actual command to preverify `HelloWorld.class`. In this case, you want the *SRC_DIR* and *DEST_DIR* to be the same directory:

```
C:\>%SUNJ2MEHOME%\bin\perverify.exe
        -classpath %SUNJ2MEHOME%\lib\midpapi.zip
        -d c:\J2MEBook\chapter3
        c:\J2MEBook\chapter3
```

Creating the JAR File

Next, you need to package the MIDlet into a *MIDlet suite*, which is a single JAR file. This unique deployment requirement is mandated by most MIDP devices. The same thing is true for our test environment, the J2MEWTK MIDP emulator.

The following command uses the `jar` utility that comes with JDK1.3 to archive and compress the class files into a package:

```
C:\>c:\JDK1.3\bin\jar cmf MANIFEST.MF HelloWorld.jar HelloWorld.class
```

Chapter 4, "Packaging and Deploying Java Wireless Applications," discusses packaging MIDlets and deploying MIDlet suites in more detail.

Execute the MIDlet from the Application Descriptor

Finally, you can run your `HelloWorld` MIDlet. Following is the syntax of how to run the program on the J2MEWTK's emulator (`C:\J2MEBook\chapter3` is the directory where we put `HelloWorld`'s source code and class files. If you need to run the program from a different location, you need to modify the `%CODEPATH%` environment variable to point to your own directory.)

```
C:\>set CODEPATH=c:\J2MEBOOK\chapter3
C:\>set CLASSPATH=%SUNJ2MEHOME%\lib\kvem.jar;%SUNJ2MEHOME%\lib\kenv.zip;
%SUNJ2MEHOME%\lib\lime.jar;%CODEPATH%

C:\>c:\jdk1.3\bin\java.exe -Dkvem.home=%SUNJ2MEHOME%
                    -classpath %CLASSPATH%
                    com.sun.kvem.midp.Main DefaultGrayPhone
                    -descriptor HelloWorld.jad
```

The first two commands set the environment variable `CODEPATH` to the directory where `HelloWorld` files are stored and `CLASSPATH` to the J2MEWTK's CLDC and MIDP library packages.

The third command starts up the emulator program (`com.sun.kvem.midp.Main`) to run your MIDlet program. The file `HelloWorld.jad` is the application descriptor file for the application. (Application descriptors are discussed in Chapter 4.) `DefaultGrayPhone` is one of the four device types supported by the emulator; the other three are `DefaultColorPhone`, `MinumumPhone`, and `Pager`. More information about the specifications of the four device types can be found in the documentation that comes with the J2MEWTK package.

Figures 3.3, 3.4, and 3.5 show the `HelloWorld` MIDlet running on the different device types supported by the J2MEWTK's emulator.

FIGURE 3.3

Hello World MIDlet on the `DefaultGrayPhone` *and the* `DefaultColorPhone`.

FIGURE 3.4
Hello World MIDlet on the MinimumPhone.

FIGURE 3.5
Hello World MIDlet on the Pager.

So far, you have completed your first MIDlet program. The next section takes a look at the features that are not supported by J2ME.

Internationalization in MIDlets

According to a recent study, the number of wireless subscribers worldwide will reach one billion by 2004. Roughly 70% of the subscribers are in Asia and Europe. To compete in this global market, you need to think about how to develop your J2ME applications to support different languages and localities. Internationalization and localization should be an integral part of your development strategy.

Internationalization is the process of designing an application so that it can be adapted to various languages and regions without engineering changes. This process usually requires that applications not contain hard-coded messages, text labels, and so on.

Localization is the process adapting software for a specific region or language by adding locale-specific components and translating text. This process includes translating text and changing the date, time, currency, and so on to conform to local cultural standards.

The Java 2 Standard Edition provides a variety of classes to deal with internationalization and localization, such as the `Locale`, `DateFormat`, and `ResourceBundle` classes in the `java.util` package, and the `Reader` and `Writer` classes in the `java.io` package.

Unfortunately, the localization classes such as `Locale`, `DateFormat`, and `ResourceBundle` are not supported in the current release of CLDC 1.0. They were removed from CLDC in order to keep down the package size.

CLDC defines the `InputStreamReader` and `OutputStreamWriter` classes in the `java.io` package to support internationalization. These two classes provide the necessary functionality to handle 16-bit Unicode characters.

You can use two approaches to support localization and internationalization in your J2ME applications. The first is to simulate the missing localization classes in your programs to deal with the formatting of dates, times, currencies, and so on.

The second approach is to develop a localized version of your application for each language and country you target and put these localized versions of your software on the OTA Web server. Then, you let your Web server detect the user's locale based on the header information sent by the device, and serve up the appropriate localized version. This way, you don't have to deal with localization inside your application. The code size will be smaller as well.

Getting Locale and Character Encoding Information

In CLDC, a `microedition.encoding` property is defined to give you the system default character encoding. In Sun's CLDC reference implementation, `ISO8859_1` (Latin-1) is the default character encoding. Foreign vendors may provide different character encoding in their own implementations. For example, in NTT DoCoMo's J2ME implementation, `Shift-JIS` is the default character encoding for Japanese characters.

Java uses Unicode as its native character encoding. Specifically, the `char` data type in Java is 16-bits wide and represents a Unicode character.

> **NOTE**
>
> The *Unicode standard* is a universal character encoding standard used to represent text for a computer to process. Unicode provides a unique number for every character. You can find more information about Unicode at
> `http://www.unicode.org/index.html`.

In MIDP, a `microedition.locale` property is defined to give you the current language code and country code. The format of a valid locale is the language code in lowercase concatenated with the country code in uppercase, separated by a hyphen (`-`). For example, the value `en-US` stands for English (`en` is the language code) and United States (`US` is the country code), and the value `zh-CN` stands for Simplified Chinese and China.

The language code and the country code are defined by the ISO-639 and ISO-3166 standards, which can be found at `http://www.ics.uci.edu/pub/ietf/http/related/iso639.txt` and `ftp://ftp.ripe.net/iso3166-countrycodes/`.

The following two statements can be used to get the values of the encoding and locale properties:

```
String encoding = System.getProperty("microedition.encoding");
String locale_str = System.getProperty("microedition.locale");
```

Using Unicode in J2ME

To support foreign languages, your MIDlet programs must deal with Unicode characters. These two classes are designed for reading and writing the 16-bit Unicode characters: `InputStreamReader` and `OutputStreamWriter`.

They are used to bridge the gap between the byte stream and the character stream. The following are the constructors of the two classes:

```
InputStreamReader(InputStream is);
InputStreamReader(InputStream is, String enc)
OutputStreamWriter(OutputStream is);
OutputStreamWriter(OutputStream is, String enc)
```

The `InputStreamReader` class is used to convert an input byte stream into an input Unicode character stream based on the encoding specified by the parameter `enc`. If the parameter `enc` is missing from the constructor, the system default encoding (`microedition.encoding`) will be used.

The `OutputStreamWriter` class is used to convert an output byte stream to an output Unicode character stream based on the encoding specified by the parameter `enc`. If the parameter `enc` is missing from the constructor, the system default encoding (`microedition.encoding`) will be used.

If the character encoding specified by `enc` is not supported, an `UnsupportedEncodingException` will be thrown from the constructors.

InputStreamReader Methods

The methods defined in `InputStreamReader` are as follows:

```
InputStreamReader(InputStream is)
InputStreamReader(InputStream is, String enc)
void close()
```

The `mark()` method marks the present position in the stream:

```
void mark(int limit)
```

This method tells whether the `mark()` operation is supported:

```
boolean markSupported()
```

The following method reads a single character:

```
int read()
```

This method reads characters into a portion of an array:

```
int read(char[] cbuf, int off, int len)
```

The `ready()` method tells whether this stream is ready to be read:

```
boolean ready()
```

The `reset()` method resets the stream:

```
void reset()
```

The `skip()` method skips characters:

```
long skip(long n)
```

OutputStreamWriter Methods

The methods defined in `OutputStreamWriter` are as follows:

```
OutputStreamWriter(OutputStream os)
OutputStreamWriter(OutputStream os, String enc)
void close() Close the stream.
```

The `flush()` method flushes the stream:

```
void flush()
```

The following method writes a portion of an array of characters:

```
void write(char[] cbuf, int off, int len)
```

This method writes a single character:

```
void write(int c)
```

This method writes a portion of a string:

```
void write(String str, int off, int len)
```

Cross-Device MIDlet Development

MIDP devices usually fall into two categories: cell phones and two-way pagers. The sizes and shapes of these devices sometimes are very different. Capabilities such as storage, network, and input device vary from device to device as well.

J2ME is designed to support a variety of small devices. The goal of the J2ME CLDC is to provide a "common denominator" development platform for mobile devices across different profiles such as MIDP and the upcoming PDA profile (PDAP), whereas MIDP provides such a platform across different devices such as Motorola's iDEN 3000 and RIM's Blackberry. This layered design makes the "write once, run anywhere" paradigm possible across different devices.

But portability is not a given. It is still very challenging for you to achieve cross-device portability while taking full advantage of device-specific functionality. It's your responsibility to understand the boundaries of the cross-device common denominators so that you can judge whether to compromise portability in exchange for device-specific functionality.

CLDC is one of the natural boundaries of portability. It is a set of class libraries that are upward compatible with the Connected Device Configuration (CDC) and J2SE and portable across different profiles built on top of CLDC. Therefore, programs developed using CLDC classes are portable among all the CLDC devices. In MIDP, things such as high-level GUI elements, persistent storage, and http communication are portable across different wireless devices, but low-level GUI elements, datagrams, and socket communication are not.

Tiered Components

One of the common practices in cross-device MIDlet development is to separate your application into tiered components. By doing so, you can separate the portable components from the device-specific components. Then, if full portability is not possible, you still can achieve partial portability.

For example, it makes sense to separate the GUI component and network component from your business logic component and data model component, because the GUI and network components tend to be more device-specific. By separating them, you will be able to effectively render the business logic and data on different types of device displays and over different types of networks.

This doesn't mean your GUI and network component are not portable across MIDP devices. As long as you stay away from the low-level GUI classes such as `Canvas` and `Graphics` and non-http network communication such as datagram and socket in MIDP, your programs are safe.

Various Devices

Devices from the same manufacturer sometimes share a very similar design. Most of these devices are supported by the same J2ME implementation. Developing cross-device MIDlets for these devices is a little easier. In these cases, an adaptive GUI component with device-specific parameters stored in a resource file will do the trick. In the previous section, you saw how to access the resource files at runtime.

So far, Motorola and RIM are committed to supporting fully compliant CLDC/MIDP implementations on their wireless devices. LG Telecom supports a combination of a standard CLDC implementation and a non-standard MIDP implementation. And NTT DoCoMo released its own proprietary Java platform for two of its i-Mode phones. (Its implementation, called DoJa, is not compatible with the CLDC and MIDP specifications, and its programs are called iApplis instead of MIDlets. To support i-Mode phones, you have to port all your MIDlet programs specifically for DoCoMo's platform. We hope this situation will change in the future as J2ME matures.) You can find more information on NTT DoCoMo's J2ME implementation in Appendix D, "NTT DoCoMo's Java for i-Mode."

CLDC Limitations

CLDC and KVM are designed for devices with limited resources. It is impossible for them to support all the features and functionality that the J2SE offers. Some of the features in J2SE are removed from CLDC and KVM to reduce their footprints and to improve runtime performance.

You must be aware of certain limitations on J2ME before you begin designing and developing J2ME applications.

No Floating-Point Support

CLDC doesn't include floating-point support. As a result, the primitive data types `float` and `double` are not allowed in your J2ME programs. The same thing is true of the two type wrapper classes `java.lang.Float` and `java.lang.Double`.

If you have to use floating-point computations in your J2ME programs, the alternative solution is to use a software package such as MathFP to simulate floating-point calculations with fixed-point integers. This package can be found at

`http://home.rochester.rr.com/ohommes/MathFP`.

No Finalization

Finalization is a process in which the garbage collector gives an object an opportunity to clean itself up before being garbage collected. More specifically, the cleanup code is put in the `finalize()` method, which is called by the garbage collector. CLDC libraries do not include the method `finalize()` from the `Object` class. The reason that finalization is not supported in CLDC is to simplify the garbage collection of KVM.

Limited Internationalization Support

CLDC provides only very basic internationalization support with its `java.io.InputStreamReader` and `java.io.OutputStreamWriter` classes. These classes allow applications to convert a byte stream to a Unicode character stream and back. Other localization-related classes such as `Locale`, `ResourceBundle`, and `DateFormat` are not defined in J2ME.

Error-Handling Limitations

The Java language includes two categories of exceptions: `java.lang.Error` and `java.lang.Exception`. Both derive from the class `java.lang.Throwable`. The `Error` exceptions (classes derived from class `Error`) are unrecoverable. On the other hand, the `Exceptions` (classes derived from class `Exception`) are recoverable. CLDC generally supports recoverable exception handling.

Only limited support is available for error handling in CLDC. There are only two error classes defined in CLDC: `java.lang.VirtualMachineError` and `java.lang.OutOfMemoryError`. Most of the error classes are removed, for two reasons:

- In embedded systems, recovery from error conditions is usually highly device-specific. Application programmers should not be expected to handle these device-specific errors.
- The `Error` exceptions are usually unrecoverable. Implementing full error-handling capabilities is rather expensive, and also imposes significant overhead on the resource-constrained CLDC devices.

KVM Limitations

Because the KVM is the underlying Java virtual machine that supports the CLDC libraries, features that are not supported in CLDC are also removed from the KVM. These unsupported features include floating-point support, finalization support, and device-specific error handling.

Because J2ME provides a limited version of the Java security model, certain features that may pose security problems are eliminated from the KVM as well. The following sections describe these features.

No Java Native Interface (JNI)

KVM doesn't support JNI for two reasons. First, according to the security model of the CLDC, the application programmer can't download any new libraries containing native functionality, or access any native functions that are not part of the Java libraries. Second, implementing JNI is considered too memory intensive on CLDC devices.

No User-Defined Class Loaders

The KVM doesn't support user-defined class loaders due to security concerns. The built-in class loader in KVM cannot be overridden, replaced, or reconfigured by the user.

No Reflection, RMI, or Object Serialization

There is no reflection feature in KVM, which means that CLDC programs cannot inspect the contents of classes, objects, methods, and so on. Consequently, all the features that depend on reflection are also not supported; they include Remote Method Invocation (RMI) and object serialization.

No Thread Groups or Daemon Threads

KVM fully supports multi-threaded applications, but does not support thread groups or daemon threads. You must use explicit collection objects to store the thread objects for performing group operations.

Weak Reference

Weak reference allows a program to be notified when the collector has determined that an object has become eligible for reclamation. The KVM does not support this feature.

Security in J2ME

The fundamental purpose of the security of a computer system is to protect system resources from malicious or unintentional access. Dynamically downloading content and applications required by the CLDC specification makes network security even more crucial. Java is designed from the ground up with security in mind. As always, J2SE comes with rich security features such as byte code verification and a security manager. Unfortunately, the size of the J2SE code devoted to security is far beyond the memory budget of a resource-constrained wireless devices. J2ME security features have to be tailored to meet the requirements of wireless devices.

Class File Verification and Preverification

When each Java class file is loaded, the class file has to be checked for validity. Traditionally in J2SE, the verification process is performed at runtime by the Java Virtual Machine (JVM). However, due to the resource constraints on wireless devices, the class verification of KVM is performed partially off-device and partially on-device to improve runtime performance. The off-device verification process is referred to as *preverification*.

The preverified class file can be loaded to the virtual machine for further in-device verification. The off-device preverifier together with the in-device preverifier guarantee language safety and integrity at runtime.

Sandbox Model

J2ME borrowed the *sandbox* security model from J2SE. The essence of the sandbox model in J2ME is that a Java application must run in a closed environment in which the application can only access those APIs that have been defined by the configuration, profiles, and licensee open classes supported by the device. More specifically, the sandbox model means that:

- Java class files have been properly verified and are guaranteed to be valid Java applications.

- Only a limited, predefined set of Java APIs is available to the application programmer, as defined by the CLDC, profiles, and licensee open classes.

- The downloading and management of Java applications on the device takes place at the native code level inside the virtual machine, and no user-definable class loaders are provided, in order to prevent the programmer from overriding the standard class loading mechanisms of the virtual machine.

- The set of native functions accessible to the virtual machine is closed, meaning that the application programmer cannot download any new libraries containing native functionality, or access any native functions that are not part of the Java libraries provided by the CLDC, profiles, or licensee open classes.

Summary

This chapter covered the basics of J2ME MIDP programming. You learned about the classes available in CLDC and MIDP libraries. The CLDC libraries provide the fundamental system classes, Generic Connection framework, and basic data types. The MIDP libraries provide device-dependent classes for the user interface, persistent storage, MIDlet, and extended network capability.

You also learned about the MIDlet, the MIDlet's life cycle model, and the Application Management Software that controls the MIDlet's life cycle.

In this chapter you wrote a simple "Hello World" program to understand the basic process of creating, compiling, preverifying, packaging, and executing a MIDlet.

At the end of this chapter, you learned about internationalization and cross-device development of MIDlets. We showed you some of the limitations of CLDC and KVM compared to J2SE's class libraries and virtual machine. Finally, we discussed some issues concerning J2ME's security.

Packaging and Deploying Java Wireless Applications

IN THIS CHAPTER

Overview

At the end of Chapter 3, "Java Wireless Programming Basics," you saw how to write a simple MIDlet program (the HelloWorld MIDlet), but we didn't explain the details of how the HelloWorld MIDlet is packaged and deployed. This chapter continues on that topic and talks about MIDlet packaging and deployment.

MIDlet Suite

The packaging and deployment of J2ME Mobile Information Device profile (MIDP) applications are quite different from their counterparts in J2SE.

First, all the class files of MIDlet applications have to be packaged into a single JAR file. Each JAR file may contain more than one MIDlet application. This group of MIDlet applications forms a *MIDlet suite*.

The JAR file can then be downloaded and installed onto wireless devices via a serial cable connected to a PC or via a wireless network. Once the JAR file is installed, a menu entry will appear for every MIDlet in the MIDlet suite. Users can choose and execute a MIDlet application from the startup menu.

> **NOTE**
>
> All MIDP devices are required to support the JAR file format. Some vendors may choose to additionally support the more compact file formats, such as ZIP.

Figure 4.1 shows the startup menu of a commercial J2ME application, MobileOrganizer, developed by the authors. You can see what it looks like when there is more than one MIDlet in a MIDlet suite. MobileOrganizer is a MIDlet suite with three MIDlets: MobileCalendar, MobileContact, and MobileEmail packaged into a single JAR file.

As shown in Figure 4.1, the application displays a menu entry for each of the three MIDlets in this MIDlet suite. Users can choose a menu entry to start the corresponding MIDlet.

In the following sections, we will discuss two files that are related to MIDlet packaging and deployment: the *manifest* and the *application descriptor*. The manifest is used in MIDlet packaging to describe the contents of a MIDlet suite's JAR file. The application descriptor is used in MIDlet deployment to describe the menu entries, JAR file location, and so on of a MIDlet suite.

FIGURE 4.1
A MIDlet suite's startup menu.

Manifest

A *manifest* file must be included with the MIDlet suite's JAR file. This file describes the contents of the JAR file and includes information such as the name, version, and vendor of the MIDlet suite. It also contains an entry for each MIDlet in the MIDlet suite.

The manifest file contains a list of MIDlet attributes represented as name-value pairs separated by colons. Using these attributes, developers can clearly describe to end users what MIDlets are packaged in the MIDlet suite. Table 4.1 shows all the predefined MIDlet attributes of the manifest file. The attributes in bold are mandatory fields; the rest of the attributes are optional.

TABLE 4.1 Predefined Manifest File Attributes

Attribute Name	Description
MIDlet-Name	The name of the MIDlet suite that identifies the MIDlets to the user.
MIDlet-Version	The version number of the MIDlet suite.
MIDlet-Vendor	The organization that provides the MIDlet suite.
MIDlet-Icon	The name of a PNG file within the JAR file used to represent the MIDlet suite. This file should be used when the Application Management Software displays an icon to identify the suite.
MIDlet-Description	The description of the MIDlet suite.
MIDlet-Info-URL	A URL for information further describing the MIDlet suite.

TABLE 4.1   Continued

Attribute Name	Description
MIDlet-<n>	The name, icon, and class of the *n*th MIDlet in the JAR file, separated by commas. The lowest value of <*n*> must be 1, and consecutive ordinals must be used.
	Name is used to identify this MIDlet to the user.
	Icon is the name of an image (PNG) within the JAR for the icon of the *n*th MIDlet.
	Class is the name of the class extending the MIDlet class for the *n*th MIDlet. The class must have a public no-args constructor.
MIDlet-Jar-URL	The URL from which the JAR file can be loaded.
MIDlet-Jar-Size	The size of the JAR file in bytes.
MIDlet-Data-Size	The minimum number of bytes of persistent data required by the MIDlet. The device may provide additional storage according to its own policy. The default is zero.
MicroEdition-Profile	The J2ME profile required, using the same format and value as the system property microedition.profiles (for example, MIDP-1.0).
MicroEdition-Configuration	The J2ME configuration required, using the same format and value as the system property microedition.configuration (for example, CLDC-1.0).

The following is the manifest file MANIFEST.MF for the HelloWorld program shown in Chapter 3:

```
MIDlet-Name: Hello World
MIDlet-Vendor: Sams Publishing
MIDlet-Version: 1.0
MIDlet-1: HelloWorld, /Icon.png, HelloWorld
MicroEdition-Configuration: CLDC-1.0
MicroEdition-Profile: MIDP-1.0
MIDlet-Data-Size: 0
```

The name of the MIDlet suite is Hello World. The vendor name is Sams Publishing, and the version of the package is 1.0. The attribute MIDlet-1 is used for the only MIDlet in this MIDlet suite. If the MIDlet suite includes more than one MIDlet, a separate entry of MIDlet-<n> must be added, where *n* is a consecutive number.

In the MIDlet-1 field, the first HelloWorld value is the name of the MIDlet, /Icon.png is the icon file for the MIDlet, and the second HelloWorld value is the class name of the MIDlet.

The icon image is a small icon placed next to menu items. In Figure 4.2, the Icon.png file is displayed next to the HelloWorld menu item.

FIGURE 4.2

HelloWorld*'s startup menu.*

Packaging MIDlet Applications

A typical MIDlet suite's JAR file includes all the class files of your MIDlet applications, the resource files, and the manifest file. The class files must be preverified bytecodes. The resource files usually include text files and image files that are used by the MIDlets at runtime.

All the MIDlets within one MIDlet suite can share class files. If you are shipping multiple MIDlet applications in one package, it makes sense to design your applications so that common class files and resource files are shared among these MIDlets. This file sharing will help you reduce your package size.

If you choose to use third-party class libraries in your MIDlets, you have to include the third party's class files in your JAR file as well, unless the class files have already been preloaded on the devices by the manufacturer.

You can package MIDlets into a JAR file using the following command. The example used here is the HelloWorld example from Chapter 3. The files that need to be put in the JAR file include the preverified class file HelloWorld.class, the icon file Icon.png, and the manifest file MANIFEST.MF:

```
c:>c:\jdk1.3\bin\jar cvmf MANIFEST.MF HelloWorld.jar HelloWorld.class icon.png
```

jar is an archive utility that comes with the JDK1.3. The command-line options cvmf are as follows: c creates a new archive, v specifies verbose output of messages, m says to include manifest information from the specified manifest file (in our case, MANIFEST.MF), and f speci-fies the archive filename (in our case, HelloWorld.jar).

The command-line outputs of the jar command are as follows:

```
added manifest
adding: HelloWorld.class(in = 1418) (out= 642)(deflated 54%)
adding: Icon.png(in = 190) (out= 191)(deflated 0%)
```

The percentages after deflated indicate the compression ratio of the archived files.

> **NOTE**
>
> You can find more information about Java's jar utility at
> http://java.sun.com/docs/books/tutorial/jar/index.html.

Application Descriptor

The *application descriptor* shares the same format as the manifest file, but it serves a totally different purpose. The manifest is used in the packaging of a MIDlet suite, whereas the application descriptor is used in the deployment of a MIDlet suite, especially in the Over-The-Air (OTA) deployment process (discussed in the section "Over-The-Air MIDlet Deployment," later in this chapter). Before a JAR file is downloaded to the device, the application descriptor is checked by the Application Management Software to make sure that the MIDlet suite is suited to the device. This step is especially useful in unstable and low-bandwidth wireless networks.

Unlike the manifest, the application descriptor is not included in the JAR file. The file extension for the application descriptor must be .jad.

Because the application descriptor is mainly used for deployment, its mandatory attributes are a little different from those in a manifest file.

Predefined Attributes

The following seven predefined attributes are mandatory for the application descriptor:

```
MIDlet-Name
MIDlet-Version
MIDlet-Vendor
MIDlet-Jar-URL
MIDlet-Jar-Size
MicroEdition-Profile
MicroEdition-Configuration
```

The following four predefined attributes are optional:

```
MIDlet-Description
MIDlet-Icon
MIDlet-Info-URL
MIDlet-Data-Size
```

Before the MIDlet suite's JAR file is downloaded to a device, the seven mandatory attributes in its application descriptor are checked by the Application Management Software to make sure the application is suitable for the device. For example, if the device doesn't support the profile or the version of the profile specified in the `MicroEdition-Profile` attribute, the JAR file will not be downloaded. If the JAR file size specified in the `MIDlet-Jar-URL` attribute is too big to fit on the device, the JAR file will not be downloaded either.

In Chapter 3, we used the following command to execute the `HelloWorld` example:

```
C:\>c:\jdk1.3\bin\java.exe -Dkvem.home=%SUNJ2MEHOME%
                           -classpath %CLASSPATH%
                           com.sun.kvem.midp.Main DefaultGrayPhone
                           -descriptor HelloWorld.jad
```

The `HelloWorld.jad` file is the application descriptor used in the `HelloWorld` example:

```
MIDlet-Name: HelloWorld
MIDlet-Version: 1.0
MIDlet-Vendor: Sams Publishing
MIDlet-1: HelloWorld, /Icon.png, HelloWorld
MIDlet-Data-Size: 0
MIDlet-Description: Our First MIDlet Example.
MIDlet-Jar-Size: 1510
MIDlet-Jar-URL: HelloWorld.jar
MicroEdition-Configuration: CLDC-1.0
MicroEdition-Profile: MIDP-1.0
Language-Support: English
Target-Device: Motorola Condor
Display-Width: 140
Display-Height: 100
```

It tells J2MEWTK's emulator where the JAR file is located, how big the JAR file is, the version of the MIDP, and so on. If the package is to be deployed remotely over the wireless network, the value of the `MIDlet-Jar-URL` field needs to be changed to a Web URL that tells where the JAR file can be downloaded. For example:

```
MIDlet-Jar-URL: http://www.webyu.com/midlets/HelloWorld.jar
```

Even though the manifest and the application descriptor are used for different purposes, certain attributes in the two files must be identical. Otherwise, the MIDlet suite will not be downloaded to the device. These attributes are `MIDlet-Name`, `MIDlet-Version`, and `MIDlet-Vendor`.

4

PACKAGING AND
DEPLOYING JAVA
APPLICATIONS

Defining Your Own Attributes

Besides these predefined attributes, you can also define your own attributes in the application descriptor. These user-defined fields cannot begin with *MIDlet-*.

All attributes in the application descriptor and manifest are accessible from the MIDlets at runtime. For example, in the `HelloWorld.jad` file, four application-specific attributes (`Language-Support`, `Target-Device`, `Display-Width`, and `Display-Height`) are used as configuration parameters. The `Display-Width` and `Display-Height` fields describe the form factors of the target devices. By accessing these parameters at runtime, the MIDlets can dynamically adapt themselves to different target devices. As a result, the same JAR file can support a variety of devices. All you have to do is create a device-specific application descriptor file for every target device.

In the section "Runtime Access to the Manifest, Application Descriptor, and Resource Files," we will talk about how to access the manifest file, the application descriptor, and the resource files from a MIDlet at runtime.

Using J2ME Wireless Toolkit's IDE to Package and Deploy MIDlets

So far, you have learned how to use the command line to compile MIDlets, preverify MIDlets, create a manifest, create an application descriptor, and package these components into a MIDlet suite. Doing these steps manually helps you better understand the various processes involved in developing and deploying MIDlets. But doing so is time-consuming and error-prone. In this section, we will show you how the J2ME Wireless Toolkit's IDE can help you streamline all these tasks into one easy step.

You have two options when using the J2ME Wireless Toolkit's IDE: You can use the stand-alone `KToolbar` that comes with the Toolkit, or you can use Forte for Java's IDE in conjunction with the J2ME Wireless Toolkit.

`%J2MEWTK%` and `%FORTE4J%` are the two environment variables used in next two sections. `%J2MEWTK%` is the installation directory of J2ME Wireless Toolkit; in our case, it is `c:\applications\J2MEWTK`. `%FORTE4J%` is the installation directory of Forte for Java; in our case, it is `c:\applications\forte4j`.

Using J2ME Wireless Toolkit's `KToolbar`

If you haven't installed the J2ME Wireless Toolkit, please refer to the section "Setting Up the Development Environment" in Chapter 2, "Java for Wireless Devices," for instructions on how to install the Toolkit.

The following steps show you how to use the KToolbar development environment to set up a project for the HelloWorld example, to create the manifest and application descriptor, and to package the application:

1. In Microsoft Windows, choose Start, Programs, J2ME Wireless Toolkit 1.0.1, KToolbar to start the KToolbar development environment. Figure 4.3 shows the KToolbar startup screen.

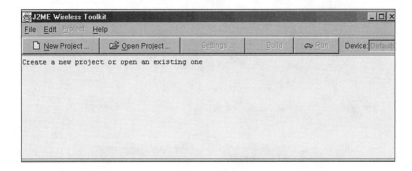

FIGURE 4.3

KToolbar's *startup menu.*

2. Click on the New Project button on the startup screen to create a new project called HelloWorld. Name the MIDlet class HelloWorld as well, as shown in Figure 4.4.

FIGURE 4.4

KToolbar's *Create New Project dialog box.*

3. A project setting window will open, as shown in Figure 4.6. This screen allows you to modify the MIDlet attributes for the manifest and application descriptor. Figure 4.5 shows all the mandatory attributes in the application descriptor and manifest.

4. Click on the Optional tab on the project setting screen. You will see a list of optional MIDlet attributes, as shown in Figure 4.6. Here, You can add and modify optional MIDlet attributes and user-defined attributes.

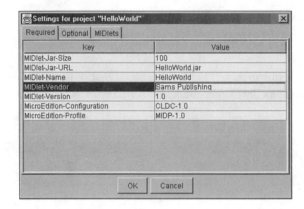

FIGURE 4.5

KToolbar*'s project setting screen for editing mandatory MIDlet attributes.*

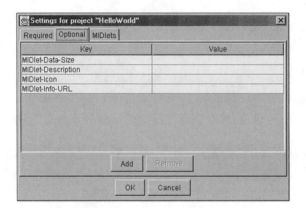

FIGURE 4.6

KToolbar*'s project setting screen for editing optional fields.*

5. Click on the MIDlets tab on the project setting screen to add and delete MIDlets in the MIDlet suite. As shown in Figure 4.7, the HelloWorld MIDlet has been already added to the MIDlet suite.

6. Once the new project HelloWorld is created, a project directory is created under %J2MEWTK%\apps\HelloWorld. Several subdirectories are created in this directory as well: bin, classes, res, src, and tmpclasses. Copy all Java source files (HelloWorld.java) to the %J2MEWTK%\apps\HelloWorld\src directory, which is the project's source code directory. If you'd like to package resource files with the MIDlet suite, you can copy them into the %J2MEWTK%\apps\HelloWorld\res directory, which is the project's resource file directory. The resource files under the res directory will be automatically packaged into the JAR file.

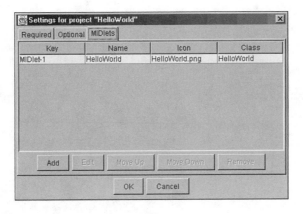

FIGURE 4.7
KToolbar's *project setting screen for editing MIDlet entries.*

7. Go back to KToolbar's main screen and click on the Build button. KToolbar will compile, preverify, generate the manifest and application descriptor, and package the JAR file in one step.

8. The packaged JAR file, the generated application descriptor, and the generated manifest can be found under the %J2MEWTK%\apps\HelloWorld\bin directory, which is the project's deployment directory.

You can find more information regarding how to use the J2ME Wireless Toolkit's KToolbar development environment in the User Guide that comes with the Toolkit installation.

Using Forte for Java's IDE

The previous section discussed how to use the standalone KToolbar of the J2ME Wireless Toolkit to package MIDlets. This section shows you how to use Forte for Java's IDE to perform the same task. If you haven't installed Forte for Java and the J2ME Wireless Toolkit, please refer to the installation instructions in Chapter 2. Forte for Java must be installed before the J2ME Wireless Toolkit is installed. When the J2ME Wireless Toolkit is installed, select the Integrated option to make sure that the J2ME Wireless Toolkit is integrated with Forte for Java.

The following steps show you how to use Forte for Java's IDE to set up a project to package your HelloWorld example:

1. In Microsoft Windows, choose Start, Programs, Forte for Java CE, Forte for Java CE to start the Forte for Java development environment. Figure 4.8 shows the IDE. If %FORTE4J%\Development is not shown in the Explorer window, choose File, Mount Filesystem to mount that directory. In our case, that's the c:\applications\forte4j\Development directory.

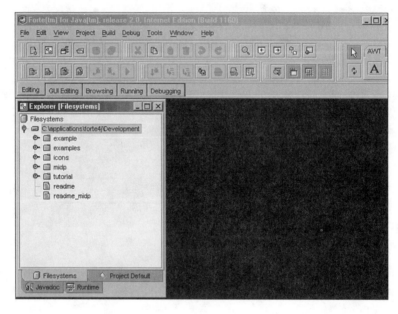

FIGURE 4.8
Forte for Java's startup screen.

2. Right-click on c:\applications\forte4j\Development in the Explorer window. Figure 4.9 shows the resulting pop-up menu. Select the New Package menu item to create a new package called HelloWorld.

FIGURE 4.9
Forte for Java's pop-up menu for creating a new package.

3. Right-click on the HelloWorld package in the Explorer window and select New, MIDP, EmptyClass to create a class called HelloWorld, as shown in Figure 4.10.

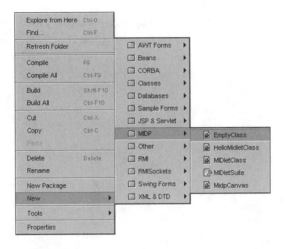

FIGURE 4.10

Forte for Java's pop-up menu for adding a class to the HelloWorld *package.*

4. Copy the contents of HelloWorld.java shown in Listing 3.1 into the Source Editor of the HelloWorld class as shown in Figure 4.11. Save the class.

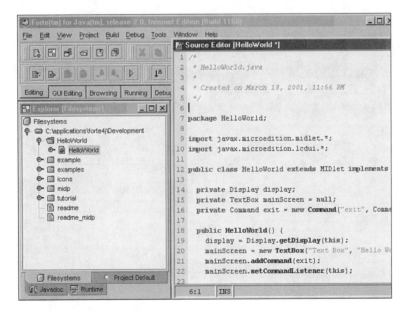

FIGURE 4.11

Forte for Java's Source Editor for editing HelloWorld.java.

4

PACKAGING AND DEPLOYING JAVA APPLICATIONS

5. Right-click again on the `HelloWorld` package in the Explorer window. Select New, MIDP, MIDletSuite to create a MIDlet suite called `HelloWorld`, as shown in Figure 4.12. A project setting windows will open, as shown in Figure 4.13. Use this screen to add, edit, or delete the MIDlet attributes for the manifest and application descriptor.

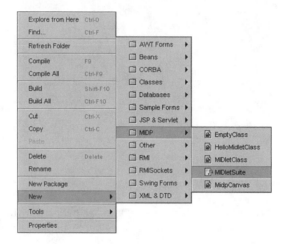

FIGURE 4.12

Forte for Java's pop-up menu for creating the `HelloWorld` *MIDlet suite.*

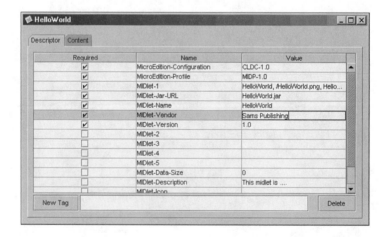

FIGURE 4.13

Forte for Java's project setting screen for editing MIDlet attributes for the manifest and application descriptor.

6. Click on the Content tab on the project setting screen as shown in Figure 4.14. Use this screen to add MIDlets to the MIDlet suite. Select the HelloWorld MIDlet from the left window, and click on the Add button to add it to the MIDlet suite.

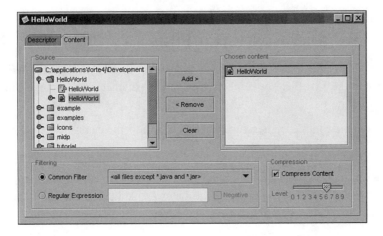

FIGURE 4.14
Forte for Java's project setting screen for adding MIDlets to the MIDlet suite.

7. Right-click on the HelloWorld MIDlet suite in the Explorer window and select Update JAR, as shown in Figure 4.15. Forte for Java will compile, preverify, generate the manifest and application descriptor, and package the JAR file for the HelloWorld application. All the files associated with the HelloWorld MIDlet suite are placed in the %FORTE4J%\Development\HelloWorld directory.

FIGURE 4.15
Forte for Java's pop-up menu for compiling and packaging the HelloWorld MIDlet suite.

4

PACKAGING AND
DEPLOYING JAVA
APPLICATIONS

Now you have created a `HelloWorld` MIDlet suite that's ready for deployment. You can find more information regarding how to use Forte for Java's IDE to package MIDlets in the User Guide that comes with the J2ME Wireless Toolkit installation.

Runtime Access to the Manifest, Application Descriptor, and Resource Files

At runtime, a MIDlet can access the manifest, application descriptor, and user-defined resource files packaged in the JAR file. The resource files can be parameter files, images files, license key files, and so on.

The attributes in the application descriptor and the manifest file can be retrieved by using the

`javax.microedition.midlet.MIDlet.getAppPorperty(String propertyname)`

method. The values of the attributes are retrieved from the combination of the application descriptor file and the manifest. If the same attributes are defined in both files, the values of the attributes in the application descriptor overwrite the values from the manifest.

The contents of the user-defined resource files can be retrieved by using the method

`java.lang.Class.getResourceAsStream(String filename)`

Listing 4.1 shows how to access the attributes in `ResourceDemo.jad` and `MANIFEST.MF`, and how to retrieve the contents of `readme.txt` from a MIDlet at runtime.

The attributes of the application descriptor `ResourceDemo.jad` are as follows:

```
MIDlet-1: ResourceDemo, /Icon.png, ResourceDemo
MIDlet-Data-Size: 0
MIDlet-Description: This midlet is a demo MIDlet application.
MIDlet-Jar-Size: 4616
MIDlet-Jar-URL: ResourceDemo.jar
MIDlet-Name: ResourceDemo
MIDlet-Vendor: Sams Publishing
MIDlet-Version: 1.0
MicroEdition-Configuration: CLDC-1.0
MicroEdition-Profile: MIDP-1.0
Target-Devices: Sun Javaphone, Motorola Condor
```

The attributes of the manifest are listed here:

```
MIDlet-1: ResourceDemo, /Icon.png,  ResourceDemo
MIDlet-Data-Size: 0
MIDlet-Name: ResourceDemo
MIDlet-Vendor: Sams Publishing
MIDlet-Version: 1.0
MicroEdition-Configuration: CLDC-1.0
MicroEdition-Profile: MIDP-1.0
```

The values of MIDlet-Name, MIDlet-Version, and MIDlet-Vendor must be the same in both files. The values of other attributes can be different.

The resource file readme.txt must be packaged in the JAR file as well, so that the MIDlet can access it:

```
C:\>c:\jdk1.3\bin\jar cmf MANIFEST.MF
     ResourceDemo.jar ResourceDemo.class Icon.png readme.txt
```

LISTING 4.1   ResourceDemo.java

```
import java.io.*;
import javax.microedition.midlet.*;

public class ResourceDemo extends MIDlet{

  public ResourceDemo() {
  }

  public void startApp() throws MIDletStateChangeException {

    // retrieve the properties defined in
    // descriptor and manifest
    System.out.println(
      "Retrieving the predefined properties:");
    System.out.println(
      "-----------------------------------------");

    String vendor = getAppProperty("MIDlet-Vendor");
    String desc = getAppProperty("MIDlet-Description");
    String devices = getAppProperty("Target-Devices");
    String size = getAppProperty("Display-Size");

    // print the values of these properties to standard output
    System.out.println("MIDlet-Vendor: " + vendor);
    System.out.println("MIDlet-Description: " + desc);
    System.out.println("Target-Devices: " + devices);
    System.out.println("Display-Size: " + size);

    System.out.println();

    // retrieve the contents of a resource file
    System.out.println(
      "Retrieving the resource file - readme.txt");
    System.out.println(
      "-----------------------------------------");
```

LISTING 4.1 Continued

```java
    InputStream is =
      this.getClass().getResourceAsStream("readme.txt");
    try {
      if ( is != null ) {
        int ch;
        while ( (ch = is.read()) != -1) {
          // print out the contents of the readme file
          System.out.print((char) ch);
        }
        is.close();
      }
    } catch (IOException e) {
      System.out.println(e);
    }
  }

  public void pauseApp() {
  }

  public void destroyApp(boolean unconditional) {
  }
}
```

The MIDlet program in Listing 4.1 retrieves four attribute values from the application descriptor and manifest by using the getAppProperty() method. These attributes are MIDlet-Vendor, MIDlet-Description, Target-Devices, and Display-Size. Because the Display-Size attribute is not defined in the two files, the value returned from getAppProperty() is null.

The second part of the program obtains an InputStream on the readme.txt file by using the method

```
this.getClass().getResourceAsStream("readme.txt")
```

It then reads the contents character by character until the end of the file and prints them out to the standard output. The following is the output from the ResourceDemo program:

```
Retrieving the predefined properties:
- - - - - - - - - - - - - - - - - - - - - - - - - - - - - - - - - - - - -
MIDlet-Vendor: Sams Publishing
MIDlet-Description: This midlet is a demo MIDlet application.
Target-Devices: Sun Javaphone, Motorola Condor
Display-Size: null

Retrieving the resource file - readme.txt
- - - - - - - - - - - - - - - - - - - - - - - - - - - - - - - - - - - - -
```

At run time, a MIDlet application can access all the non-class files that are packaged within the MIDlet Suite JAR file by using methods on java.lang.Class.getResourceAsStream().

Over-The-Air MIDlet Deployment

There are several ways to deploy MIDlet applications. First, a MIDlet suite can be loaded to a device via a serial cable connected to the PC. However, this loading process is usually reserved for the manufacturer to preload the K Virtual Machine (KVM), the Connected Limited Device Configuration (CLDC) and MIDP libraries, and built-in MIDlets onto devices before they are shipped to the end users.

MIDlets can also be downloaded to a device via a wireless network, very similar to downloading Java applets to your PC over the Internet. This process, illustrated in Figure 4.16, is called Over-The-Air (OTA) MIDlet deployment. OTA installation is a cost-effective way of deploying applications for both device manufacturers and the software developers. It also gives users full control over which applications to download and execute on their wireless devices.

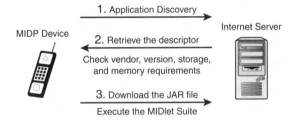

FIGURE 4.16
Over-The-Air MIDlet deployment.

The process can be best described in the following steps:

1. Application Discovery: The MIDP devices provide mechanisms that allow users to discover or be notified of the MIDlet suites that can be downloaded to the device. For example, users can use the on-device browser (for example, WAP, i-Mode browsers) to identify MIDlet suites to download. Once the user sees a link to an application descriptor in the browser, he or she can select the link to begin the installation process.

2. Download and verify the application descriptor: The application descriptor is downloaded onto the device. The Application Management Software examines the name, vendor, version, size, and CLDC/MIDP versions of the application descriptor to make sure that the MIDlets are appropriate for the current execution environment on the device.

The Application Management Software also makes sure that any old or same version of the existing MIDlet suite is ignored and only the upgraded or new MIDlet suite is downloaded.

3. Download and execute the MIDlet suite: Once the application descriptor is verified, the Application Management Software begins downloading the JAR file from the location specified in the `MIDlet-Jar-URL` attribute. Once the download is complete, the Application Management Software checks the values of the key fields in the application descriptor against those in the manifest to make sure they match. If the key values are identical, the MIDlet suite is loaded and ready for execution. Otherwise, the MIDlet suite is rejected.

Serving an Application Descriptor

In order to serve an application descriptor from your Web server, you need to add the following MIME type to your Web server's configuration file:

```
text/vnd.sun.j2me.app-descriptor jad
```

For example, on our Apache/Linux Web server, you can either add a new MIME entry in the MIME type configuration file `mime.types` or add the following line in Apache's configuration file `httpd.conf`:

```
AddType text/vnd.sun.j2me.app-descriptor .jad
```

The configuration file and its syntax vary from server to server; please consult your Web server vendor for detail information.

OTA Example

The following example shows you how the OTA process works in an emulator environment. We took the JAR file and application descriptor of the `HelloWorld` example and put them on our book companion Web site. You can use the following command to start the OTA installation process:

```
C:\>c:\midp-fcs\bin\midp.exe
    -transient http://www.webyu.com/midlets/HelloWorld.jad HelloWorld
```

To run this example, you need to download and install Sun's MIDP reference implementation package. This package is different from Sun's J2MEWTK and can be downloaded from `http://www.sun.com/software/communitysource/midp/download.html`. On our laptop, we installed the package in the `C:\midp-fcs` directory. The MIDP reference implementation package comes with its own emulator. The command-line option `transient` indicates that you want to run a MIDlet named `HelloWorld` from an application descriptor at the specified Web URL `http://www.webyu.com/midlets/Helloworld.jad`.

The following is the message generated from the execution:

```
the path is ./transapps/Hello World/HelloWorld.jar
Good - Required Manifest values match app descriptor
```

The MIDP emulator first verifies the attributes in the application descriptor. If everything looks fine, it then downloads the JAR file and begins executing the program.

Figure 4.17 shows the HelloWorld MIDlet executing via the OTA process.

FIGURE 4.17
The HelloWorld MIDlet.

Summary

An application developed with J2ME MIDP is called a MIDlet. MIDlets are packaged together to form an application bundle known as a MIDlet suite. The MIDlet suite is packaged in JAR file format for deployment. A manifest that describes the MIDlets in the MIDlet suite must be included in the JAR file. The MIDlet suite can be downloaded to the wireless device via the Over-The-Air deployment process, and an application descriptor is needed for this process.

4

PACKAGING AND
DEPLOYING JAVA
APPLICATIONS

Developing Wireless Applications Using Java

IN THIS PART

Central Components of the UI for Wireless Devices

IN THIS CHAPTER

Introduction

J2ME will run on a variety of consumer devices, from smart cards and cell phones all the way to TV set-top boxes and home appliances. The display devices and their resources are quite different. Sun Microsystems recognizes this situation, so no *über* user interface (UI) class is defined in J2ME. Instead, the user interface API is defined in the profile for a specific group of devices. For example, the UI API for mobile information devices (MID), such as cell phones and pagers, is defined in the MID profile (MIDP); and the UI API for personal digital assistants (PDA), such as Palm Pilots, is defined in the PDA profile (PDAP).

The user interface API of J2SE is defined in the Abstract Window Toolkit (AWT), which is mainly designed and optimized for desktop computers with pointer devices, large displays, and sufficient resources. Wireless devices' displays are much smaller than those of common desktop systems, and the primary input devices are keypads instead of pointer devices. In addition, the dynamic event-handling model used in AWT is a resource-intensive process, and it's not suitable for resource-limited wireless devices. Many desktop-based features in AWT, such as window management and layout management, are not useful for wireless devices due to their limited display size. Simply tailoring a subset of AWT to fit the needs of MIDs is difficult because of the internal dependency of AWT. Thus, the MIDP expert group decided not to subset AWT but rather to define a whole new UI API for wireless devices. The UI API is included in the package javax.microedition.lcdui.

The UI defined in MIDP is logically composed of two sets of APIs: high level and low level. The high-level API emphasizes portability, which is achieved by employing a high level of abstraction. The actual drawing and processing user interactions are performed by implementations. Applications that use the high-level API have little control over the visual appearance of components, and can only access high-level UI events. On the other hand, using the low-level API, an application has full control of appearance, and can directly access input devices and handle primitive events generated by user interaction. However, the low-level API may be device-dependent, so applications using it may not be portable. You should consider using the high-level API and the device-independent features of the low-level API in your applications whenever possible.

This chapter talks about the basics of developing user interfaces for J2ME MIDP applications. The next two chapters discuss UI development using the high-level API and the low-level API.

Displayable and Display

One of central functions of a user interface is to present information to users. In J2ME MIDP, a Displayable object contains information to be presented, and a Display object manages which Displayable object will be visible to users.

Displayable

The central abstraction of the MIDP's UI is a `Displayable` class. A `Displayable` is an object that encapsulates device-specific graphics rendering and can be placed on the display.

The UI defined in MIDP is logically composed of two APIs: the high level and the low level. The `Screen` class is a `Displayable` that implements the high-level API. The `Canvas` class is a `Displayable` that implements the low-level API.

The sizes and shapes of MIDs' displays are quite different. For example, Figure 5.1 shows, from left to right, a pager's display and two different sizes of cell-phone displays. Because the high-level API takes care of different display sizes, applications developed with it do not need to deal explicitly with different display sizes. However, applications developed with low-level APIs must deal with different sizes when they paint to the display.

FIGURE 5.1

Displays of mobile information display devices: a pager, a cell phone with a large screen, and a cell phone with a small screen.

There are three categories of `Displayables`, as shown in Figure 5.2:

- Structure-predefined `Screen` (`Alert`, `List`, and `TextBox`): These screens usually encapsulate complex interface components. Applications cannot add other components to these screens.

- Generic `Screen` (`Form`): Applications can populate these screens with text, images, and simple sets of related UI components.

- `Canvas`: Applications have full control of the appearance of components and can directly access low-level events.

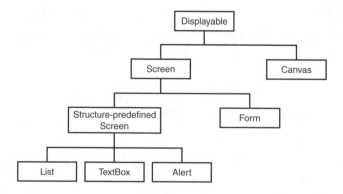

FIGURE 5.2

Hierarchical structure of Displayables.

Here are the methods defined in a Displayable class:

```
void addCommand(Command cmd)
boolean isShown()
void removeCommand(Command cmd)
void setCommandListener(CommandListener l)
```

All Displayables may have Commands and Commandlisteners registered to receive the command events. Command and CommandListener are discussed in the section "Events and Event Handling" later in the chapter.

Screen

The Screen is a subclass of Displayable that implements the high-level API. It is the superclass of Alert, Form, List, and TextBox. A Screen can contain an optional title and ticker-tape (a piece of text that runs continuously across the display).

Screen is an abstract class. Its methods, which define how contents are displayed and how contents interact with the user, are abstract methods. These methods need to be implemented by Screen's subclasses. Only the methods for refreshing displayed contents are implemented in the Screen class. However, you cannot extend the Screen class directly because its abstract methods are not accessible from outside the javax.microedition.lcdui package.

The following methods are provided for a Screen class:

```
Ticker getTicker()
String getTitle()
void setTicker(Ticker ticker)
void setTitle(String s)
```

A `Ticker` class implements a ticker-tape. A `Ticker` object can be constructed using the `Ticker(String str)` method. The `Ticker`'s text can be set or retrieved using the `Ticker.setString(String str)` or `Ticker.getString()` method.

A `Ticker` object can be attached to a `Screen` by using `setTicker(Ticker)`, and it can be removed from a `Screen` by using `setTicker(null)`. One `Ticker` object can be shared by multiple `Screens`.

The animated effect of ticker text can be accomplished by scheduling the painting of the text with `TimerTask` and `Timer`. The painting schedule is implementation dependent; applications have no control on it.

Canvas

The `Canvas` class is a subclass of `Displayable` that implements the low-level API. Using this class, applications have full control over what to display and how to display it. Applications can also directly access low-level events, such as key events. `Canvas` is an abstract class. Applications have to subclass the `Canvas` class in order to use it. How to use the `Canvas` class is discussed in detail in Chapter 7, "Using Low-Level APIs in UI Development."

Display

The `Display` class represents the display manager. It provides the following methods for retrieving properties of the device and for requesting objects to be displayed on the device:

```
void callSerially(Runnable r)
Displayable getCurrent()
static Display getDisplay(MIDlet m)
boolean isColor()
int numColors()
void setCurrent(Alert alert, Displayable nextDisplayable)
void setCurrent(Displayable nextDisplayable)
```

`Display` is a *singleton* in a MIDlet application. That means there is only one instance of `Display` per MIDlet; the application can get a reference to that instance by calling the `getDisplay()` method. The application can call the `getDisplay()` method any time from the beginning of the `MIDlet.startApp()` call until the return of `MIDlet.destroyApp()` call. The `Display` object returned by all calls to `getDisplay()` will remain the same during this time.

The Current `Displayable`

At any time, an application can have at most one `Displayable` object that it intends to show on the display device and through which user interaction occurs. This `Displayable` is referred to as the *current* `Displayable`. Users can only interact with the current `Displayable`.

The `Display` class has a `getCurrent()` method for retrieving the current `Displayable` and two methods for setting the current `Displayable`:

```
void setCurrent(Displayable nextDisplayable)
void setCurrent(Alert alert, Displayable nextDisplayable)
```

The `Alert` class is a subclass of `Screen`. (We will discuss why the

```
setCurrent(Alert alert, Displayable nextDisplayable)
```

method is necessary when we discuss the `Alert` class in Chapter 6, "Using High-Level APIs in UI Development.")

The application has control over its current `Displayable` and can call `Display.setCurrent()` at any time. Any threads of the MIDlet can set or retrieve the current `Displayable` using the `Display.setCurrent()` or `Display.getCurrent()` method.

The example in Listing 5.1 creates two `Forms`. A `Ticker` object is created and is shared by the two `Forms`. The application switches the current `Displayable` every five seconds by calling `setCurrent()`.

LISTING 5.1   TestScreen1.java

```java
import javax.microedition.midlet.*;
import javax.microedition.lcdui.*;

public class ScreenTest1 extends MIDlet {
    private Display display;
    private Form s1;
    private Form s2;
    public ScreenTest1() {
        s1 = new Form("Screen 1");
        s2 = new Form("Screen 2");
        Ticker t= new Ticker("This is a test for switching screen. "+
                             "Screen 1 and 2 are switched every 5 seconds.");
        s1.setTicker(t);
        s2.setTicker(t);
    }
    public void startApp() throws MIDletStateChangeException {
        display=Display.getDisplay(this);
        display.setCurrent(s1);
        new Thread(new ScreenTestRun()).start();
    }

    /**
     * Pause the MIDlet
     */
```

LISTING 5.1   Continued

```
public void pauseApp() {
}

/**
 * Called by the framework before the application is unloaded
 */
public void destroyApp(boolean unconditional) {
    display=null;
    s1=null;
    s2=null;
}

class ScreenTestRun implements Runnable {
    public void run() {
        while(true) {
            try {
                Thread.sleep(5000);
                if(display.getCurrent()==s1) {
                    display.setCurrent(s2);
                }
                else {
                    display.setCurrent(s1);
                }
            }catch(Exception e){}
        }
    }
}
}
```

If you run the MIDlet, you will see the display switching between screens similar to Figure 5.3 and Figure 5.4.

The Foreground and Background Application

Users may have several MIDlet applications running simultaneously on the same device. However, the device has only one display on which to make a MIDlet's current `Displayable` visible. If a MIDlet's current `Displayable` is actually visible on the display device, the MIDlet is said to be in the *foreground,* and user input events will be delivered to it. A *background* MIDlet has access to neither the display nor input devices.

A MIDlet application can put itself into the background using `Display.setCurrent(null)`. However, this call does not actually set the current `Displayable` to null. For example, suppose the current `Displayable` is cD. After the application calls `Display.setCurrent(null)`, the call `getCurrent()` still returns cD. An application can bring itself back to the foreground using `Display.setCurrent(Display.getCurrent())`.

FIGURE 5.3
Set current Displayable; *the first screen.*

FIGURE 5.4
Set current Displayable; *the second screen.*

Even though an application's current Displayable may not physically be drawn on the display, the application is still aware of its current Displayable. The current Displayable is significant, even for background applications, because it is always the one that will be shown next time the application is brought into the foreground.

Each MIDlet application has its own current Displayable. The getCurrent() method returns the MIDlet's current Displayable, regardless of the MIDlet's foreground/background state. And changing a MIDlet's current Displayable by calling setCurrent() will not affect any other MIDlet's current Displayable.

Switching between the SQL foreground and background applications is under the control of the Application Management Software (AMS). There is a detailed discussion of the AMS in Chapter 4, "Packaging and Deploying Java Wireless Applications."

System Screens

Typically, the current screen of the foreground MIDlet will be visible on the display. However, under certain circumstances, the system may create a screen that temporarily obscures the application's current screen. These screens are referred to as *system screens*. This may occur if the system needs to show a menu of commands or if the system requires the user to edit text on a separate screen instead of within a text field inside a Form.

Even though the system screen obscures the application's screen, the notion of the current Displayable does not change. While a system screen is visible, a call to getCurrent() will return the application's current Displayable, not the system screen. The value returned by a currentDisplayable.isShown() call is false while the current Displayable is obscured by a system screen.

Image

The Image class is used to hold graphical image data. Image objects exist in offscreen memory independently of the display device. An Image object can be painted to a Canvas, or be placed within a Form, an Alert, a List element, or a ChoiceGroup element.

The following methods of Image are provided in the API:

```
static Image createImage(byte[] imageData, int imageOffset, int imageLength)
static Image createImage(Image source)
static Image createImage(int width, int height)
static Image createImage(String name)
Graphics getGraphics()
int getHeight()
int getWidth()
boolean isMutable()
```

Images are either *mutable* or *immutable* depending upon how they are created.

Immutable Images

Immutable Images are generally created by loading image data from resource bundles, files, or the network. They cannot be modified once created. Images to be placed within Alert, Choice, or ImageItem objects are required to be immutable.

Creating Immutable Images from Files

An immutable `Image` can be created from a resource file included in the MIDlet suite using

```
Image.createImage(String name)
```

Image data stored in the file has to be in one of the image formats supported by the implementation. The Portable Network Graphics (PNG) format must be supported by all implementations. The GIF format is supported by some implementations. For example, Sun's emulator version 1.0b supports the GIF format, but the new version 1.01 does not. Motorola's emulator does not support the GIF format. The format of the image will be auto-detected based on the first few bytes of the image file. If the image file is not found or the image format is not recognized, an `IOException` will be thrown. J2SE provides a method `ImageIO.getReaderFormatNames()` to list all supported image formats; J2ME does not. With J2ME, you must use trial and error to test whether other image formats are supported.

Creating Immutable Images from Byte Arrays

You don't always need to include image files that you want to display in the MIDlet suite. You can

- Store the image file data to persistent storage and then read it to byte arrays as necessary.
- Download the image files from the Internet into byte arrays when the data is needed.
- Store the image file data into byte arrays and include the byte arrays in the program.

Then, you can create an immutable `Image` from a byte array using the method

```
Image.createImage(byte[] imageData, int imageOffset, int imageLength)
```

For example, you can convert a PNG image as shown in Figure 5.5 into a byte array using any hex editor for Windows or using the Unix hexdump utility xxd. Then, you can create an immutable `Image` as follows:

```
byte data[] = {
        (byte)0x89, (byte)0x50, (byte)0x4e, (byte)0x47, (byte)0x0d,
(byte)0x0a,
        (byte)0x1a, (byte)0x0a, (byte)0x00, (byte)0x00, (byte)0x00,
(byte)0x0d,
        (byte)0x49, (byte)0x48, (byte)0x44, (byte)0x52, (byte)0x00,
(byte)0x00,
        (byte)0x00, (byte)0x20, (byte)0x00, (byte)0x00, (byte)0x00,
(byte)0x20,
        (byte)0x01, (byte)0x00, (byte)0x00, (byte)0x00, (byte)0x00,
(byte)0x5b,
        (byte)0x01, (byte)0x47, (byte)0x59, (byte)0x00, (byte)0x00,
(byte)0x00,
        (byte)0x04, (byte)0x67, (byte)0x41, (byte)0x4d, (byte)0x41,
(byte)0x00,
```

```
                (byte)0x01, (byte)0x86, (byte)0xa0, (byte)0x31, (byte)0xe8,
        (byte)0x96,
                (byte)0x5f, (byte)0x00, (byte)0x00, (byte)0x00, (byte)0x5b,
        (byte)0x49,
                (byte)0x44, (byte)0x41, (byte)0x54, (byte)0x78, (byte)0x9c,
        (byte)0x2d,
                (byte)0xcc, (byte)0xb1, (byte)0x09, (byte)0x03, (byte)0x30,
        (byte)0x0c,
                (byte)0x05, (byte)0xd1, (byte)0xeb, (byte)0xd2, (byte)0x04,
        (byte)0xb2,
                (byte)0x4a, (byte)0x20, (byte)0x0b, (byte)0x7a, (byte)0x34,
        (byte)0x6f,
                (byte)0x90, (byte)0x15, (byte)0x3c, (byte)0x82, (byte)0xc1,
        (byte)0x8d,
                (byte)0x0a, (byte)0x61, (byte)0x45, (byte)0x07, (byte)0x51,
        (byte)0xf1,
                (byte)0xe0, (byte)0x8a, (byte)0x2f, (byte)0xaa, (byte)0xea,
        (byte)0xd2,
                (byte)0xa4, (byte)0x84, (byte)0x6c, (byte)0xce, (byte)0xa9,
        (byte)0x25,
                (byte)0x53, (byte)0x06, (byte)0xe7, (byte)0x53, (byte)0x34,
        (byte)0x57,
                (byte)0x12, (byte)0xe2, (byte)0x11, (byte)0xb2, (byte)0x21,
        (byte)0xbf,
                (byte)0x4b, (byte)0x26, (byte)0x3d, (byte)0x1b, (byte)0x42,
        (byte)0x73,
                (byte)0x25, (byte)0x25, (byte)0x5e, (byte)0x8b, (byte)0xda,
        (byte)0xb2,
                (byte)0x9e, (byte)0x6f, (byte)0x6a, (byte)0xca, (byte)0x30,
        (byte)0x69,
                (byte)0x2e, (byte)0x9d, (byte)0x29, (byte)0x61, (byte)0x6e,
        (byte)0xe9,
                (byte)0x6f, (byte)0x30, (byte)0x65, (byte)0xf0, (byte)0xbf,
        (byte)0x1f,
                (byte)0x10, (byte)0x87, (byte)0x49, (byte)0x2f, (byte)0xd0,
        (byte)0x2f,
                (byte)0x14, (byte)0xc9, (byte)0x00, (byte)0x00, (byte)0x00,
        (byte)0x00,
                (byte)0x49, (byte)0x45, (byte)0x4e, (byte)0x44, (byte)0xae,
        (byte)0x42,
                (byte)0x60, (byte)0x82};
};

Image img = Image.createImage(data, 0, data.length);
```

The byte array is the contents of an image file. So, the supported image formats and format detection are the same as just discussed.

5

CENTRAL
COMPONENTS OF
THE UI

FIGURE 5.5
A immutable Image *created from a byte array.*

Creating Immutable Images from Other Images

An immutable Image can also be created from a source image:

```
Image.createImage(Image source)
```

The source Image can be either mutable or immutable.

Mutable Images

Mutable Images are created in offscreen memory. They are like offscreen display devices or canvases. The application may paint into them after having created a Graphics object expressly. A mutable Image can be created using

```
Image.createImage(int width, int height)
```

Mutable Images can be used in the double-buffering technique, which is covered in Chapter 7.

Properties of Images

All Image objects have three properties: height, width, and isMutable. Applications can retrieve the property values using the getHeight(), getWidth(), and isMutable() methods, respectively. If an image is mutable, applications can create Graphics objects that render to this image using the getGraphics() method.

Events and Event Handling

A user interface has two central pieces: a screen on which to present information to users, and responses to user interactions. The UI defined in MIDP is event driven. Events are generated in response to user interactions, and event handlers then process these events. Similar to the high-level and low-level APIs for `Displayable`, there are also high-level and low-level events and corresponding event-handling mechanisms.

High-Level Events and Event Handling

The high-level event model delegated is delegation based, similar to the model used in J2SE AWT version 1.1 and beyond. This model has two components: event sources and event listeners. An event is generated from a source and is then from its source to an event listener. Then, the event handling method of the listener processes this event. The event delegation model is illustrated in Figure 5.6.

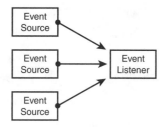

FIGURE 5.6

High-level event-handling model.

An *event listener* is an interface that contains event-handling methods. Any class can implement an event listener. An event listener object can be registered to `Displayables` (event sources) to listen for interesting events. This event-handling model consists of the following steps:

1. A class implements an event listener interface, `XYZListener`.
2. The listener object is registered to a UI component (event source) using `addXYZListener(XYXListener)`.
3. The `XYZListener` object listens for `XYZ` events.
4. The UI component fires an `XYZ` event.
5. The `XYZListener` acts upon the `XYZ` event.
6. Go back to step 3.

The MIDP UI uses two types of high-level events: the `Command` event and the `ItemStateChanged` event. Correspondingly, the events have two types of event listeners: `CommandListener` and `ItemStateListener`, respectively.

Any `Displayables` can be the event source of `Command` events. Only a `Form` can be the source of `ItemStateChanged` events. `Command` and the `Command` event are discussed next, and `ItemStateChanged` and `ItemStateListener` are discussed in Chapter 6.

Command

The Command class is a construct that encapsulates the semantic information of an action (event). The actual action (event handling) that happens when a Command is activated is defined in an interface CommandListener. When a Command is activated, an event is generated and passed to a registered CommandListener object.

A Command object contains three pieces of information:

- **Label:** A string that represents the meaning of the Command. It is what the application requests to show to users.
- **Type:** An integer that specifies the intent of this Command. The defined types are BACK, CANCEL, HELP, EXIT, ITEM, OK, SCREEN, and STOP.
- **Priority:** An integer that indicates the importance of the Command. The lower the number, the more important the Command.

A Command object can be constructed using

```
Command(String label, int commandType, int priority)
```

Once a Command is created, its information cannot be changed. The Command's information can be retrieved using the following methods:

```
int getCommandType()
String getLabel()
int getPriority()
```

Commands can be added to any Displayable (either a Screen or a Canvas) using

```
Displayable.addCommand(Command)
```

or can be removed from a Displayable using

```
Displayable.removeCommand(Command)
```

One Command object can be added to multiple Displayables.

Command Type

The Command type simply provides hints for Command mapping by MIDP implementations. The example in Listing 5.2 adds an Exit Command to a screen. The command type is Command.EXIT. The MIDP implementation will map the Command to a certain soft-button where a native Exit operation is placed. The command mapping is implementation dependent. When you run the MIDlet from Listing 5.2 on Sun's emulator, you will see the Exit Command mapped to the upper-left key (see Figure 5.7). If you run the MIDlet on Motorola's emulator, you will see the Command is mapped to upper-right key, as shown in Figure 5.8.

LISTING 5.2   CommandTest1.java

```java
import javax.microedition.midlet.*;
import javax.microedition.lcdui.*;

public class CommandTest1 extends MIDlet {
    private Display display;
    private Form s1;
    public CommandTest1() {
        display=Display.getDisplay(this);
        s1 = new Form("Screen with Exit");
        Command exitCommand = new Command("Exit", Command.EXIT, 1);
        s1.addCommand(exitCommand);
    }
    public void startApp() throws MIDletStateChangeException {
        display.setCurrent(s1);
    }

    /**
     * Pause the MIDlet
     */
    public void pauseApp() {
    }

    /**
     * Called by the framework before the application is unloaded
     */
    public void destroyApp(boolean unconditional) {
        display=null;
        s1=null;
    }
}
```

FIGURE 5.7

The mapping of the Exit Command *on Sun's emulator.*

FIGURE 5.8

The mapping of the Exit Command *on Motorola's emulator.*

Command **Priority**

The priority of a Command describes the importance of this Command relative to other Commands on the same screen. The command priority values are integers, and a lower number indicates greater importance. (In Sun's emulator, the interpretation of command priority values is reversed from the MIDP specification. It interprets the Command with a larger priority value indicating more importance.) The MIDP's UI has no command layout manager to manage how Commands are displayed on the device screen. The implementation will decide how Commands are mapped to soft-buttons based on the types, priorities, and number of Commands.

Typically, the implementation first chooses the placement of a Command based on its priority. The Command with the highest priority is placed in a position where the user can trigger it directly. Which soft-button the Command is mapped to is based on the Command type, as shown earlier. If all the Commands have the same priority, the first added Command is selected first. If there are more than two Commands (assuming there are only two soft-buttons), Commands with lower priority are placed on a menu that is associated with a soft-button.

The example in Listing 5.3 adds three Commands of different types and priorities to a screen.

LISTING 5.3   CommandTest2.java

```
import javax.microedition.midlet.*;
import javax.microedition.lcdui.*;

public class CommandTest2 extends MIDlet {
    private Display display;
```

LISTING 5.3 Continued

```
public void startApp() throws MIDletStateChangeException {
    display=Display.getDisplay(this);
    Form s1 = new Form("Screen with 3 commands");
    Command okCommand = new Command("OK",Command.OK,1);
    Command backCommand = new Command("Back",Command.BACK,2);
    Command exitCommand = new Command("Exit",Command.EXIT,3);

    s1.addCommand(okCommand);
    s1.addCommand(backCommand);
    s1.addCommand(exitCommand);

    display.setCurrent(s1);
}

/**
 * Pause the MIDlet
 */
public void pauseApp() {
}

/**
 * Called by the framework before the application is unloaded
 */
public void destroyApp(boolean unconditional) {
    display=null;
}
}
```

If you run the MIDlet on Sun's emulator, you will see that the Commands are mapped as shown in Figure 5.9. The Back Command has the highest priority in its interpretation, so it is mapped directly to the right soft-button. The other two Commands are contained in a menu mapped to the left soft-button. If you press the right soft-button, you will see the two Commands as shown in Figure 5.10.

If the MIDlet is executed on Motorola's emulator, the Commands will be mapped as shown in Figure 5.11. The OK Command, which has the highest priority, is mapped to the right soft-button. The other Commands are contained in a menu mapped to the left soft-button. If the left soft-button is pressed, the two Commands will be displayed as shown in Figure 5.12.

If you have to add more than two Commands to a screen, the Command that you use most often should have the highest priority and should be added first. Then add the Command with the second-highest priority, the one with the third-highest priority, and so on.

5

CENTRAL COMPONENTS OF THE UI

Figure 5.9

Mapping more than two Commands *to soft-buttons on Sun's emulator. The* Command *with the highest priority is mapped to a soft-button.*

Figure 5.10

Mapping more than two Commands *to soft-buttons on Sun's emulator. The* Commands *with lower priorities are mapped to a menu.*

CommandListener

CommandListener is an interface that provides the Command event processing method

```
void commandAction(Command c, Displayable d)
```

where the Displayable d is the event source. Any class can implement this interface to become a CommandListener object. A CommandListener object can listen to multiple Displayables. However, a Displayable can have at most one registered CommandListener at a time. A Displayable object can set its CommandListener using

```
Displayable.setCommandListener(CommandListener cl)
```

FIGURE 5.11

Mapping more than two Commands *to soft-buttons on Motorola's emulator. The* Command *with the highest priority is mapped to a soft-button.*

FIGURE 5.12

Mapping more than two Commands *to soft-buttons on Motorola's emulator. The* Commands *with lower priorities are mapped to a menu.*

If a Displayable already has a registered CommandListener, the call to setCommandListener (CommandListener cl) will replace the old CommandListener with this new one. If you want to remove the registered CommandListener of a Displayable, you can use

```
Displayable.setCommandListener(null)
```

Implementing `CommandListener` with Outer Classes

The `CommandListener` interface can be implemented by an outer class in a MIDlet application.
In the example in Listing 5.4, the MIDlet class implements the `CommandListener`. Two screens
are created, each with a `Command` added. The `CommandListener` will listen to `Command` events
from both screens by registering to both screens as follows:

```
s1.setCommandListener(this);
...
s2.setCommandListener(this);
```

The `Command` events come from two sources. So, in the `CommandAction()` method, the application has to differentiate which `Command` is fired and which `Displayable` it comes from, as follows:

```
if(d==s1 && c==changeCommand) {
...
}
else if(d==s2 && c==changeCommand) {
...
}
```

LISTING 5.4   CommandListenerTest1.java

```java
import javax.microedition.midlet.*;
import javax.microedition.lcdui.*;

public class CommandListenerTest1 extends MIDlet implements CommandListener{
    private Display display;
    private Command changeCommand= new Command("Change",Command.OK,1);
    private Form s1,s2;

    public CommandListenerTest1() {
        display=Display.getDisplay(this);
        s1 = new Form("Screen1");
        s1.addCommand(changeCommand);
        s1.setCommandListener(this);

        s2 = new Form("Screen2");
        s2.addCommand(changeCommand);
        s2.setCommandListener(this);
    }

    public void startApp() throws MIDletStateChangeException {
        display.setCurrent(s1);
    }

    /**
     * Pause the MIDlet
```

LISTING 5.4   Continued

```
    */
    public void pauseApp() {
    }

    /**
     * Called by the framework before the application is unloaded
     */
    public void destroyApp(boolean unconditional) {
        s1=null;
        s2=null;
        display=null;
    }

    public void commandAction(Command c,Displayable d) {
        if(d==s1 && c==changeCommand) {
            display.setCurrent(s2);
            System.out.println("changed to screen 2");
        }
        else if(d==s2 && c==changeCommand) {
            display.setCurrent(s1);
            System.out.println("Changed to screen 1");
        }
    }
}
```

If you run the MIDlet, you will see a screen as shown in Figure 5.13. If you choose the Change Command, the screen will change as shown in Figure 5.14. If you choose the Change Command in this screen, the screen will change back to the one shown in Figure 5.13.

FIGURE 5.13

CommandListener *demo: the first screen.*

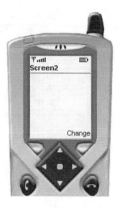

FIGURE 5.14

CommandListener *demo: the second screen.*

Implementing `CommandListener` with Inner Classes

The `CommandListener` interface can also be implemented by an inner class in a MIDlet application. In the example in Listing 5.5, a class `Screen1` is created by extending `Form`. The `Screen1` class implements the `CommandListener` interface. The `CommandListener` object is registered to listen for `Command` events originated from itself using

```
s1.setCommandListener(s1);
```

The `Command` action is very simple. It just tells users the `Command` is activated. If you run the example, you will see a screen as shown in Figure 5.15. If you choose the OK `Command`, you will see the following line as output from the terminal:

```
OK is pressed.
```

LISTING 5.5   CommandListenerTest2.java

```java
import javax.microedition.midlet.*;
import javax.microedition.lcdui.*;

public class CommandListenerTest2 extends MIDlet {
    private Display display;
    private Command okCommand= new Command("OK",Command.OK,1);
    private Screen1 s1;

    public CommandListenerTest2() {
        display=Display.getDisplay(this);
        s1 = new Screen1("Screen 1");
        s1.addCommand(okCommand);
```

LISTING 5.5   Continued

```
        s1.setCommandListener(s1);
    }

    public void startApp() throws MIDletStateChangeException {
        display.setCurrent(s1);
    }

    /**
     * Pause the MIDlet
     */
    public void pauseApp() {
    }

    /**
     * Called by the framework before the application is unloaded
     */
    public void destroyApp(boolean unconditional) {
        s1=null;
        display=null;
    }

    class Screen1 extends Form implements CommandListener {
        public Screen1(String title) {
            super(title);
        }
        public void commandAction(Command c,Displayable d) {
            if(c==okCommand) {
                System.out.println("OK is pressed.");
            }
        }
    }
}
```

Other Events and Event Listeners

In addition to the Command event and the CommandListener, J2ME MIDP provides two other types of events (ItemStateChanged and record-related events that include recordAdded, recordChanged, and recordDeleted events) and two types of event listener interfaces (ItemStateListener and RecordListener, respectively).

The only source of an ItemStateChanged event is a Form. So an ItemStateListener can only be registered to a Form. This topic is discussed in the section "Form and Items" in Chapter 6.

The RecordStore, record, record-related events, and RecordListener are not part of the UI. They are discussed in Chapter 8, "Persistent Storage."

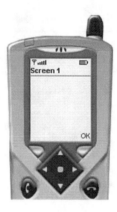

FIGURE 5.15
The CommandListener *interface implemented by an inner class.*

Delegation-Based Event Handling in J2SE Versus J2ME

In J2SE, an event can be delivered to multiple event listeners that are registered to the event source. While in J2ME, a Command event or an ItemStateChanged event can only be delivered to one event listener that is registered to the event source. The current registered event listener will replace the previous one. This is accomplished by the function

```
Displayable.setCommandListener(CommandListener)
```

or

```
Form.setItemStateListener(ItemStateListener)
```

However, a record event can be delivered to multiple RecordListeners. The listener registering method

```
RecordStore.addRecordListener(RecordListener listener)
```

adds the listener to a listener list rather than replacing the previous one.

Low-Level Events and Event Handling

Low-level events include key-pressed events, key-released events, paint events, and so on. Applications cannot access low-level events originated from the Displayables that implement the high-level API. Only low-level events associated with Displayables that implement the low-level API are accessible to applications.

Canvas is a subclass of Displayable that implements the low-level API. The low-level event-handling model is similar to the inheritance-based event model used in AWT version 1.0 and 1.02. To handle an event, you have to extend the component class and overwrite its appropriate event-handling routine. We will discuss low-level events and event handling further when we discuss the Canvas class in Chapter 7.

Low-Level and High-Level Event Handling Commonality

High-level and low-level event handling have one thing in common: Calls to event-handling methods are made on the same thread where the event occurs. Event-handling methods should promptly return. Otherwise applications will be blocked.

For example, if a CommandListener method does not return or the return is delayed, the system may be blocked. What do you do when you have functions that cannot return immediately? One solution is to use the Runnable interface to put time-consuming parts of the code on separate threads. In Listing 5.6, we deliberately slow down the process of counting numbers. As a result, the counting will take about 10 seconds to finish. In the commandAction() method, we use

```
new Thread(new Count(max)).start();
```

to start a counting process on a new thread; the commandAction() method returns right away. The Thread class and Runnable interface are contained in J2ME's java.lang package, which is a subset of J2SE's java.lang. The Count class implements the Runnable interface. In the Count.run() method, a Gauge is updated to report progress when every 10% of the work is done during the counting process. Form, TextField, Gauge, and StringItem are used in Listing 5.6. We'll discuss how to use them in Chapter 6.

LISTING 5.6   CountDemo.java

```
import javax.microedition.midlet.*;
import javax.microedition.lcdui.*;

public class CountDemo extends MIDlet implements CommandListener{
    private Form     mainscreen;
    private Form     infoscreen;
    private Command tryCommand = new Command("Try", Command.OK, 1);
    private Command againCommand = new Command("Again", Command.OK, 1);
    private Command exitCommand = new Command("Exit", Command.EXIT, 1);
    private Display display;

    public CountDemo() {
        mainscreen= new Form("Count demo");
```

LISTING 5.6   Continued

```java
        mainscreen.addCommand(tryCommand);
        mainscreen.addCommand(exitCommand);
        mainscreen.setCommandListener(this);

        //first create a textfield
        mainscreen.append(new TextField(
                "How many seconds does it take to count from 1 to ",
            "15000",50, TextField.NUMERIC));

        //create an empty info screen
        infoscreen= new Form("");
        infoscreen.setCommandListener(this);

        //retrieve display object
        display=Display.getDisplay(this);
    }

    public void startApp() throws MIDletStateChangeException {
        display.setCurrent(mainscreen);
    }

    /**
     * Pause the MIDlet
     */
    public void pauseApp() {
    }

    /**
     * Called by the framework before the application is unloaded
     */
    public void destroyApp(boolean unconditional) {
    }

    public void commandAction(Command c, Displayable d) {
        if(d==mainscreen) {
            if(c==tryCommand) {
                int max=Integer.parseInt(
                    ((TextField)mainscreen.get(0)).getString());
                infoscreen.append(new Gauge(
                                    "Counting in progress",false,
                                    max,1));
                display.setCurrent(infoscreen);
```

LISTING 5.6   Continued

```
                new Thread(new Count(max)).start();
            }
            else if(c==exitCommand) {
                destroyApp(true);
                notifyDestroyed();
            }
        }
        else if(d==infoscreen) {
            //set it for next try
            infoscreen.delete(0);
            infoscreen.removeCommand(againCommand);
            display.setCurrent(mainscreen);
        }
    }
}

class Count implements Runnable{
    int max;
    public Count(int n) {
        max=n;
    }

    public void run() {
        long c= System.currentTimeMillis();
        int sum=0;
        for(int i=1; i<max; i++) {
            sum++;
            if(i*10%max==0) {
                Gauge g= (Gauge) infoscreen.get(0);
                g.setValue(i);
                try {
                    Thread.sleep(1000);
                }catch(Exception e) {}
            }
        }
        c=(System.currentTimeMillis()-c)/1000;
        infoscreen.delete(0);
        infoscreen.append(new StringItem(
            "Count result:\n","It takes "+c+ " seconds."));
        infoscreen.addCommand(againCommand);
    }
}
}
```

When you run this MIDlet, you will see a screen like Figure 5.16. If you activate the Try Command, you will see an information screen, as shown in Figure 5.17. The gauge will be updated as counting progresses. When the counting process finishes, a result screen similar to Figure 5.18 will appear to show the result and inform you to continue.

FIGURE 5.16

Putting the time-consuming part of an event-handling method into a separate thread: starting screen.

FIGURE 5.17

The thread updates the information screen.

FIGURE 5.18
The thread updates the result screen.

Summary

This chapter covered two central pieces of MIDP's user interface programming: a display for presenting information and event-handling models to respond to user interactions. The `Displayable` class is the central abstraction of the display device of a wireless device. The `Display` class is a display manager that controls which `Displayable` to show on the display.

There are two types of `Displayables`: those that implement the high-level API and those that implement the low-level API. Each individual subclass of `Displayable` is discussed in Chapters 6 and 7.

There are also two types of events and event-handling models. This chapter discussed the high-level events and event-handling model. The low-level events and event-handling model are discussed in Chapter 7.

Using High-Level APIs in UI Development

IN THIS CHAPTER

Introduction

Chapter 5, "Central Components of the UI for Wireless Devices," discussed two central pieces of user interface development: `Display`/`Displayable` and event/event handling. The `Displayable` class has two subclasses: the `Screen` class, which implements the high-level API; and the `Canvas` class, which implements the low-level API. The high-level API emphasizes portability across different devices. The low-level API emphasizes flexibility and controls. There are two categories of subclasses of `Screen`: `List`, `TextBox`, and `Alert` classes whose structures are predefined; and `Form` class whose structure is generic and defined by applications. This chapter discusses subclasses of `Screen`. We will leave the discussion of `Canvas` to Chapter 7, "Using Low-Level APIs in UI Development."

List and Choice

When an application starts, it will often present a menu that contains several choices of functions you can select. `List` and `ChoiceGroup` both display a list of choices that can be selected. They both implement the `Choice` interface defined in the `javax.microedition.lcdui` package. The `Choice` interface and the `List` class are discussed in this section, and the `ChoiceGroup` class will be discussed later in the section "Form and `Items`."

List

The `List` class is a structure-predefined `Screen` that implements the `Choice` interface. Two constructors are provided in the API of `javax.microedition.lcdui` package:

```
List(String title, int listType)
List(String title, int listType, String[] stringElements, Image[]
imageElements)
```

The first constructor creates an empty `List`; choice elements can be added later. The second constructor creates a `List` with the initial elements provided. The `stringElements` array must be non-null, and every array element must also be non-null. The length of the `stringElements` array determines the number of elements in the `List`. The `imageElements` array may be null to indicate that the `List` elements have no images. If the `imageElements` array is not null, it must be the same length as the `stringElements` array. Individual elements of the `imageElements` array may be null to indicate the absence of an image for the corresponding `List` element.

All the methods for accessing and modifying a `List` are defined in the `Choice` interface.

The `Choice` Interface

The `Choice` interface defines an API for UI components implementing selections from a predefined number of elements/choices. Two UI components implement the interface: the `List` discussed in this section, and the `ChoiceGroup` discussed later in this chapter.

Using High-Level APIs in UI Development

CHAPTER 6

111

6

USING HIGH-
LEVEL APIs IN UI
DEVELOPMENT

The following methods are provided through the `Choice` interface:

```
int append(String stringPart, Image imagePart)
void delete(int elementNum)
Image getImage(int elementNum)
int getSelectedFlags(boolean[] selectedArray_return)
int getSelectedIndex()
String getString(int elementNum)
void insert(int elementNum, String stringPart, Image imagePart)
boolean isSelected(int elementNum)
void set(int elementNum, String stringPart, Image imagePart)
void setSelectedFlags(boolean[] selectedArray)
void setSelectedIndex(int elementNum, boolean selected)
int size()
```

Types of `Choices`

There are three types of `Choice` objects: implicit-choice (valid only for `List`), exclusive-choice, and multiple-choice:

- Exclusive-choice: Exactly one element must be selected at any given time unless there is no choice element.

- Implicit-choice: A special exclusive choice, where the focused element is implicitly selected when a `Command` is initiated. It can only be used for a `List`.

- Multiple-choice: Any number of elements (including none) in any combination can be selected at any time.

The types of `Choices` differentiate themselves by their visual appearance. In Listing 6.1, three different types of `Lists` are created.

LISTING 6.1   ListTest1.java

```
import javax.microedition.midlet.*;
import javax.microedition.lcdui.*;

public class ListTest1 extends MIDlet implements CommandListener{
    private List[] lists;
    private Command nextCommand = new Command("Next",
                                              Command.SCREEN, 1);
    private Command exitCommand = new Command("Exit",
                                              Command.EXIT, 1);
    private String[] options={"Option A","Option B","Option C"};
    private Display display;

     public ListTest1() {
         lists = new List[3];
```

LISTING 6.1 Continued

```java
        //create an implicit list
        lists[0]= new List("Implicit-choice list",List.IMPLICIT,
                            options, null);
        //Add commands
        lists[0].addCommand(nextCommand);
        lists[0].addCommand(exitCommand);
        lists[0].setCommandListener(this);

        //create an exclusive list
        lists[1]= new List("Exclusive-choice list",
                            List.EXCLUSIVE,
                            options, null);
        lists[1].addCommand(nextCommand);
        lists[1].addCommand(exitCommand);
        lists[1].setCommandListener(this);

        //create a multiple choice list
        lists[2]= new List("Multiple-choice list",
                            List.MULTIPLE,
                            options, null);
        lists[2].addCommand(nextCommand);
        lists[2].addCommand(exitCommand);
        lists[2].setCommandListener(this);

        display=Display.getDisplay(this);
    }
    public void startApp() throws MIDletStateChangeException {
        display.setCurrent(lists[0]);
    }

    /**
     * Pause the MIDlet
     */
    public void pauseApp() {
    }

    /**
     * Called by the framework before the application is unloaded
     */
    public void destroyApp(boolean unconditional) {
        //clear everything
        lists=null;
        nextCommand = null;
        exitCommand = null;
```

LISTING 6.1   Continued

```
        display=null;
    }

    public void commandAction(Command c, Displayable d) {
        if(c==nextCommand) {
            List l=null;
            for(int i=0; i<3; i++) {
                if(d==lists[i]) l=lists[(i+1)%3];
            }
            display.setCurrent(l);
        }
        else if(c==exitCommand) {
            destroyApp(true);
            notifyDestroyed();
        }
    }
}
```

If you run the MIDlet, you will see an implicit-choice List in the first screen, shown in Figure 6.1. The focused element in an implicit-choice List is the selected element. If you choose the Next Command, you will see an exclusive-choice List similar to Figure 6.2. Each element of the exclusive-choice List has a radio-button icon. If you choose the Next command again, you will see a multiple-choice List similar to Figure 6.3. Each element of the multiple-choice List has a checkbox icon associated with it.

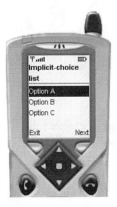

FIGURE 6.1

An implicit-choice List.

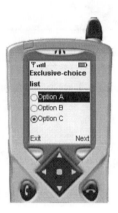

FIGURE 6.2

An exclusive-choice List.

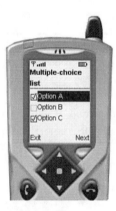

FIGURE 6.3

A multiple-choice List.

Choice Elements

A Choice object presents users a series of elements to choose from. Each choice element is composed of a text string and an optional image.

Indexing

The number of elements in a Choice object can be retrieved using the size() method. Elements within the Choice object are referred to by their indexes, which are consecutive integers in the range from 0 to size()-1, with 0 referring to the first element and size()-1 to the last element.

Using High-Level APIs in UI Development

CHAPTER 6

115

6

USING HIGH-
LEVEL APIs IN UI
DEVELOPMENT

Choice Element Images

The image of a choice element can be null if the application does not set it. If the application does provide an image, the implementation may choose to ignore the image if it exceeds the capacity of the device to display it. If the implementation displays the image, it will be displayed adjacent to the text string and the pair will be treated as a unit. The image of a choice element must be immutable. Applications can set the image part of the `elementNum` choice element using

```
void set(int elementNum, String stringPart, Image imagePart)
```

and retrieve the image part using

```
Image getImage(int elementNum)
```

The example in Listing 6.2 creates an implicit-choice `List` with three elements. Two images are created. The image portions of the first two elements are set using the `set()` method. The results of this code are shown in Figure 6.4.

LISTING 6.2   ListTest2.java

```
import javax.microedition.midlet.*;
import javax.microedition.lcdui.*;

public class ListTest2 extends MIDlet implements CommandListener{
    private List list;
    private Command exitCommand = new Command("Exit",
                                        Command.EXIT, 1);
    private String[] options={"Option A","Option B","Option C"};
    private Display display;

    public ListTest2() {
        //create an implicit list
        list= new List("Implicit-choice list",List.IMPLICIT,
                    options, null);
        try {
            Image img0= Image.createImage("/open.png");
            list.set(0,"Open",img0);
            Image img1= Image.createImage("/smallDuke.png");
            list.set(1,"Duke",img1);
        }catch(Exception e){
            System.out.println("Error: "+e.getMessage());
        }
        //Add commands
```

LISTING 6.2 Continued

```
        list.addCommand(exitCommand);
        list.setCommandListener(this);

        display=Display.getDisplay(this);
    }
    public void startApp() throws MIDletStateChangeException {
        display.setCurrent(list);
    }

    /**
     * Pause the MIDlet
     */
    public void pauseApp() {
    }

    /**
     * Called by the framework before the application is unloaded
     */
    public void destroyApp(boolean unconditional) {
        //clear everything
        list=null;
        exitCommand = null;
        display=null;
    }

    public void commandAction(Command c, Displayable d) {
        if(c==exitCommand) {
            destroyApp(true);
            notifyDestroyed();
        }
    }
}
```

Be aware:

- Resource filenames are case sensitive. For example, "duke.png" and "Duke.png" are different.

- Images of choice elements in the same List can be mixture of null and images of different sizes.

- If images of choice elements are not null, they must be immutable.

Using High-Level APIs in UI Development

CHAPTER 6

117

6

USING HIGH-
LEVEL APIs IN UI
DEVELOPMENT

FIGURE 6.4

A List *whose elements contain both images and text strings.*

Choice Element Text Strings

A choice element's text string is the element's label. It must be set and cannot be null. If an element (image and text string) is too long to be displayed on a single line, it may be wrapped to multiple lines. If an element is wrapped, then the second and subsequent lines show a clear indication to users that they are part of the same element and are not new elements, such as the example shown in Figure 6.5.

The text string of an element can be set using the method

```
set(int elementNum, String stringPart, Image imagePart)
```

or retrieved using the method

```
getString(int elementNum)
```

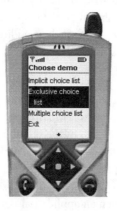

FIGURE 6.5

A List *in which the second element is too long to fit on a single line.*

Choice Element Selected Property

The selected state of an element is a property of the element. This state stays with the element if other elements are inserted or deleted, causing elements to be shifted around. When a new element is inserted or appended, it is always unselected (except in the special case of adding an element to an empty exclusive Choice object).

Users can interact with a Choice object and select or unselect an element using a dedicated Select or Go function key of the device. For example, Sun's emulator uses the center-arrow key for the Select function, and Motorola's emulator uses the FIRE key, the second button on the right side.

Applications can set the selected states of elements using

```
setSelectedFlags(boolean[] selectedArray)
```

or

```
setSelectedIndex(int elementNum, boolean selected)
```

When an element is selected, the element is shown using a distinct visual representation. For example, in Figure 6.2, Option C of the exclusive Choice is selected; and in Figure 6.3, Options A and C of the multiple Choice are selected. The focused element of an implicit-choice List is selected. In Figure 6.1, the element Option A is selected.

Modifying Choice Objects

An element can be added to a Choice object using either of these methods:

```
append(String stringPart, Image imagePart)
insert(int elementNum, String stringPart, Image imagePart)
```

After an element is added, its image or text string can be modified by using the set() method. An element can be removed from a Choice object by using the delete(int elementNum) method. If a List object is currently shown on the display, the display will be automatically refreshed to reflect any changes to the List, such as addition or deletion of elements, or changes of elements' images or text strings.

User Interaction

When a Choice object is present on the display, users can select/unselect an element, move from element to element, and possibly scroll. Moving operations will change which element is focused but won't change the selected state of the previously or currently focused element, except for an implicit-choice List. Because the focused element in an implicit-choice List is always the selected element, moving the focused element will change which element is selected. The moving and scrolling operations do not cause application-visible events. The system notifies the application either when an application-defined Command is fired, or when a selection state of a ChoiceGroup element is changed.

Implicit-choice Lists

An implicit-choice List is a special exclusive Choice object. Exactly one element of the List must be selected at any time, unless the List is empty. A static Command SELECT_COMMAND is associated with an implicit-choice List. When users select an element within an implicit-choice List by pressing the Select key, the SELECT_COMMAND will be fired; a Command event will then be generated and delivered to a CommandListener registered for the List.

An implicit-choice List can be used to construct menus by associating logical commands with elements. In this case, no application-defined Commands have to be attached. Applications just have to register a CommandListener that is called when users activate the Select function.

The example in Listing 6.3 creates an implicit-choice List and registers a CommandListener to the List.

LISTING 6.3   ListTest3.java

```
import javax.microedition.midlet.*;
import javax.microedition.lcdui.*;

public class ListTest3 extends MIDlet implements CommandListener{
    private List list;
    private Command exitCommand = new Command("Exit",
                                            Command.EXIT, 1);
    private String[] options={"Option A","Option B","Option C"};
    private Display display;

    public ListTest3() {
        //create an implicit list
        list= new List("Implicit-choice list",List.IMPLICIT,
                        options, null);
        //Add commands
        list.addCommand(exitCommand);
        list.setCommandListener(this);

        display=Display.getDisplay(this);
    }
    public void startApp() throws MIDletStateChangeException {
        display.setCurrent(list);
    }

    /**
     * Pause the MIDlet
     */
```

Listing 6.3   Continued

```java
public void pauseApp() {
}

/**
 * Called by the framework before the application is unloaded
 */
public void destroyApp(boolean unconditional) {
    //clear everything
    list=null;
    exitCommand = null;
    display=null;
}

public void commandAction(Command c, Displayable d) {
    if(d==list && c==List.SELECT_COMMAND) {
        System.out.println(options[list.getSelectedIndex()]+
                            " is selected");
    }
    else if(c==exitCommand) {
        destroyApp(true);
        notifyDestroyed();
    }
}
}
```

In the `commandAction()` method, the application has to check from which `List` object the static `SELECT_COMMAND` is fired as follows:

```java
if(d==list && c==List.SELECT_COMMAND) {
    System.out.println(options[list.getSelectedIndex()]+" is selected");
}
```

If you run the MIDlet, you will see the implicit-choice `List`. You can change the focused element using the arrow keys. If you have element Option B focused as shown in Figure 6.6 and you press the Select button, the MIDlet will output the following line to the terminal:

```
Option B is selected.
```

The selected element of an implicit-choice `List` is the focused element. Changing the focused element will trigger a selection-state change for both the current and previous focused elements. This type of `List` differs from the exclusive-choice or multiple-choice `List`s, in that users have to press the Select button to change the selected state of the focused element.

Using High-Level APIs in UI Development

CHAPTER 6

121

6

USING HIGH-
LEVEL APIs IN UI
DEVELOPMENT

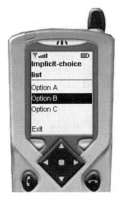

FIGURE 6.6

An implicit-choice List *with Option B in focus.*

List Example

The example in Listing 6.4 shows the usage of the three types of Lists.

LISTING 6.4 ListTest.java

```java
import javax.microedition.midlet.*;
import javax.microedition.lcdui.*;

public class ListTest extends MIDlet implements CommandListener{
    private List menu;
    private List implicit_list;
    private List exclusive_list;
    private List multiple_list;
    private Command okCommand = new Command("OK", Command.OK, 1);
    private Command backCommand = new Command("Back", Command.BACK, 1);
    private String[] options={"Option A","Option B","Option C"};
    private Display display;

    public ListTest() {
        //create an implicit choice list, and use it as start menu
        menu= new List("Choose demo", List.IMPLICIT);
        menu.append("Implicit choice list",null);
        menu.append("Multiple choice list",null);
        menu.insert(1, "Exclusive choice list",null);
        menu.append("Exit",null);
        menu.setCommandListener(this);

        //create an implicit list
        implicit_list= new List("Implicit-choice list",
```

LISTING 6.4 Continued

```
                                List.IMPLICIT,
                                options, null);
        implicit_list.addCommand(backCommand);
        implicit_list.setCommandListener(this);

        //create an exclusive list
        exclusive_list= new List("Exclusive-choice list",
                                List.EXCLUSIVE,
                                options, null);
        exclusive_list.addCommand(okCommand);
        exclusive_list.addCommand(backCommand);
        exclusive_list.setCommandListener(this);

        //create a multiple choice list
        multiple_list= new List("Multiple-choice list",
                                List.MULTIPLE,
                                options, null);
        multiple_list.addCommand(okCommand);
        multiple_list.addCommand(backCommand);
        multiple_list.setCommandListener(this);

        display=Display.getDisplay(this);
    }
    public void startApp() throws MIDletStateChangeException {
        display.setCurrent(menu);
    }

    /**
     * Pause the MIDlet
     */
    public void pauseApp() {
    }

    /**
     * Called by the framework before the application is unloaded
     */
    public void destroyApp(boolean unconditional) {
    }

    public void commandAction(Command c, Displayable d) {
        if(d==menu && c==List.SELECT_COMMAND) {
            switch(menu.getSelectedIndex()) {
            case 0: //implicit choice list
                display.setCurrent(implicit_list);
```

LISTING 6.4 Continued

```
                break;
            case 1: //exclusive choice list
                display.setCurrent(exclusive_list);
                break;
            case 2: //multiple choice list
                display.setCurrent(multiple_list);
                break;
            case 3: //exit
                destroyApp(true);
                notifyDestroyed();
                break;
            default:
            }
        }
        else if(d==implicit_list && c==List.SELECT_COMMAND) {
            System.out.println(options[((List)d).getSelectedIndex()]+
                                " is selected");
        }
        else if(d==exclusive_list && c==okCommand) {
            System.out.println(options[((List)d).getSelectedIndex()]+
                                " is selected");
        }
        else if(d==multiple_list && c==okCommand) {
            //report which options are selected
            boolean[] selected= new boolean[options.length];
            ((List)d).getSelectedFlags(selected);
            for(int i=0; i<options.length; i++) {
                if(selected[i]) {
                    System.out.println(options[i]+" is selected");
                }
            }
        }
        else if(c==backCommand) {
            display.setCurrent(menu);
        }
    }
}
```

First, an empty implicit-choice List is created. Then elements are added using the append()
and insert() methods. The implicit-choice List is used as a startup menu when the application starts (see Figure 6.5). Next, three Lists of different types are created. From the start
menu, you can select one type of List. If you select Multiple Choice List from the start menu,

you will see a screen like Figure 6.7. If you select both Option A and Option C and click OK, you will see the following output:

```
Option A is selected.
Option C is selected.
```

You can choose the Back command and go back to the start menu for more testing.

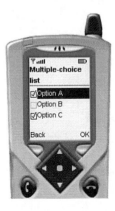

FIGURE 6.7
A multiple-choice List.

TextBox

The TextBox class is a structure-predefined Screen that allows the user to enter and edit text. A TextBox object can be created using its constructor:

```
TextBox(String title, String text, int maxSize, int constraints)
```

The following TextBox methods are provided in the API:

```
void delete(int offset, int length)
int getCaretPosition()
int getChars(char[] data)
int getConstraints()
int getMaxSize()
String getString()
void insert(char[] data, int offset, int length, int position)
void insert(String src, int position)
void setChars(char[] data, int offset, int length)
void setConstraints(int constraints)
int setMaxSize(int maxSize)
void setString(String text)
int size()
```

Maximum Size

The content of a TextBox is stored in a char array. As a result, a textbox has a maximum number of characters that can be stored in the object at any time (its *capacity*). The maximum size can be set when the TextBox is constructed using

```
TextBox(String title, String text, int maxSize, int constraints)
```

or set using the setMaxSize() method after the TextBox object is created. The maximum size of a TextBox can be retrieved by calling the getMaxSize() method. Because wireless devices are resource-limited, an upper limit is imposed on the maximum size by the actual MIDP implementation. The actual maximum size assigned to a TextBox is limited to that number.

The maximum size limit is checked when a TextBox object is constructed, when the user is editing text within a TextBox, and when the application program calls methods to modify the TextBox's contents. If the text exceeds the limit at any time, an IllegalArgumentException will be thrown.

The text contained within a TextBox may be longer than can be displayed at one time. If this is the case, the implementation will let the user scroll to view and edit any part of the text. This scrolling action does not trigger any application-visible events.

Input Constraints

The TextBox allows you to specify *input constraints*. The different constraints allow the application to restrict user input in a variety of ways. The TextBox class shares the same input constraints that are defined in the TextField class. The five input constraint constants defined in the TextField are summarized in Table 6.1.

TABLE 6.1 Input Constraints of the TextField That Are Shared by the TextBox

Name	Description
ANY	Constant 0 is assigned to it. The user is allowed to enter any text.
EMAILADDR	Constant 1 is assigned to it. The user is allowed to enter an e-mail address.
NUMERIC	Constant 2 is assigned to it. The user is allowed to enter only an integer value. The integer value can be negative.
PHONENUMBER	Constant 3 is assigned to it. The user is allowed to enter a phone number and some optional non-numerical characters. The exact set of acceptable characters is implementation dependent.
URL	Constant 4 is assigned to it. The user is allowed to enter a URL.

One modifier constant PASSWORD is defined in the TextField, and constant 0x10000 is assigned to it. The PASSWORD modifier can be combined with other constraints by using the | (logical or) operator. In such cases, the acceptable set of characters is determined by the other constraints; however, the actual text will be masked and displayed as a string of asterisks (*) so that the real text string is not visible to users. If you use PASSWORD alone as an input constraint, the behavior is equivalent to a combination of PASSWORD and ANY constraints.

Applications can set the input constraint of a TextBox when it is constructed, or set it using the setConstraints() method. If the text string in the constructor violates the input constraint or the text already in the TextBox violates the newly set input constraints, the text will be reset to empty.

The input constraints can be retrieved using the getConstraints() method. However the return value of the getConstraints() method may be the result of input constraints combining with the PASSWORD modifier. To mask the PASSWORD modifier, a constant CONSTRAINT_MASK is defined in the TextField class. The constant 0xFFFF is assigned to CONSTRAINT_MASK. The application should use the logical AND operation with a value returned by the getConstraints() method and CONSTRAINT_MASK to determined the current input constraint.

Editing or Retrieving Text from a TextBox

The following methods can be used for editing the text in a TextBox:

```
void delete(int offset, int length)
void insert(char[] data, int offset, int length, int position)
void insert(String src, int position)
void setChars(char[] data, int offset, int length)
void setString(String text)
```

Any changes to the text in a TextBox that violate its input constraints will be discarded, and an IllegalArgumentException will be thrown. Applications can retrieve the contents of a TextBox into a character array using getChars(char[] data) or into a string using the getString() method. The number of characters in the TextBox can be retrieved by calling the size() method.

User Interaction

Users can edit the contents of a TextBox using a device's keypad. TextBoxes with different input constraints will respond differently to key input. The key setting is implementation specific for each device. On Sun's emulator, the * key is the SHIFT key which has a special function: It's used to switch key input modes among number, lowercase, uppercase, and a list of special characters. On Motorola's emulator, pressing the * key removes a character following the caret, and the 1 key provides a list of special characters to choose from.

User interactions, including traversing and editing text, do not generate any events that are accessible to applications.

TextBox Example

The example in Listing 6.5 shows how TextBoxes with different types of input constraints behave. If you start the MIDlet, you will see a start menu as shown in Figure 6.8. If you select Any Character, you will see the screen in Figure 6.9. If you go back and select Password, you will see a screen like Figure 6.10; the contents of the TextBox are masked with asterisks. If you choose the OK Command, you can see the unmasked contents:

```
text=This is my info:
Constaint=Any Character
Modifier=PASSWORD
```

If you select Number or Phone from the start menu, you will see an empty TextBox. Even though the text of the TextBox is set, it is not numeric-only; so, the resulting text is empty.

LISTING 6.5   TextBoxTest.java

```java
import javax.microedition.midlet.*;
import javax.microedition.lcdui.*;

public class TextBoxTest extends MIDlet implements CommandListener{
    private List      startmenu;
    private TextBox textBox;
    private Command okCommand = new Command("OK", Command.OK, 1);
    private Command backCommand = new Command("Back", Command.BACK, 1);
    /**
     * These are the labels for the supported textboxes.
     */
    private static final String[] textBoxLabels = {
            "Any Character",
            "E-Mail",
            "Number",
            "Phone",
            "Url",
            "Password",
    };
    private static final String[] text = {
            "This is my info:",
            "jzhu@webyu.com",
            "91320",
            "3762659",
            "www.webyu.com",
            "1234",
    };
    /**
     * These are the supported textbox types.
     */
```

Listing 6.5 Continued

```java
    private static final int[] textBoxTypes = {
            TextField.ANY,
            TextField.EMAILADDR,
            TextField.NUMERIC,
            TextField.PHONENUMBER,
            TextField.URL,
            TextField.PASSWORD
    };

    private Display display;

    public TextBoxTest() {
        //create an implicit choice list, and use it as start menu
        startmenu= new List("Select a Text Box Type", List.IMPLICIT,
                            textBoxLabels, null);
        startmenu.setCommandListener(this);
        //retrieve display object
        display=Display.getDisplay(this);
    }

    public void startApp() throws MIDletStateChangeException {
        display.setCurrent(startmenu);
    }

    /**
     * Pause the MIDlet
     */
    public void pauseApp() {
    }

    /**
     * Called by the framework before the application is unloaded
     */
    public void destroyApp(boolean unconditional) {
        startmenu=null;
        textBox=null;
        okCommand = null;
        backCommand = null;
    }

    public void commandAction(Command c, Displayable d) {
        if(d==startmenu && c==List.SELECT_COMMAND) {
            int selected_num=startmenu.getSelectedIndex();
            textBox= new TextBox(null, "", 150,
                                textBoxTypes[selected_num]);
            textBox.addCommand(okCommand);
```

Using High-Level APIs in UI Development

CHAPTER 6

129

6

USING HIGH-
LEVEL APIS IN UI
DEVELOPMENT

LISTING 6.5 Continued

```
            textBox.addCommand(backCommand);
            textBox.setCommandListener(this);

            try {
                textBox.setString("This is my info:");
                //textBox.setString(text[selected_num]);
            }catch(Exception e) {
                System.out.println("Error: "+e.getMessage());
            }

            textBox.setTitle(textBoxLabels[selected_num]);
            display.setCurrent(textBox);
        }
        else if(c==okCommand) {
            //output the text typed
            System.out.println("text="+textBox.getString());
            int constraint= TextField.CONSTRAINT_MASK&
                            textBox.getConstraints();
            System.out.println("Constaint="+
                                textBoxLabels[constraint]);
            if(textBox.getConstraints()>=TextField.PASSWORD) {
                System.out.println("Modifier=PASSWORD");
            }
        }
        else if(c==backCommand) {
            display.setCurrent(startmenu);
        }
    }
}
```

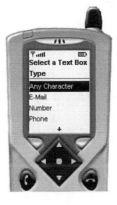

FIGURE 6.8

The start menu for the TextBox *test.*

FIGURE 6.9

A TextBox *with the* TextBox.ANY *input constraint.*

FIGURE 6.10

A TextBox *with the* TextBox.PASSWORD *input constraint.*

Alert

An Alert is a structure-predefined Screen that shows data (text and image) to the user and waits for a certain period of time (timeout) before proceeding to the next screen. There are two constructor methods:

```
Alert(String title)
Alert(String title, String alertText, Image alertImage, AlertType alertType)
```

Using High-Level APIs in UI Development

CHAPTER 6

131

6

USING HIGH-
LEVEL APIS IN UI
DEVELOPMENT

Timeout

The timeout period of an `Alert` is measured in milliseconds. It can be set to an implementation-specific default value when the `Alert` is constructed, or it can be set using the `setTimeout()` method. The application also can set the alert time to infinity with the `setTimeout(Alert.FOREVER)` call, in which case the `Alert` is considered to be *modal*. If an `Alert` is modal, users have to explicitly dismiss it by activating a Done `Command` within the `Alert`. Doing so is equivalent to an immediate timeout.

The timeout value of an `Alert` can be retrieved with the `getTimeout()` method. The default timeout value specified by the implementation can be retrieved with the `getDefaultTimeout()` method.

Current `Displayable`

Applications will proceed to the next screen after an `Alert` screen times out. If an `Alert` screen is the current `Displayable` and it's going to time out, the implementation needs to know which `Displayable` object will be shown next on the display. Therefore, when the application sets an `Alert` object as the current screen, it should set the next `Displayable` at the same time. To do so, the application calls the method

```
Display.setCurrent(Alert alert, Displayable nextDisplayable)
```

In this call, the `alert` cannot be null and `nextDisplayable` cannot be an `Alert` or null. A `NullPointerException` will be thrown if `alert` or `nextDisplayable` is null; an `IllegalArgumentException` will be thrown if `nextDisplayable` is an `Alert`.

When the user dismisses an alert, or the alert times out, the `nextDisplayable` will be set current.

If an `Alert` screen is set to current using `display.setCurrent(alert)` without designating the next `Displayable`, the implementation will interpret the call as follows:

```
display.setCurrent(alert, display.getCurrent())
```

Application-Defined `Commands`

The `Alert` class is a special subclass of `Displayable`. It overwrites `Displayable`'s `addCommand()` and `setCommandListener()` methods. An `Alert` screen does not accept application-defined `Commands`, so the `Alert.addCommand()` method always throws an `IllegalStateException` when it is called. In addition, applications cannot register a `CommandListener` to an `Alert` screen, so `Alert.setCommandListener()` method will always throw an `IllegalStateException` when it is called.

AlertTypes

The intended use for an `Alert` is to inform users about errors and other exceptional conditions. Each `Alert` may have an `AlertType` to indicate its nature. The `AlertType` of an `Alert` can be null or one of five predefined `AlertType`s: ALARM, CONFIRMATION, ERROR, INFO, and WARNING. It can be set when the `Alert` is constructed or set with the `setType()` method, and it can be retrieved using the `getType()` method.

Each `AlertType` can play a sound with the `playSound()` method to give a hint about an error or progress.

Alert Images and Strings

An `Alert` provides information to users with its image and string. Both of them can be null. If the image is not null, it must be immutable. The `Alert`'s image and string can be set when the `Alert` is constructed with

```
Alert(String title, String alertText, Image alertImage, AlertType alertType)
```

Or, they can be set using the `setImage()` and `setString()` methods. They can be retrieved with the `getImage()` and `getString()` methods.

In the example in Listing 6.6, a `TextBox` is created to allow users to type a six-character word (see Figure 6.11). If you type in **mobile** and choose the OK `Command`, you will see an `Alert` screen like Figure 6.12. If you type a word such as **motor** and choose OK, you will see an `Alert` screen like Figure 6.13.

LISTING 6.6   AlertTest.java

```java
import javax.microedition.midlet.*;
import javax.microedition.lcdui.*;

public class AlertTest extends MIDlet implements CommandListener{
    private TextBox textBox;
    private Command okCommand = new Command("OK", Command.OK, 1);
    private Command exitCommand = new Command("EXIT", Command.EXIT, 1);
    private Display display;

    public AlertTest() {
        //create an exclusive list
        textBox= new TextBox("Type in a 6-character word",
```

LISTING 6.6   Continued

```
                                "", 20, TextField.ANY);
    textBox.addCommand(okCommand);
    textBox.addCommand(exitCommand);
    textBox.setCommandListener(this);

    //retrieve display object
    display=Display.getDisplay(this);
}

public void startApp() throws MIDletStateChangeException {
    display.setCurrent(textBox);
}

/**
 * Pause the MIDlet
 */
public void pauseApp() {
}

/**
 * Called by the framework before the application is unloaded
 */
public void destroyApp(boolean unconditional) {
    textBox=null;
    okCommand = null;
    exitCommand = null;
    display=null;
}

public void commandAction(Command c, Displayable d) {
    if(d==textBox && c==okCommand) {
        String t=textBox.getString();
        if(t.length()==6) {
            Alert info= new Alert("Success",
                                  "Good word. Try again.",
                                  null,
                                  AlertType.INFO);
            info.setTimeout(Alert.FOREVER);
            display.setCurrent(info,textBox);
        }
        else {
```

LISTING 6.6 Continued

```java
            Image err_img= null;
            //create error image
            try {
                err_img=Image.createImage("/error.png");
            }catch(Exception e){
                System.out.println("image is not created.");
            }
            Alert error= new Alert("Error",
                                    "Sorry not right. Try again.",
                                    err_img,
                                    AlertType.ERROR);
            error.setTimeout(Alert.FOREVER);
            display.setCurrent(error,textBox);
        }
    }
    else if(c==exitCommand) {
        destroyApp(true);
        notifyDestroyed();
    }
  }
}
```

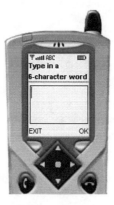

FIGURE 6.11

A TextBox *for users to type in words.*

Using High-Level APIs in UI Development

CHAPTER 6

135

6

USING HIGH-
LEVEL APIs IN UI
DEVELOPMENT

FIGURE 6.12
An alert screen informs users that they've succeeded.

FIGURE 6.13
An alert screen informs users that they've made an error.

Form and Items

A `Form` is a `Screen` that can contain an arbitrary mixture of `Items`, such as image, text, and choice.

You can construct a `Form` object two ways: create an empty `Form` that contains no `Items` with

`Form(String title)`

or create a `Form` with initial `Items` using

`Form(String title, Item[] items)`

The number of `Items` within a `Form` can be retrieved by calling the `size()` method. `Items` are referred to by their indexes, which are consecutive integers in the range from zero to `size()-1`, with zero referring to the first item and `size()-1` to the last item.

Applications can use the following methods to edit `Items` within a `Form`:

```
int append(Image img)
int append(Item item)
int append(String str)
void delete(int itemNum)
void insert(int itemNum, Item item)
void set(int itemNum, Item item)
```

The `Items` within a `Form` can be retrieved using the `get(int itemNum)` method.

An `Item` may be placed within at most one `Form`. If the application attempts to place an `Item` into a `Form`, and the `Item` is already owned by this or another `Form`, an `IllegalStateException` will be thrown. The application must remove the `Item` from its current container `Form` before inserting it into the new `Form`.

The following sections discuss each individual `Item`; then how a `Form` manages its `Items` is discussed.

Item

The `Item` class is the superclass for components that can be added to a `Form`. Each `Item` has a label field, which is a string that is attached to the `Item`. The label is typically displayed near the component when it appears within a screen.

The hierarchical class structure of `Items` is shown in Figure 6.14.

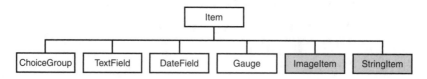

FIGURE 6.14
The hierarchical structures of the `Item` class.

The `ChoiceGroup`, `Gauge`, `DateField`, and `TextField` are focusable items whose values can be interactively changed by users. The `StringItem` and `ImageItem` are nonfocusable items whose contents can only be changed by applications, not by users.

StringItem

A `StringItem` object contains a label and a display-only text string. Users cannot interact with a `StringItem` to change its contents; only applications can modify its contents using the `setText()` method. A `StringItem` object can be constructed with the method

```
StringItem(String label, String text)
```

The text string of a `StringItem` can be retrieved using `getText()` method.

ImageItem

An `ImageItem` object may contain an immutable `Image` object. It can be constructed using

```
ImageItem(String label, Image img, int layout, String altText)
```

Layout

Each `ImageItem` object has a layout parameter that specifies how the object is aligned on the screen. The layout directive's values and their meanings are summarized in Table 6.2.

TABLE 6.2   Layout Directives for `ImageItems`

Layout Directive	Description
LAYOUT_DEFAULT	Its value is 0. Use the default formatting of the image's container.
LAYOUT_LEFT	Its value is 1. Image should be close to the left edge of the drawing area.
LAYOUT_RIGHT	Its value is 2. Image should be close to the right edge of the drawing area.
LAYOUT_CENTER	Its value is 3. Image should be horizontally centered.
LAYOUT_NEWLINE_BEFORE	Its value is 0x100. A new line should be started before the image is drawn.
LAYOUT_NEWLINE_AFTER	Its value is 0x200. A new line should be started after the image is drawn.

Layout values can be combined with the | operator (ORed) to achieve desired effects. The MIDP documentation contains some implicit rules for how the layout directives can be combined:

- `LAYOUT_DEFAULT` cannot be combined with any other directive. In fact, any other option will override `LAYOUT_DEFAULT`, because its value is 0.
- `LAYOUT_LEFT+LAYOUT_RIGHT` is equal to `LAYOUT_CENTER`.

- LAYOUT_CENTER cannot be combined with LAYOUT_LEFT or LAYOUT_RIGHT.
- It usually makes sense to combine LAYOUT_LEFT, LAYOUT_RIGHT, and LAYOUT_CENTER with LAYOUT_NEWLINE_BEFORE and LAYOUT_NEWLINE_AFTER. For example, with directives LAYOUT_CENTER+LAYOUT_NEWLINE_BEFORE+LAYOUT_NEWLINE_AFTER, the ImageItem object will be positioned in the horizontal center, and will start with a new line and end with a new line.

The layout value of an ImageItem can be set with the setLayout() method or retrieved using the getLayout() method.

The layout value of an ImageItem is merely a suggestion. Because of device constraints, such as limited screen size, the implementation may choose to ignore layout directives.

Alternative Text

If the image cannot be displayed because it exceeds the capacity of the display, a text string specified by the altText parameter will be displayed instead. The alternative text can be set or retrieved using the setAltText() or getAltText() method.

ChoiceGroup

A ChoiceGroup class is an Item that implements the Choice interface. ChoiceGroup's implementation of Choice is similar to that of List, except that there is no implicit-choice type of ChoiceGroup. The appearances of exclusive and multiple-choice ChoiceGroups are similar to those of the corresponding List types, shown in Figures 6.2 and 6.3. The constructor methods for a ChoiceGroup are the following:

```
ChoiceGroup(String label, int choiceType)
ChoiceGroup(String label, int choiceType, String[] stringElements,
            Image[] imageElements)
```

The other methods of a ChoiceGroup class are implementations of the Choice interface. They are similar to corresponding methods of a List class.

Gauge

A Gauge is an Item that displays a bar graph of a value in the range from zero to a maxValue. A Gauge object can be constructed as follows:

```
Gauge(String label, boolean interactive, int maxValue, int initialValue)
```

The following methods of a Gauge class are provided in the API:

```
int getMaxValue()
int getValue()
boolean isInteractive()
void setMaxValue(int maxValue)
void setValue(int value)
```

Using High-Level APIs in UI Development

CHAPTER 6

139

6

USING HIGH-
LEVEL APIs IN UI
DEVELOPMENT

The device can only display a small number of bars. If the number of different possible values set by maxValue is greater than the number of bars that can be displayed, the values will be *binned* into a smaller set of values for display purposes. For example, ten bars can be displayed on the device, and the maxValue is set to 99. Then, values zero to nine are treated as the same value, values 10 to 19 are treated as the same value, and so forth.

A Gauge can be interactive or noninteractive. Users can change a Gauge's value interactively when it is interactive. Only applications can change a Gauge's value when it is noninteractive. There may be visual differences for gauges in interactive and noninteractive modes. Applications can set or retrieve the Gauge's value with the setValue() method or the getValue() method, respectively, at any time, regardless of the interaction mode.

The example in Listing 6.7 creates two different types of Gauges. If you run the MIDlet on Sun's emulator and select Interactive Gauge from the start menu shown in Figure 6.15, you will see a screen like Figure 6.16. You can interactively adjust the Gauge's value using the left and right arrows. If you select Non-interactive Gauge from the start menu, you will see a screen like Figure 6.17.

LISTING 6.7   GaugeTest.java

```java
import javax.microedition.midlet.*;
import javax.microedition.lcdui.*;

public class GaugeTest extends MIDlet implements CommandListener{
    private Form  form;
    private List  startmenu;
    private String choices[]={"Interactive Gauge","Non-interactive Gauge"};
    private Command backCommand = new Command("Back", Command.BACK, 1);
    private Command exitCommand = new Command("EXIT", Command.EXIT, 1);
    private Display display;

    public GaugeTest() {
        //create a list as start menu
        startmenu= new List("Choose a Gauge type", List.IMPLICIT,
                            choices, null);
        startmenu.addCommand(exitCommand);
        startmenu.setCommandListener(this);

        //create a form to manage a gauge
        form= new Form("Gauge Test");
        form.addCommand(backCommand);
        form.setCommandListener(this);
```

LISTING 6.7 Continued

```java
        //retrieve display object
        display=Display.getDisplay(this);
    }

    public void startApp() throws MIDletStateChangeException {
        display.setCurrent(startmenu);
    }

    /**
     * Pause the MIDlet
     */
    public void pauseApp() {
    }

    /**
     * Called by the framework before the application is unloaded
     */
    public void destroyApp(boolean unconditional) {
        form=null;
        startmenu=null;
        backCommand = null;
        exitCommand = null;
        display=null;
    }

    public void commandAction(Command c, Displayable d) {
        if(d==startmenu && c==List.SELECT_COMMAND) {
            if(form.size()>0) form.delete(0);
            if(startmenu.getSelectedIndex()==0) {
                form.append(new Gauge("Interactive Gauge",true,10,4));
            }
            else {
                form.append(new Gauge("Non-interactive Gauge",
                                    false, 10, 4));
            }
            display.setCurrent(form);
        }
        else if(c==backCommand) {
            display.setCurrent(startmenu);
        }
        else if(c==exitCommand) {
            destroyApp(true);
            notifyDestroyed();
        }
    }
}
```

Using High-Level APIs in UI Development

CHAPTER 6

141

6

USING HIGH-
LEVEL APIS IN UI
DEVELOPMENT

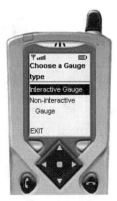

FIGURE 6.15

A start menu for gauge test.

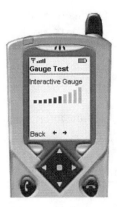

FIGURE 6.16

An interactive Gauge.

DateField

A DateField is an editable Item for presenting date and time (calendar) information. A DateField object can be constructed using one of the following constructors:

```
DateField(String label, int mode)
DateField(String label, int mode, TimeZone timeZone)
```

There are three input modes:

- DATE: Users can only set date information.
- TIME: Users can only set time information (hours, minutes). In this mode the date components should be set to the *zero epoch* value of January 1, 1970 and should not be accessed.
- DATE_TIME: Users can set both clock time and date values.

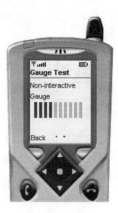

FIGURE 6.17

A non-interactive Gauge.

The input mode can be set or retrieved with setInputMode(int mode) or getInputMode(),
respectively. When the input mode is set to DATE mode, the time information will be set to
zero. When the input mode is set to TIME mode, the date information will be set to zero.

The Date value of a DateField can be set using the setDate() method and retrieved with the
getDate() method.

The example in Listing 6.8 displays date/time information using a DateField set to different
input modes.

LISTING 6.8   DateFieldTest.java

```
import javax.microedition.midlet.*;
import javax.microedition.lcdui.*;
import java.util.Date;

public class DateFieldTest extends MIDlet implements CommandListener{
    private Form   form;
    private List   startmenu;
    private long   date, time;
    // one day in millis
    private long   dayInMillis=24*60*60*1000;
    private String choices[]={"DATE mode","TIME mode", "DATE_TIME mode"};
    private Command backCommand = new Command("Back", Command.BACK, 1);
    private Command okCommand = new Command("OK", Command.OK, 1);
    private Command exitCommand = new Command("EXIT", Command.EXIT, 1);
    private Display display;

    public DateFieldTest() {
        //create a list as start menu
```

Using High-Level APIs in UI Development

CHAPTER 6

143

6

USING HIGH-
LEVEL APIs IN UI
DEVELOPMENT

LISTING 6.8 Continued

```java
        startmenu= new List("Choose a input mode", List.IMPLICIT,
                            choices, null);
        startmenu.addCommand(exitCommand);
        startmenu.setCommandListener(this);

        //create a form to manage a gauge
        form= new Form("DateField Test");
        DateField df=new DateField("", DateField.DATE_TIME);
        time=System.currentTimeMillis()%dayInMillis;
        date=System.currentTimeMillis()-time;
        df.setDate(new Date(date+time));
        form.append(df);
        form.addCommand(okCommand);
        form.addCommand(backCommand);
        form.setCommandListener(this);

        //retrieve display object
        display=Display.getDisplay(this);
    }

    public void startApp() throws MIDletStateChangeException {
        display.setCurrent(startmenu);
    }

    /**
     * Pause the MIDlet
     */
    public void pauseApp() {
    }

    /**
     * Called by the framework before the application is unloaded
     */
    public void destroyApp(boolean unconditional) {
        form=null;
        startmenu=null;
        backCommand = null;
        okCommand=null;
        exitCommand = null;
        display=null;
    }

    public void commandAction(Command c, Displayable d) {
        if(d==startmenu && c==List.SELECT_COMMAND) {
```

LISTING 6.8 Continued

```
            DateField df= (DateField) form.get(0);
            //save the date/time information has been set
            if(df.getInputMode()==DateField.DATE) {
                date=df.getDate().getTime();
            }
            else if(df.getInputMode() == DateField.TIME) {
                time=df.getDate().getTime();
            }
            else {
                time=df.getDate().getTime()%dayInMillis;
                date=df.getDate().getTime()-time;
            }
            //set time and input mode
            df.setLabel(choices[startmenu.getSelectedIndex()]);
            switch(startmenu.getSelectedIndex()) {
            case 0:
                df.setInputMode(DateField.DATE);
                df.setDate(new Date(date));
                break;
            case 1:
                df.setInputMode(DateField.TIME);
                df.setDate(new Date(time));
                break;
            case 2:
                df.setInputMode(DateField.DATE_TIME);
                df.setDate(new Date(date+time));
                break;
            }
            display.setCurrent(form);
        }
        else if(d==form && c==okCommand) {//get time
            DateField df= (DateField) form.get(0);
            System.out.println("Time set in millis: "+df.getDate().getTime());
        }
        else if(c==backCommand) {
            display.setCurrent(startmenu);
        }
        else if(c==exitCommand) {
            destroyApp(true);
            notifyDestroyed();
        }
    }
}
```

Using High-Level APIs in UI Development

CHAPTER 6

145

6

USING HIGH-
LEVEL APIs IN UI
DEVELOPMENT

When the input mode is set to DATE or TIME, the time or date component, respectively, will be set to zero. To save the date or time component when the input mode of the DateField is switched, you can use the following code in the commandAction() method:

```
public void commandAction(Command c, Displayable d) {
    if(d==startmenu && c==List.SELECT_COMMAND) {
        DateField df= (DateField) form.get(0);
        //save the date/time information has been set
        if(df.getInputMode()==DateField.DATE) {
            date=df.getDate().getTime();
        }
        else if(df.getInputMode() == DateField.TIME) {
            time=df.getDate().getTime();
        }
        else {
            time=df.getDate().getTime()%dayInMillis;
            date=df.getDate().getTime()-time;
        }
    ...
}
```

If you run the MIDlet on Sun's emulator, you will see a start screen like Figure 6.18. If you select DATE Mode, you will see date information displayed in a screen similar to Figure 6.19. To set the date value, you can press the Select button and a system screen with a calendar like Figure 6.20 will pop up. After you select a day, choose the Save command to accept the change; you will see the date value of the DateField changed accordingly.

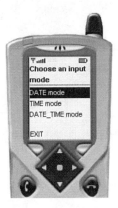

FIGURE 6.18

A start menu for DateField *test.*

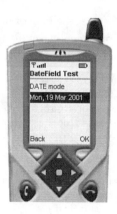

FIGURE 6.19

A DateField *in* DateField.DATE *mode.*

FIGURE 6.20

A system screen that contains a calendar, which is used to provide date information for a DateField.

If you select TIME Mode from the start menu, you will see a screen like Figure 6.21. If you press the Select key, a clock will pop up, as shown in Figure 6.22, to allow you to set the time. After setting the time, choose Save; the time value will be reflected in the DateField.

Using High-Level APIs in UI Development

CHAPTER 6

147

6

USING HIGH-
LEVEL APIs IN UI
DEVELOPMENT

FIGURE 6.21

A DateField *in* DateField.TIME *mode.*

FIGURE 6.22

A system screen that contains a clock, which is used to set the time information in a DateField*.*

If you select DATE_TIME Mode from the start menu, you will see a screen like Figure 6.23. To change the date or time component of the DateField, you can move focus to the appropriate field using the arrow keys and press the Select button. A calendar like Figure 6.20 or a clock like Figure 6.22 will pop up.

The visual presentation of the DateField on Motorola's emulator, shown in Figure 6.24, is quite different from Sun's emulator. To change DateField values on Motorola's emulator, you can move focus to the desired field using the left and right arrow keys, and edit its value using the keypad.

FIGURE 6.23

A DateField *in* DateField.DATE_TIME *mode.*

FIGURE 6.24

A DateField *in* DateField.DATE_TIME *mode on a Motorola's emulator.*

TextField

A TextField class is an Item that contains a text string that can be interactively edited by users. A TextField object can be constructed using

TextField(String label, String text, int maxSize, int constraints)

A TextField and a TextBox are very similar. They both contain a text string, and both have a maximum number of characters that can be stored in the object at any time. They share the concept of input constraints. In addition, the set of methods for editing and retrieving the text string is the same for both TextField and TextBox.

The difference between a `TextField` and a `TextBox` is whose subclass it is. A `TextBox` is a subclass of `Screen`, so it can be put directly on the display. A `TextField` is a subclass of `Item`, so it must be put in a `Form` to be displayed.

Form

The `Form` class is the most important component in developing UI for MIDP devices. It gives developers the flexibility to construct new screens.

Layout Management

The MIDP implementation dictates the actual layout of `Items` within a `Form`. The layout policy of a `Form` on most devices is vertical. A new line is always started for focusable `Items` such as `TextFields`, `DateFields`, `Gauges`, or `ChoiceGroups`. `StringItems` and `ImageItems`, which do not involve user interactions, behave differently. They are filled in horizontal lines, unless a newline is embedded in the string or layout directives of an `ImageItem` force a new line. The contents of a `StringItem` or `ImageItem` will be wrapped (for text) or clipped (for images) to fit the width of the display, and scrolling will occur vertically as necessary. There is no horizontal scrolling.

In Listing 6.9, a `StringItem`, `ImageItem`, `ChoiceGroup`, `TextField`, `DateField`, and `Gauge` object are created and added to a `Form`. If you run the MIDlet, you will see screens like Figure 6.25.

LISTING 6.9   FormTest1.java

```
import javax.microedition.midlet.*;
import javax.microedition.lcdui.*;

public class FormTest1 extends MIDlet implements CommandListener{
    private Form    mainscreen;
    private Command okCommand = new Command("OK", Command.OK, 1);
    private Command exitCommand = new Command("Exit", Command.EXIT, 1);
    private Display display;

    public FormTest1() {
        mainscreen= new Form("Form demo");
        mainscreen.addCommand(okCommand);
        mainscreen.addCommand(exitCommand);
        mainscreen.setCommandListener(this);

        //first create a stringItem
        mainscreen.append(new StringItem("StringItem Test",
                                         "The following is Duke."));
```

LISTING 6.9   Continued

```
        //create an imageItem
        Image img=null;
        try {
            img= Image.createImage("/Duke.png");
        } catch (Exception e) {}
        mainscreen.append(new ImageItem("ImageItem test",
                                        img,
                                        ImageItem.LAYOUT_CENTER,
                                        "Image can not display"));

        //create exclusive choice
        String[] editable_choices={"editable", "uneditable"};
        mainscreen.append(new ChoiceGroup("Gauge option", Choice.EXCLUSIVE,
                                        editable_choices, null));
        //create a textfield
        mainscreen.append(new TextField("TextField", "", 20, TextField.ANY));

        //create a datefield
        mainscreen.append(new DateField("DateField", DateField.DATE));

        //create a Gauge
        mainscreen.append(new Gauge("Gauge Test", true, 100, 50));

        //retrieve display object
        display=Display.getDisplay(this);
    }

    public void startApp() throws MIDletStateChangeException {
        display.setCurrent(mainscreen);
    }

    /**
     * Pause the MIDlet
     */
    public void pauseApp() {
    }

    /**
     * Called by the framework before the application is unloaded
     */
    public void destroyApp(boolean unconditional) {
        //clear everything
        mainscreen=null;
        okCommand = null;
```

Using High-Level APIs in UI Development

CHAPTER 6

151

6

USING HIGH-
LEVEL APIS IN UI
DEVELOPMENT

LISTING 6.9 Continued

```
        exitCommand = null;
        display=null;
    }

    public void commandAction(Command c, Displayable d) {
    if(c==okCommand) {
    }
    else if(c==exitCommand) {
        destroyApp(true);
        notifyDestroyed();
    }
    }
}
```

FIGURE 6.25
A Form *that contains a* StringItem. *The text string of the* StringItem *does not start from a new line.*

You may notice an undesirable effect: The text of the StringItem does not start from a new line. To overcome this effect, you can add a new line return, as follows:

```
mainscreen.append(new StringItem("StringItem Test",
                            "\nThe following is Duke."));
```

If you run the modified MIDlet, you will see a screen like Figure 6.26.

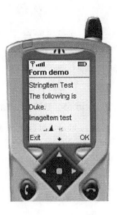

FIGURE 6.26

A Form *that contains a* StringItem. *The text string of the* StringItem *is forced to start on a new line.*

The default layout behaviors of ImageItem on Sun's emulator are that an ImageItem object starts with a new line and ends with a new line to separate it from the previous and next Items in the Form. That is, the ImageItem.LAYOUT_NEWLINE_AFTER and ImageItem.LAYOUT_ NEWLINE_AFTER directives are combined to be the default. Thus,

```
mainscreen.append(new ImageItem("ImageItem test",
                                img,
                                ImageItem.LAYOUT_CENTER,
                                "Image can not display"));
```

is equivalent to

```
mainscreen.append(new ImageItem("ImageItem test",
                                img,
                                ImageItem.LAYOUT_CENTER|
                                ImageItem.LAYOUT_NEWLINE_BEFORE|
                                ImageItem.LAYOUT_NEWLINE_AFTER,
                                "Image can not display"));
```

NOTE

The scrolling behaviors within a Form are different on Sun's emulator and Motorola's. On Motorola's emulator, when you press the up and down arrow keys, you can traverse Items within a Form, but not elements within an Item, such as a ChoiceGroup. To change the focused element of a ChoiceGroup on Motorola's emulator, you have to use the right and left arrow keys.

Using High-Level APIs in UI Development

CHAPTER 6

153

6

USING HIGH-
LEVEL APIs IN UI
DEVELOPMENT

ItemStateChanged Events and ItemStateListener

When a Form is present on the display, the user can move or scroll from Item to Item within it. These moving and scrolling operations do not cause application-visible events. When the user modifies the state of an interactive Item contained within a Form, such as editing the text of a TextField, or selecting/unselecting elements of a ChoiceGroup, an ItemStateChanged event will be generated. Only user interactions with interactive Items can trigger generation of ItemStateChanged events. If an application sets item values, no ItemStateChanged events are generated. For example, setting the text string of a TextField using the setString() method does not generate an ItemStateChanged event.

There is an ItemStateListener interface for ItemStateChanged events. The ItemStateChanged event-handling model is delegation-based, like the command event-handling model. Any class can implement the ItemStateListener interface. Then, the ItemStateListener object is registered to a Form using the Form.setItemStateListener() method. All ItemStateChanged events from the Form will be delivered to the ItemStateListener for processing. A Form object can have at most one registered ItemStateListener at a time. An ItemStateListener can listen to multiple Forms. The event processing method of the ItemStateListener interface is

```
public void itemStateChanged(Item item)
```

Only the state-changing Item is passed to the itemStateChanged() method. No information about which Form the event originated in is passed to the event processing method.

However, in the command event-handling model, both the Command and the Displayable from which the Command is fired are passed to the event processing method:

```
public void commandAction(Command c, Displayable d)
```

This is the case because a Command can be added to multiple Displayables, whereas an Item can be added to at most one Form. Thus, given an Item, applications can uniquely identify the source of the ItemStateChanged event.

In Listing 6.10, the outer class implements the ItemStateListener interface, and is registered to a Form.

LISTING 6.10   FormTest2.java

```
import javax.microedition.midlet.*;
import javax.microedition.lcdui.*;

public class FormTest2 extends MIDlet
                    implements CommandListener,
                             ItemStateListener{
```

LISTING 6.10   Continued

```java
private Form     mainscreen;
private Command okCommand = new Command("OK", Command.OK, 1);
private Command exitCommand = new Command("Exit", Command.EXIT, 1);
private Display display;

public FormTest2() {
    mainscreen= new Form("Form demo");
    mainscreen.addCommand(okCommand);
    mainscreen.addCommand(exitCommand);
    mainscreen.setCommandListener(this);
    mainscreen.setItemStateListener(this);

    //create exclusive choice
    String[] editable_choices={"interactive", "noninteractive"};
    mainscreen.append(new ChoiceGroup("Gauge option", Choice.EXCLUSIVE,
                                 editable_choices, null));

    //create a textfield
    mainscreen.append(new TextField("Reset Gauge value", "10", 20,
                             TextField.NUMERIC));
    //create a Gauge
    mainscreen.append(new Gauge("Gauge Test", true, 100, 10));

    //retrieve display object
    display=Display.getDisplay(this);
}

public void startApp() throws MIDletStateChangeException {
    display.setCurrent(mainscreen);
}

/**
 * Pause the MIDlet
 */
public void pauseApp() {
}

/**
 * Called by the framework before the application is unloaded
 */
public void destroyApp(boolean unconditional) {
    //clear everything
    mainscreen=null;
    okCommand = null;
```

Listing 6.10 Continued

```
            exitCommand = null;
            display=null;
    }

    public void commandAction(Command c, Displayable d) {
        if(c==okCommand) {
        }
        else if(c==exitCommand) {
            destroyApp(true);
            notifyDestroyed();
        }
    }

    public void itemStateChanged(Item item) {
        if(item==mainscreen.get(0)) {//option for setting gauge
            ChoiceGroup c= (ChoiceGroup) item;
            if(c.getString(c.getSelectedIndex()).equals("interactive")) {
                System.out.println("Switch to interactive gauge.");
                mainscreen.delete(mainscreen.size()-1);
                mainscreen.append(new Gauge("Gauge Test",true,100,50));
            }
            else if(c.getString(c.getSelectedIndex()).equals("noninteractive"))
{
                System.out.println("Switch to non-interactive gauge.");
                mainscreen.delete(mainscreen.size()-1);
                mainscreen.append(new Gauge("Gauge Test",false,100,50));
            }
        }
        else if(item==mainscreen.get(1)) {//textfield
            TextField tf= (TextField) item;
            System.out.println("textfield: "+tf.getString());
            int value=Integer.parseInt(tf.getString());
            Gauge g= (Gauge)mainscreen.get(mainscreen.size()-1);
            g.setValue(value);
        }
    }
}
```

If you start the MIDlet, you will see a screen like Figure 6.27. If you scroll the screen down to the end, you will see a Gauge as shown in Figure 6.28. If you change the selection of the ChoiceGroup from Interactive to Non-interactive, you will see the Gauge changed accordingly, as shown in Figure 6.29. If you change the contents of the TextField, you will see that the Gauge changes, too.

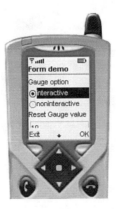

FIGURE 6.27

A Form *for testing* ItemStateListener.

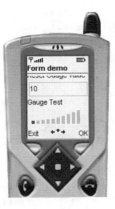

FIGURE 6.28

A Form *for testing* ItemStateListener; *the* Gauge *is interactive.*

The way an ItemStateChanged event is generated from a TextField is different on Sun's emulator than it is on Motorola's. On Sun's emulator, the event is generated after you choose the Save Command of the system screen when you edit the text of a TextBox. On Motorola's emulator, every editing action of the TextField triggers an ItemStateChanged event.

On both emulators the contents of the TextField are updated before the ItemStateChanged event is delivered to an ItemStateListener. Thus, in the itemStateChanged() method, the contents of the TextField retrieved using the getString() method already reflect the modification.

Using High-Level APIs in UI Development

CHAPTER 6

157

6

USING HIGH-
LEVEL APIS IN UI
DEVELOPMENT

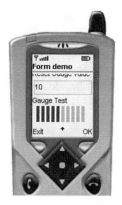

FIGURE 6.29

A Form *for testing* ItemStateListener. *The Gauge changes to noninteractive mode in response to a new* ChoiceGroup *selection.*

Example

In this book, you will gradually build an application called MobileScheduler that allows users to organize their appointments. In this chapter, you will build MobileScheduler's graphical user interface. Other functional components such as synchronization and local storage will be added in later chapters.

There are three files in this example: Scheduler.java, AppointmentForm.java, and SynchOptionForm.java. Scheduler.java in Listing 6.11 is the main program. It creates an implicit-choice List menu as the starting menu, shown as Figure 6.30. A new AppointmentForm is created if Add Appointment is selected. A new SynchOptionForm is created if Synch Setup is selected. If Exit is selected, the program terminates.

The AppointmentForm class in Listing 6.12 creates a Form containing three TextFields for appointment length, location, and subject, and a DateField for appointment date, shown in Figure 6.31. It also creates a Save Command for saving data. After editing the appointment date, length, location, and subject in the Form, you can choose the Save Command, and the contents of the those fields are output to the terminal as follows:

```
Appointment:
Time: February 5, 2001  8:30
Length (Min): 30
Where:  conference room
Subject: Status meeting
```

The `SynchOptionForm` class in Listing 6.13 creates a `Form` containing `TextFields` with different input constraints. These TextFields are for the URL, username, password, and synch schedule, shown in Figure 6.32. The class then creates a `ChoiceGroup` with Manual and Automatic options. If you select Automatic in the `ChoiceGroup`, an extra `TextField` for the frequency of automatic synchronizing appointments will be added to the `Form`. You probably need to scroll to the bottom of the `Form` in order to see the frequency `TextField`.

You can also set a rule that users must provide a username and the URL of the synchronizing server. If you choose the Save `Command` before setting those fields, an `Alert` screen is created to display the warning message, as in Figure 6.33. By dismissing the `Alert` screen, you return to the point before you chose Save, and continue editing. When all the required fields are set, you can choose Save. The contents of those fields will be output to the terminal, as follows:

```
url address: www.webyu.com/appointmentSynchServlet
username: someone
password: test
Synch schedule: Manual
```

LISTING 6.11   `Scheduler.java`

```java
import java.util.Calendar;
import javax.microedition.midlet.*;
import javax.microedition.lcdui.*;

public class Scheduler extends MIDlet implements CommandListener{
    private Calendar          calendar;
    private List              menu;
    private AppointmentForm   appForm=null;
    private SynchOptionForm   soForm=null;
    private String[]          options={"Add Appointment",
                                       "Synch Setup",
                                       "Exit"};

    private Display           display;

    public Scheduler() {
        //create an implicit choice list, and use it as start menu
        menu= new List("Scheduler", List.IMPLICIT,options,null);
        menu.setCommandListener(this);

        //get a calendar
        calendar=Calendar.getInstance();

        //retrieve display
        display=Display.getDisplay(this);
    }
```

LISTING 6.11 Continued

```java
public void startApp() throws MIDletStateChangeException {
    display.setCurrent(menu);
}

/**
 * Pause the MIDlet
 */
public void pauseApp() {
}

/**
 * Called by the framework before the application is unloaded
 */
public void destroyApp(boolean unconditional) {
    //clear everything
    menu= null;
    calendar=null;
    display=null;
    appForm = null;
    soForm = null;
}

public void commandAction(Command c, Displayable d) {
    if(d==menu && c==List.SELECT_COMMAND) {
        switch(menu.getSelectedIndex()) {
        case 0: //Add appointment
            if(appForm==null) {
                //create a new appointment form
                appForm = new AppointmentForm(display,menu);
            }
            appointmentForm.addNew(calendar.getTime());
            display.setCurrent(appForm);
            break;
        case 1: //synchronization set up
            if(soForm==null) {
                //synchsetting
                soForm = new SynchOptionForm(display,menu);
            }
            display.setCurrent(soForm);
            break;
        case 2: //exit
            destroyApp(true);
            notifyDestroyed();
            break;
```

LISTING 6.11   Continued

```
              default:
              }
          }
      }
}
```

LISTING 6.12   AppointmentForm.java

```java
import javax.microedition.midlet.*;
import javax.microedition.lcdui.*;
import java.util.Date;
import java.util.Calendar;

public class AppointmentForm extends Form implements CommandListener{
    private Display display;
    private Displayable parent;
    private Command saveCommand = new Command("Save", Command.OK, 1);
    private Command cancelCommand = new Command("Cancel", Command.CANCEL, 1);
    private static String months[] = {"January", "February", "March", "April",
                            "May", "June", "July", "August", "September",
                            "October", "November", "December"};

    public AppointmentForm(Display d, Displayable p) {
        super("New Appointment");
        display=d;
        parent=p;
        addCommand(saveCommand);
        addCommand(cancelCommand);
        setCommandListener(this);

        //Appointment Time
        DateField df= new DateField("Date and Time",DateField.DATE_TIME);
        df.setDate(new Date(System.currentTimeMillis()));
        append(df);

        //Appointment Length
        append(new TextField("Length (Min)", "30", 10, TextField.NUMERIC));

        //Appointment location
        append(new TextField("Where", "", 50, TextField.ANY));
```

Using High-Level APIs in UI Development

CHAPTER 6

161

6

USING HIGH-
LEVEL APIs IN UI
DEVELOPMENT

LISTING 6.12   Continued

```java
        //Subject
        append(new TextField("Subject", "", 50, TextField.ANY));
    }

    public void addNew(Date date) {
        //Appointment Time
        DateField df= (DateField) get(0);
        df.setDate(date);

        //Appointment Length
        TextField tf_length= (TextField) get(1);
        tf_length.setString("30");

        //Appointment location
        TextField tf_location= (TextField) get(2);
        tf_location.setString("");

        //Appointment subject
        TextField tf_subject= (TextField) get(3);
        tf_subject.setString("");
    }

    public void commandAction(Command c, Displayable d) {
        if(c==saveCommand) {//display
            System.out.println("Appointment:");
            Calendar cal= Calendar.getInstance();
            cal.setTime(((DateField)get(0)).getDate());
            System.out.println("Time: "+months[cal.get(Calendar.MONTH)]+" "+
                            cal.get(Calendar.DAY_OF_MONTH)+", "+
                            cal.get(Calendar.YEAR)+" "+
                            cal.get(Calendar.HOUR_OF_DAY)+":"+
                            cal.get(Calendar.MINUTE));
            for(int i=1; i<size(); i++) {
                TextField tf= (TextField) get(i);
                System.out.println(tf.getLabel()+": "+tf.getString());
            }
            display.setCurrent(parent);
        }
        else if(c==cancelCommand) {
            display.setCurrent(parent);
        }
    }
}
```

LISTING 6.13   SynchOptionForm.java

```java
import javax.microedition.midlet.*;
import javax.microedition.lcdui.*;

public class SynchOptionForm extends Form
                                implements CommandListener,
                                           ItemStateListener{
    private Command saveCommand = new Command("Save", Command.OK, 1);
    private Command cancelCommand = new Command("Cancel", Command.CANCEL, 1);
    private Display display;
    private Displayable parent;

    public SynchOptionForm(Display d, Displayable p) {
        super("Synchronization Setting");
        display=d;
        parent=p;
        addCommand(saveCommand);
        addCommand(cancelCommand);
        setCommandListener(this);
        setItemStateListener(this);

        //url
        append(new TextField("url address", "", 50,
                            TextField.URL));

        //user name
        append(new TextField("username", "", 30,
                            TextField.ANY));
        //password
        append(new TextField("password", "", 30,
                            TextField.PASSWORD));

        //create exclusive choice
        String[] choices={"Manual", "Automatic"};
        append(new ChoiceGroup("Synch schedule",Choice.EXCLUSIVE,
                            choices,null));
    }

    public void commandAction(Command c, Displayable d) {
        if(c==saveCommand) {
            //url and user name must be set
            if(((TextField) get(0)).getString().length()==0 ) {
                Alert a = new Alert("Error", "url address must be set.", null,
                                AlertType.ERROR);
                a.setTimeout(Alert.FOREVER);
                display.setCurrent(a,this);
```

Using High-Level APIs in UI Development

CHAPTER 6

163

6

USING HIGH-
LEVEL APIS IN UI
DEVELOPMENT

LISTING 6.13   Continued

```
                return;
            }
            else if(((TextField) get(1)).getString().length()==0 ) {
                Alert a = new Alert("Error", "username must be set.",null,
                                    AlertType.ERROR);
                a.setTimeout(Alert.FOREVER);
                display.setCurrent(a,this);
                return;
            }

            for(int i=0; i<3; i++) {
                TextField t= (TextField) get(i);
                System.out.println(t.getLabel()+": "+t.getString());
            }
            ChoiceGroup cg= (ChoiceGroup)get(3);
            if(cg.getString(cg.getSelectedIndex()).equals("Manual")) {
                System.out.println(cg.getLabel()+": Manual");
            }
            else {
                System.out.println(cg.getLabel()+": Automatic");
                TextField t= (TextField) get(4);
                System.out.println(t.getLabel()+": "+t.getString());
            }
            display.setCurrent(parent);
        }
        else if(c==cancelCommand) {
            display.setCurrent(parent);
        }
    }

    public void itemStateChanged(Item item) {
        //option for setting synch schedule
        if(item==get(3)) {
            ChoiceGroup c= (ChoiceGroup) item;
            if(c.getString(c.getSelectedIndex()).equals("Automatic")) {
                append(new TextField("Frequency (Min)","30",10,
                                     TextField.NUMERIC));
            }
            else if(c.getString(c.getSelectedIndex()).equals("Manual")) {
                delete(size()-1);
            }
        }
    }
}
```

FIGURE 6.30

The start menu of the scheduler.

FIGURE 6.31

The Form *for creating a new appointment.*

Using High-Level APIs in UI Development

CHAPTER 6

165

6

USING HIGH-
LEVEL APIS IN UI
DEVELOPMENT

FIGURE 6.32

The Form for setting synchronization options.

FIGURE 6.33

The error alert screen.

Summary

This chapter covered basic user interface development using subclasses of Screen. The Screen class is a Displayable that implements the high-level API. There are three structure-predefined subclasses of a Screen: List, TextBox, and Alert. In addition, Screen has a generic subclass: Form. Applications can combine arbitrary number of Items in a Form.

Only high-level events (Command events and ItemStateChanged events) from a Screen are accessible to applications. If applications need to access low-level events, such as key events, or they need to have more control over where UI elements should be put, then a Canvas class should be used. The Canvas class is covered in Chapter 7.

Using Low-level APIs in UI Development

IN THIS CHAPTER

Introduction

Chapter 6, "Using High-Level APIs in UI Development," discussed developing user interfaces for wireless devices using MIDP UI's high-level API. The high-level API emphasizes portability. It uses a high abstraction approach to shield detail implementations from developers. As a result, applications have no control over how or where their contents will be drawn on the display, and have access only to high-level events. MIDP UI's low-level API, on the other hand, gives applications full control over the appearance of the contents drawn on the display and access to low-level events. However, applications developed with low-level APIs may not be portable across devices if device-specific features are used.

The low-level API consists of two parts: the Canvas class, upon which you can perform graphics operations and where low-level events are delivered; and the Graphics class, which is used to render text and images, draw, and fill shapes.

In this chapter, we will first discuss the basics of Canvas, and then discuss how to draw contents to a Canvas object using the Graphics class with the paint() method of the Canvas. We will also talk about low-level events and their event-handling methods.

Canvas Basics

The Canvas class is the subclass of Displayable that implements the low-level API. It provides a paint method and several methods for handling low-level events that applications can override. The paint() method of the Canvas class is declared abstract, so the Canvas class is an abstract class. An application must extend the Canvas class in order to use it. The application is required to provide an implementation of the paint() method when subclassing the Canvas class. The low-level event handling methods are not declared abstract, and their default implementations are empty (that is, they do nothing). Thus, the application does not need to provide an implementation for every event-handling method. The application only needs to override the event-handling methods the application is interested in.

Any classes that need to handle low-level events and to issue graphics calls for drawing on the display have to extend the Canvas class as follows:

```
class TestCanvas extends Canvas {
...
    void paint(Graphics g) {
    ...
    }
...
}
```

The Canvas Size

The actual size of the drawing area on a display varies from device to device. Applications should not assume any default values but should instead query the dimensions by calling the `getHeight()` and the `getWidth()` methods. Table 7.1 shows the drawing area sizes of some phone models.

TABLE 7.1   Display Sizes of Different Phones (Measured in Pixels)

Phone Model	Width	Height
Sun's color phone	96	100
Sun's minimum phone	88	54
Sun's pager	120	60
Motorola's iDEN3000	111	100
Motorola's StarTac	98	49
Motorola's iDEN1000	96	48
Motorola's Condor	160	280

Events

The primary use of the `Canvas` class is to access and handle low-level events. But high-level events can also originate from a `Canvas` object. Like other subclasses of `Displayable`, an application can add `Commands` to a `Canvas` using the `addCommand()` method, and register a `CommandListener` to a `Canvas` using the `setCommandListener()` method.

Graphics

The `Graphics` class provides simple 2D geometric rendering capabilities. It is very similar to the `java.awt.Graphics` class in J2SE. The following methods are defined for drawing text, images, and lines; drawing and filling rectangles; and drawing arcs on the display:

```
void clipRect(int x, int y, int width, int height)
void drawArc(int x, int y, int width, int height, int startAngle,
            int arcAngle)
void drawChar(char character, int x, int y, int anchor)
void drawChars(char[] data, int offset, int length, int x, int y,
              int anchor)
void drawImage(Image img, int x, int y, int anchor)
void drawLine(int x1, int y1, int x2, int y2)
void drawRect(int x, int y, int width, int height)
```

```
void drawRoundRect(int x, int y, int width, int height, int arcWidth,
                   int arcHeight)
void drawString(String str, int x, int y, int anchor)
void drawSubstring(String str, int offset, int len, int x, int y,
                   int anchor)
void fillArc(int x, int y, int width, int height, int startAngle,
             int arcAngle)
void fillRect(int x, int y, int width, int height)
void fillRoundRect(int x, int y, int width, int height, int arcWidth,
                   int arcHeight)
int getBlueComponent()
int getClipHeight()
int getClipWidth()
int getClipX()
int getClipY()
int getColor()
Font getFont()
int getGrayScale()
int getGreenComponent()
int getRedComponent()
int getStrokeStyle()
int getTranslateX()
int getTranslateY()
void setClip(int x, int y, int width, int height)
void setColor(int RGB)
void setColor(int red, int green, int blue)
void setFont(Font font)
void setGrayScale(int value)
void setStrokeStyle(int style)
void translate(int x, int y)
```

The only drawing mode provided by the Graphics class is pixel replacement. Under this mode, the destination pixel value is replaced by the current pixel value specified in the graphics object being used for rendering. No facility for combining pixel values, such as raster-ops or alpha blending, is provided by the Graphics class.

Obtaining a Graphics Object

A Graphics object can be rendered directly to the display or to an offscreen image buffer. The destination of rendered graphics depends on the provenance of the Graphics object.

The only way to obtain a Graphics object for rendering to the display is through the paint(Graphics g) method of a Canvas object. Applications can draw contents onto the Canvas object using this Graphics object only for the duration of the paint() method.

Drawing and Filling Rectangles

The `Graphics` class provides two sets of operations for drawing and filling rectangles. One set is for drawing straight-angle rectangles:

```
void drawRect(int x, int y, int width, int height)
void fillRect(int x, int y, int width, int height)
```

The other set is for drawing round-angle rectangles:

```
void drawRoundRect(int x, int y, int width, int height, int
                  arcWidth, int arcHeight)
void fillRoundRect(int x, int y, int width, int height, int
                  arcWidth, int arcHeight)
```

The corner arc is a 90-degree fixed-angle arc. The arc parameters will be discussed in the next section.

Be aware that the area affected by a fill operation differs slightly from the area affected by a draw operation given the same coordinates, as already illustrated in Figures 7.2 and 7.3.

The example in Listing 7.4, shown in Figure 7.8, demonstrates a 2D bar plot using the `fillRect()` method.

LISTING 7.4   `PlotBarTest.java`

```
import javax.microedition.midlet.*;
import javax.microedition.lcdui.*;
import java.lang.Math;

public class PlotBarTest extends MIDlet {
    private Display display;
    int v1[]={10,30,40,70,50};
    int v2[]={30,90,50,60,65};
    int maxX;
    int maxY;
    public PlotBarTest() {
        display=Display.getDisplay(this);
        maxX=Math.max(v1.length,v2.length)-1;
        maxY=0;
        for(int i=0; i<v1.length; i++) {
            maxY=Math.max(maxY,v1[i]);
        }
        for(int i=0; i<v2.length; i++) {
            maxY=Math.max(maxY,v2[i]);
        }
```

Using Low-Level APIs in UI Development

CHAPTER 7

171

7

USING LOW-LEVEL
APIs IN UI
DEVELOPMENT

Applications can obtain a `Graphics` object for rendering to an offscreen image buffer by call-ing the `getGraphics()` method on the desired image. A `Graphics` object so obtained may be held indefinitely by the application, and rendering requests may be issued on this graphics object at any time.

The Coordinate System

As shown in Figure 7.1, the graphics coordinate system is anchored in the upper-left corner of a drawing space, with x values increasing to the right, and y values increasing downward.

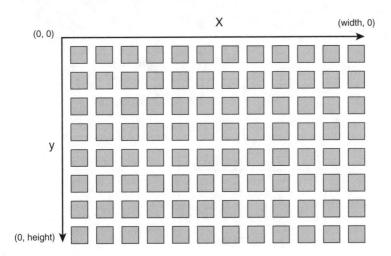

FIGURE 7.1
The Graphics coordinate system.

The coordinate system represents locations between pixels, not the pixels themselves. For example, the first pixel in the upper-left corner of the display lies in the square bounded by coordinates (0,0), (1,0), (0,1), (1,1).

Operations that draw outlines of shapes traverse a coordinate path with a pen that hangs beneath and to the right of the path. The size of the pen is one pixel wide and one pixel high by default. Thus, the pixels that lie to the right or beneath a coordinate on the drawing path will be affected by the drawing operation. For example, the call `drawRect(2,2,3,3)` will pro-duce the result shown in Figure 7.2.

The filling operations are different from the drawing operations. Only the pixels that are enclosed by the drawing path are affected. For example, the call `fillRect(2,2,3,3)` will pro-duce the result shown in Figure 7.3.

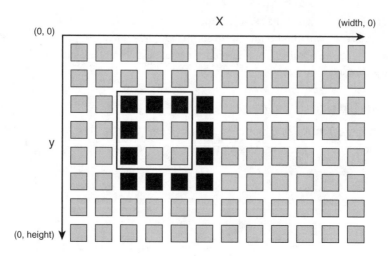

FIGURE 7.2
A drawing path.

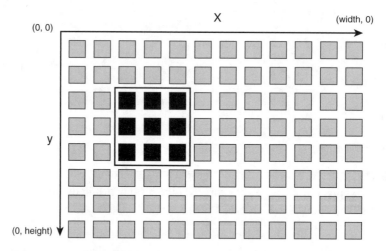

FIGURE 7.3
A filling operation.

Drawing and Filling Shapes

The `Graphics` class provides the following methods for rendering lines, arcs, and rectangles:

```
void drawArc(int x, int y, int width, int height, int
          startAngle, int arcAngle)
void drawLine(int x1, int y1, int x2, int y2)
```

```
void drawRect(int x, int y, int width, int height)
void drawRoundRect(int x, int y, int width, int height, int
                   arcWidth, int arcHeight)
void fillArc(int x, int y, int width, int height, int
             startAngle, int arcAngle)
void fillRect(int x, int y, int width, int height)
void fillRoundRect(int x, int y, int width, int height, int
                   arcWidth, int arcHeight)
```

The `Graphics` class maintains a set of parameters used for graphics rendering, which includes color, font, and stroke styles.

Color

A 24-bit color model is provided in the low-level API, with 8 bits each for the red, green, and blue components of a color. Because not all devices support the full 24-bit color, the MIDP implementation will map colors requested by the application into colors available on the device. An application can query whether a color is supported by the device using the `Display.isColor()` method. It can query how many distinct colors (if `isColor()` is true) or gray levels (if `isColor()` is false) can be represented on the device by calling the `Display.numColors()` method.

The following methods are provided in the `Graphics` class for setting or retrieving the color parameter maintained in a `Graphics` object:

```
int getColor()
int getBlueComponent()
int getGreenComponent()
int getRedComponent()
int getGrayScale()
void setColor(int RGB)
void setColor(int red, int green, int blue)
void setGrayScale(int value)
```

Normally, before an application draws contents to a display or image, it needs to set background and foreground colors. In J2SE, the `setBackGround()` and `setForeGround()` methods are provided for this purpose. However, only a single `setColor()` method is provided in the `Graphics` class. To set the background color of a drawing area, the application has to call the `setColor()` method and then the `fillRect()` method. After setting the background color, the application has to call the `setColor()` method again to set the foreground color.

The example in Listing 7.1 creates a color palette. Before drawing to a `Canvas` object, you should always query the dimensions of the available drawing area by using the `Canvas.getWidth()` and `Canvas.getHeight()` methods. If the application doesn't assume any specific display dimension, it can improve its portability across different devices.

LISTING 7.1   ColorTest.java

```java
import javax.microedition.midlet.*;
import javax.microedition.lcdui.*;

public class ColorTest extends MIDlet {
    private Display display;

    public ColorTest() {
        display=Display.getDisplay(this);
    }

    public void startApp() throws MIDletStateChangeException {
        display.setCurrent(new ColorTestCanvas(display.isColor()));
    }

    /**
     * Pause the MIDlet
     */
    public void pauseApp() {
    }

    /**
     * Called by the framework before the application is unloaded
     */
    public void destroyApp(boolean unconditional) {
    }

    class ColorTestCanvas extends Canvas {
        boolean isColor;

        public ColorTestCanvas(boolean _isColor) {
            isColor=_isColor;
        }

        public void paint(Graphics g) {
            //drawing area dimension
            int width=this.getWidth();
            int height=this.getHeight();

            //create an 8x8 palette
            int nrow=8;
            int ncol=8;
            /*  the dimension of each palette is deltaX, deltaY
             *  the gap between palettes is 3-pixel wide
             */
```

LISTING 7.1 Continued

```
int gap=3;
int deltaX=(width-(ncol+1)*gap)/ncol;
int deltaY=(height-(nrow+1)*gap)/nrow;

if(isColor) {
    //set background to white
    g.setColor(0xFFFFFF);
    g.fillRect(0,0,width,height);

    int deltaColor=0xFF/4;
    int red=0;
    int green=0;
    int blue=0;
    for(int i=0; i<nrow; i++) {
        for(int j=0; j<ncol; j++) {
            /*get the red, green and blue
             *components of the foreground
             *color
             */
            red+=deltaColor;
            if(red>0xFF) {
                red-=0xFF;
                green+=deltaColor;
                if(green>0xFF) {
                    green-=0xFF;
                    blue+=deltaColor;
                }
            }
            g.setColor(red, green, blue);
            int x=gap*(j+1)+j*deltaX;
            int y=gap*(i+1)+i*deltaY;
            g.fillRect(x,y,deltaX,deltaY);
        }
    }
}
//gray scale version
else {
    //set background to white
    g.setGrayScale(0xFF);
    g.fillRect(0,0,width,height);

    int deltaGrayScale=0xFF/(nrow*ncol);
    for(int i=0; i<nrow; i++) {
        for(int j=0; j<ncol; j++) {
```

LISTING 7.1   Continued

```
                        //set the foreground color
                        int n=(i+1)*ncol+j;
                        g.setGrayScale(deltaGrayScale*n);
                        int x=gap*(j+1)+j*deltaX;
                        int y=gap*(i+1)+i*deltaY;
                        g.fillRect(x,y,deltaX,deltaY);
                }
            }
        }
    }
}
```

If the display supports color, the background is set by calling `setColor(0xFFFFFF)` and `fillRect(0,0,width,height)`. The color of each block is set with `setColor(int red, int green, int green)`. The resulting MIDlet is shown in Figure 7.4.

FIGURE 7.4

The color palette: color version.

If the display does not support color, the background color and colors of the palette blocks are set to grayscale by using the `setGrayScale()` method. The resulting MIDlet is shown in Figure 7.5.

FIGURE 7.5
The color palette: grayscale version.

Stroke Styles

The Graphics class provides two stroke styles for drawing lines, arcs, and rectangles: DOTTED and SOLID. The stroke styles have no effect on filling arcs and rectangles. Applications can set or retrieve stroke style information using the following two methods:

```
int getStrokeStyle()
void setStrokeStyle(int style)
```

When you're using the SOLID stroke style, the pixels on the drawing path will be set with the current color. When you're using the DOTTED stroke style, only a subset of pixels (known as *dots*) on the drawing path will be set with the current color. The spaces between the dots are left untouched. The frequency and length of dots is implementation-dependent. The endpoints of lines and arcs are not guaranteed to be drawn, nor are the corner points of rectangles guaranteed to be drawn.

Drawing Lines

A line can be drawn by using the following method defined in the Graphics class:

```
public void drawLine(int x1, int y1, int x2, int y2)
```

This method draws a line between the coordinates (x1,y1) and (x2,y2) using the current color and stroke style. The line thickness is always one pixel. The pixels that are set with the current color are to the right of and beneath the coordinate path.

For example, Listing 7.2 draws two axes for a plot. The result is depicted in Figure 7.6. Similar to the illustration in Figure 7.2, the pixels affected by the drawLine() method lie to the right and beneath the drawing path.

LISTING 7.2   LineTest.java

```java
import javax.microedition.midlet.*;
import javax.microedition.lcdui.*;

public class LineTest extends MIDlet {
    private Display display;

    public LineTest() {
        display=Display.getDisplay(this);
    }

    public void startApp() throws MIDletStateChangeException {
        display.setCurrent(new LineTestCanvas());
    }

    /**
     * Pause the MIDlet
     */
    public void pauseApp() {
    }

    /**
     * Called by the framework before the application is unloaded
     */
    public void destroyApp(boolean unconditional) {
    }

    class LineTestCanvas extends Canvas {
        public void paint(Graphics g) {
            //drawing area dimension
            int width=this.getWidth();
            int height=this.getHeight();

            //set background to white
            g.setColor(0xFFFFFF);
            g.fillRect(0,0,width,height);

            //set foreground color to black
            g.setColor(0x000000);
            //draw two axes
            g.drawLine(0,height,0,0);
            g.drawLine(0,height-1,width,height-1);
        }
    }
}
```

Using Low-Level APIs in UI Development

CHAPTER 7

179

7

USING LOW-LEVEL
APIS IN UI
DEVELOPMENT

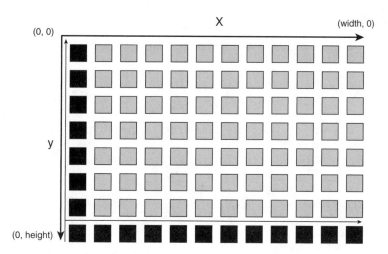

FIGURE 7.6

The result of drawing lines.

The example in Listing 7.3 draws a 2D plot using the drawLine() method. The plot coordinate system is different from the Graphics coordinate system: Its origin is at the lower-left corner, and its coordinates increase to the right and up. Thus, in the drawLine() method, you transform the y coordinate as height-y. The resulting MIDlet is shown in Figure 7.7. Here you use different stroke styles to differentiate two curves. You can also combine different stroke styles and colors to differentiate more curves.

LISTING 7.3   Plot2DTest.java

```java
import javax.microedition.midlet.*;
import javax.microedition.lcdui.*;
import java.lang.Math;

public class Plot2DTest extends MIDlet {
    private Display display;
    int v1[]={10,30,40,70,50};
    int v2[]={30,90,50,60,65};
    int maxX;
    int maxY;
    public Plot2DTest() {
        display=Display.getDisplay(this);
        maxX=Math.max(v1.length,v2.length)-1;
        maxY=0;
        for(int i=0; i<v1.length; i++) {
            maxY=Math.max(maxY,v1[i]);
        }
```

LISTING 7.3 Continued

```
            for(int i=0; i<v2.length; i++) {
                maxY=Math.max(maxY,v2[i]);
            }
            maxY+=10;
    }

    public void startApp() throws MIDletStateChangeException {
        display.setCurrent(new Plot2DTestCanvas(v1, v2, maxX, maxY));
    }

    /**
     * Pause the MIDlet
     */
    public void pauseApp() {
    }

    /**
     * Called by the framework before the application is unloaded
     */
    public void destroyApp(boolean unconditional) {
    }

    class Plot2DTestCanvas extends Canvas {
        int v1[];
        int v2[];
        int maxX, maxY;
        public Plot2DTestCanvas(int[] v1, int[] v2, int maxX,
                    int maxY) {
            this.v1=v1;
            this.v2=v2;
            this.maxX=maxX;
            this.maxY=maxY;
        }

        public void paint(Graphics g) {
            //drawing area dimension
            int width=this.getWidth();
            int height=this.getHeight();

            //set background to white
            g.setColor(0xFFFFFF);
            g.fillRect(0,0,width,height);

            //set foreground color to black
            g.setColor(0x000000);
```

LISTING 7.3   Continued

```
        //draw two axels
        g.drawLine(0,height,0,0);
        g.drawLine(0,height-1,width,height-1);

        //determine x scale
        int deltaX=width/maxX;
        int deltaY=height/maxY;

        //plot the first curve
        for (int i=0; i<v1.length-1; i++) {
            g.drawLine(deltaX*i,height-deltaY*v1[i],
                    deltaX*(i+1), height-deltaY*v1[i+1]);
        }

        //plot the second curve using the dotted line
        g.setStrokeStyle(Graphics.DOTTED);
        for (int i=0; i<v2.length-1; i++) {
            g.drawLine(deltaX*i,height-deltaY*v2[i],
                    deltaX*(i+1), height-deltaY*v2[i+1]);
        }
    }
  }
}
```

FIGURE 7.7

A 2D plot.

LISTING 7.4 Continued

```java
        maxY+=10;
    }

    public void startApp() throws MIDletStateChangeException {
        display.setCurrent(new PlotBarTestCanvas(v1, v2, maxX, maxY));
    }

    /**
     * Pause the MIDlet
     */
    public void pauseApp() {
    }

    /**
     * Called by the framework before the application is unloaded
     */
    public void destroyApp(boolean unconditional) {
    }

    class PlotBarTestCanvas extends Canvas {
        int v1[];
        int v2[];
        int maxX, maxY;
        int colors[]={0xFF0000,0x00FFFF};
        public PlotBarTestCanvas(int[] v1, int[] v2, int maxX, int maxY) {
            this.v1=v1;
            this.v2=v2;
            this.maxX=maxX;
            this.maxY=maxY;
        }

        public void paint(Graphics g) {
            //drawing area dimension
            int width=this.getWidth();
            int height=this.getHeight();

            //set background to white
            g.setColor(0xFFFFFF);
            g.fillRect(0,0,width,height);

            //set foreground color to black
            g.setColor(0x000000);
            //draw two axels
```

LISTING 7.4   Continued

```
                g.drawLine(0,height,0,0);
                g.drawLine(0,height-1,width,height-1);

                //determine x/y scale
                int deltaX=width/(maxX+1);
                int deltaY=height/maxY;
                //determine bar width
                int barWidth=deltaX/4;

                //plot the first function using color[0]
                g.setColor(colors[0]);
                for (int i=0; i<v1.length; i++) {
                    g.fillRect(deltaX*i, height-deltaY*v1[i],
                               barWidth, deltaY*v1[i]);
                }

                //plot the second curve using color[1]
                g.setColor(colors[1]);
                for (int i=0; i<v2.length; i++) {
                    g.fillRect(deltaX*i+barWidth, height-deltaY*v2[i],
                               barWidth, deltaY*v2[i]);
                }
            }
        }
    }
```

FIGURE 7.8

A bar plot.

Drawing and Filling Arcs

The `Graphics` class also provides methods for drawing or filling a circular or elliptical arc covering the specified rectangle:

```
void drawArc(int x, int y, int width, int height, int
            startAngle, int arcAngle)
void fillArc(int x, int y, int width, int height, int
            startAngle, int arcAngle)
```

Angles are interpreted such that 0 degrees is at the 3 o'clock position. A positive value indicates a counterclockwise rotation, and a negative value indicates a clockwise rotation.

The center of the arc is the center of the rectangle whose origin is (x,y) and whose size is specified by the `width` and `height` arguments. The resulting arc covers an area `width+1` pixels wide by `height+1` pixels tall.

For example, the call

```
g.drawArc(10, 10, width-12, height-12, 30, 45)
```

will produce a result depicted in Figure 7.9.

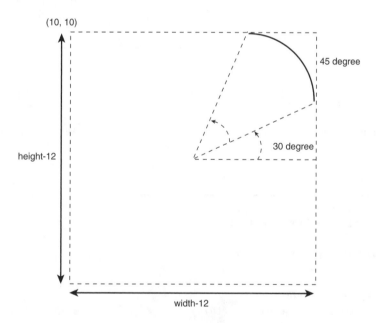

FIGURE 7.9

Drawing an arc.

The round corner of a rectangle is a special arc. For example, the call

`g.drawRoundRect(x, y, width, height, arcWidth, arcHeight)`

will create a rectangle with corners as depicted in Figure 7.10.

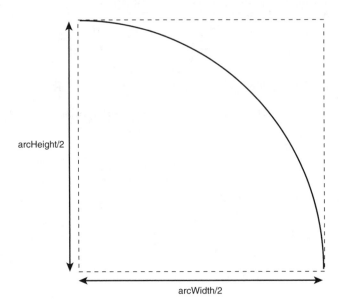

FIGURE 7.10

Drawing round corners on a rectangle.

The example in Listing 7.5, shown in Figure 7.11, draws a pie chart using the `fillArc()` method.

LISTING 7.5   `PieChartTest.java`

```java
import javax.microedition.midlet.*;
import javax.microedition.lcdui.*;

public class PieChartTest extends MIDlet {
    private Display display;

    public PieChartTest() {
        display=Display.getDisplay(this);
    }

    public void startApp() throws MIDletStateChangeException {
        int v1[]={10,30,40,70,50};
```

LISTING 7.5 Continued

```java
        display.setCurrent(new PieChartTestCanvas(v1));
    }

    /**
     * Pause the MIDlet
     */
    public void pauseApp() {
    }

    /**
     * Called by the framework before the application is unloaded
     */
    public void destroyApp(boolean unconditional) {
    }

    class PieChartTestCanvas extends Canvas {
        int v[];
        int colors[]={0xFF0000, 0x0000FF, 0x00FF00, 0x00FFFF,
                      0xFF00FF, 0xFFFF00};
        public PieChartTestCanvas(int[] v) {
            this.v=v;
        }

        public void paint(Graphics g) {
            //drawing area dimension
            int width=this.getWidth();
            int height=this.getHeight();

            //set background to white
            g.setColor(0xFFFFFF);
            g.fillRect(0,0,width,height);

            //determine angle scale
            int sum=0;
            for(int i=0; i<v.length; i++) {
                sum+=v[i];
            }

            /*
             *there is no floating point operation.
             *This is the trick to get around it.
```

LISTING 7.5 Continued

```
        */
        int deltaAngle=360*100/sum;

        int edge=3;
        //pie chart diameter
        int diameter;
        if(width>height) diameter=height-edge*2;
        else diameter=width-edge*2;

        int startAngle=0;
        for (int i=0; i<v.length; i++) {
            g.setColor(colors[i%colors.length]);
            g.fillArc(edge, edge, diameter, diameter, startAngle,
                    deltaAngle*v[i]/100);
            startAngle+=deltaAngle*v[i]/100;
        }
    }
  }
}
```

FIGURE 7.11

Plotting a pie chart.

Drawing Text

The Graphics class provides the following methods for rendering text:

```
void drawChar(char character, int x, int y, int anchor)
void drawChars(char[] data, int offset, int length, int x,
          int y, int anchor)
```

```
void drawString(String str, int x, int y, int anchor)
void drawSubstring(String str, int offset, int len, int x,
                   int y, int anchor)
```

In addition to color and stroke-style parameters, a `Graphics` object also maintains a font parameter for rendering text.

Font

The `Font` class represents fonts and font metrics. `Font` objects cannot be created by applications. Instead, applications can query for fonts based on font attributes using the method

```
static Font getFont(int face, int style, int size).
```

The `Font` attributes are `style`, `size`, and `face`. There are four possible values for font style: `STYLE_BOLD`, `STYLE_ITALIC`, `STYLE_PLAIN`, and `STYLE_UNDERLINED`. There are three choices of font size: `SIZE_LARGE`, `SIZE_MEDIUM`, and `SIZE_SMALL`. And there are three choices for font face: `FACE_MONOSPACE`, `FACE_PROPORTIONAL`, and `FACE_SYSTEM`.

Values for the `style` attribute can be combined using the logical `OR` operator, whereas values for the other attributes cannot be combined. You can retrieve the default font using the `Font.getDefaultFont()` method.

The font attributes can be retrieved using the following methods of the `Font` class:

```
int getFace()
int getSize()
int getStyle()
boolean isBold()
boolean isItalic()
boolean isPlain()
boolean isUnderlined()
```

The font dimension is illustrated in Figure 7.12. The font dimension and the width of characters can be queried using the following methods:

```
int charsWidth(char[] ch, int offset, int length)
int charWidth(char ch)
int getBaselinePosition()
int getHeight()
int stringWidth(String str)
int substringWidth(String str, int offset, int len)
```

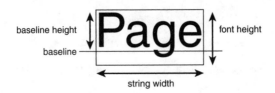

FIGURE 7.12

Font dimensions.

Anchor Points

The drawing of text is based on *anchor points*. Anchor points are used to minimize the amount of computation required when applications place text.

An anchor point has three horizontal constants: LEFT, HCENTER, and RIGHT. It also uses four vertical constants: TOP, BASELINE, VCENTER, and BOTTOM. The definition of the anchor point must be one of the horizontal constants combined with the TOP, BASELINE, or BOTTOM constant using the logical OR operator. You can't use the VCENTER value in the anchor point parameter of a text-drawing call, because vertical centering of text is not considered useful, is hard to specify, and is burdensome to implement.

The actual position of the text's bounding box relative to the (x,y) location is determined by the anchor point. For example, the call

```
g.drawString("testing", x, y, Graphics.BOTTOM|Graphics.LEFT)
```

will produce the result depicted in Figure 7.13. And the call

```
g.drawString("testing", x, y,Graphics.TOP|Graphics.RIGHT)
```

will produce the result shown in Figure 7.14.

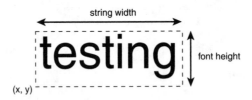

FIGURE 7.13

An anchor point (bottom-left) for drawing text.

FIGURE 7.14
An anchor point (top-right) for drawing text.

The size of the bounding box for a piece of text is defined by the `stringWidth(String str)` method and the `getHeight()` method of the font in which it is drawn. This box includes inter-line and inter-character spacing. This space appears below and to the right of the pixels actually belonging to the characters drawn, as shown in Figure 7.13 and Figure 7.14.

Drawing Images

The `Graphics` class provides one image-drawing method:

```
public void drawImage(Image img, int x, int y, int anchor)
```

The image can be either mutable or immutable. The anchor point definition is similar to the one discussed in the previous section for text-drawing operations. The only difference is that `BASELINE` is replaced with `VCENTER` for placing images. The example in Listing 7.6 draws an image at the center of the canvas as shown in Figure 7.15.

LISTING 7.6 `ImageTest.java`

```java
import javax.microedition.midlet.*;
import javax.microedition.lcdui.*;
import java.io.*;
public class ImageTest extends MIDlet {
    private Display display;
    private ImageView iv;

    public ImageTest() {
        Image img=null;
        try {
            img= Image.createImage("/bigDuke.png");
        }catch(Exception e) {
            System.out.println(e.getMessage());
        }
        iv = new ImageView(img);
    }
```

LISTING 7.6   Continued

```java
public void startApp() throws MIDletStateChangeException {
    display=Display.getDisplay(this);
    display.setCurrent(iv);
}

/**
 * Pause the MIDlet
 */
public void pauseApp() {
}

/**
 * Called by the framework before the application is unloaded
 */
public void destroyApp(boolean unconditional) {
}

class ImageView extends Canvas {
    Image img;
    public ImageView(Image i) {
        img=i;
    }

    public void paint(Graphics g) {
        g.drawImage(img, getWidth()/2, getHeight()/2,
                    g.HCENTER|g.VCENTER);
    }
}
}
```

FIGURE 7.15

Drawing images to the canvas.

Translating Coordinate Systems

By default, the origin of a `Graphics` object's coordinate system is at the upper-left corner. The `Graphics` class provides a method for translating the origin of the coordinate system:

```
void translate(int x, int y)
```

This method translates the origin to the point (x,y) of the current coordinate system. The coordinate of the translated origin can be retrieved using the following methods:

```
public int getTranslateX()
public int getTranslateY()
```

The coordinate values returned by these methods are not relative to the previous coordinate system. The values are in the `Graphics` default coordinate system.

The example in Listing 7.7 draws a stack of rectangles. It uses the same parameters for the `fillRect()` calls but shifts the origin of the coordinate system after each call.

LISTING 7.7   `TranslateTest.java`

```java
import javax.microedition.midlet.*;
import javax.microedition.lcdui.*;

public class TranslateTest extends MIDlet {
    private Display display;

    public TranslateTest() {
        display=Display.getDisplay(this);
    }

    public void startApp() throws MIDletStateChangeException {
        display.setCurrent(new TranslateTestCanvas());
    }

    /**
     * Pause the MIDlet
     */
    public void pauseApp() {
    }

    /**
     * Called by the framework before the application is unloaded
     */
    public void destroyApp(boolean unconditional) {
    }

    class TranslateTestCanvas extends Canvas {
        public void paint(Graphics g) {
```

LISTING 7.7 Continued

```
            //drawing area dimension
            int width=this.getWidth();
            int height=this.getHeight();

            //set background to white
            g.setColor(0xFFFFFF);
            g.fillRect(0,0,width,height);

            //set foreground color to black
            g.setColor(0x000000);

            int n=6;
            int deltaX=width/n;
            int deltaY=height/n;
            for(int i=0; i<n; i++) {
                g.fillRect(0,0,deltaX,deltaY);
                g.translate(deltaX, deltaY);
                System.out.println("Origin: "+g.getTranslateX()+
                                ", "+g.getTranslateY());
            }
        }
    }
}
```

When you run the MIDlet, you will see a display like Figure 7.16 and output from the terminal as follows:

```
Origin: 16, 16
Origin: 32, 32
Origin: 48, 48
Origin: 64, 64
Origin: 80, 80
Origin: 96, 96
```

Coordinate translation is very important in situations where the size of the display is too small to fit the whole picture and you need scrolling in order to show the complete drawing. It is commonly used in programming games. The example in Listing 7.8 tries to show a really big image. However, only part of the image can be shown at any one time, such as shown in Figure 7.17. You can use coordinate translation to shift the area that is displayed. In this example, users can use Left and Right Commands to scroll the image to left and right to see the hidden parts of the image. For example, if you click the Right Command, you will see a screen like Figure 7.18. Since the Graphics object is destroyed at the end of the paint() method, you have to remember the current coordinate system by maintaining two parameters, transX and transY, in the TestCanvas class.

Using Low-Level APIs in UI Development

CHAPTER 7

195

7

USING LOW-LEVEL
APIs IN UI
DEVELOPMENT

FIGURE 7.16

Translating the Graphics *coordinate system.*

LISTING 7.8   DisplayBigImageTest.java

```java
import javax.microedition.midlet.*;
import javax.microedition.lcdui.*;

public class DisplayBigImageTest extends MIDlet
                                 implements CommandListener {
    private Display display;
    private TestCanvas tc;
    private Command leftCommand = new Command("Left",
                                            Command.SCREEN, 1);
    private Command rightCommand = new Command("right",
                                            Command.SCREEN, 1);
    public DisplayBigImageTest() {
        Image img=null;
        try {
            img= Image.createImage("/realBigDuke.PNG");
        }catch(Exception e) {
            System.out.println(e.getMessage());
        }
        tc = new TestCanvas(img);
        tc.addCommand(rightCommand);
        tc.addCommand(leftCommand);
        tc.setCommandListener(this);
        display=Display.getDisplay(this);
    }
```

Listing 7.8   Continued

```java
public void startApp() throws MIDletStateChangeException {
    display.setCurrent(tc);
}

/**
 * Pause the MIDlet
 */
public void pauseApp() {
}

/**
 * Called by the framework before the application is unloaded
 */
public void destroyApp(boolean unconditional) {
}

public void commandAction(Command c, Displayable d) {
    int stepX=tc.getWidth()/4;
    int stepY=tc.getHeight()/4;
    if(d==tc && c==leftCommand) {
        tc.increaseXY(stepX,0);
        tc.repaint();
    }
    else if(d==tc && c==rightCommand) {
        tc.increaseXY(-stepX,0);
        tc.repaint();
    }
}

class TestCanvas extends Canvas {
    private Image img;
    private int    transX=0;
    private int    transY=0;
    public TestCanvas(Image img) {
        this.img=img;
        transX=0;
        transY=0;
    }
    public void increaseXY(int x, int y) {
        transX+=x;
        transY+=y;
    }

    public void paint(Graphics g) {
        //drawing area dimension
```

LISTING 7.8 Continued

```
            int width=this.getWidth();
            int height=this.getHeight();

            //set background to white
            g.setColor(0xFFFFFF);
            g.fillRect(0,0,width,height);

            g.translate(transX, transY);
            g.drawImage(img,0,0, g.TOP|g.LEFT);
        }
    }
}
```

FIGURE 7.17

Display a big image using coordinate translation: first screen.

FIGURE 7.18

Display a big image using coordinate translation: after scrolling to right.

Clips

Occasionally, you may want to set up a working area in a canvas, or only render contents to a small area of a canvas. The Graphics class provides *clip* functionality to support this operation. The clip is a rectangular area. Only pixels that lie entirely within the clip rectangle are affected by graphics operations. Pixels outside the clip rectangle are not touched by any graphics operations.

The Graphics class provides this method to define a clip:

```
void setClip(int x, int y, int width, int height)
```

The meanings of the parameters are the same as those of the drawRect() method.

The following operation intersects the current clip rectangle with a given rectangle:

```
void clipRect(int x, int y, int width, int height)
```

It is legal to specify a clipping rectangle whose width or height is zero or negative. In this case, the clipping rectangle is considered to be empty, and no pixels will be modified by any graphical operations.

The offset and dimensions of the current clip can be retrieved using these methods:

```
int getClipHeight()
int getClipWidth()
int getClipX()
int getClipY()
```

The example in Listing 7.9, shown in Figure 7.19, illustrates another way to draw stacked rectangles using clips. In the loop of the paint() method

```
public void paint(Graphics g) {
...
    for(int i=0; i<n; i++) {
        g.setClip(width-deltaX*(i+1),deltaY*i,deltaX,deltaY);
        g.fillRect(0,0,width,height);
    }
..
}
```

each operation tries to fill the complete screen. But because the clip area is a small rectangle, only the small rectangle within the clip is filled with the current color.

LISTING 7.9   ClipTest.java

```java
import javax.microedition.midlet.*;
import javax.microedition.lcdui.*;

public class ClipTest extends MIDlet {
    private Display display;

    public ClipTest() {
        display=Display.getDisplay(this);
    }

    public void startApp() throws MIDletStateChangeException {
        display.setCurrent(new ClipTestCanvas());
    }

    /**
     * Pause the MIDlet
     */
    public void pauseApp() {
    }

    /**
     * Called by the framework before the application is unloaded
     */
    public void destroyApp(boolean unconditional) {
    }

    class ClipTestCanvas extends Canvas {
        public void paint(Graphics g) {
            //drawing area dimension
            int width=this.getWidth();
            int height=this.getHeight();

            //set background to white
            g.setColor(0xFFFFFF);
            g.fillRect(0,0,width,height);

            //set foreground color to black
            g.setColor(0x000000);

            int n=6;
            int deltaX=width/n;
            int deltaY=height/n;
            for(int i=0; i<n; i++) {
                g.setClip(width-deltaX*(i+1),deltaY*i,deltaX,deltaY);
```

LISTING 7.9   ClipTest.java

```
            g.fillRect(0,0,width,height);
        }
    }
  }
}
```

FIGURE 7.19
Clipping graphics.

Low-level Events and Event Handling

The Canvas class implements the low-level UI API, and is responsible for handling low-level events, such as key and pointer (if supported by the device) events.

If you recall from Chapter 6, each high-level event has a corresponding event listener interface. Applications can define listeners and register them with instances of the Screen classes. If the Canvas class used the same event-handling model for low-level events, then several new listener interfaces would need to be created, one for each kind of event that might be delivered. This approach would increase the API's complexity. An alternative event-handling model, which is similar to the inheritance-based event model in AWT 1.0 and AWT 1.02 of J2SE, is used in the low-level API. That is, all the events are delivered to the Canvas, and applications must filter out events in which they had no interest.

Event-Handling Methods

The Canvas object defines several methods that are called by the MIDP implementation. These methods deliver low-level events to the application for processing. The set of methods is as follows:

```
showNotify()
hideNotify()
keyPressed()
keyRepeated()
keyReleased()
pointerPressed()
pointerDragged()
pointerReleased()
paint()
```

These methods are all called serially by the MIDP implementation on the application's running thread. Thus, any event-handling method will block the application and other event-handling methods until it returns.

If the Canvas object has a registered CommandListener object, then the CommandListener's commandAction() method is also called serially along with the methods just listed.

Except for the paint() method, the default implementations of these methods are empty. The paint() method is declared abstract, so any subclass of Canvas has to provide an implementation of the method. If applications want to respond to certain events of interest, they can override their event-handling methods with their own implementations.

Show and Hide Events

The showNotify() method is called prior to a Canvas object being made visible on the display. The hideNotify() method is called after the Canvas object has been removed from the display. The change in the visibility state of a Canvas may be caused by the Application Management Software moving MIDlets between foreground and background states, or by the system obscuring the Canvas with system screens. Thus, the calls to showNotify() and hideNotify() are not under the control of the MIDlet and may occur fairly frequently.

The key event methods, pointer event methods, paint() method, and commandAction() method will be called only while the Canvas object is visible on the device. These methods will therefore be called on this Canvas object only after a call to showNotify() and before a call to hideNotify(). After hideNotify() has been called, none of the key, pointer, paint(), and commandAction() methods will be called until after a subsequent call to showNotify() has returned.

Key Events

Applications receive key events when users press a key on the keypad.

Key Codes and Key Names

Every key is assigned a *key code*. The key code values are unique for each hardware key, unless two keys are obvious synonyms for each other. MIDP defines the following key codes: KEY_NUM0, KEY_NUM1, KEY_NUM2, KEY_NUM3, KEY_NUM4, KEY_NUM5, KEY_NUM6, KEY_NUM7, KEY_NUM8, KEY_NUM9, KEY_STAR, and KEY_POUND. These key codes correspond to keys on a standard telephone keypad.

These key code values are equal to the Unicode encoding for the character that represents the key; for example, KEY_NUM0, corresponding to 0 on the keypad, is equal to 48. Other keys may be present on the keypad, and they will generally have negative key code values that are distinct from those just listed, which are positive values.

Each key on the keypad has a name. A key's name can be queried using the getKeyName() method of the Canvas class.

There are three types of key event-handling methods:

```
protected void keyPressed(int keyCode)
protected void keyReleased(int keyCode)
protected void keyRepeated(int keyCode)
```

A key-repeated event is generated when users press the same key consecutively twice in a short time. Some devices support the key-repeated event, and some don't. To check whether the device supports the key-repeated event, applications can use this method:

```
public boolean hasRepeatEvents()
```

The example in Listing 7.10 demonstrates how to handle key-pressed events. For example, if you press key 7, you will see the display shown in Figure 7.20.

LISTING 7.10   KeyEventTest.java

```
import javax.microedition.midlet.*;
import javax.microedition.lcdui.*;

public class KeyEventTest extends MIDlet {
    private Display display;

    public KeyEventTest() {
        display=Display.getDisplay(this);
    }
```

LISTING 7.10   Continued

```java
public void startApp() throws MIDletStateChangeException {
    display.setCurrent(new KeyEventTestCanvas());
}

/**
 * Pause the MIDlet
 */
public void pauseApp() {
}

/**
 * Called by the framework before the application is unloaded
 */
public void destroyApp(boolean unconditional) {
}

class KeyEventTestCanvas extends Canvas {
    String str="";
    public void paint(Graphics g) {
        int width=this.getWidth();
        int height=this.getHeight();

        //set background to white
        g.setColor(0xFFFFFF);
        g.fillRect(0,0,width,height);

        //set foreground color to black
        g.setColor(0x000000);
        Font f=Font.getDefaultFont();
        g.drawString("Press a key",5,5,g.TOP|g.LEFT);
        g.drawString(str,5,5+f.getHeight(),g.TOP|g.LEFT);
    }

    public void keyPressed(int keycode) {
        str=getKeyName(keycode)+" is pressed";
        repaint();
    }
}
}
```

The changes made to all subclasses of Screen are automatically reflected to the display. Applications do not need to refresh the display. For Canvas, refreshing the screen is not done automatically. Applications have to use the repaint() method to update the screen when changes occur, as shown in Listing 7.10. Applications can repaint part of the canvas or the whole canvas when needed.

FIGURE 7.20
Testing event handling.

Game Actions

Many applications need arrow key events and gaming-related events. MIDP defines the following game actions: UP, DOWN, LEFT, RIGHT, FIRE, GAME_A, GAME_B, GAME_C, and GAME_D. Each key code may be mapped to at most one game action. However, a game action may be associated with more than one key code. The key codes and game actions can be translated back and forth using the following methods:

```
public int getKeyCode(int gameAction)
public int getGameAction(int keyCode)
```

How the game action is mapped into key codes is implementation dependent. For example, on some devices, the game actions UP, DOWN, LEFT, and RIGHT may be mapped to the four navigation arrow keys. On other devices, a possible mapping would be on the number keys 2, 4, 6, and 8. The application should translate a key code into a game action using the getGameAction() method to improve portability.

The example in Listing 7.11 demonstrates game actions. If you run the MIDlet, you will see a black box as shown in Figure 7.21. You can use the arrow keys to move the little black box around on the display. If the box hits the borders, it wraps around to the other side. In this example, the method

```
public final void repaint(int x, int y, int width, int height)
```

is used to update only a region of the canvas.

LISTING 7.11   GameActionTest).java

```java
import javax.microedition.midlet.*;
import javax.microedition.lcdui.*;

public class GameActionTest extends MIDlet {
    private Display display;

    public GameActionTest() {
        display=Display.getDisplay(this);
    }

    public void startApp() throws MIDletStateChangeException {
        display.setCurrent(new GameActionTestCanvas());
    }

    /**
     * Pause the MIDlet
     */
    public void pauseApp() {
    }

    /**
     * Called by the framework before the application is unloaded
     */
    public void destroyApp(boolean unconditional) {
    }

    class GameActionTestCanvas extends Canvas {
        int width, height;
        int deltaX, deltaY;
        int x,y;

        public GameActionTestCanvas() {
            //draw a 8x10 net
            deltaX=this.getWidth()/8;
            deltaY=this.getHeight()/10;
            width=deltaX*8;
            height=deltaY*10;
            x=0;
            y=0;
        }
        public void paint(Graphics g) {
            //set background to white
```

LISTING 7.11   Continued

```java
        g.setColor(0xFFFFFF);
        g.fillRect(0,0,width,height);

        //set foreground color to black
        g.setColor(0x000000);
        g.fillRect(x,y,deltaX,deltaY);
    }

    public void keyPressed(int keycode) {
        switch(getGameAction(keycode)) {
        case Canvas.DOWN:
            y+=deltaY;
            if(y>=height) {
                y-=height;
                repaint(x,0,deltaX,height);
            }
            else {
                repaint(x,y-deltaY,deltaX,2*deltaY);
            }
            break;
        case Canvas.UP:
            y-=deltaY;
            if(y<0) {
                y+=height;
                repaint(x,0,deltaX,height);
            }
            else {
                repaint(x,y,deltaX,2*deltaY);
            }
            break;
        case Canvas.LEFT:
            x-=deltaX;
            if(x<0) {
                x+=width;
                repaint(0,y,width,deltaY);
            }
            else {
                repaint(x,y,deltaX*2,deltaY);
            }
            break;
        case Canvas.RIGHT:
            x+=deltaX;
            if(x>=width) {
                x-=width;
```

Using Low-Level APIs in UI Development

CHAPTER 7

207

7

USING LOW-LEVEL
APIs IN UI
DEVELOPMENT

LISTING 7.11 Continued

```
                repaint(0,y,width,deltaY);
        }
        else {
            repaint(x-deltaX,y,deltaX*2,deltaY);
        }
        break;
    default:
        }
    }
  }
}
```

FIGURE 7.21

Testing game actions.

Conflict with Commands

Like other subclasses of the Displayable class, it is possible to add Commands to a Canvas object and register a CommandListener to the Canvas object.

Commands are mapped to keys and menus in a device-specific fashion. For some devices, the keys used for Commands may overlap with the keys that will deliver key events to the Canvas class. If this is the case, the device will provide a means to solve the conflict. Applications don't need to handle the conflict.

Pointer Events

For a touch-sensitive screen, a pointer can be any object that is used to press on the screen. It can be a stylus, a pen, or a finger. There are three types of pointer events: pointer press events, pointer release events, and pointer drag events. Accordingly, there are three types of pointer event-handling methods:

```
protected void pointerPressed(int x, int y)
protected void pointerReleased(int x, int y)
protected void pointerDragged(int x, int y)
```

Parameters x and y are pointer position relative to the Canvas.

Some MIDP devices support pointer events; most devices don't. To check a device's support for the pointer press or release event, you can use this method:

```
public boolean hasPointerEvents()
```

Event if a device supports pointer press and release events, it may not support pointer drag events. The Canvas class provides the following method to check whether pointer drag events are supported:

```
public boolean hasPointerMotionEvents()
```

On the emulator, you can set the device property file to enable pointer events. For example, to enable pointer press and release events on Motorola's emulator, you can set

```
mousesupport=true
```

And to enable pointer drag events, you can set

```
mousemotionsupport=false
```

With pointer events enabled, you can build more user-friendly user interfaces similar to the PalmOS. The example in Listing 7.12 shows a pointer-based user menu as shown in Figure 7.22. If you already enabled the pointer events, you can click a menu item and the pointerPressed() method will determine which item you choose. Then, the label string of the selected icon will be shown on the display. For example, if you click the Open option, you will see a screen like Figure 7.23.

LISTING 7.12 PointerMenu.java

```
/*
 * This menu simulates a PalmOS like menu.
 * You can move the mouse to the item you want to select, and
 * click the mouse button (either right or left).  You will see
 * an enlarge icon.
 */

import javax.microedition.midlet.*;
import javax.microedition.lcdui.*;
```

LISTING 7.12 Continued

```
public class PointerMenu extends MIDlet {
    Display display;
    PointerMenuCanvas   pmc;

    public PointerMenu() {
        display = Display.getDisplay(this);
        pmc= new PointerMenuCanvas();
    }

    public void startApp () {
        display.setCurrent(pmc);
    }


    /**
     * Pause the MIDlet
     */
    public void pauseApp() {
    }

    /**
     * Called by the framework before the application is unloaded
     */
    public void destroyApp (boolean unconditional) {
        pmc=null;
        display=null;
    }

    class PointerMenuCanvas extends Canvas {
        String iconFiles[]={"/new.png", "/open.png","/delete.png",
                            "/copy.png","/save.png","/exit.png"};
        String iconLabels[]={"New", "Open", "Delete", "Copy",
                            "Save", "Exit"};
        Image   icons[]= new Image[iconFiles.length];
        int   nrow=3;
        int   ncol=2;
        int   width, height;
        int deltax, deltay;

        public PointerMenuCanvas() {
            for(int i=0; i<iconFiles.length; i++) {
                try{
                    icons[i]= Image.createImage(iconFiles[i]);
                }catch (Exception e) {
```

LISTING 7.12 Continued

```
                    System.out.println("Error: "+ e.getMessage());
            }
        }
        width=getWidth();
        height=getHeight();
        deltax=width/ncol;
        deltay=height/nrow;
    }

    protected void paint(Graphics g) {
        //clear screen
        g.setGrayScale(255);
        g.fillRect(0, 0, width, height);
        g.setGrayScale(0);
        g.setFont(Font.getFont(Font.FACE_SYSTEM, Font.STYLE_BOLD,
                Font.SIZE_SMALL));
        for(int r=0; r<nrow; r++) {
            for(int c=0; c<ncol; c++) {
                Image img= icons[r*ncol+c];
                g.drawImage(img, c*deltax, r*deltay,
                        Graphics.LEFT | Graphics.TOP);
                g.drawString(iconLabels[r*ncol+c],
                            c*deltax+img.getWidth()+3,
                            r*deltay+img.getHeight(),
                            g.LEFT|g.BASELINE);
            }
        }
    }

    protected void pointerPressed(int x, int y) {
        //determine which row and column
        int r=y/deltay;
        int c=x/deltax;
        int index=r*ncol+c;

        //act accordingly
        if(index==nrow*ncol-1) {
            destroyApp(true);
        notifyDestroyed();
        }
        else {
            display.setCurrent(
                new FunctionCanvas(this,
```

LISTING 7.12   Continued

```
                                                iconLabels[index]));
            }
        }
    }

    class FunctionCanvas extends Canvas implements CommandListener {
        Displayable menu;
        Command backCommand = new Command("Back", Command.BACK, 1);
        String text;

        public FunctionCanvas(Displayable d, String message) {
            menu=d;
            text=message;
            this.addCommand(backCommand);
            this.setCommandListener(this);
        }

        protected void paint(Graphics g) {
            g.setGrayScale(0);
            g.setFont(Font.getFont(Font.FACE_SYSTEM, Font.STYLE_BOLD,
                                Font.SIZE_LARGE));
            g.drawString(text, 10, 10, g.TOP|g.LEFT);
        }

        public void commandAction (Command c, Displayable s) {
            if(c==backCommand) {
                display.setCurrent(menu);
            }
        }
    }
}
```

Refreshing the Display

When a Screen object is on the display, any changes made to the Screen object will be automatically reflected to the display; applications do not need to refresh the display. However, when a Canvas object is the display, applications must handle refreshing the display when changes are made to the Canvas object. The Canvas class provides two methods for refreshing the display:

```
public final void repaint(int x, int y, int width, int height)
public final void repaint()
```

If the Canvas is not visible on the display, calls to these two methods have no effect.

FIGURE 7.22
A pointer-based menu.

FIGURE 7.23
A screen after the Open icon is selected.

The first method requests a repaint for the specified region of the canvas. Calling this method may result in subsequent call to paint(), where the passed Graphics object's clip region will include at least the specified region.

The second method requests a repaint for the entire Canvas. The effect is equivalent to

```
repaint(0, 0, getWidth(), getHeight());
```

Repainting of the `Canvas` is done asynchronously. The `repaint()` methods will return without waiting for the call to the `paint()` method to finish.

To synchronize with the `paint()` routine, you can use either `Display.callSerially()` or `serviceRepaints()`, or you can code explicit synchronization into your `paint()` routine.

The `Display.callSerially(Runnable r))` method causes the `Runnable` object r to have its `run()` method called soon after completion of the `Displayable`'s repaint cycle. It can be used to generate animation effects. For example, in Listing 7.13, after a frame of an image has been painted, the `run()` method is called to set up the next frame of the image to be painted. As a result, you will see an image like that shown in Figure 7.24 moving back and forth.

LISTING 7.13   WavingDuke.java

```java
import javax.microedition.midlet.*;
import javax.microedition.lcdui.*;

public class WavingDuke extends MIDlet {
    private Display display;

    public WavingDuke() {
    }

    public void startApp() throws MIDletStateChangeException {
        display=Display.getDisplay(this);
        WavingDukeCanvas wdc= new WavingDukeCanvas();
        display.setCurrent(wdc );
        wdc.startAnimation();
    }

    /**
     * Pause the MIDlet
     */
    public void pauseApp() {
    }

    /**
     * Called by the framework before the application is unloaded
     */
    public void destroyApp(boolean unconditional) {
    }

    class WavingDukeCanvas extends Canvas implements Runnable {
        Image img[] = new Image[2];
        int currentFrame;
```

Listing 7.13   Continued

```
public WavingDukeCanvas() {
    try {
        img[0] = Image.createImage("/bigDuke.png");
    } catch (Exception e) {
        System.out.println("Error: "+ e.getMessage());
    }
    try {
        img[1] = Image.createImage("/bigDuke15.png");
    } catch (Exception e) {
        System.out.println("Error: "+ e.getMessage());
    }
    currentFrame=0;
}

public void paint(Graphics g) {
    g.drawImage(img[currentFrame], getWidth()/2,
                getHeight()/2, g.HCENTER|g.VCENTER);
}
//start animation
public void startAnimation() {
    repaint();
    display.callSerially(this);
}

public void run() { // called after previous repaint is finished
    try {
        Thread.sleep(200);
        currentFrame=(currentFrame+1)%2;
        repaint();
        display.callSerially(this);
    } catch(Exception e) {}
}
}
}
```

The Canvas class provides a method to flush any pending repaint requests:

```
public final void serviceRepaints()
```

As a result of a call to this method, several repaint requests may cause one single call to paint(). This method blocks until the pending repaint requests have been serviced and the call to the application's paint() method returns.

FIGURE 7.24

A screen shot of moving Duke.

The synchronization of refreshing the display is very important for animation and game appli-cations. For example, an application has several threads to request repainting a canvas. To get an immediate response for a repaint request, you can use the serviceRepaints() method. However, if several repaint requests result in one call to paint(), you may get a corrupted screen. To avoid the problem, you can set a limit so that only one thread can request a repaint at a time. And, after the request, you can enforce having the request served immediately as follows:

```
public class TestThread extends Thread {
...
    public void run() {
        ...
        synchronized (repaintLock) {
            myCanvas.repaint(x, y, width, height);
            myCanvas.serviceRepaints();
        }
    }
}
```

Calendar Example

In Chapter 6, you started to build an application MobileScheduler. You already have the pieces for inputting appointments. In this chapter, you will build a monthly schedule viewer to display appointment information. It also let users select a day and view all the appointments on that day.

The example in Listing 7.14 is the MIDlet that will create an object of the MonthlyScheduleViewer class found in Listing 7.15.

In Listing 7.14, you assume that an appointment is scheduled on March 1, 2001, and you remember the date that contains appointments using a hash table. (This program is also used later in testing a double-buffering version of MonthlyScheduleViewer. For now, we've just commented out related segments.)

Listing 7.15 creates a schedule viewer, shown in Figure 7.25. If there are appointments on a date, the date will be specially marked in the viewer, as March 1, 2001 is shaded in Figure 7.25. A selected date is saved in the Calendar object, and the selected date is highlighted on the viewer.

Users can use the arrow keys to change the selected date. In the keyPressed() method, the key code is translated to game actions. The game actions UP, DOWN, RIGHT, and LEFT move the selected date on the viewer accordingly.

Be aware that the areas for drawing command labels are different in Sun's and Motorola's implementations. The area for drawing command labels is not part of a canvas on Sun's emulator. However, it is part of the canvas drawing area on Motorola's emulator. To avoid overlapping the schedule viewer with command labels, leave a rectangular area at the bottom of the canvas for command labels; the rectangle's height is defined by the command_height parameter. If you compile and execute the MIDlet on Motorola's emulator, you will see a schedule viewer like Figure 7.26.

LISTING 7.14   ScheduleViewTest.java

```java
import javax.microedition.midlet.*;
import javax.microedition.lcdui.*;
import java.util.Calendar;
import java.util.Hashtable;

public class ScheduleViewerTest extends MIDlet implements CommandListener {
    private Display display;
    private List menu;
    private Calendar calendar;
    private MonthlyScheduleViewer viewer;
    //private MonthlyScheduleViewer_DB viewerDB;
    private Hashtable app_table;

    public ScheduleViewerTest() {
        display=Display.getDisplay(this);

        //create a implicit list for starting menu
        String elements[]={"Monthly Schedule viewer",
```

LISTING 7.14 Continued

```
                            "Monthly Schedule viewer (double buffering)",
                            "Exit"};

    menu=new List("Main menu",List.IMPLICIT,elements,null);
    menu.setCommandListener(this);
    calendar=Calendar.getInstance();
    app_table= new Hashtable();
    app_table.put("3/1/2001",new Object());
    viewer=null;
    //viewerDB=null;
}

public void startApp() throws MIDletStateChangeException {
    display.setCurrent(menu);
}

/**
 * Pause the MIDlet
 */
public void pauseApp() {
}

/**
 * Called by the framework before the application is unloaded
 */
public void destroyApp(boolean unconditional) {
}

public void commandAction(Command c, Displayable d) {
    if(c==List.SELECT_COMMAND) {
        List l= (List) d;
        switch (l.getSelectedIndex()) {
        case 0:
            if(viewer==null)
                viewer= new MonthlyScheduleViewer(
                            display, menu,
                            calendar, app_table);
            display.setCurrent(viewer);
            break;
        case 1:
            /*if(viewerDB==null)
                viewerDB= new MonthlyScheduleViewer_DB(
                            display, menu,
                            calendar, app_table);
```

LISTING 7.14   Continued

```
                    display.setCurrent(viewerDB);
                     */
                    break;
                case 2:
                    destroyApp(true);
            notifyDestroyed();
                    break;
            }
            }
        }
    }
```

LISTING 7.15   MonthlyScheduleViewer.java

```java
import java.util.Calendar;
import java.util.Date;
import java.util.Hashtable;
import javax.microedition.io.*;
import javax.microedition.lcdui.*;
import javax.microedition.midlet.*;

/**
 * A simple Monthly Schedule Viewer
 * If there are appointments on a day, that day will be highlighted with
 * APPOINTMENT_COLOR.
 * There is selected day that is saved in calendar.  Users can navigate
 * the viewer using arrow keys. The selected day is differentiated from
 * others using the reversed background and foreground colors
 */

public class MonthlyScheduleViewer extends Canvas implements CommandListener{
    private Display        display;
    private Displayable    parent;
    private Calendar       calendar;
    private Hashtable      app_table;
    private Command backCommand = new Command("Back", Command.BACK, 1);

    /**
     * parameters for month views
     */
    final String days[] = {"S", "M", "T", "W", "T", "F", "S"};

    final String months[] = {"January", "February", "March", "April",
                             "May", "June", "July", "August",
```

LISTING 7.15 Continued

```java
                            "September", "October", "November",
                            "December"};

    final int DaysInMonth[] = {31, 28, 31, 30, 31, 30,
                                31, 31, 30, 31, 30, 31};

    /**
     *Background color
     */
    final int BACKGROUND_COLOR= 0xFFFFFF; //white
    /**
     *Foreground color
     */
    final int FOREGROUND_COLOR = 0x000000; //black
    /**
     *Appointment color
     */
    final int APPOINTMENT_COLOR = 0x00FF00; //green
    /**
     *  calendar information
     */
    int day_of_month;
    int day_of_week;
    int week_of_month;
    int month;
    int days_in_month;
    int year;
    int hour;

    //canvas dimensions
    int width, height;
    //font for title
    Font flabel;
    int header_height,command_height;
    final long  dayinmillis=24*60*60*1000;
    //number of rows and columns
    int nrow, ncolumn;
    //cell dimensions
    int xdelta, ydelta;
    //calendar dimensions
    int xdim, ydim;
```

LISTING 7.15 Continued

```java
//top position after drawing header information
int xtop, ytop;


public MonthlyScheduleViewer(Display d, Displayable p,
                            Calendar c, Hashtable a) {
    display = d;
    parent =p;
    calendar=c;
    app_table=a;

    //get dimension information
    width=getWidth();
    height=getHeight();
    flabel= Font.getFont(Font. FACE_SYSTEM, Font.STYLE_BOLD,
                        Font.SIZE_MEDIUM);
    header_height=flabel.getHeight()-1;
    command_height=header_height-2;
    //x dimension information is fixed
    ncolumn=7;

    //row/column dimensions
    xdelta = width/ncolumn;

    //calculate the calendar dimension
    xdim=xdelta*ncolumn;

     //top position after drawing header information
     xtop=(width-xdim)/2;

    addCommand(backCommand);
    setCommandListener(this);
}

private void initCalendarInfo() {
    day_of_month= calendar.get(Calendar.DAY_OF_MONTH);
    day_of_week= calendar.get(Calendar.DAY_OF_WEEK)-1;
    week_of_month=1;
    if(day_of_month-day_of_week-1>0) {
        week_of_month+=(day_of_month-day_of_week-1)/7;
        if((day_of_month-day_of_week-1)%7!=0) week_of_month++;
    }

    //month is 1 off;
    month=calendar.get(Calendar.MONTH);
```

LISTING 7.15 Continued

```
        days_in_month=DaysInMonth[month];
        year=calendar.get(Calendar.YEAR);
        if(month==1) { //check leap year
            if(year%4==0) {
                days_in_month++;
            }
        }
        hour=calendar.get(Calendar.HOUR_OF_DAY);
    }

    public void commandAction(Command c, Displayable d) {
    if(c==backCommand) {
            display.setCurrent(parent);
        }
    }

    public void paint(Graphics g) {
            initCalendarInfo();

            //clear canvas
            g.setColor(BACKGROUND_COLOR);
            g.fillRect(0,0,width,height);

            g.setColor(FOREGROUND_COLOR);
            //paint header information at the top
            g.setFont(flabel);
            String header = months[month]+", " +year;
            g.drawString(header,0,header_height-2,g.BASELINE|g.LEFT);

            //y dimension varies depending on month
            nrow= numberOfRows();

            //row/column dimensions
            ydelta=(height-header_height-command_height)/nrow;

            //calculate the calendar dimension
            ydim=ydelta*nrow;

            //top position after drawing header information
            ytop=header_height+(height-header_height-
                                command_height-ydim)/2;

            //reset font
            Font fcal=Font.getFont(Font. FACE_SYSTEM,
```

LISTING 7.15   Continued

```
                                     Font.STYLE_PLAIN, Font.SIZE_SMALL);
    g.setFont(fcal);

    //Draw week Headers
    for(int i=0; i<ncolumn; i++) {
        g.drawString(days[i],
        xtop+i*xdelta+(xdelta-fcal.stringWidth(days[i]))/2,
        ytop+(ydelta-fcal.getHeight())/2+1,
        g.TOP|g.LEFT);
    }

    //draw days
    //calculate the day_of_week for the first day of the month
    int day_of_week_of_first_of_month=(7-(day_of_month-1-
                                      day_of_week)%7)%7;
    int xoff=day_of_week_of_first_of_month;
    int yoff=1;
    for(int i=1; i<=days_in_month; i++) {
        //check whether there are appointments on that day;
        boolean hasAppointment;
        if(app_table.get((month+1)+"/"+i+"/"+year)!=null) {
            hasAppointment=true;
        }
        else {
            hasAppointment=false;
        }

        //if there are appointments on that day, reset the
        //background color
        if(hasAppointment) {
            g.setColor(APPOINTMENT_COLOR);
            g.fillRect(xtop+xoff*xdelta, ytop+yoff*ydelta,
                       xdelta, ydelta);
            g.setColor(FOREGROUND_COLOR);
        }

        //highlight the current day
        if(i==day_of_month) {
            g.setColor(FOREGROUND_COLOR);
            g.fillRect(xtop+xoff*xdelta,
                       ytop+yoff*ydelta,
                       xdelta, ydelta);
            if(hasAppointment) {
                g.setColor(APPOINTMENT_COLOR);
            }
```

LISTING 7.15   Continued

```
            else {
                g.setColor(BACKGROUND_COLOR);
            }
        }

        g.drawString(String.valueOf(i),
                     xtop+xoff*xdelta+(xdelta-
                     fcal.stringWidth(String. valueOf(i)))/2,
                     ytop+yoff*ydelta+(ydelta-
                                      fcal.getHeight())/2+1,
                     g.TOP|g.LEFT);


        xoff++;
        if(xoff>=7) {
            xoff=xoff%7;
            yoff++;
        }
        g.setColor(FOREGROUND_COLOR);
    }

    //draw outline of calendar
    g.drawRect(xtop, ytop, xdim, ydim);

    //draw cell lines
    for(int i=1;  i<nrow;  i++) {
        g.drawLine(xtop,ytop+i*ydelta, xtop+xdim,
                   ytop+i*ydelta);
    }
    for(int i=1;  i<ncolumn;  i++) {
        g.drawLine(xtop+i*xdelta, ytop,
                   xtop+i*xdelta, ytop+ydim);
    }
}

public int numberOfRows() {
    int Nrow=2; //current row and week header row
    if(day_of_month-day_of_week-1>0) {
        Nrow+=(day_of_month-day_of_week-1)/7;
        if((day_of_month-day_of_week-1)%7!=0) Nrow++;
    }

    if(days_in_month-day_of_month-6+day_of_week>0) {
        Nrow+=(days_in_month-day_of_month-6+day_of_week)/7;
```

LISTING 7.15   Continued

```
            if((days_in_month-day_of_month-6+day_of_week)%7!=0)
                Nrow++;
        }
        return Nrow;
    }

    public void keyPressed(int keycode) {
        Date dtmp=calendar.getTime();
        int day_of_week_of_first_of_month=(7-(day_of_month-1-
                                        day_of_week)%7)%7;

        switch (getGameAction(keycode)) {
        case Canvas.UP:
            dtmp.setTime(dtmp.getTime()-dayinmillis*7);
            calendar.setTime(dtmp);
            if(day_of_month >calendar.get(Calendar.DAY_OF_MONTH)) {
                repaint(
                    xtop+xdelta*day_of_week,
                    ytop+ydelta*((day_of_week_of_first_of_month+
                                day_of_month-1)/7),
                    xdelta, ydelta*2);
            }
            else { //repaint the whole screen
                repaint();
            }
            break;
        case Canvas.DOWN:
            dtmp.setTime(dtmp.getTime()+dayinmillis*7);
            calendar.setTime(dtmp);
            if(day_of_month <calendar.get(Calendar.DAY_OF_MONTH)) {
                repaint(
                    xtop+xdelta*day_of_week,
                    ytop+ydelta*((day_of_week_of_first_of_month+
                                day_of_month-1)/7+1),
                    xdelta, ydelta*2);
            }
            else { //repaint the whole screen
                repaint();
            }
            break;
        case Canvas.LEFT:
            dtmp.setTime(dtmp.getTime()-dayinmillis);
            calendar.setTime(dtmp);
            if(day_of_month >calendar.get(Calendar.DAY_OF_MONTH)) {
```

LISTING 7.15   Continued

```
                    if(day_of_week>
                       calendar.get(Calendar.DAY_OF_WEEK)-1) {
                         //same line
                         repaint(
                           xtop+xdelta*(day_of_week-1),
                           ytop+ydelta*((day_of_week_of_first_of_month+
                                         day_of_month-1)/7+1),
                           xdelta*2, ydelta);
                    }
                    else {
                         repaint(
                           xtop,
                           ytop+ydelta*((day_of_week_of_first_of_month+
                                         day_of_month-1)/7),
                           xdim, ydelta*2);
                    }
                }
                else { //repaint the whole screen
                    repaint();
                }
                break;
            case Canvas.RIGHT:
                dtmp.setTime(dtmp.getTime()+dayinmillis);
                calendar.setTime(dtmp);
                if(day_of_month <calendar.get(Calendar.DAY_OF_MONTH)) {
                    if(day_of_week<
                       calendar.get(Calendar.DAY_OF_WEEK)-1) {
                         //same line
                         repaint(
                           xtop+xdelta*(day_of_week),
                           ytop+ydelta*((day_of_week_of_first_of_month+
                                         day_of_month-1)/7+1),
                           xdelta*2, ydelta);
                    }
                    else {
                         repaint(
                           xtop,
                           ytop+ydelta*((day_of_week_of_first_of_month+
                           day_of_month-1)/7+1),
                           xdim, ydelta*2);
                    }
                }
                else { //repaint the whole screen
                    repaint();
```

LISTING 7.15   Continued

```
            }
        break;
    default:
        break;
    }
  }
}
```

FIGURE 7.25
A monthly schedule viewer on Sun's emulator.

FIGURE 7.26
A monthly schedule viewer on Motorola's emulator.

Using Low-Level APIs in UI Development

CHAPTER 7

227

7

USING LOW-LEVEL
APIS IN UI
DEVELOPMENT

Double Buffering

When the execution speed of the underlying K Virtual Machine (KVM) is slow, sometimes you may notice flickering when you change the selected date using the arrow keys in the previous section's MonthlySchedulerViewer example. The flickering is due to the fact that the MIDlet has to clear the drawing area with the background color before new contents are rendered to the area. You can use a common technique known as *double buffering* to eliminate the flickering problem.

Double buffering is a simple concept. Instead of rendering contents (drawing or clearing) directly to a drawing area of a canvas, you can create an offscreen image that is essentially a copy of the canvas's drawing area. When it is time to update the canvas's drawing area, the application first updates the offscreen image exactly as it would do to render directly to the canvas. After the offscreen image is updated, the application then copies the image to the canvas. In other words, every time the buffer is drawn to the real screen, it is complete—with no interim state of screen clearing.

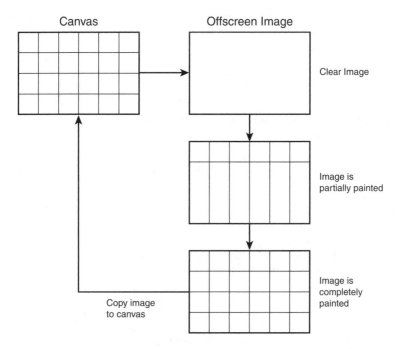

FIGURE 7.27

The process to update a Canvas *using an offscreen image.*

Some MIDP implementations already use double buffering for the Graphics object used in rendering contents to a canvas. You can check whether the Graphics object used in a canvas is double buffered by the implementation using this method of the Canvas class:

```
public boolean isDoubleBuffered()
```

The Canvas classes of both Sun's and Motorola's implementation use double buffering.

The double-buffering technique can be easily implemented by the application as well. First an offscreen image of the same size as the canvas is created as follows:

```
buffer_image=Image.createImage(width,height);
```

Then you need to obtain a Graphics object for rendering contents to the image:

```
bg= buffer_image.getGraphics();
```

Life Cycle of a Graphics Object

A Graphics object for an offscreen image can be obtained by calling the getGraphics() method of the image. It can be held indefinitely by the application. If the Graphics object isn't explicitly released, the application can drain all system resources quickly. Thus, after using the Graphics object, you need to dispose of it by using

```
bg=null;
```

The example in Listing 7.16 is the double-buffering version of Listing 7.15. You can uncomment the segments related to MonthlyScheduleViewer_DB in Listing 7.14 and test the double-buffering version of the viewer.

LISTING 7.16   MonthlyScheduleView_DB.java

```java
import java.util.Calendar;
import java.util.Date;
import java.util.Hashtable;
import javax.microedition.io.*;
import javax.microedition.lcdui.*;
import javax.microedition.midlet.*;

/**
 * Monthly schedule viewer, this example uses double buffers for painting
 */
public class MonthlyScheduleViewer_DB extends Canvas implements
CommandListener{
    private Display        display;
    private Displayable    parent;
    private Calendar       calendar;
```

LISTING 7.16 Continued

```java
private Hashtable          app_table;
private Command            backCommand = new Command("Back",
                                               Command.BACK, 1);
private Image              buffer_image=null;

/**
 * parameters for month views
 */
String days[] = {"S", "M", "T", "W",
                 "T", "F", "S"};

String months[] = {"January", "February", "March", "April",
                   "May", "June", "July", "August", "September",
                   "October", "November", "December"};

int DaysInMonth[] = {31, 28, 31, 30, 31, 30,
                     31, 31, 30, 31, 30, 31};

/**
 *Background color
 */
final int BACKGROUND_COLOR= 0xFFFFFF; //white
/**
 *Foreground color
 */
final int FOREGROUND_COLOR = 0x000000; //black
  /**
 *Appointment color
 */
final int APPOINTMENT_COLOR = 0x00FF00; //green
/**
 *  calendar information
 */
int day_of_month;
int day_of_week;
int week_of_month;
int month;
int days_in_month;
int year;
int hour;

//canvas dimensions
int width, height;
//font for title
```

LISTING 7.16 Continued

```java
Font flabel;
int header_height,command_height;
final long  dayinmillis=24*60*60*1000;
//number of rows and columns
int nrow, ncolumn;
//cell dimensions
int xdelta, ydelta;
//calendar dimensions
int xdim, ydim;
//top position after drawing header information
int xtop, ytop;

public MonthlyScheduleViewer_DB(Display d, Displayable p,
                               Calendar c, Hashtable a) {
    display = d;
    parent =p;
    calendar=c;
    app_table=a;

    //get dimension information
    width=getWidth();
    height=getHeight();

    //create buffer image
    try {
        buffer_image=Image.createImage(width,height);
    }catch(Exception e) {}
    flabel= Font.getFont(Font. FACE_SYSTEM, Font.STYLE_BOLD,
                        Font.SIZE_MEDIUM);
    header_height=flabel.getHeight()+1;
    command_height=header_height-2;
    //x dimension information is fixed
    ncolumn=7;

    //row/column dimensions
    xdelta = width/ncolumn;

    //calculate the calendar dimension
    xdim=xdelta*ncolumn;

    //top position after drawing header information
    xtop=(width-xdim)/2;
```

Using Low-Level APIs in UI Development

CHAPTER 7

231

7

USING LOW-LEVEL
APIS IN UI
DEVELOPMENT

LISTING 7.16   Continued

```
        addCommand(backCommand);
        setCommandListener(this);
    }


    private void initCalendarInfo() {
        day_of_month= calendar.get(Calendar.DAY_OF_MONTH);
        day_of_week= calendar.get(Calendar.DAY_OF_WEEK)-1;
        week_of_month=1;
        if(day_of_month-day_of_week-1>0) {
            week_of_month+=(day_of_month-day_of_week-1)/7;
            if((day_of_month-day_of_week-1)%7!=0) week_of_month++;
        }

        //month is 1 off;
        month=calendar.get(Calendar.MONTH);
        days_in_month=DaysInMonth[month];
        year=calendar.get(Calendar.YEAR);
        if(month==1) { //check leap year
            if(year%4==0) {
                days_in_month++;
            }
        }
        hour=calendar.get(Calendar.HOUR_OF_DAY);
    }

    public void commandAction(Command c, Displayable d) {
    if(c==backCommand) {
            display.setCurrent(parent);
        }
    }

    public void paint(Graphics g) {
            initCalendarInfo();
            Graphics bg=null;
            if(buffer_image!=null) {
                bg= buffer_image.getGraphics();
            }

            if(bg==null) {
                bg=g;
            }
```

LISTING 7.16 Continued

```
//clear canvas
bg.setColor(BACKGROUND_COLOR);
bg.fillRect(0,0,width,height);

bg.setColor(FOREGROUND_COLOR);
//paint header information at the top
bg.setFont(flabel);
String header = months[month]+", " +year;
bg.drawString(header, 0, header_height-2,
              bg.BASELINE|bg.LEFT);

//y dimension varies depending on month
nrow= numberOfRows();

//row/column dimensions
ydelta=(height-header_height-command_height)/nrow;

//calculate the calendar dimension
ydim=ydelta*nrow;

//top position after drawing header information
ytop=header_height+(height-header_height-
                    command_height-ydim)/2;

//reset font
Font fcal=Font.getFont(Font.FACE_SYSTEM, Font.STYLE_PLAIN,
                       Font.SIZE_SMALL);
bg.setFont(fcal);

//Draw week Headers
for(int i=0; i<ncolumn; i++) {
    bg.drawString(days[i],
    xtop+i*xdelta+(xdelta-fcal.stringWidth(days[i]))/2,
    ytop+(ydelta-fcal.getHeight())/2+1,
    bg.TOP|bg.LEFT);
}

//draw days
//calculate the day_of_week for the first day of the month
int day_of_week_of_first_of_month=
        (7-(day_of_month-1-day_of_week)%7)%7;
int xoff=day_of_week_of_first_of_month;
int yoff=1;
for(int i=1; i<=days_in_month; i++) {
```

LISTING 7.16 Continued

```
//check whether there are appointments on that day;
boolean hasAppointment;
if(app_table.get((month+1)+"/"+i+"/"+year)!=null) {
    hasAppointment=true;
}
else {
    hasAppointment=false;
}

//if there are appointments on that day,
//reset the background color
if(hasAppointment) {
    bg.setColor(APPOINTMENT_COLOR);
    bg.fillRect(xtop+xoff*xdelta, ytop+yoff*ydelta,
                xdelta, ydelta);
    bg.setColor(FOREGROUND_COLOR);
}

//highlight the current day
if(i==day_of_month) {
    bg.setColor(FOREGROUND_COLOR);
    bg.fillRect(xtop+xoff*xdelta, ytop+yoff*ydelta,
                xdelta, ydelta);
    if(hasAppointment) {
        bg.setColor(APPOINTMENT_COLOR);
    }
    else {
        bg.setColor(BACKGROUND_COLOR);
    }
}

bg.drawString(
    String.valueOf(i),
    xtop+xoff*xdelta+(xdelta-
        fcal.stringWidth(String.valueOf(i)))/2,
    ytop+yoff*ydelta+(ydelta-fcal.getHeight())/2+1,
    bg.TOP|bg.LEFT);

xoff++;
if(xoff>=7) {
    xoff=xoff%7;
    yoff++;
}
```

LISTING 7.16 Continued

```java
            bg.setColor(FOREGROUND_COLOR);
        }

        //draw outline of calendar
        bg.drawRect(xtop, ytop, xdim, ydim);

        //draw cell lines
        for(int i=1; i<nrow; i++) {
            bg.drawLine(xtop, ytop+i*ydelta, xtop+xdim,
                        ytop+i*ydelta);
        }
        for(int i=1; i<ncolumn; i++) {
            bg.drawLine(xtop+i*xdelta, ytop, xtop+i*xdelta,
                        ytop+ydim);
        }

        //check where have we been drawing
        if(bg!=g) {//we have double buffers
            g.drawImage(buffer_image,0,0,g.TOP|g.LEFT);
            bg=null;
        }
    }

    public int numberOfRows() {
        int Nrow=2; //current row and week header row
        if(day_of_month-day_of_week-1>0) {
            Nrow+=(day_of_month-day_of_week-1)/7;
            if((day_of_month-day_of_week-1)%7!=0) Nrow++;
        }

        if(days_in_month-day_of_month-6+day_of_week>0) {
            Nrow+=(days_in_month-day_of_month-6+day_of_week)/7;
            if((days_in_month-day_of_month-6+day_of_week)%7!=0)
                Nrow++;
        }
        return Nrow;
    }

    public void keyPressed(int keycode) {
        Date dtmp=calendar.getTime();
        int day_of_week_of_first_of_month=(7-(day_of_month-1
                                        -day_of_week)%7)%7;

        switch (getGameAction(keycode)) {
        case Canvas.UP:
```

LISTING 7.16   Continued

```
                dtmp.setTime(dtmp.getTime()-dayinmillis*7);
                calendar.setTime(dtmp);
                repaint();
                break;
        case Canvas.DOWN:
                dtmp.setTime(dtmp.getTime()+dayinmillis*7);
                calendar.setTime(dtmp);
                repaint();
                break;
        case Canvas.LEFT:
                dtmp.setTime(dtmp.getTime()-dayinmillis);
                calendar.setTime(dtmp);
                repaint();
                break;
        case Canvas.RIGHT:
                dtmp.setTime(dtmp.getTime()+dayinmillis);
                calendar.setTime(dtmp);
                repaint();
                break;
        default:
                break;
        }
    }
}
```

Limitations

By using the double-buffering technique, applications can eliminate the flickering problem. However, you may find the application responds slower to key events. This is because copying offscreen images to a canvas is a slow process.

In addition, double buffering takes up a lot of memory and some devices may not even support it. An alternative remedy to the flickering problem is to carefully erase only the parts of the screen that change, as opposed to the whole screen.

Summary

This chapter covered the usage of the Canvas and Graphics classes that implement the low-level MIDP API. Using Canvas, applications have full control over the appearance of what you want to draw. Applications can also access low-level events such as key events.

Persistent Storage

IN THIS CHAPTER

Overview

Wireless devices, such as cell phones and pagers, normally have two types of memory: memory for running applications and memory for persistent storage. Data stored in persistent storage outlasts application programs that operate on that data. Users can store personal preference settings and/or information that can be dynamically changed over time in persistent storage.

A *database*, by definition, is a large, persistent, integrated collection of dynamic data that provides some operations to describe, establish, manipulate, and access this data. J2ME MIDP defines a simple record-oriented database system called a *record management system (RMS)*. Each table of the database system is called a record store, and each entry in a record store is called a record. The APIs for creating a record store and accessing and manipulating its records are described in the `javax.microedition.rms` package. This package defines two classes, three interfaces, and five exceptions:

- **Classes**—`RecordStore`, `RecordEnumeration`
- **Interfaces**—`RecordComparator`, `RecordFilter`, `RecordListener`
- **Exceptions**—`InvalidRecordIDException`, `RecordStoreException`, `RecordStoreFullException`, `RecordStoreNotFoundException`, `RecordStoreNotOpenException`

In the MIDP specification, `RecordEnumeration` is defined as an interface. However, an implementation of MIDP must provide an implementation of this interface. You don't need to implement the interface to use it. So, it is treated as a regular class in this chapter.

This chapter discusses how to create, delete, and access a record store and how to manipulate its records.

Record Stores

The RMS in MIDP is a flat-file database system. A record store, which is equivalent to a table in a database, is a file that consists of a collection of records. A record store is represented by a `RecordStore` class. Here are the rules regarding record store names:

1. Record store names are case sensitive and may consist of any combination of up to 32 Unicode characters.
2. Record stores created by MIDlets within a MIDlet suite are located in the same directory. However, record store files created by MIDlets within different MIDlet suites are located in different directories. (This rule is not true for MotoSDK version 0.7.)
3. Record store names must be unique within a MIDlet suite.
4. Record stores created by MIDlets within one MIDlet suite are not accessible to MIDlets within other MIDlet suites.

Operations on a Record Store

The `RecordStore` class provides the following methods to create/open, close, and delete a record store, respectively:

```
public static RecordStore openRecordStore(String recordStoreName,
                                          boolean createIfNecessary)
public void closeRecordStore()
public static void deleteRecordStore(String recordStoreName)
```

MIDlets can create a record store using

```
RecordStore.openRecordStore(recordStoreName, true)
```

If the record store specified by `recordStoreName` does not exist, a record store with `recordStoreName` will be created. If the record store already exists, no new record store will be created and the record store with `recordStoreName` will be opened.

MIDlets can open an existing record store with

```
RecordStore.openRecordStore(recordStoreName, false)
```

If the record store exists, it will be opened. However, if the record store does not exist, then a `RecordStoreNotFoundException` will be thrown. You can use this method to test whether a record store file exists, like this:

```
public boolean exist(String recordStoreName) {
    boolean existF=true;
    RecordStore rs=null;
    if(recordStoreName.length()>32) return false;
    try {
        rs=RecordStore.openRecordStore(recordStoreName,false);
    }catch(RecordStoreNotFoundException e) {existF=false;}
    catch(Exception e){}
    finally{
        try{
            rs.close();
        }catch(Exception e){}
    }
    return existF;
}
```

Each record store contains at least a header field (the information maintained in the header is discussed in the following section, "The Record Store Header"). If not enough memory is allocated for a header, the record store will not be created and a `RecordStoreFullException` will be thrown. If other problems occur, such as a record store name that is too long or a corrupted record store file, then a `RecordStoreException` will be thrown.

For example, the MIDlet in Listing 8.1 will create a record store called `file1`.

LISTING 8.1 RecordStoreTest1.java

```java
import javax.microedition.midlet.*;
import javax.microedition.rms.*;

public class RecordStoreTest1 extends MIDlet {
    public RecordStoreTest1() {
    }
    public void startApp() throws MIDletStateChangeException {
        RecordStore rs=null;
        try {
            rs = RecordStore.openRecordStore("file1",true);
            System.out.println("record store file1 is opened.");
        }catch(Exception e){
            System.out.println("Error: "+e.getMessage());
        }finally{
            //close the record store
            try {
                rs.closeRecordStore();
                System.out.println("record store file1 is closed");
            }catch (Exception e){
                System.out.println("Error: "+e.getMessage());
            }
        }
        destroyApp(true);
        notifyDestroyed();
    }

    /**
     * Pause the MIDlet
     */
    public void pauseApp() {
    }

    /**
     * Called by the framework before the application is unloaded
     */
    public void destroyApp(boolean unconditional) {
    }
}
```

If this MIDlet is within the MIDlet suite Chapter8 and you run it using Sun's emulator, you will find the record store file in [J2MEWTKDIR]\nojam\Chapter8 with the name file1.db, where J2MEWTKDIR is the directory in which J2MEWTK is installed. If you start the ktoolbar program from a command prompt or run the MIDlet from command line, you will find the file under the directory `$Current_DIR\nojam\Chapter8`, where `$Current_DIR` is the directory from which you start `ktoolbar` or the MIDlet. If you would like to start `ktoolbar` or a MIDlet from the command line, you should start from the same directory every time. Otherwise, you will not find the same record store you create before.

If you run the MIDlet using Motorola's emulator, you will find the record store `file1.db` in `[MOTOSDKDIR]\lib\resources\1`, where `MOTOSDKDIR` is the directory in which MotoSDK is installed. (Currently, MotoSDK does not differentiate MIDlet suites, so all record stores are located in the same directory.)

A record store should be closed with `closeRecordStore()` when you finish using it. (As long as the record store is open, it consumes resources of the wireless devices.) Each process or thread that opens a record store should call the close method explicitly. The `closeRecordStore()` method does not actually close the record store file; it just notifies the application manager that this process or thread has finished using the record store. The record store file will not *actually* close until all processes that have opened the record store call `closeRecordStore()`.

When a record store is no longer needed, you can delete it using the `deleteRecordStore(String recordStoreName)` method. Before you can delete a record store, the record store must be closed. Otherwise, a `RecordStoreException` will be thrown.   The name rules also apply here; a MIDlet can only delete record stores associated with its MIDlet suite. If the record store is not found, a `RecordStoreNotFoundException` will be thrown. When a MIDlet suite is removed from a wireless device, all the record stores associated with it will also be removed.

The Record Store Header

Similar to other flat-file databases, a record store contains a header and many data blocks. Each data block is a record within the record store. Data blocks are linked together as a linked list, and each block maintains a pointer to the next block. To make such a flat-file database work, the header must maintain a link to the first data block and a link to the first block of free space. The header of a record store also maintains the following information:

1. The number of records in the record store. The initial value is zero. When a new record is added, this value increases by one. When a record is deleted, it decreases by one.

2. Version number. The initial version number is implementation dependent (normally, it is zero). The version number increments by a positive integer greater than zero (usually one). Each time a record store is modified (a record is added, modified, or deleted), the version number is incremented. This incrementing enables MIDlets to quickly tell if the record store has been modified by other processes or threads.

3. Last modified time. The time the record store was last modified, in the same format used by `System.currentTimeMillis()`. This value is complementary to the version number; they change together.

4. Next `recordId`. The `recordId` of the next record to be added to the record store. When the `addRecord()` method is called, the next `recordId` increases by one. This method can be useful for setting up pseudo-relational relationships. That is, if you have two or more record stores whose records need to refer to one another, you can predetermine the `recordIds` of the records that will be created in one record store, before populating the fields and allocating the records in another record store.

The header information of a record store can be retrieved by using the following methods of the `RecordStore` class:

```
public long getLastModified()
public int getNextRecordID()
public int getNumRecords()
public int getVersion()
```

Additional Record Store Data

Some information about a record. store is not maintained in its header, but is provided through implementations. For example

```
public int getSizeAvailable()
```

returns the amount of additional room (in bytes) available for this record store to grow. Note that this is not necessarily the amount of extra MIDlet-level data that can be stored, because implementations may store additional data structures with each record to support integration with native applications, synchronization, and so on.

The method

```
public int getSize()
```

returns the amount of space, in bytes, that the record store occupies. The size returned includes any overhead associated with the implementation, such as the data structures used to hold the state of the record store.

The method

```
public static String[] listRecordStores()
```

returns an array of the names of record stores owned by the MIDlet suite. Note that if the MIDlet suite does not have any record stores, this function will return null.

Record Store Limitations

The RMS in MIDP is a bare-bones database system. The API provides only a minimum set of operations that allow you to initialize, update, and retrieve data. The schema of each record store is very simple: an integer `recordId` as the primary key and a byte array as a record field. Many popular database features, such as transaction control, crash recovery, and data integrity control, are not supported by RMS.

Multiple MIDlets within a MIDlet suite or multiple threads of a MIDlet can open and access the same record store simultaneously. All record store operations are atomic, synchronous, and serialized, thus guaranteeing that no corruption will occur due to simultaneous accesses. Any operations (both reads and writes) will lock the record store until they finish. If a MIDlet uses multiple threads to access a record store, it is the MIDlet's responsibility to coordinate these accesses—otherwise, unintended consequences may result. For example, suppose you want to set up pseudo-relational relationships as mentioned earlier. One thread `t1` predetermines the next `recordId` of record store A using the `getNextRecordID()` method and puts the `recordId` into a record of record store B. Before thread `t1` creates a record in record store A, another thread `t2` adds a record into record store A. At this time, the relationship between record stores A and B is corrupted. Coordinating threads `t1` and `t2` is the application's responsibility.

Records

Entries in a record store are called records. These records are represented by byte arrays and are uniquely identified by `recordId`s. Records can be added, deleted, retrieved, and modified from an opened record store with the following methods in the API:

```
public int addRecord(byte[] data, int offset, int numBytes)
public void deleteRecord(int recordId)
public int getRecord(int recordId, byte[] buffer, int offset)
public byte[] getRecord(int recordId)
public void setRecord(int recordId, byte[] newData, int offset, int numBytes)
```

Adding Records

The first record created in a record store will have a `recordId` value of 1. Each subsequent record added to the record store will be assigned a `recordId` one greater than the record added before it. For example, the MIDlet in Listing 8.2 adds two records to the record store `file1` that you created when executing Listing 8.1.

LISTING 8.2   RecordStoreTest2.java

```java
import javax.microedition.midlet.*;
import javax.microedition.rms.*;
public class RecordStoreTest2 extends MIDlet {
    public RecordStoreTest2() {
    }
    public void startApp() throws MIDletStateChangeException {
        RecordStore rs=null;
        try {
            rs = RecordStore.openRecordStore("file1",true);
            byte data[]= new byte[4];
            for(int j=0; j<2; j++) {
                int i=rs.getNextRecordID();
                data[0] = (byte)((i >> 24) & 0xff);
                data[1] = (byte)((i >> 16) & 0xff);
                data[2] = (byte)((i >> 8) & 0xff);
                data[3] = (byte)(i & 0xff);
                System.out.println("record "+rs.addRecord(data,0,4)+
                                   " is added.");

            }
        }catch(Exception e){}
        finally{
            //close the record store
            try {
                rs.closeRecordStore();
            }catch (Exception e){}
        }
        destroyApp(true);
        notifyDestroyed();
    }
    /**
     * Pause the MIDlet
     */
    public void pauseApp() {
    }

    /**
     * Called by the framework before the application is unloaded
     */
    public void destroyApp(boolean unconditional) {
    }
}
```

If you run the MIDlet in Listing 8.2 multiple times, you will get the following results:

```
Adding Record to rMS........
record 1 is added.
Adding Record to rMS........
record 2 is added.
Adding Record to rMS........
record 3 is added.
Adding Record to rMS........
record 4 is added.
...
```

The text `Adding Record to rMS........` is a system message that appears when adding records.

Deleting Records

You can delete a record from a record store by calling `deleteRecord(int recordId)`. If the method is called before the record store is open, a `RecordStoreNotOpenException` will be thrown. If the record specified by the `recordId` does not exist in the record store, an `InvalidRecordIDException` will be thrown. If another general record store exception occurs, a `RecordStoreException` will be thrown.

The `recordIds` of deleted records are not reused; the primary key of the next new record, `nextRecordID`, increases by one over that of the previous new record.

Deleting a record does not make the record store file smaller; the data block of the deleted record is just marked free for future use. The example in Listing 8.3 adds two records and then removes one from the record store `file1`.

LISTING 8.3   RecordStoreTest3.java

```java
import javax.microedition.midlet.*;
import javax.microedition.rms.*;

public class RecordStoreTest3 extends MIDlet {
    public RecordStoreTest3() {
    }
    public void startApp() throws MIDletStateChangeException {
        RecordStore rs=null;
        try {
            rs = RecordStore.openRecordStore("file1",true);
            byte data[]= new byte[4];
            for(int j=0; j<2; j++) {
                int i=rs.getNextRecordID();
                data[0] = (byte)((i >> 24) & 0xff);
```

LISTING 8.3   Continued

```
                    data[1] = (byte)((i >> 16) & 0xff);
                    data[2] = (byte)((i >> 8) & 0xff);
                    data[3] = (byte)(i & 0xff);
                    System.out.println("record "+rs.addRecord(data,0,4)+
                                        " is added.");
                }
                try {
                    rs.deleteRecord(2);
                    System.out.println("record 2 is deleted.");
                }catch(InvalidRecordIDException e) {
                    System.out.println("record 2 does not exist");
                }
            }catch(Exception e){}
            finally{
                //close the record store
                try {
                    rs.closeRecordStore();
                }catch (Exception e){}
            }
            destroyApp(true);
            notifyDestroyed();
        }

        /**
         * Pause the MIDlet
         */
        public void pauseApp() {
        }

        /**
         * Called by the framework before the application is unloaded
         */
        public void destroyApp(boolean unconditional) {
        }
}
```

When you run the MIDlet in Listing 8.3 for the first time, you will get output similar to the following:

```
Adding Record to rMS.........
record 7 is added.
Adding Record to rMS.........
record 8 is added.
record 2 is deleted.
```

When you run it again, you will see output like this:

```
Adding Record to rMS.........
record 9 is added.
Adding Record to rMS.........
record 10 is added.
record 2 does not exist.
```

Two more records are added, and their recordIds are consecutive from the previous run. The record with a recordId value of 2 is not deleted, because that record no longer exists in the record store.

Monitoring Record Changes

A record store can monitor changes that happen to it using the RecordListener interface. When a change is made to the record store, an event is delivered to the registered RecordListener. (The event-handling model is the same as the delegation-based event-handling model discussed in Chapter 5, "Central Components of the UI for Wireless Devices.") Three types of events—recordChanged, recordAdded, and recordDeleted—can be delivered to a RecordListener. These events are handled by the following methods of the RecordListener interface:

```
void recordAdded(RecordStore recordStore, int recordId)
void recordChanged(RecordStore recordStore, int recordId)
void recordDeleted(RecordStore recordStore, int recordId)
```

The RecordStore class provides the following methods to add or remove a RecordListener:

```
public void addRecordListener(RecordListener listener)
public void removeRecordListener(RecordListener listener)
```

Unlike a Displayable, which can have at most one registered CommandListener, or a Form, which can have at most one registered ItemStateListener, a RecordStore object can have multiple registered RecordListeners.

For instance, suppose you want to keep two record stores synchronized. You can do so using a RecordListener as shown in Listing 8.4. When records in record store rs1 are modified, the changes will be automatically reflected in record store rs2.

LISTING 8.4   RecordListenerTest.java

```
import javax.microedition.midlet.*;
import javax.microedition.rms.*;

public class RecordListenerTest extends MIDlet implements RecordListener {
    RecordStore rs1=null;
    RecordStore rs2=null;
```

8

PERSISTENT
STORAGE

LISTING 8.4 Continued

```java
public RecordListenerTest() {
}

public void startApp() throws MIDletStateChangeException {
    //open two record stores
    try {
        rs1 = RecordStore.openRecordStore("test1",true);
        rs1.addRecordListener(this);
    }catch(Exception e) {}
    try {
        rs2 = RecordStore.openRecordStore("test2",true);
    }catch(Exception e) {}

    //add two records to rs1
    byte data[]= new byte[4];
    for(int j=0; j<2; j++) {
        try {
            int i=rs1.getNextRecordID();
            data[0] = (byte)((i >> 24) & 0xff);
            data[1] = (byte)((i >> 16) & 0xff);
            data[2] = (byte)((i >> 8) & 0xff);
            data[3] = (byte)(i & 0xff);
            System.out.println("record #"+rs1.addRecord(data,0,4)+
                               " is added to record store 1");
        }catch (Exception e){}
    }

    //modified the second last added record
    try {
        int id=rs1.getNextRecordID()-2;
        data=rs1.getRecord(id);
        data[0]+=1;
        rs1.setRecord(id, data, 0, 4);
      System.out.println("record #"+id+" of record store 1 is modified.");
    }catch(Exception e) {}

    //delete the last added
    try {
        int id=rs1.getNextRecordID()-1;
        rs1.deleteRecord(id);
        System.out.println("record #"+id+" of record store 1 is deleted.");
    }catch (Exception e){}

    // end
```

LISTING 8.4   Continued

```java
    destroyApp(true);
    notifyDestroyed();
}


/**
 * Pause the MIDlet
 */
public void pauseApp() {
}


/**
 * Called by the framework before the application is unloaded
 */
public void destroyApp(boolean unconditional) {
    //close the two record stores
    try {
        if(rs1!=null) rs1.closeRecordStore();
    }catch(Exception e){}
    try {
        if(rs2!=null) rs2.closeRecordStore();
    }catch (Exception e){}
}


//implement RecordListener
public void recordAdded(RecordStore rs, int rid) {
    if(rs==rs1) {
        try {
            byte data[]=rs.getRecord(rid);
            int id=rs2.addRecord(data, 0, data.length);
            System.out.println("record #"+id+
                               " is added to record store 2.");
        }catch(Exception e) {}
    }
}
public void recordChanged(RecordStore rs, int rid) {
    if(rs==rs1) {
        try {
            byte data[]=rs.getRecord(rid);
            rs2.setRecord(rid, data, 0, data.length);
            System.out.println("record #"+rid+
                               " of record store 2 is modified.");
        }catch(Exception e) {}
    }
}
```

LISTING 8.4   Continued

```
public void recordDeleted(RecordStore rs, int rid) {
    if(rs==rs1) {
        try {
            rs2.deleteRecord(rid);
            System.out.println("record #"+rid+
                               " of record store 2 is deleted.");
        }catch(Exception e) {}
    }
}
}
```

If you run the MIDlet, you will see output like following:

```
Adding Record to rMS.........
Adding Record to rMS.........
record #1 is added to record store 2.
record #1 is added to record store 1.
Adding Record to rMS.........
Adding Record to rMS.........
record #2 is added to record store 2.
record #2 is added to record store 1.
record #1 of record store 2 is modified.
record #1 of record store 1 is modified.
record #2 of record store 2 is deleted.
record #2 of record store 1 is deleted.
```

Record store rs2 automatically copies record changes made to record store rs1.

RecordEnumeration

After records are deleted, recordIds of records in the record store are no longer consecutive. You can retrieve all the records using the MIDlet shown in Listing 8.5, but it is *not* a good and efficient way to do so.

LISTING 8.5   RecordStoreList1.java

```
import javax.microedition.midlet.*;
import javax.microedition.rms.*;

public class RecordStoreList1 extends MIDlet {
    public RecordStoreList1() {
    }
    public void startApp() throws MIDletStateChangeException {
        RecordStore rs=null;
```

LISTING 8.5 Continued

```
        try {
            rs = RecordStore.openRecordStore("file1", true);
            byte data[];
            System.out.println(rs.getNumRecords()+
                              " records are in the record store.");
            for(int i=1; i<rs.getNextRecordID(); i++) {
                try{
                    data=rs.getRecord(i);
                    System.out.println("record "+i+" is retrieved.");
                }catch (Exception e) {}
            }
        }catch(Exception e){}
        finally{
            //close the record store
            try {
                rs.closeRecordStore();
            }catch (Exception e){}
        }
        destroyApp(true);
        notifyDestroyed();
    }

    /**
     * Pause the MIDlet
     */
    public void pauseApp() {
    }

    /**
     * Called by the framework before the application is unloaded
     */
    public void destroyApp(boolean unconditional) {
    }
}
```

If you run the MIDlet in Listing 8.5, you will get output as follows:

```
9 records are in the record store.
record 1 is retrieved.
record 3 is retrieved.
record 4 is retrieved.
...
```

This is a trial-and-error way to retrieve all records: If the record specified by the recordId exists, it will be retrieved with the getRecord() method; but if the record identified by the recordId does not exist, an InvalidRecordIDException will be thrown. If many records have been deleted since the record store was created, getting records with this MIDlet will be very inefficient.

The API of RMS provides a better way to traverse all records in a record store. RecordEnumeration is a class representing a bidirectional record store record enumerator. MIDP defines RecordEnumeration as an interface, because the detailed implementations are left for device manufacturers. Any device manufacturers that implement J2ME MIDP must implement RecordEnumeration. For developers like us, the RecordEnumeration is a solid class.

A RecordEnumeration is similar to a double-linked list with each node representing a recordId. The RecordEnumeration logically maintains a sequence of the recordIds of the records in a record store. The RecordStore class provides the method for creating a RecordEnumeration:

```
public RecordEnumeration enumerateRecords(RecordFilter filter,
                        RecordComparator comparator, boolean keepUpdated)
```

If a RecordEnumeration is created with keepUpdated set to true, the enumerator will keep its enumeration current with any changes in the record store's records. If the RecordEnumeration is created with keepUpdated set to false, the MIDlet is responsible for updating the enumerator with the rebuild() method. If the enumeration is not kept current, it may return recordIds for records that have been deleted, or it may miss records that are added later. When keepUpdated is set to true, performance may be penalized because some unnecessary enumeration updates can be triggered by changes in the record store. For example, when both the filter and comparator are set to null, a data change in a record should not trigger an update of the enumerator. A MIDlet also can wait to update the enumerator until all changes are done, if the enumerator is not used between changes.

The keepUpdated setting of a RecordEnumeration object can be changed with the method

```
void keepUpdated(boolean keepUpdated)
```

The setting can be retrieved by calling the method

```
boolean isKeptUpdated()
```

Accessing and Traversing Records

The API of the RecordEnumeration class provides the following methods to access or traverse all records in a record store:

```
void destroy()
boolean hasNextElement()
boolean hasPreviousElement()
byte[] nextRecord()
int nextRecordId()
int numRecords()
byte[] previousRecord()
int previousRecordId()
void rebuild()
void reset()
```

If you need to use the enumerator multiple times, remember to use the reset() method to reset the current node (pointer) to the first recordId in the linked list. The example in Listing 8.6 lists all records with even recordIds and then lists all records with odd recordIds.

LISTING 8.6   RecordStoreList2.java

```
import javax.microedition.midlet.*;
import javax.microedition.rms.*;

public class RecordStoreList2 extends MIDlet {
    public RecordStoreList2() {
    }
    public void startApp() throws MIDletStateChangeException {
        RecordStore rs=null;
        RecordEnumeration re=null;
        try {
            rs = RecordStore.openRecordStore("file1", true);
            byte data[];
            re= rs.enumerateRecords(null, null, false);
            System.out.println(re.numRecords()+
                            " records are in the record store.");
            System.out.println("records with even recordIds:");
            for(int i=1; i<=re.numRecords(); i++) {
                try{
                    int j=re.nextRecordId();
                    if(j%2==0) {
                        data=rs.getRecord(j);
                        System.out.println("record "+j+" is retrieved.");
                    }
                }catch (Exception e) {}
            }
            System.out.println("records with odd recordIds:");
            /* now the current pointer points to the last node of the
             * enumerator.  To use it again, you have to reset it.
             */
```

8

Listing 8.6   Continued

```
            re.reset();
            while(re.hasNextElement()) {
                try{
                    int j=re.nextRecordId();
                    if(j%2==1) {
                        data=rs.getRecord(j);
                        System.out.println("record "+j+" is retrieved.");
                    }
                }catch (Exception e) {}
            }
        }catch(Exception e){}
        finally{
            //detroy the record enumerator
            try {
                re.destroy();
            }catch(Exception e){}
            //close the record store
            try {
                rs.closeRecordStore();
            }catch (Exception e){}
        }
        destroyApp(true);
        notifyDestroyed();
    }

    /**
     * Pause the MIDlet
     */
    public void pauseApp() {
    }

    /**
     * Called by the framework before the application is unloaded
     */
    public void destroyApp(boolean unconditional) {
    }
}
```

When you run the MIDlet in Listing 8.6, you will see output like the following:

```
9 records are in the record store.
records with even recordIds:
record 4 is retrieved.
record 6 is retrieved.
record 8 is retrieved.
```

```
record 10 is retrieved.
records with odd recordIds:
record 1 is retrieved.
record 3 is retrieved.
record 5 is retrieved.
...
```

Record 2 is not retrieved because it was deleted from the record store when you ran the MIDlet in Listing 8.3.

Creating Tables with Multiple Columns

Generally, a database table has multiple columns. A record in a record store has only one data field, which is represented by a byte array. However, you can pack multiple fields into a single record using UTF-8 encoding, so that the record store is equivalent to a multiple-column table. J2ME's java.io package inherits the classes DataInputStream, DataOutputStream, ByteArrayInputStream, and ByteArrayOutputStream from J2SE's java.io package. You can use these classes to pack and unpack different data types into and out of byte arrays.

For example, suppose you want to store an appointment record with the following four fields: time (long integer), length (integer), location (string), and subject (string). You can create this class for appointments:

```
public class Appointment  {
    private int  id;
    private long time;
    private int length;
    private String location;
    private String subject;
...
}
```

The id in the class corresponds to the recordId in the record store. If you want to save an appointment record to a record store, you can first pack all the fields into a byte array like this:

```
public class Appointment  {
...
    /* convert to the byte array that will be saved in the record store*/
    public byte[] toBytes() {
        byte data[]=null;
        try {
            ByteArrayOutputStream baos= new ByteArrayOutputStream();
            DataOutputStream dos= new DataOutputStream(baos);
            dos.writeLong(time);
            dos.writeInt(length);
            dos.writeUTF(location);
```

```
            dos.writeUTF(subject);
            data=baos.toByteArray();

            baos.close();
            dos.close();
        }catch(Exception e) {}
        return data;
    }
    ...
}
```

Then, you can save the byte array to the record store as follows:

```
public class CalendarDB  {
    RecordStore rs=null;
...
    //save an appointment (new and old)
    public boolean save(Appointment app) {
        if(rs==null) return false;

        boolean success=false;
        try {
            byte[] data= app.toBytes();
            int id= app.getId();
            if(id==0) {//create a new record
                id=rs.addRecord(data,0,data.length);
                app.setId(id);
            }
            else {//update the old record
                rs.setRecord(id, data, 0, data.length);
            }
            success=true;
        }catch(Exception e){
            System.out.println("Error: "+e.getMessage());
        }
        return success;
    }
    ...
}
```

In the `CalendarDB.save()` method, the appointment's `id` is a flag that indicates whether this appointment record is an old appointment or a new one. If the appointment is a new one, a new record is created with

```
id=rs.addRecord(data,0,data.length);
```

and a new `recordId` is assigned to the appointment's `id` as

`app.setId(id);`

If the appointment already exists in the record store, it is updated with

`rs.setRecord(id,data,0,data.length);`

> **CAUTION**
>
> There is a bug in the `RecordStore.setRecord()` method of Sun's J2ME toolkit. If the length of the new record's data is larger than the length of the old data, the record store will be corrupted.

In Chapter 6, "Using High-Level APIs in UI Development," you saw a UI program `AppointmentForm.java` that takes user input and outputs the result to a terminal. Now you can link the UI part with a record store and save users' input as follows (the complete program is listed in the section "Sample Application: Mobile Scheduler" later in the chapter):

```
public class AppointmentForm extends Form implements CommandListener{
    private Display display;
    private Displayable parent;
    private Command saveCommand = new Command("Save", Command.OK, 2);
    private Command deleteCommand = new Command("Delete",Command.OK,2);
    private Command cancelCommand = new Command("Cancel", Command.CANCEL, 1);
    private Appointment app;

    private CalendarDB calendarDB;
...
    public void commandAction(Command c, Displayable d) {
        if(c==saveCommand) {
            //time
            app.setTime(((DateField)get(0)).getDate().getTime());
            TextField tf;
            //length
            tf= (TextField) get(1);
            app.setLength(Integer.parseInt(tf.getString()));
            //location
            tf= (TextField) get(2);
            app.setLocation(tf.getString());
            //subject
```

```
            tf= (TextField) get(3);
            app.setSubject(tf.getString());

            //create an alert
            Alert saveInfo= new Alert("Save Appointment", "",
                                    null, AlertType.INFO);
            saveInfo.setTimeout(Alert.FOREVER);
            if(calendarDB.save(app)) {
                saveInfo.setString("Success!");
            }
            else {
                saveInfo.setString("Fail!");
            }
            display.setCurrent(saveInfo,parent);
        }
        else if(c==deleteCommand) {
            //create an alert
            Alert deleteInfo= new Alert("Delete Appointment", "",
                                    null, AlertType.INFO);
            deleteInfo.setTimeout(Alert.FOREVER);
            if(calendarDB.delete(app)) {
                deleteInfo.setString("Success!");
            }
            else {
                deleteInfo.setString("Fail!");
            }
            display.setCurrent(deleteInfo,parent);
        }
        else if(c==cancelCommand) {
            display.setCurrent(parent);
        }
    }
}
```

For instance, suppose you want to create an appointment with these values

time: 1/1/01, 19:00

length: 120 minutes

location: Universal city

subject: new year celebration

and then save it. Because Motorola's emulator gives better performance when used with record stores, we will use it in the rest of this chapter. You can start the Scheduler MIDlet and select the Add Appointment function. After you input all the information (see Figure 8.1), click Save. If the appointment is saved properly, you will see a success message, as shown as Figure 8.2.

FIGURE 8.1

Adding an appointment.

FIGURE 8.2

After successfully adding an appointment.

After you save appointments, you want to retrieve them for review. The next example shows how to retrieve and display all the appointments in the record store:

```
public class CalendarDB  {
    RecordStore rs=null;
...
```

```
public Vector retrieveAll() {
    RecordEnumeration re=null;
    Vector apps= new Vector();
    try {
        re = rs.enumerateRecords(null, null, false);
        while(re.hasNextElement()) {
            int rec_id=re.nextRecordId();
            apps.addElement(new Appointment(rec_id,
                                            rs.getRecord(rec_id)));

        }
    }catch(Exception e) {}
    finally{
        //destroy the enumerator
        if(re!=null) re.destroy();
    }
    return apps;
}
...
}
```

The retrieveAll() method creates a RecordEnumeration for use in stepping through all the records. After a record is retrieved with rs.getRecord(rec_id), the byte array is parsed to get the value of each field in the appointment record as follows:

```
public class Appointment  {
...
    /* rec is the byte array saved in record store */
    public Appointment (int _id, byte[] rec) {
        id=_id;
        init_app(rec);
    }

    /* rec is the byte array saved in record store */
    public void init_app(byte[] rec) {
        // parse the record
        ByteArrayInputStream bais= new ByteArrayInputStream(rec);
        DataInputStream dis= new DataInputStream(bais);
        try {
            time=dis.readLong();
            length=dis.readInt();
            location=dis.readUTF();
            subject=dis.readUTF();
        }catch(Exception e){}
    }
...
}
```

You can add the Retrieve Appointments function to the Scheduler MIDlet (see the section "Sample Application: Mobile Scheduler"). If you run the Scheduler MIDlet and invoke Retrieve Appointments, you will see all the appointments listed as in Figure 8.3. If you select an appointment in the list, the appointment's detail information will be shown, as in Figure 8.4. From here, you can edit the appointment or you can save it or delete it by selecting the appropriate menu item (see Figure 8.5).

FIGURE 8.3

List all appointments.

FIGURE 8.4

Edit an appointment selected from the list.

FIGURE 8.5

Available operations on a selected appointment.

The `RecordFilter` and `RecordComparator` Interfaces

In general, you will insert appointments into the record store whenever you need to. But when you view or retrieve appointments, you usually want to sort them by appointment time and filter out appointments that are too old. The RMS package provides two interfaces, `RecordFilter` and `RecordComparator`, to meet this need.

The `RecordFilter` interface has only one function:

```
public boolean matches(byte[] candidate)
```

You can define criteria for selecting a record in this method. Listing 8.7 defines an `AppointmentFilter` class that implements the `RecordFilter` interface. Any appointments that are later than a cutoff time will pass through the filter.

LISTING 8.7   `AppointmentFilter.java`

```
/*
 * AppointmentFilter.java
 *
 */

import javax.microedition.rms.*;
```

LISTING 8.7   Continued

```java
public class AppointmentFilter implements RecordFilter{
    private long cutoff;
    public AppointmentFilter (long _cutoff) {
        cutoff=_cutoff;
    }

    public boolean matches(byte[] candidate) {
        Appointment app= new Appointment();
        app.init_app(candidate);

        if (app.getTime()>cutoff) {
            return true;
        }
        else {
            return false;
        }
    }
}
```

The `RecordComparator` interface provides an easy way to sort records. It also has only one function:

```java
int compare(byte[] rec1, byte[] rec2)
```

The return value must be one of three constants—PRECEDES, FOLLOWS, and EQUIVALENT—that indicates the ordering of the two records. If rec1 precedes rec2 in the sort order, the function returns `RecordComparator.PRECEDES`. If rec1 follows rec2 in the sort order, the function returns `RecordComparator.FOLLOWS`. If rec1 and rec2 are equivalent in terms of sort order, the function returns `RecordComparator.EQUIVALENT`.

To sort appointments by appointment time, you can create an `AppointmentComparator` class as shown in Listing 8.8. This class implements the `RecordComparator` interface.

LISTING 8.8   `AppointmentComparator.java`

```java
/*
 * AppointmentComparator.java
 *
 */

import javax.microedition.rms.*;
public class AppointmentComparator implements RecordComparator{
    public int compare(byte[] rec1, byte[] rec2) {
```

LISTING 8.8 Continued

```
            Appointment app1= new Appointment();
            app1.init_app(rec1);
            Appointment app2= new Appointment();
            app2.init_app(rec2);

            if (app1.getTime()==app2.getTime()) {
                return RecordComparator.EQUIVALENT;
            }
            else if(app1.getTime()<app2.getTime()) {
                return RecordComparator.PRECEDES;
            }
            else {
                return RecordComparator.FOLLOWS;
            }
        }
    }
}
```

The compare() method of the AppointmentComparator class determines the order of two records by appointment time. For instance, suppose you don't want to see any appointments that are 90 days old and you want to sort appointments by time. You can use AppointmentFilter and AppointmentComparator to modify the retrieveAll() method in the CalendarDB class as follows:

```
public class CalendarDB  {
    public Vector retrieveAll() {
        RecordEnumeration re=null;
        Vector apps= new Vector();
        try {
            //cutoff is 90 days old
            long cutoff=System.currentTimeMillis()-
                        new Integer(90).longValue()*24*60*60000;
            RecordFilter rf = new AppointmentFilter(cutoff);
            RecordComparator rc = new AppointmentComparator();
            re = rs.enumerateRecords(rf,rc,false);
            while(re.hasNextElement()) {
                int rec_id=re.nextRecordId();
                apps.addElement(new Appointment(rec_id,rs.getRecord(rec_id)));
            }
        }catch(Exception e) {}
        finally{
            //destroy the enumerator
            if(re!=null) re.destroy();
        }
        return apps;
    }
```

Sample Application: Mobile Scheduler

Chapter 6 presented the `Scheduler.java` MIDlet. To save appointment data on wireless devices, you need to use a record store. The ability to retrieve appointments has also been added. After all appointments are retrieved, they can be displayed in a list or can be graphically displayed using the `MonthlyScheduleViewer` developed in Chapter 7, "Using Low-Level APIs in UI Development." The updated `Scheduler.java` shown in Listing 8.9 links together pieces of programs developed in Chapters 6, 7, and this chapter.

LISTING 8.9   Scheduler.java

```java
import java.util.*;
import javax.microedition.midlet.*;
import javax.microedition.lcdui.*;

public class Scheduler extends MIDlet implements CommandListener{
    private Calendar          calendar;
    private List              menu;
    private AppointmentForm   appForm=null;
    private List              appList=null;
    private SynchOptionForm   soForm=null;
    private MonthlyScheduleViewer   monthlyviewer=null;
    private String[]          options={"Add Appointment",
                                       "Retrieve Appointments",
                                       "Synch Option Setup",
                                       "Calendar view"};

    private Display       display;
    private Command       backCommand= new Command("Back",Command.BACK,1);
    private Command       exitCommand = new Command("Exit",Command.EXIT,1);
    private Command       detailCommand =
                          new Command("Detail",Command.SCREEN, 1);

    private CalendarDB    calendarDB;
    private Vector        apps;
    private Hashtable     app_table;
    private SynchOption    so;
    public Scheduler() {
        //create an implicit choice list, and use it as start menu
        menu= new List("Scheduler", List.IMPLICIT,options,null);
        menu.addCommand(exitCommand);
        menu.setCommandListener(this);

        //get a calendar
        calendar=Calendar.getInstance();
```

LISTING 8.9 Continued

```java
            //open the record store that stores appointments
            calendarDB = new CalendarDB();
            //retrieve synchoption
            so = new SynchOption();

            //retrieve display
            display=Display.getDisplay(this);
    }
    public void startApp() throws MIDletStateChangeException {
        display.setCurrent(menu);
    }

    /**
     * Pause the MIDlet
     */
    public void pauseApp() {
    }

    /**
     * Called by the framework before the application is unloaded
     */
    public void destroyApp(boolean unconditional) {
        //close record store
        calendarDB.close();
        //clear everything
        menu= null;
        calendar=null;
        display=null;
        appForm = null;
        appList =null;
        apps=null;
        soForm = null;
        monthlyviewer=null;
    }

    public void commandAction(Command c, Displayable d) {
        if(d==menu && c==List.SELECT_COMMAND) {
            switch(menu.getSelectedIndex()) {
            case 0: //Add appointment
                //create a new appointment from
                appForm = new AppointmentForm(display, menu, calendarDB);
                appForm.setAppointment(new Appointment(calendar.getTime()));
                display.setCurrent(appForm);
                break;
```

LISTING 8.9 Continued

```
        case 1: //retrieve appointments
            //create an appointment list
            appList = new List("Appointments",List.IMPLICIT);
            appList.addCommand(backCommand);
            appList.setCommandListener(this);

            //retrieve all the appointments
            apps= calendarDB.retrieveAll();
            for(int i=0; i<apps.size(); i++) {
                Appointment app= (Appointment) apps.elementAt(i);
                StringBuffer sb = new StringBuffer();
                sb.append(app.getTimeString()).append(" ").
                        append(app.getSubject());
                appList.append(sb.toString(),null);
            }
            display.setCurrent(appList);
            break;
        case 2: //synchronization set up
            if(soForm==null) {
                //synchsetting
                soForm = new SynchOptionForm(display,menu,so);
            }
            display.setCurrent(soForm);
            break;
        case 3: // monthly schedule view
            //retrieve all the appointments
            apps= calendarDB.retrieveAll();
            app_table= new Hashtable();
            for(int i=0; i<apps.size(); i++) {
                Appointment app= (Appointment) apps.elementAt(i);
                String key=app.getTimeString();
                key=key.substring(0, key.indexOf(' '));
                app_table.put(key, new Object());
            }
            monthlyviewer= new MonthlyScheduleViewer(calendar, app_table);
            monthlyviewer.addCommand(detailCommand);
            monthlyviewer.addCommand(backCommand);
            monthlyviewer.setCommandListener(this);
            display.setCurrent(monthlyviewer);
            break;
        default:
        }
    }
    else if(d==menu && c==exitCommand ) {
        destroyApp(true);
```

LISTING 8.9   Continued

```java
                notifyDestroyed();
        }
        else if(d==appList) {
            if(c==List.SELECT_COMMAND) {
                //create a new appointment from
                appForm = new AppointmentForm(display,menu,calendarDB);
                appForm.setAppointment(
                  (Appointment)apps.elementAt(appList.getSelectedIndex()));
                display.setCurrent(appForm);
            }
            else if(c==backCommand) {
                display.setCurrent(menu);
            }
        }
        else if(d==monthlyviewer) {
            if(c==backCommand) {
                display.setCurrent(menu);
            }
            else {//detail command
                //create an appointment list
                appList = new List("Appointments",List.IMPLICIT);
                appList.addCommand(backCommand);
                appList.setCommandListener(this);

                //retrieve all the appointments
                apps= calendarDB.retrieveAllByDate(calendar);
                for(int i=0; i<apps.size(); i++) {
                    Appointment app= (Appointment) apps.elementAt(i);
                    StringBuffer sb = new StringBuffer();
                    sb.append(app.getTimeString()).append(" ").
                            append(app.getSubject());
                    appList.append(sb.toString(),null);
                }
                display.setCurrent(appList);
            }
        }
    }
}
```

We've already discussed the functions that add new appointments and retrieve all appointments. You also need to change (or edit) and cancel (or delete) appointments. These functions are added to AppointmentForm.java (Listing 8.10).

LISTING 8.10   AppointmentForm.java

```java
import javax.microedition.midlet.*;
import javax.microedition.lcdui.*;
import java.util.Date;
import java.util.Calendar;

public class AppointmentForm extends Form implements CommandListener{
    private Display display;
    private Displayable parent;
    private Command saveCommand = new Command("Save", Command.OK, 2);
    private Command deleteCommand = new Command("Delete",Command.OK,2);
    private Command cancelCommand = new Command("Cancel", Command.CANCEL, 1);
    private Appointment app;

    private CalendarDB calendarDB;
    public AppointmentForm(Display d, Displayable p, CalendarDB calDB) {
        super("Appointment");
        display=d;
        parent=p;
        calendarDB=calDB;
        addCommand(cancelCommand);
        addCommand(saveCommand);
        addCommand(deleteCommand);
        setCommandListener(this);

        //Appointment Time
        DateField df= new DateField("Date and Time",DateField.DATE_TIME);
        df.setDate(new Date(System.currentTimeMillis()));
        append(df);

        //Appointment Length
        append(new TextField("Length (Min)", "30", 10,TextField.NUMERIC));

        //Appointment location
        append(new TextField("Location","",50,TextField.ANY));

        //Subject
        append(new TextField("Subject","",50,TextField.ANY));
    }

    public void setAppointment(Appointment _app) {
        app= _app;
        //Appointment Time
```

LISTING 8.10   Continued

```java
        DateField df= (DateField) get(0);
        df.setDate(new Date(app.getTime()));

        //Appointment Length
        TextField tf_length= (TextField) get(1);
        tf_length.setString(String.valueOf(app.getLength()));

        //Appointment location
        TextField tf_location= (TextField) get(2);
        tf_location.setString(app.getLocation());

        //Appointment subject
        TextField tf_subject= (TextField) get(3);
        tf_subject.setString(app.getSubject());
    }

    public void commandAction(Command c, Displayable d) {
        if(c==saveCommand) {
            //time
            app.setTime(((DateField)get(0)).getDate().getTime());
            TextField tf;
            //length
            tf= (TextField) get(1);
            app.setLength(Integer.parseInt(tf.getString()));
            //location
            tf= (TextField) get(2);
            app.setLocation(tf.getString());
            //subject
            tf= (TextField) get(3);
            app.setSubject(tf.getString());

            //create an alert
            Alert saveInfo=
                new Alert("Save Appointment","",null,AlertType.INFO);
            saveInfo.setTimeout(Alert.FOREVER);
            if(calendarDB.save(app)) {
                saveInfo.setString("Success!");
            }
            else {
                saveInfo.setString("Fail!");
            }
            display.setCurrent(saveInfo,parent);
        }
        else if(c==deleteCommand) {
```

LISTING 8.10   Continued

```
                //create an alert
                Alert deleteInfo=
                    new Alert("Delete Appointment","",null,AlertType.INFO);
                deleteInfo.setTimeout(Alert.FOREVER);
                if(calendarDB.delete(app)) {
                    deleteInfo.setString("Success!");
                }
                else {
                    deleteInfo.setString("Fail!");
                }
                display.setCurrent(deleteInfo,parent);
            }
            else if(c==cancelCommand) {
                display.setCurrent(parent);
            }
        }
    }
}
```

All methods related to the record store are provided in the `CalendarDB` class in Listing 8.11. It uses a `calendarDB` record store to save all appointment records. (You can give the file any name you like.)

LISTING 8.11   `CalendarDB.java`

```
/*
 * CalendarDB.java
 *
 */

import java.io.*;
import java.util.*;
import javax.microedition.rms.*;

public class CalendarDB  {
    RecordStore rs=null;
    public CalendarDB () {
        //the file to store the db is "calendarDB"
        String file="calendarDB";
        try {
            // open a record store named file
            rs = RecordStore.openRecordStore(file,true);
```

LISTING 8.11 Continued

```java
        }catch(Exception e) {
            System.out.println("Error: "+e.getMessage());
        }
    }

    //close the record store
    public void close() {
        if(rs!=null) {
            try {
                rs.closeRecordStore();
            }catch (Exception e){}
        }
    }

    //delete a record
    public boolean delete(Appointment app) {
        boolean success=false;
        int id=app.getId();
        if(id==0) return false;

        try {
            rs.deleteRecord(id);
            success=true;
        }catch(Exception e) {}

        return success;
    }

    public Appointment getAppointmentById(int id) {
        Appointment app=null;
        try {
            byte data[]=rs.getRecord(id);
            app= new Appointment (id, data);
        }catch(Exception e) {}
        return app;
    }

    //retrieve all appointments
    public Vector retrieveAll() {
        RecordEnumeration re=null;
        Vector apps= new Vector();
        try {
            //cutoff is 90 days old
            long cutoff=System.currentTimeMillis()-
```

LISTING 8.11 Continued

```
                        new Integer(90).longValue()*24*60*60000;
        RecordFilter rf = new AppointmentFilter(cutoff);
        RecordComparator rc = new AppointmentComparator();
        re = rs.enumerateRecords(rf,rc,false);
        while(re.hasNextElement()) {
            int rec_id=re.nextRecordId();
            apps.addElement(new Appointment(rec_id,rs.getRecord(rec_id)));
        }
    }catch(Exception e) {}
    finally{
        //destroy the enumerator
        if(re!=null) re.destroy();
    }
    return apps;
}

//retrieve all appointments on a single date
public Vector retrieveAllByDate(Calendar calendar) {
    RecordEnumeration re=null;
    Vector apps= new Vector();
    try {
        RecordFilter rf = new AppointmentDateFilter(calendar);
        RecordComparator rc = new AppointmentComparator();
        re = rs.enumerateRecords(rf,rc,false);
        while(re.hasNextElement()) {
            int rec_id=re.nextRecordId();
            apps.addElement(new Appointment(rec_id,rs.getRecord(rec_id)));
        }
    }catch(Exception e) {}
    finally{
        //destroy the enumerator
        if(re!=null) re.destroy();
    }
    return apps;
}

//save an appointment (new and old)
public boolean save(Appointment app) {
    if(rs==null) return false;

    boolean success=false;
    try {
        byte[] data= app.toBytes();
        int id= app.getId();
```

LISTING 8.11   Continued

```
            if(id==0) {//create a new record
                id=rs.addRecord(data,0,data.length);
                app.setId(id);
            }
            else {//update the old record
                rs.setRecord(id, data, 0, data.length);
            }
            success=true;
        }catch(Exception e){
            System.out.println("Error: "+e.getMessage());
        }
        return success;
    }
}
```

A method to pack appointment fields into a byte array using UTF-8 encoding is added to the Appointment class. A method to construct an appointment from a UTF-8 encoded byte array is added as well. The updated Appointment.java is shown in Listing 8.12.

LISTING 8.12   Appointment.java

```
/*
 * Appointment.java
 *
 */

import java.util.Calendar;
import java.util.Date;
import java.util.Vector;
import java.io.DataInputStream;
import java.io.DataOutputStream;
import java.io.ByteArrayInputStream;
import java.io.ByteArrayOutputStream;
import javax.microedition.rms.*;


public class Appointment  {
    private int   id;
    private long time;
    private int length;
    private String location;
    private String subject;

    /* default constructor */
    public Appointment () {
```

LISTING 8.12 Continued

```
        id=0;
        time=0;
        length=0;
        location="";
        subject="";
    }

    public Appointment(int _id,long _time, int _length, String _location,
                    String _subject) {
        this();
        id=_id;
        time=_time;
        length=_length;
        location=_location;
        subject=_subject;
    }

    public Appointment(Date date) {
        this();
        time=date.getTime();
        length=30;
    }

    /* rec is the byte array saved in record store */
    public Appointment (int _id, byte[] rec) {
        id=_id;
        init_app(rec);
    }

    /* rec is the byte array saved in record store */
    public void init_app(byte[] rec) {
        // parse the record
        ByteArrayInputStream bais= new ByteArrayInputStream(rec);
        DataInputStream dis= new DataInputStream(bais);
        try {
            time=dis.readLong();
            length=dis.readInt();
            location=dis.readUTF();
            subject=dis.readUTF();
        }catch(Exception e){}
    }

    /* convert to the byte array that will be saved in the record store*/
    public byte[] toBytes() {
```

LISTING 8.12   Continued

```java
        byte data[]=null;
        try {
            ByteArrayOutputStream baos= new ByteArrayOutputStream();
            DataOutputStream dos= new DataOutputStream(baos);
            dos.writeLong(time);
            dos.writeInt(length);
            dos.writeUTF(location);
            dos.writeUTF(subject);
            data=baos.toByteArray();

            baos.close();
            dos.close();
        }catch(Exception e) {}
        return data;
    }

    /* get the appointment time in display format */
    public String getTimeString() {
        StringBuffer sb= new StringBuffer();
        Calendar cal= Calendar.getInstance();
        cal.setTime(new Date(time));
        sb.append(cal.get(Calendar.MONTH)+1).append("/");
        sb.append(cal.get(Calendar.DAY_OF_MONTH)).append("/");
        sb.append(cal.get(Calendar.YEAR)).append(" ");
        sb.append(cal.get(Calendar.HOUR_OF_DAY)).append(":");
        if(cal.get(Calendar.MINUTE)<10) sb.append(0);
        sb.append(cal.get(Calendar.MINUTE));

        return sb.toString();
    }

    public int  getId() {return id;}
    public void setId(int _id) { id=_id;}
    public long getTime() {return time;}
    public  void setTime(long _time){time=_time;}
    public int  getLength(){return length;}
    public void setLength(int _length) {length=_length;}
    public String getLocation() {return location;}
    public void setLocation(String _location){location=_location;}
    public String getSubject() {return subject;}
    public void setSubject(String _subject) {subject=_subject;}
}
```

The `SynchOption` setting is saved to a record store with the name `synchOption`. Methods to save a setting to the record store and to retrieve a setting from the record store are added to the updated `SynchOption.java` (see Listing 8.13).

LISTING 8.13   `SynchOption.java`

```java
import java.io.*;
import javax.microedition.rms.*;

public class SynchOption {
    private String url;
    private String user;
    private String passwd;
    private boolean autoSynch;
    private int     frequency;
    private String file="synchOption";

    public SynchOption(){
        //default value
        url="";
        user="";
        passwd="";
        autoSynch=false;
        frequency=0;

        RecordStore rs=null;
        try {
            // open a record store named file
            rs = RecordStore.openRecordStore(file,true);
            if(rs.getNumRecords()>0) {
                byte data[]=rs.getRecord(1);
                // parse the record
                ByteArrayInputStream bais= new ByteArrayInputStream(data);
                DataInputStream dis= new DataInputStream(bais);
                try {
                    url=dis.readUTF();
                    user=dis.readUTF();
                    passwd=dis.readUTF();
                    autoSynch=dis.readBoolean();
                    frequency=dis.readInt();
                }catch(Exception e) {}
                dis.close();
            }
        }catch(Exception e) {
            System.out.println("Error: "+e.getMessage());
```

LISTING 8.13 Continued

```java
        }finally {
            if(rs!=null) {
                try {
                    rs.closeRecordStore();
                }catch(Exception e) {}
            }
        }
    }

    public boolean save() {
        //convert to byte array
        byte data[]=null;
        try {
            ByteArrayOutputStream baos= new ByteArrayOutputStream();
            DataOutputStream dos= new DataOutputStream(baos);

            dos.writeUTF(url);
            dos.writeUTF(user);
            dos.writeUTF(passwd);
            dos.writeBoolean(autoSynch);
            dos.writeInt(frequency);
            data=baos.toByteArray();
            //close
            baos.close();
            dos.close();
        }catch(Exception e) {}

        boolean success=false;
        //save data to file
        RecordStore rs=null;
        try {
            // open a record store named file
            rs = RecordStore.openRecordStore(file,true);
            if(rs.getNumRecords()>0) {
                rs.setRecord(1, data, 0, data.length);
            }
            else {
                rs.addRecord(data,0,data.length);
            }
            success=true;
        }catch(Exception e) {
            System.out.println("Error: "+e.getMessage());
        }finally {
            if(rs!=null) {
```

LISTING 8.13   Continued

```
                try{
                    rs.closeRecordStore();
                }catch(Exception e) {}
            }
        }
        return success;
    }

    public String getUrl() {
        return url;
    }
    public String getUser() {
        return user;
    }
    public String getPasswd() {
        return passwd;
    }
    public boolean getAutoSynch() {
        return autoSynch;
    }
    public int getFrequency() {
        return frequency;
    }

    public void setUrl(String url) {
        this.url=url;
    }
    public void setUser(String user) {
        this.user=user;
    }
    public void setPasswd(String passwd) {
        this.passwd=passwd;
    }
    public void setAutoSynch(boolean autoSynch) {
        this.autoSynch=autoSynch;
    }
    public void setFrequency(int frequency) {
        this.frequency=frequency;
    }
}
```

8

PERSISTENT
STORAGE

In `MonthlyScheduleView.java`, developed in Chapter 7, a day that has appointments is highlighted in the viewer. From the viewer, you know a day has appointments; now, you want to know how many appointments are on that day and what they are. In `Scheduler.java`, a

Detail command is added to the MonthlyScheduleViewer object. If you click the Detail command, all appointments on the selected day will be retrieved and listed. The appointment filter that selects appointments on a single day is shown in Listing 8.14.

LISTING 8.14   AppointmentDateFilter.java

```java
/*
 * AppointmentDateFilter.java
 * Only the appointment that has the same date will match.
 */
import java.util.*;
import javax.microedition.rms.*;

public class AppointmentDateFilter implements RecordFilter{
    private long cutoff0;
    private long cutoff1;
    public AppointmentDateFilter (Calendar calendar) {
        long dayInMillis=24*60*60*1000;
        cutoff0=calendar.getTime().getTime()/dayInMillis*dayInMillis;
        cutoff1=cutoff0+dayInMillis;
    }

    public boolean matches(byte[] candidate) {
        Appointment app= new Appointment();
        app.init_app(candidate);

        if (app.getTime()>=cutoff0 && app.getTime()<cutoff1) {
            return true;
        }
        else {
            return false;
        }
    }
}
```

SynchOptionForm.java from Chapter 6 and MonthlyScheduleView.java from Chapter 7 are used in this application. We haven't modified them; thus, they are not listed here, but are included on this book's Web site.

Now you have a complete local application that can store, retrieve, and edit your appointments. All the appointments can be summarized in a list or be graphically presented in monthly calendar view. Suppose you have appointments as shown in Figure 8.3. If you go to the monthly schedule viewer, you will see a display like Figure 8.6. You can change the selected date to March 10, 2001 using the arrow keys; then, choose the Detail command. You will see the appointments on that day, as shown in Figure 8.7. From the list, you can edit or delete selected appointments.

FIGURE 8.6

Monthly schedule viewer. The days with appointments are highlighted.

FIGURE 8.7

Listing of appointments on a selected day.

To make the application more useful, it should have the ability to synchronize with your appointments stored on a networked data server. In later chapters, we will discuss network connections and XML. In Chapter 12, "Data Synchronization for Wireless Applications," this application will be converted to a network application with the addition of synchronization functions.

Summary

MIDP defines a record-oriented database, RMS, for storing persistent data. A set of APIs for managing the database is provided in the package `javax.microedition.rms`. This package defines a `RecordStore` class for representing a record store. Each record store is a file that functions similarly to a table in a database. Each record in a record store contains an integer `recordId` as its primary key and a byte array that holds data.

The `RecordStore` class provides methods for adding, modifying, and deleting records. The `RecordEnumeration` class provides methods to enumerate all records. Even though a record in a record store has only one data field, it can be used to store a record with multiple columns by using UTF-8 coding. In the `javax.microedition.rms` package, two interfaces (`RecordComparator` and `RecordFilter`) are provided for selecting and sorting records. Another interface, `RecordListener`, is provided for monitoring record changes in a record store.

Basic Network Programming in J2ME MIDP

IN THIS CHAPTER

Overview

The biggest advantages of a wireless device are its connectivity and accessibility. Wireless devices keep people connected to the outside world all the time and from virtually any place. The functionality of these wireless devices has changed significantly in the last couple of years, as increased wireless network coverage area, higher data transfer bandwidth, and improved wireless technology have become available. Cell phones are no longer just for conversation purposes; increasingly, they are becoming "mobile information devices" that allow people to access enterprise data and business/personal information in a timely fashion.

Network programming plays an important role in developing wireless applications that take advantage of the connectivity these devices have to offer. This chapter is intended to help you understand and learn the important concepts in network programming with J2ME MIDP. The first part of the chapter explains the main difference between network programming with J2SE and with J2ME.

Next, the concept of the Generic Connection framework is introduced and explained. The latter part of the chapter examines several sample MIDlet applications using different types of network communications available in the Generic Connection framework: namely, sockets (in the section "Wireless Network Programming Using Sockets"), datagrams ("Wireless Network Programming Using Datagrams"), and HTTP communication ("Wireless Network Programming Using `HttpConnection`").

Network Programming with J2SE Versus J2ME

For those who have developed network applications using Java 2 Standard Edition, network programming is fairly simple and straightforward; J2SE provides network libraries that are rich in functionality. Approximately 60 classes are available in the `java.io` package to support file input and output, and approximately 20 classes are available in the `java.net` package to support networking.

However, most of the classes in these two packages are designed to support traditional computer systems with enough CPU power, sufficient memory, and sufficient disk storage. The total static size of these class files is approximately 200 kilobytes. These packages are too big to fit in the typical wireless device, which has very limited computing power and a total memory and storage budget of a few hundred kilobytes.

Size is not the only issue when dealing with wireless devices. Java 2 Micro Edition needs to support a variety of mobile devices. The networking and file I/O capability varies significantly from one wireless device to another, so the requirements for networking and file I/O libraries are very different. For example, some wireless carriers use packet-switched networks, whereas others use circuit-switched networks. The difference between the two networks requires two different communication abstractions in Java libraries: datagram-based communication for packet-switched networks and socket-based communication for circuit-switched networks. Vendors that support datagram-based communication may not be interested in supporting socket-based connections and vice versa.

> **Note**
>
> A *circuit-switched network* creates telecommunication connections by setting up an end-to-end circuit. The circuit remains open for the duration of the communication, and a fixed share of network resources is tied up; no one else can use those resources until the connection is closed. The main advantage of a circuit-switched network is that performance guarantees can be offered.
>
> A *packet-switched network* creates telecommunication connections by breaking up the information to be sent into packets of bytes, sending them along a network with other information streams, and reassembling the original information flow at the other end. The main advantage of a packet-switched network is that it makes very efficient use of fixed capacity. The disadvantage is that the quality of service of an information channel cannot be guaranteed.

The file I/O for wireless devices falls into a similar situation. These file accesses are highly device specific and require different implementations. Due to strict memory limitations, the vendors who support one type of file I/O mechanism generally do not want to support another.

The networking in J2ME has to be very flexible to support a variety of devices and has to be very device specific at the same time. To meet these challenges, the Generic Connection framework is first introduced in the CLDC. The idea of the Generic Connection framework is to define the abstractions of the networking and file I/O as generally as possible to support a broad range of handheld devices, and leave the actual implementations of these abstractions to individual device manufacturers. These abstractions are defined as Java interfaces. The device manufacturers choose which one to implement in their MIDP implementations or PDAP implementations based on the actual device capabilities.

The Generic Connection Framework

The Generic Connection framework is introduced in J2ME's CLDC to reflect the requirements of small-footprint networking and file I/O for a broad range of mobile devices.

To meet the small-footprint requirement, the Generic Connection framework generalizes the functionality of J2SE's network and file I/O classes from J2SE's `java.io` and `jave.net` packages. It is a precise functional subset of J2SE classes, but much smaller in size. These J2ME classes and interfaces are all included in a single package, `javax.microedition.io`.

9

BASIC NETWORK
PROGRAMMING IN
J2ME MIDP

To meet the extendibility and flexibility requirement, the Generic Connection framework uses a set of related abstractions for different forms of communications, represented by seven connection interfaces: `Connection`, `ContentConnection`, `DatagramConnection`, `InputConnection`, `OutputConnection`, `StreamConnection`, and `StreamConnectionNotifier`.

The Generic Connection framework supports the following basic forms of communications. All the connections are created by one common method, `Connector.open()`:

HTTP:

```
Connector.open("http://www.webyu.com");
```

Sockets:

```
Connector.open("socket://localhost:80");
```

Datagrams:

```
Connector.open("datagram://www.webyu.com:9000");
```

Serial Port:

```
Connector.open("comm:0;baudrate=9600");
```

File:

```
Connector.open("file:/foo.dat");
```

This flexible design makes adding a new form of communication much easier without causing major structural changes to the class libraries.

Figure 9.1 shows the hierarchical relationships between these connection interfaces.

Connection Interfaces

As shown in Figure 9.1, `Connection` is the base interface, the root of the connection interface hierarchy. All the other connection interfaces derive from `Connection`. `StreamConnection` derives from `InputConnection` and `OutputConnection`. It defines both the input and output capabilities for a stream connection. `ContentConnection` derives from `StreamConnection`. It adds three methods for MIME data handling to the input and output methods in `StreamConnection`. Finally, `HttpConnection` derives from `ContentConnection`.

The `HttpConnection` is not part of the Generic Connection framework. Instead, it is defined in the MIDP specification that is targeted at cellular phones and two-way pagers. `HttpConnection` contains methods and constants specifically to support the HTTP 1.1 protocol. The `HttpConnection` interface must be implemented by all MIDP implementations, which means the `HttpConnection` will be a concrete class in the actual MIDP implementations. The http communication capability is expected to be available on all MIDP devices.

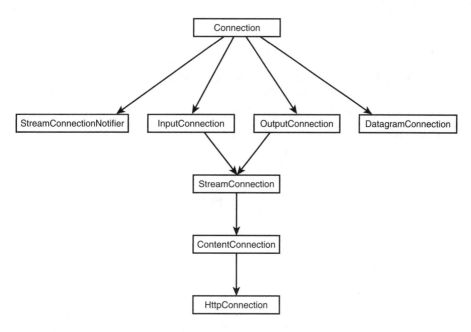

FIGURE 9.1

The connection interface hierarchy.

Why are these connections defined as interfaces instead of concrete classes? Because the Generic Connection framework specifies only the basic framework of how these connection interfaces should be implemented. The actual implementations are left to individual device manufacturers' profile implementations (MIDP or PDAP). As discussed in the previous section, individual device manufacturers may be interested in implementing only a subset of these connection interfaces based on the capabilities of their devices. The documentation of each manufacturer's J2ME MIDP SDK should indicate which connection interfaces are implemented and which are not.

Creating Network Connections

So far we have talked about the different kinds of connections. You may wonder how the connections are created and how to use them.

The Connector class is the core of the Generic Connection framework, because all connections are created by the static open() method in the Connector class. Different types of communication are created from the same method. The connection type can be file I/O, serial port communication, datagram connection, or an HTTP connection, depending on the string parameter passed to the method. Such a design makes the J2ME implementation more extensible and flexible in supporting new devices and product.

The method's signature is as follows:

```
Connection open(String connect_string)
```

The `connect_string` has a format of `{protocol}:[{target}][{params}]`, which is similar to the commonly used URL format, such as `http://www.somewhere.com`. It consists of three parts: `protocol`, `target`, and `params`.

`protocol` dictates what type of connection will be created by the `open()` method. There are several possible values for `protocol`, as listed in Table 9.1.

TABLE 9.1 Protocol Values

Value	Connection Usage
file	File I/O
comm	Serial port communication
socket	TCP/IP socket communication
datagram	Datagram communication
http	Accessing Web servers

`target` can be a hostname, a network port number, a file name, or a communication port number.

`params` is optional. It specifies the additional information needed to complete the connect string.

The following examples demonstrate how to use the `open()` method to create different types of communication based on different protocols:

HTTP communication:

```
Connection hc = Connector.open("http://www.webyu.com")
```

Socket communication:

```
Connection sc = Connector.open("socket://localhost:9000")
```

Datagram communication:

```
Connection dc = Connector.open("datagram://www.webyu.com:9000")
```

Serial port communication:

```
Connection cc = Connector.open("comm:0;baudrate=9000")
```

File I/O:

```
Connection fc = Connector.open("file:/foo.dat")
```

> **NOTE**
>
> Actual support for these protocols varies from vendor to vendor. Of all the J2ME MIDP implementations we have evaluated (Sun's J2ME Wireless Toolkit, MotoSDK from Motorola, and RIMSDK from Research in Motion), MotoSDK supports all three networking protocols that we are concerned with in this chapter: `socket` (TCP/IP), `datagram` (UDP), and `http` (HTTP). For this reason, all the sample codes in this chapter are compiled and run under MotoSDK (release 0.7).
>
> A `ConnectionNotFoundException` will be thrown if your MIDlet program tries to create a connection based on a protocol that is not supported by your device manufacturer's MIDP implementation.
>
> Even though we said that Sun's J2ME Wireless Toolkit only supports the http communication, there is actually an undocumented feature that will let you run socket or datagram programs under the Toolkit if you set the environment variable `ENABLE_CLDC_PROTOCOLS=INTUITIVE_TOOLKIT`. Because it is an undocumented feature that is not officially supported by Sun, we chose not to use Sun's J2ME Wireless Toolkit to run our samples in this chapter.

The Methods in the `Connector` Class

This section takes a close look at the `Connector` class. The `Connector` class is the only concrete class in Generic Connection framework in CLDC. It contains seven `static` methods:

```
static Connection open(String connectString)
```

This method creates and opens a new `Connection` based on the `connectString`.

```
static Connection open(String connectString, int mode)
```

This method creates and opens a new `Connection` based on the `connectString`. The additional `mode` parameter specifies the access mode for the connection. There are three access modes: `Connector.READ`, `Connector.READ_WRITE`, and `Connector.WRITE`. If mode is not specified, the default value is `Connector.READ_WRITE`. The validity of the actual setting is protocol dependent. If the access mode is not allowed for a protocol, an `IllegalArgumentException` will be thrown.

```
static Connection open(String connectString, int mode, boolean timeouts)
```

This method creates and opens a new `Connection` based on the `connectString`. The additional `timeouts` parameter is a Boolean flag that dictates whether the method will throw a timeout exception `InterruptedIOException`. The default `timeouts` value is `false`, which indicates that no exception will be thrown.

```
static DataInputStream openDataInputStream(String connectString)
```

This method creates and opens a new `DataInputStream` based on the `connectString`.

```
static DataOutputStream openDataOutputStream(String connectString)
```

This method creates and opens a `DataOutputStream` from the `connectString`.

```
static InputStream openInputStream(String connectString)
```

This method creates and opens a new `InputStream` from the `connectString`.

```
static OutputStream openOutputStream(String connectString)
```

This method creates and opens a new `OutputStream` from the `connectString`.

The last four I/O stream-creation methods combine creating the connection and opening the input/output stream into one step. For example, the following statement

```
DataInputStream dis = Connector.openDataInputStream(http://www.webyu.com);
```

is the equivalent of the following two statements:

```
InputConnection ic = (InputConnection)
  Connector.open("http://www.webyu.com", Connector.READ, false);
DataInputStream dis = ic.openDataInputStream();
```

An `IllegalArgumentException` will be thrown if a malformed `connectString` is received. A `ConnectionNotFoundException` will be thrown if the protocol specified in `connectString` is not supported. An `IOException` will be thrown for other types of I/O errors.

Listing 9.1 contains an example of how an http connection is created and how a `DataInputStream` is opened on top of the connection.

LISTING 9.1   Listing1.txt

```
/**
 * This sample code block demonstrates how to open an
 * http connection, how to establish an InputStream from
 * this http connection, and how to free them up after use.
 **/

// include the networking class libraries
import javax.microedition.io.*;
// include the I/O class libraries
import java.io.*;

// more code here ...

// define the connect string with protocol: http
// and hostname: 64.28.105.110
String connectString = "http://64.28.105.110";
```

LISTING 9.1 Continued

```
InputConnection hc = null;
DataInputStream dis = null;

// IOException must be caught when Connector.open() is called
try {
    // an http connection is established with read access.
    // The returned object is cast into an InputConnection object.
    hc = (InputConnection)
      Connector.open(connectString, Connector.READ, false);

    // an InputStream is created on top of the InputConnection
    // object for read operations.
    dis = hc.openDataInputStream();

    // perform read operations here ...

} catch (IOException e) {
    System.err.println("IOException:" + e);
} finally {
    // free up the I/O stream after use
    try { if (dis != null ) dis.close(); }
    catch (IOException ignored) {}

    // free up the connection after use
    try { if ( hc != null ) hc.close(); }
    catch (IOException ignored) {}
}

// more code here ...
```

Connection Interfaces

This section takes a look at all the connection interfaces defined in the
javax.microedition.io package including the seven connections from the Generic
Connection framework in CLDC and the HttpConnection in MIDP:

```
Connection
ContentConnection
DatagramConnection
InputConnection
OutputConnection
StreamConnection
StreamConnectionNotifier
HttpConnection
```

Connection

The Connection interface has one method:

```
void close()
```

This method closes the connection.

InputConnection

The InputConnection interface has two methods:

```
DataInputStream openDataInputStream()
```

This method opens a data input stream from the connection.

```
InputStream openInputStream()
```

This method opens an input stream from the connection.

OutputConnection

The OutputConnection interface has two methods:

```
DataOutputStream openDataOutputStream()
```

This method opens a data output stream from the connection.

```
OutputStream openOutputStream()
```

This method opens an output stream from the connection.

DatagramConnection

The DatagramConnection interface is used to create a datagram for a UDP communication. More details regarding this interface are discussed in the section "Wireless Network Programming Using Datagrams." This interface has eight methods:

```
int getMaximumLength()
```

This method returns the maximum length that is allowed for a datagram packet.

```
int getNominalLength()
```

This method returns the nominal length for datagram packets.

```
Datagram newDatagram(byte[] buf, int size)
```

This method creates a new Datagram object. buf is the placeholder for the data packet, and size is the length of the buffer to be allocated for the Datagram object.

```
Datagram newDatagram(byte[] buf, int size, String addr)
```

This method creates a new Datagram object. The additional parameter addr specifies the destination of this datagram message. It is in the format
{protocol}://[{host}]:{port}.

```
Datagram newDatagram(int size)
```

This method creates a new `Datagram` object with an automatically allocated buffer with length `size`.

```
Datagram newDatagram(int size, String addr)
```

This method creates a new `Datagram` object. `addr` specifies the destination of this datagram message.

```
void receive(Datagram dgram)
```

This method receives a `Datagram` object dgram from the remote host.

```
void send(Datagram dgram)
```

This method sends a `Datagram` object dgram to the remote host.

StreamConnection

The `StreamConnection` interface offers both send and receive capabilities for socket-based communication. All four of its methods are inherited from `InputConnection` and `OutputConnection`:

```
DataInputStream openDataInputStream()
InputStream openInputStream()
DataOutputStream openDataOutputStream()
OutputStream openOutputStream()
```

StreamConnectionNotifier

The `StreamConnectionNotifier` interface has one method:

> ```
> StreamConnection acceptAndOpen()
> ```
>
> This method returns a `StreamConnection` that represents a server-side socket connection to communicate with a client.

ContentConnection

The `ContentConnection` interface extends from `StreamConnection` and adds three methods to determine an HTTP stream's character encoding, MIME type, and size:

> ```
> String getEncoding()
> ```
>
> This method returns the value of the `content-encoding` in the HTTP header of an HTTP stream.
>
> ```
> long getLength()
> ```
>
> This method returns the value of the `content-length` in the HTTP header of an HTTP stream.
>
> ```
> String getType()
> ```
>
> This method returns the value of the `content-type` in the HTTP header of an HTTP stream.

The methods inherited from `StreamConnection` are as follows:

```
DataInputStream openDataInputStream()
InputStream openInputStream()
DataOutputStream openDataOutputStream()
OutputStream openOutputStream()
```

HttpConnection

The `HttpConnection` extends from `ContentConnection`. It adds the following methods to support the HTTP 1.1 protocol:

```
long getDate()
long getExpiration()
String getFile()
String getHeaderField(int index)
String getHeaderField(String name)
long getHeaderFieldDate(String name, long def)
int getHeaderFieldInt(String name, int def)
String getHeaderFieldKey(int n)
String getHost()
long getLastModified()
int getPort()
String getProtocol()
String getQuery()
String getRef()
String getRequestMethod()
String getRequestProperty(String key)
int getResponseCode()
String getResponseMessage()
String getURL()
void setRequestMethod(String method)
void setRequestProperty(String key, String value)
```

The `HttpConnection` interface is mandatory for all MIDP vendor implementations. However, the underlying support mechanisms could be different from vendor to vendor. Some vendors may support the HTTP stack on top of non-IP–based protocols such as WSP transport or TL/PDC-P, and other vendors may use HTTP over TCP/IP. To support the HTTP protocol on MIDP devices, non-IP networks may have to install gateways in order to convert HTTP requests from the wireless network format to a TCP/IP format to be able to access the Internet.

Figure 9.2 illustrates the possible implementations of `HttpConnection`, based on different wireless network infrastructures.

The section "Wireless Network Programming Using `HttpConnection`" discusses `HttpConnection` in detail.

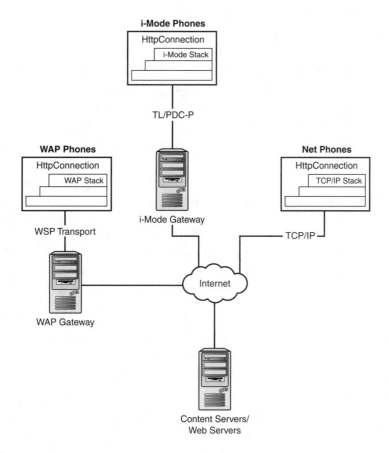

FIGURE 9.2

Implementations of HttpConnection *on different underlying transports.*

Wireless Network Programming Using Sockets

A *socket* is one end-point of a two-way communication link between programs running on the network. A socket connection is the most basic low-level reliable communication mechanism between a wireless device and a remote server or between two wireless devices. The socket communication capability provided with some of the mobile devices in J2ME enables a variety of client/server applications. Using the socket connection to SMTP and POP3 servers, an e-mail client on wireless devices can send or receive regular Internet e-mail messages.

Socket use gives J2ME developers the flexibility to develop all kinds of network applications for wireless devices. However, not every wireless manufacturer supports socket communication in MIDP devices, which means that wireless applications developed using sockets could be limited to certain wireless devices and are less likely to be portable across different types of wireless networks.

To use a socket, the sender and receiver that are communicating must first establish a connection between their sockets. One will be listening for a request for a connection, and the other will be asking for a connection. Once two sockets have been connected, they may be used for transmitting data in either direction.

To receive data from the remote server, `InputConnection` has to be established and an `InputStream` must be obtained from the connection. To send data to the remote server, `OutputConnection` has to be established and an `OutputStream` must be obtained from the connection. In J2ME, three types of connections are defined to handle input/output streams: `InputConnection`, `OutputConnection`, and `StreamConnection`. As the names indicate, `InputConnection` defines the capabilities for input streams to receive data and `OutputConnection` defines the capabilities for output streams to send data. `StreamConnection` defines the capabilities for both input and output streams. When to use which connection depends on whether the data needs to be sent, received, or both.

Network programming using sockets is very straightforward in J2ME. The process works as follows:

1. A socket connection is opened with a remote server or another wireless device using `Connector.open()`.

2. `InputStream` or `OutputStream` is created from the socket connection for sending or receiving data packets.

3. Data can be sent to and received from the remote server via the socket connection by performing read or write operations on the `InputStream` or `OutputStream` object.

4. The socket connection and input or output streams must be closed before exiting the program.

The example in Listing 9.2 demonstrates how a socket connection is created and how a `DataOutputStream` is opened on top of the connection.

LISTING 9.2 Listing2.txt

```
/**
 * This sample code block demonstrates how to open a
 * socket connection, how to establish a DataOutputStream
 * from this socket connection, and how to free them up
 * after use.
 **/

// include the networking class libraries
import javax.microedition.io.*;
```

LISTING 9.2   Continued

```java
// include the I/O class libraries
import java.io.*;

// more code here ...

// define the connect string with protocol: socket,
// hostname: 64.28.105.110, and port number: 80
String connectString = "socket://64.28.105.110:80";
OutputConnection sc = null;
DataOutputStream dos = null;

// IOException must be caught when Connector.open() is called.
try {
    // a socket connection is established with the remote server.
    sc = (OutputConnection) Connector.open(socketUrlString);

    // an OutputStream is created on top of the OutputConnection
    // object for write operations.
    dos = sc.openDataOutputStream();

    // perform write operations that send data to the remote server ...

} catch (IOException e) {
    System.err.println("IOException caught:" + e)
} finally {
    // free up the I/O stream after use
    try { if (dos != null ) dos.close(); }
    catch (IOException ignored) {}

    // free up the socket connection after use
    try { if ( sc != null ) sc.close(); }
    catch (IOException ignored) {}
}

// more code here ...
```

9

BASIC NETWORK
PROGRAMMING IN
J2ME MIDP

In this example, a socket connection is established with remote server 64.28.105.110 on port 80. Port 80 is the well-known port for HTTP service. Note that we are using the socket connection to communicate with the remote server; therefore, the protocol is specified as socket. The DataOutputStream is then created on the top of the connection for sending requests to the remote server.

Sample Program

The sample program in Listing 9.3 creates a Web client session to request a page from a Web server on the Internet. Figure 9.3 illustrates the program flow of a Web client implemented using socket connections.

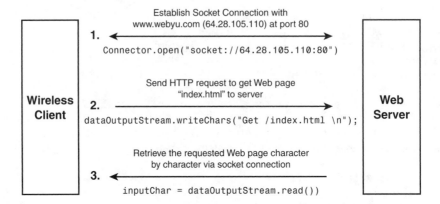

FIGURE 9.3

The program flow of a Web client implemented with sockets.

LISTING 9.3   SocketExample.java

```java
/**
 * The following MIDlet application creates socket connection with
 * a remote Web server at port 80, and then sends an HTTP request
 * to retrieve the Web page "index.html" via the connection.
 */

// include MIDlet class libraries
import javax.microedition.midlet.*;
// include networking class libraries
import javax.microedition.io.*;
// include GUI class libraries
import javax.microedition.lcdui.*;
// include I/O class libraries
import java.io.*;

public class SocketExample extends MIDlet {
    // StreamConnection allows bidirectional communication
    private StreamConnection streamConnection = null;
```

LISTING 9.3   Continued

```java
// use OutputStream to send requests
private OutputStream outputStream = null;
private DataOutputStream dataOutputStream = null;

// use InputStream to receive responses from Web server
private InputStream inputStream = null;
private DataInputStream dataInputStream = null;

// specify the connect string
private String connectString = "socket://64.28.105.110:80";

// use a StrignBuffer to store the retrieved page contents
private StringBuffer results;

// define GUI components
private Display myDisplay = null;
private Form resultScreen;
private StringItem resultField;

public SocketExample() {
    // initializing GUI display
    results = new StringBuffer();
    myDisplay = Display.getDisplay(this);
    resultScreen = new Form("Page Content:");
}

public void startApp() {
    try {
        // establish a socket connection with remote server
        streamConnection =
        (StreamConnection) Connector.open(connectString);

        // create DataOuputStream on top of the socket connection
        outputStream = streamConnection.openOutputStream();
        dataOutputStream = new DataOutputStream(outputStream);

        // send the HTTP request
        dataOutputStream.writeChars("GET /index.html \n");
        dataOutputStream.flush();

        // create DataInputStream on top of the socket connection
        inputStream = streamConnection.openInputStream();
        dataInputStream = new DataInputStream(inputStream);

        // retrieve the contents of the requested page from Web server
        int inputChar;
```

LISTING 9.3 Continued

```
        while ( (inputChar = dataInputStream.read()) != -1) {
            results.append((char) inputChar);
        }

        // display the page contents on the phone screen
        resultField = new StringItem(null, results.toString());
        resultScreen.append(resultField);
        myDisplay.setCurrent(resultScreen);

    } catch (IOException e) {
        System.err.println("Exception caught:" + e);
    } finally {
        // free up I/O streams and close the socket connection
        try {
            if (dataInputStream != null)
                dataInputStream.close();
        } catch (Exception ignored) {}
        try {
            if (dataOutputStream != null)
                dataOutputStream.close();
        } catch (Exception ignored) {}
        try {
            if (outputStream != null)
                outputStream.close();
        } catch (Exception ignored) {}
        try {
            if (inputStream != null)
                inputStream.close();
        } catch (Exception ignored) {}
        try {
            if (streamConnection != null)
                streamConnection.close();
        } catch (Exception ignored) {}
    }
}

public void pauseApp() {
}

public void destroyApp(boolean unconditional) {
}
}
```

The program first opens a socket connection with the Web server www.webyu.com at port 80. It sends an HTTP request to the Web server using the DataOutputStream established from the connection. It receives the requested content from the Web server using the DataInputStream opened from the connection. After the Web page content is completely received, the content is displayed on the emulator.

Because the program needs to perform bidirectional communication between a cell phone and a Web server, StreamConnection is used to support both the send and receive operations.

Figure 9.4 illustrates a screen shot of the Web page content displayed on the Motorola iDEN 3000 Emulator.

FIGURE 9.4

A screenshot of SocketExample.java.

So far, we have talked about how to develop wireless applications using sockets. The previous example used a socket connection to communicate with a Web server to retrieve a Web document. The next section examines how to develop J2ME applications using datagram connections to communicate with a remote server or another wireless device. This datagram communication is based on the UDP protocol.

NOTE

If you are interested in more information about different network protocols, the full specifications for UDP, TCP/IP, and HTTP can be found online at
http://info.internet.isi.edu/1/in-notes/rfc.

Wireless Network Programming Using Datagrams

A *datagram* is an independent, self-contained message sent over the network; the datagram's arrival, arrival time, and content are not guaranteed. It is a packet-based communication mechanism. Unlike stream-based communication, packet-based communication is connectionless, which means that no dedicated open connection exists between the sender and the receiver.

Packet-switched wireless networks are more likely to support this type of communication on MIDP devices. Datagrams may not be supported by circuit-switched wireless networks, which means that wireless applications developed with datagrams might be limited to certain devices and are less likely to be portable across different networks.

UDP

Datagram communication is based on UDP. The sender builds a datagram packet with destination information (an Internet address and a port number) and sends it out. Lower-level network layers do not perform any sequencing, error checking, or acknowledgement of packets. So, there is no guarantee that a data packet will arrive at its destination. The server might never receive your initial datagram—moreover, if it does, its response might never reach your wireless device. Because UDP is a not a guaranteed-delivery protocol, it is not suitable for applications such as FTP that require reliable transmission of data. However, it is useful in the following cases:

- When raw speed of the communication is more critical than transmitting every bit correctly. For example, in a real-time wireless audio/video application on a cell phone, lost data packets simply appear as static. Static is much more tolerable than awkward pauses (when socket data transmission is used) in the audio stream.

- When information needs to be transmitted on a frequent basis. In this case, losing a communication packet now and then doesn't affect the service significantly.

- When socket communication is not supported at all, which is most likely the case in a packet-switched wireless network.

Using Datagrams

Here are the typical steps for using datagram communication in MIDlet applications:

1. Establish a datagram connection.
2. Construct a send datagram object with a message body and a destination address.
3. Send the datagram message out through the established datagram connection.
4. Construct a receive datagram object with a pre-allocated buffer.

5. Wait to receive the message through the established connection using the allocated datagram buffer.

6. Free up the datagram connection after use.

The following are rules of thumb for choosing a datagram size:

*   Never exceed the maximum allowable packet size. The maximum allowable packet size can be obtained by using the method `GetMaximumLength()` in the `DatagramConnection` interface (discussed earlier in the section "The Generic Connection Framework"). This number varies from vendor to vendor.

*   If the wireless network is very reliable and most of the data transmitted will arrive at the destination, use a bigger packet size. The bigger the packet size, the more efficient the data transfer, because the datagram header causes significant overhead when the packet size is too small.

*   If the wireless network is not very reliable, packets will probably be dropped during transmission. Use a smaller packet size so that they are unlikely to be corrupted in transit.

`DatagramConnection` and `Datagram` Classes

J2ME network programming with datagrams is very similar to J2SE. Two classes are defined in J2ME to support datagram communication: `DatagramConnection` and `Datagram`.

`DatagramConnection` is one of the connection interfaces in the Generic Network framework. It defines methods to support network communication based on the UDP protocol. (These methods were discussed in the section "The Generic Connection Framework" earlier in this chapter.)

`Datagram` provides a placeholder for a datagram message. A `Datagram` object can then be sent or received through a `DatagramConnection`.

The `Datagram` class extends from the `DataInput` and `DataOutput` classes in the `java.io` package. These classes provide methods for the necessary read and write operations to the binary data stored in the datagram's buffer.

`Datagram` also defines several UDP-specific methods in addition to the methods inherited from `DataInput` and `DataOutput`. These methods are as follows:

```
String getAddress()
```
This method returns the destination address in a datagram message.

```
byte[] getData()
```
This method returns the data buffer for a datagram message.

9

BASIC NETWORK PROGRAMMING IN J2ME MIDP

```
int getLength()
```

This method returns the length of the data buffer.

```
int getOffset()
```

This method returns the offset position in the data buffer.

```
void reset()
```

This method resets the read/write pointer to the beginning of the data structure.

```
void setAddress(Datagram ref)
```

This method gets the destination address from `ref` and assigns it to the current `Datagram` object.

```
void setAddress(String addr)
```

This method sets the destination address using `addr`. The address string is in the format `{protocol}://[{host}]:{port}`.

```
void setData(byte[] buffer, int offset, int len)
```

This method sets the data buffer, offset, and length for the `Datagram` object.

```
void setLength(int len)
```

This method sets a new length for its data buffer.

The following methods in the `Datagram` class are inherited from `DataInput` for reading binary data from its data buffer:

```
boolean readBoolean()
byte readByte()
char readChar()
void readFully(byte[] b)
void readFully(byte[] b, int off, int len)
int readInt()
long readLong()
short readShort()
int readUnsignedByte()
int readUnsignedShort()
String readUTF()
int skipBytes(int n)
```

The following methods in the `Datagram` class are inherited from `DataOutput` for writing binary data to the datagram's data buffer:

```
void write(byte[] b)
void write(byte[] b, int off, int len)
void write(int b)
void writeBoolean(boolean v)
void writeByte(int v)
void writeChar(int v)
```

```
void writeChars(String s)
void writeInt(int v)
void writeLong(long v)
void writeShort(int v)
void writeUTF(String str)
```

Datagram Connections

To use datagram communication in a J2ME application, a datagram connection has to be opened first. Here is how to do that:

```
DatagramConnection dc = (DatagramConnection)
   Connector.open("datagram://localhost:9000");
```

Like other types of connections, a datagram connection is created with the open method in Connector. The connect string is in this format:

```
datagram://[{host}]:{port}
```

In the connect string, the port field is required; it specifies the target port with a host. The host field is optional; it specifies the target host. If the host field is missing in the connection string, the connection is created in "server" mode. Otherwise, the connection is created in "client" mode.

For example, here is how a "server" mode datagram connection is created:

```
DatagramConnection dc = (DatagramConnection)
   Connector.open("datagram://:9000");
```

This is the equivalent of the following:

```
DatagramConnection dc = (DatagramConnection)
   Connector.open("datagram://localhost:9000");
```

A "server" mode connection means that the connection can be used both for sending and receiving datagrams via the same port. In the previous example, the program can receive and send datagrams on port 9000.

A "client" mode datagram connection is created with host specified in the connect string:

```
DatagramConnection dc = (DatagramConnection)
   Connector.open("datagram://64.28.105.110:9000");
```

A "client" mode connection can be used only for sending datagram messages. The datagram to be sent must have the destination host and port; in this case, the host is 64.28.105.110 and the target port is 9000. When a datagram message is sent with a client mode connection, the reply-to port is always allocated dynamically.

Once a `DatagramConnection` is established, datagram messages can be sent and received using the `send` and `receive` methods.

The example in Listing 9.4 shows how to use datagrams to communicate with a remote server:

LISTING 9.4   Listing4.txt

```
/**
 * This sample code block demonstrates how a "server" mode
 * DatagramConnection is created, and how datagram
 * messages are sent and received via the connection.
 * For demostration purpose, we assume that the remote server
 * listens to port 9000 for incoming datagrams and responses
 * back with a datagram message once the incoming datagram is
 * received.. Once the message is received.
 */

import javax.microedition.io.*;
import java.io.*;
import java.lang.*;

// more code here ...

// the destination address of the datagram message to be sent.
String destAddr = "datagram://64.28.105.110:9000";

// the message string to be sent
String messageString = "REQUEST INFO";

// the DatagramConnection to be used for exchanging message with remote server
DatagramConnection datagramConnection = null;

try {
    // create a "server" mode DatagramConnection
    datagramConnection =
      (DatagramConnection) Connector.open("datagram://:9000");

    // get the length of the datagram message
    int length = messageString.length();

    byte[] messageBytes = new byte[length];

    // store the message string into a byte array
    System.arraycopy(messageString.getBytes(), 0, messageBytes, 0, length);

    // construct a Datagram object to be sent with the message byte array,
    // length of the byte array, and the destination address
```

LISTING 9.4 Continued

```
Datagram sendDatagram =
datagramConnection.newDatagram(messageBytes, length, destAddr);

// send the Datagram object to its destination
datagramConnection.send(sendDatagram);

// create a Datagram object as a place holder for receiving message
receiveDatagram = datagramConnection.newDatagram(

datagramConnection.getMaximumLength());

// wait for Datagram sent back from remote server
datagramConnection.receive(receiveDatagram);

// do something with the received Datagram ...

} catch (IOException e) {
    System.err.println("IOException Caught:" + e);
} finally {
    // free up open connection
    try { if (dc != null) dc.close();
    } catch (Exception ignored) {}
}

// more code here ...
```

Sample Program

The following sample application demonstrates datagram communication between two cell phones. It consists of two programs: DatagramClient.java and DatagramServer.java. They are running on separate emulators. DatagramClient initiates a message, sends it out to DatagramServer using port 9000, and uses the same port to receive the response back. DatagramServer receives the message sent from the DatagramClient at port 9001, reverses the message string, and sends the reversed message back to the client. In this example, the client and server programs are running on separate emulators on the same machine. But, this process could just as easily occur across the Internet.

Figure 9.5 illustrates the program flow between two J2ME programs communicating with each other using datagrams.

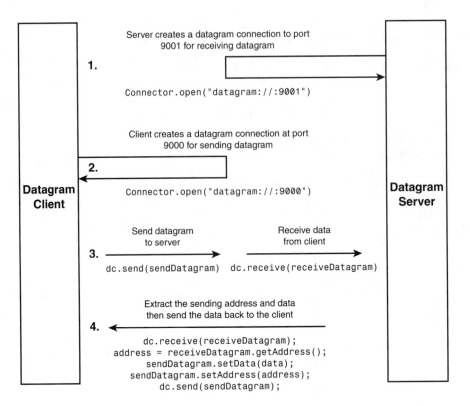

FIGURE 9.5

The program flow of the datagram sample application.

The code of the client program can be found in Listing 9.5, and the code of the server program can be found in Listing 9.6.

LISTING 9.5   `DatagramClient.java`

```
/**
 * The following MIDlet application is a datagram client program
 * that exchanges datagram  with another MIDlet application acting
 * as a datagram server program.
 */

// include MIDlet class libraries
import javax.microedition.midlet.*;
// include networking class libraries
import javax.microedition.io.*;
// include GUI class libraries
```

Listing 9.5   Continued

```java
import javax.microedition.lcdui.*;
// include I/O class libraries
import java.io.*;

public class DatagramClient extends MIDlet
implements CommandListener {
    // define the GUI components for entering the message text to be sent
    private Form mainScreen;
    private TextField sendingField;
    private Display myDisplay = null;
    private DatagramClientHandler client;

    // define the GUI components for displaying the returned message
    private Form resultScreen;
    private StringItem resultField;
    private String resultString;

    // the "send" button on the mainScreen
    Command sendCommand = new Command("SEND", Command.OK, 1);

    public DatagramClient(){
        // initialize the GUI components
        myDisplay = Display.getDisplay(this);
        mainScreen = new Form("Datagram Client");
        sendingField = new TextField(
        "Enter your message", null, 30, TextField.ANY);
        mainScreen.append(sendingField);
        mainScreen.addCommand(sendCommand);
        mainScreen.setCommandListener(this);
    }

    public void startApp() {
        myDisplay.setCurrent(mainScreen);
        client = new DatagramClientHandler();
    }

    public void pauseApp() {
    }

    public void destroyApp(boolean unconditional) {
    }

    public void commandAction(Command c, Displayable s) {
        if (c == sendCommand) {
```

LISTING 9.5   Continued

```java
            // get the message text from user input
            String sendMessage = sendingField.getString();

            // send and receive datagram messages
            try {
                resultString = client.send_receive(sendMessage);
            } catch (IOException e) {
                System.out.println("Failed in send_receive():" + e);
            }

            // display the returned message
            resultScreen = new Form("Message Confirmed:");
            resultField  = new StringItem(null, resultString);
            resultScreen.append(resultField);
            resultScreen.setCommandListener(this);
            myDisplay.setCurrent(resultScreen);
        }
    }

class DatagramClientHandler extends Object {
    private DatagramConnection dc;
    // Datagram object to be sent
    private Datagram sendDatagram;
    // Datagram object to be received
    private Datagram receiveDatagram;

    public DatagramClientHandler() {
        try {
            // establish a DatagramConnection at port 9000
            dc = (DatagramConnection)
              Connector.open("datagram://" +   ":9000");

            /* Since the datagram server program runs on the same machine
             * where the client program runs on, and the server program
             * listens to port 9001, the destination address of datagram
             * to be sent is set to "localhost:9001". If the server
             * program runs on a different machine, "localhost" in the
             * connect string needs to be replaced with that machine's ip
             * address.
             */
            sendDatagram = dc.newDatagram(
            dc.getMaximumLength(), "datagram://localhost:9001");

            // initialize the Datagram object to be received
            receiveDatagram = dc.newDatagram(dc.getMaximumLength());
```

LISTING 9.5 Continued

```
        } catch (IOException e) {
            System.out.println(e.toString());
        }
    }

    public String send_receive(String msg) throws IOException {
        int length = msg.length();
        byte[] message = new byte[length];

        // copy the send message text into a byte array
        System.arraycopy(msg.getBytes(), 0, message, 0, length);
        sendDatagram.setData(message, 0, length);
        sendDatagram.setLength(length);

        // use retval to store the received message text
        String retval = "";
        try {
            // send the message to server program
            dc.send(sendDatagram);

            // wait and receive message from the server
            dc.receive(receiveDatagram);

            // put the received message in a byte array
            byte[] data = receiveDatagram.getData();

            // transform the byte array to a string
            retval = new String(data, 0, receiveDatagram.getLength());
        } finally{
            if (dc != null) dc.close();
        }

        // return the received message text to the calling program
        return retval;
    }
  }
}
```

9

LISTING 9.6 DatagramServer.java

```
/**
 * The following MIDlet application is a datagram server program
 * that waits and receives datagram message from a client program,
 * reverses the message text, then sends the reversed text back to
```

LISTING 9.6   Continued

```java
 * the datagram client program.
 */

// include MIDlet class libraries
import javax.microedition.midlet.*;
// include networking class libraries
import javax.microedition.io.*;
// include GUI class libraries
import javax.microedition.lcdui.*;
// include I/O class libraries
import java.io.*;

public class DatagramServer extends MIDlet{
    // define the GUI components for displaying the received message
    private Display myDisplay = null;
    private Form mainScreen;
    private StringItem resultField;

    // text string for storing the received message
    private String resultString;

    public DatagramServer() {
        // initialize the GUI components
        myDisplay = Display.getDisplay(this);
        mainScreen = new Form("Message Received");
        resultField  = new StringItem(null, null);
    }

    public void startApp() {
        myDisplay.setCurrent(mainScreen);

        // perform the receive, reverse and send back tasks
        DatagramServerHandler server = new DatagramServerHandler();
        try {
            resultString = server.receive_reverse_send();
        } catch (IOException e) {
            System.out.println("Failed in receive_reverse_send():" + e);
        }

        // display the received message text
        resultField.setText(resultString);
        mainScreen.append(resultField);
    }

    public void pauseApp() {
    }
```

LISTING 9.6   Continued

```java
public void destroyApp(boolean unconditional) {
}

class DatagramServerHandler extends Object {
    // the server program listens to port 9001
    private static final String defaultPortNumber="9001";
    private String msg;
    private DatagramConnection dc;

    // define the Datagram objects for messages
    private Datagram sendDatagram;
    private Datagram receiveDatagram;

    public DatagramServerHandler() {
        try {
            // Create a "server" mode connection on the default port
            dc = (DatagramConnection)Connector.open(
            "datagram://:" + defaultPortNumber);

            // construct a Datagram object for receiving message
            receiveDatagram = dc.newDatagram(dc.getMaximumLength());

            // construct a Datagram object for sending message
            sendDatagram = dc.newDatagram(dc.getMaximumLength());

        } catch (Exception e) {
            System.out.println("Failed to initialize Connector");
        }
    }

    public String receive_reverse_send() throws IOException {
        String receiveString = "";
        try{
            // wait to receive datagram message
            dc.receive(receiveDatagram);

            // extract data from the Datagram object receiveDatagram
            byte[] receiveData = receiveDatagram.getData();
            int receiveLength = receiveDatagram.getLength();

            // store message text in receiveString
            receiveString = (new String(receiveData)).trim();

            // reverse the string
            StringBuffer reversedString =
            (new StringBuffer(receiveString)).reverse();
```

LISTING 9.6 Continued

```
                // getting the reply-to address from the Datagram object
                String address = receiveDatagram.getAddress();

                // construct the sendDatagram with the reversed text
                // and the reply-to address.
                int sendLength = reversedString.length();
                byte[] sendData = new byte[sendLength];
                System.arraycopy(reversedString.toString().getBytes(),
                0, sendData, 0, sendLength);
                sendDatagram.setData(sendData, 0, sendLength);
                sendDatagram.setAddress(address);

                // send the reversed string back to client program
                dc.send(sendDatagram);
            } finally {
                if (dc != null) dc.close();
            }
            return receiveString;
        }
    }
}
```

Figure 9.6 shows the client program before the message test message is sent to the server program. Figure 9.7 shows the server program after the message test message is received.

FIGURE 9.6

Before test message *is sent to the server.*

FIGURE 9.7

After test message *is received by the server.*

Figure 9.8 shows the client program after the reversed message string is received from the server program. The string test message is now egassem tset.

FIGURE 9.8

The reversed message egassem tset *is received from the server.*

Wireless Network Programming Using `HttpConnection`

The section "Wireless Network Programming Using Sockets," showed an example of using socket connections to communicate with a Web server using the HTTP protocol. The same thing can be done more easily with the `HttpConnection`, which is more closely tied to the HTTP protocol for communicating with Web servers. It defines several HTTP-specific methods to make HTTP-based network programming simpler and more straightforward. For example, `HttpConnection` provides methods that allow developers to obtain HTTP header information much easier.

Using `HttpConnection` as the network communication in your application offers several major advantages:

- Not every MIDP device supports socket and datagram communication. However, all MIDP devices support HTTP communication.

- Socket and datagram communications are very network dependent. Some networks may implement only one type of communication and not the other. This limitation makes your wireless application less portable.

- The mandatory support of the HTTP protocol in MIDP devices gives wireless application a high-level, standard, network-independent protocol to work with. Therefore, J2ME wireless applications developed using `HttpConnection` are very portable across different wireless networks.

- Different types of data can be encapsulated into HTTP requests easily, especially if developers use XML in their applications. Chapter 10, "Using XML in Wireless Applications," discusses in more detail how to use XML in wireless application development. HTTP communication makes it easier to deal with issues such as network security and firewalls. Because the HTTP's well-known port 80 is the least likely port blocked by firewalls.

Methods in `HttpConnection`

The `HttpConnection` interface supports a subset of the HTTP 1.1 protocol. Here are the methods defined in `HttpConnection`:

```
long getDate()
```
This method returns the value of the date field in the HTTP header. The result is the number of milliseconds since January 1, 1970, GMT.

```
long getExpiration()
```
This method returns the value of the expires field in the HTTP header. The result is the number of milliseconds since January 1, 1970, GMT. It returns 0 if the value is unknown.

```
String getFile()
```

This method returns the file portion of the URL of this `HttpConnection`. It returns `null` if there is no file.

```
String getHeaderField(int index)
```

This method returns the `String` value of a header field by `index`. It returns `null` if `index` is out of range. Because the HTTP headers returned by different Web servers are different, it is recommended that you check to see if the value is `null` before applying any operation on it. You have to know the sequence of the header fields to use this method.

```
String getHeaderField(String name)
```

This method returns the `String` value of a named header field. It returns `null` if the field is missing or malformed.

```
long getHeaderFieldDate(String name, long def)
```

This method returns the `long` value of a named header field. The value is parsed as a date. The result is the number of milliseconds since January 1, 1970, GMT. The default value `def` is returned if the field is missing or malformed.

```
int getHeaderFieldInt(String name, int def)
```

This method returns the `int` value of a named header field. The default value `def` is returned if the field is missing or malformed.

```
String getHeaderFieldKey(int index)
```

This method returns the name of a header field by index. It returns `null` if `index` is out of range. You have to know the sequence of the header fields to use this method.

```
String getHost()
```

This method returns the host information of the URL string.

```
long getLastModified()
```

This method returns the value of the `last-modified` field in the HTTP header. The result is the number of milliseconds since January 1, 1970, GMT. It returns `0` if the value is unknown.

```
int getPort()
```

This method returns the port number of the URL string. It returns `80` by default if there was no port number in the string passed to `Connector.open()`.

```
String getProtocol()
```

This method returns the protocol name of the URL string, such as `http` or `https`.

```
String getQuery()
```

This method returns the query portion of the URL string. In the HTTP protocol, a query component of a URL is defined as the text after the last question mark (?) character in the URL. For instance, the query portion of the URL string `http://64.28.105.110/servlets/webyu/Chapter9Servlet?request=gettimestamp` is `request=gettimestamp`.

```
String getRef()
```

This method returns the reference portion of the URL string. In the HTTP protocol, a reference component of a URL is defined as the text after the crosshatch character (#) in the URL. For instance, the reference portion of the URL string `http://64.28.105.110/index.html#top` is top.

```
String getRequestMethod()
```

This method returns the current request method of the `HttpConnection`. The possible values are GET, HEAD, and POST.

```
String getRequestProperty(String key)
```

This method returns the value of the general request property by the `key` property.

```
int getResponseCode()
```

This method returns the HTTP response status code. For instance

```
HTTP/1.1 200 OK
HTTP/1.1 401 Unauthorized
```

The method returns the integers 200 and 401, respectively, from the above responses.

```
String getResponseMessage()
```

This method returns the HTTP response message from a Web server. For instance, given the responses HTTP/1.1 200 **OK** and HTTP/1.1 401 **Unauthorized**, the method returns the strings OK and Unauthorized, respectively.

```
String getURL()
```

This method returns the URL string of this `HttpConnection`.

```
void setRequestMethod(String method)
```

This method sets the request method for this `HttpConnection`. The possible values are GET, POST, and HEAD. If not specified, the default HTTP request method is GET.

```
void setRequestProperty(String key, String value)
```

This method sets the general request property for this `HttpConnection`. For instance

```
setRequestProperty(
  "User-Agent",
  "Mozilla/5.001 (windows; U; NT4.0; en-us) Gecko/25250101");
```

sets a value for the request property "User-Agent" of an `HttpConnection`. If a property with the key already exists, the method overwrites its value with the new value.

The following methods are inherited from the `ContentConnection` interface:

```
String getEncoding()
long getLength()
String getType()
DataInputStream openDataInputStream()
InputStream openInputStream()
DataOutputStream openDataOutputStream()
OutputStream openOutputStream()
```

HttpConnection States

There are two possible states for an HTTP connection: Setup and Connected.

In the Setup state, the connection has not been made to the server. In the Connected state, the connection has been made, request parameters have been sent, and the response is expected in the Connected state.

The transition from the Setup state to the Connected state is caused by any method that requires data to be sent to or received from the server. The following methods cause the transition to the Connected state from a Setup state:

```
openInputStream()
openDataInputStream()
openOutputStream()
openDataOutputStream()
oetLength()
oetType()
oetEncoding()
getDate()
getExpiration()
getLastModified()
getHeaderField()
getHeaderFieldKey()
getResponseCode()
getResponseMessage()
getHeaderFieldInt()
getHeaderFieldDate()
```

The following methods may be invoked only in the Setup state:

```
setRequestMethod()
setRequestProperty()
```

The following methods may be invoked in any state:

```
close()
getRequestMethod()
getRequestProperty()
getURL()
getProtocol()
getHost()
getFile()
getRef()
getPort()
getQuery()
```

HttpConnection Request Methods

HttpConnection allows three types of requests to be sent to a Web server: GET, HEAD, and POST.

The GET method is used by programs to obtain the contents of a Web document from the specified URL. The Web server responses consist of HTTP header information about the Web document, MIME type information about the content data, and the actual content data.

The HEAD method is used by programs to obtain information about a Web document instead of retrieving the contents of the Web document. When the Web server receives a HEAD request, only the HTTP header data (without the content data) is returned.

The POST method is often used by programs to send the form information to the URL of a CGI program. Both POST and GET can be used to send data to a CGI program; the difference is that the POST method sends data via a stream while the GET method sends data via environment variables embedded in the query string.

The following examples explain how to use these request methods with HttpConnection.

Using the GET Request Method with HttpConnection

The default request method used by HttpConnection is GET. This type of request carries all the information as part of the URL string. In the following code example, a GET request is sent to server 64.28.105.110:

```
http://64.28.105.110/servlets/webyu/Chapter9Servlet?request=gettimestamp
```

The Java servlet Chapter9Servlet will accept the request, get the current local time, and send it back to the client.

In a GET request, the query string is embedded as part of the URL string. For instance, if getQuery() is called on this HTTP connection, the value request=gettimestamp will be returned. When the GET request is sent to the Java servlet, the previous environment variable request and its value are also passed along to the server program.

Listing 9.7 is a sample program that demonstrates how to send a GET request to a Web server using HttpConnection.

LISTING 9.7   HttpGET.java

```java
/**
 * The following MIDlet application demonstrates how to establish a
 * HttpConnection and uses it to send a GET request to Web server.
 */

// include MIDlet class libraries
import javax.microedition.midlet.*;
```

LISTING 9.7 Continued

```java
// include networking class libraries
import javax.microedition.io.*;
// include GUI class libraries
import javax.microedition.lcdui.*;
// include I/O class libraries
import java.io.*;

public class HttpGET extends MIDlet implements CommandListener  {

    // A default URL is used. User can change it from the GUI.
    private static String defaultURL =
    "http://64.28.105.110/servlets/webyu/Chapter9Servlet?request=gettimestamp";

    // GUI components for entering a Web URL.
    private Display myDisplay = null;
    private Form mainScreen;
    private TextField requestField;

    // GUI components for displaying server responses.
    private Form resultScreen;
    private StringItem resultField;

    // the "send" button used on mainScreen
    Command sendCommand = new Command("SEND", Command.OK, 1);
    // the "back" button used on resultScreen
    Command backCommand = new Command("BACK", Command.OK, 1);

    public HttpGET(){

        // initialize the GUI components
        myDisplay = Display.getDisplay(this);
        mainScreen = new Form("Type in a URL:");
        requestField =
        new TextField(null, defaultURL,
        100, TextField.URL);
        mainScreen.append(requestField);
        mainScreen.addCommand(sendCommand);
        mainScreen.setCommandListener(this);
    }

    public void startApp() {
        myDisplay.setCurrent(mainScreen);
    }
```

LISTING 9.7   Continued

```java
public void pauseApp() {
}

public void destroyApp(boolean unconditional) {
}

public void commandAction(Command c, Displayable s) {

    // when user clicks on the "send" button on mainScreen
    if (c == sendCommand) {

        // retrieve the Web url that user entered
        String urlstring = requestField.getString();

        // send a GET request to Web server
        String resultstring = "";
        try {
            resultstring = sendGetRequest(urlstring);
        } catch (IOException e) {
            resultstring = "ERROR";
        }

        // display the page content retrieved from Web server
        resultScreen = new Form("GET Result:");
        resultField  =
        new StringItem(null, resultstring);
        resultScreen.append(resultField);
        resultScreen.addCommand(backCommand);
        resultScreen.setCommandListener(this);
        myDisplay.setCurrent(resultScreen);

    } else if (c == backCommand) {

        // do it all over again
        requestField.setString(defaultURL);
        myDisplay.setCurrent(mainScreen);
    }
}

// send a GET request to Web server
public String sendGetRequest(String urlstring) throws IOException {

    HttpConnection hc = null;
    DataInputStream dis = null;
```

LISTING 9.7 Continued

```
        String message = "";
        try {

            // open up an HttpConnection with the Web server
            // the default request method is GET.
            hc = (HttpConnection) Connector.open(urlstring);

            // obtain a DataInputStream from the HttpConnection
            dis = new DataInputStream(hc.openInputStream());

            // retrieve the contents of the requested page from Web server
            int ch;
            while ((ch = dis.read()) != -1) {
                message = message + (char) ch;
            }
        } finally {
            if (hc != null) hc.close();
            if (dis != null) dis.close();
        }
        return message;
    }
}
```

Figure 9.9 shows a screenshot of the HttpGET program before the GET request is sent out to a Web server.

Figure 9.10 shows a screenshot of the page content retrieved from a Web URL.

FIGURE 9.9

Type in the Web URL.

FIGURE 9.10
The content of a Web document.

Using the HEAD Request Method with `HttpConnection`

HTTP servers provide a substantial amount of information in the HTTP headers that precede each response. For instance, here's a typical HTTP header returned by an Apache Web server running on Sun Solaris:

```
HTTP 1.1 200 OK
Data: Mon, 18 Oct 1999 20:06:48 GMT
Server: Apache/1.3.4 (Unix) PHP/3.0.6
Last-Modified: Mon, 18 Oct 1999
Accept-Ranges: bytes
Content-Length:  35259
Content-Type: text/html
```

In most cases, an HTTP header includes the content type of the page requested, the content length and the character set in which the content is encoded, the date and time of the response, the last modified time of the page requested, and the expiration date for caching purposes. The following are some of the most common header fields in an HTTP header:

```
Content-type
Content-length
Content-encoding
Date
Last-modified
Expires
```

When a HEAD request is sent to a Web server, only the header information will be returned. This type of request is typically used to determine if a cache entry can be reused or if it should be replaced with newer information based on the property values retrieved from the header fields.

The sample program in Listing 9.8 sends a HEAD request to Web server 64.28.105.110 and retrieves all the HTTP header information. The setRequestMethod(HttpConnection.HEAD) method is used to specify that this request is a HEAD request. The getHeaderField() method is used to retrieve the field values and the getHeaderFieldKey() method is used to retrieve the field names.

LISTING 9.8   HttpHEAD.java

```java
/**
 * The following MIDlet application demonstrates how to establish
 * an HttpConnection and use it to send a HEAD request
 * to a Web server.
 */
import javax.microedition.midlet.*;
import javax.microedition.lcdui.*;
import javax.microedition.io.*;
import java.io.*;

public class HttpHEAD extends MIDlet
implements CommandListener  {
    // A default URL is used. User can change it from the GUI.
    private static String defaultURL = "http://64.28.105.110";

    // GUI components for entering a Web URL.
    private Display myDisplay = null;
    private Form mainScreen;
    private TextField requestField;

    // GUI components for displaying server responses.
    private Form resultScreen;
    private StringItem resultField;

    // the "send" button used on mainScreen
    Command sendCommand = new Command("SEND", Command.OK, 1);
    // the "back" button used on resultScreen
    Command backCommand = new Command("BACK", Command.OK, 1);

    public HttpHEAD(){
        // initialize the GUI components
        myDisplay = Display.getDisplay(this);
```

LISTING 9.8 Continued

```java
        mainScreen = new Form("Type in a URL:");
        requestField = new TextField(
        null, defaultURL, 50, TextField.URL);
        mainScreen.append(requestField);
        mainScreen.addCommand(sendCommand);
        mainScreen.setCommandListener(this);
    }

    public void startApp() {
        myDisplay.setCurrent(mainScreen);
    }

    public void pauseApp() {
    }

    public void destroyApp(boolean unconditional) {
    }

    public void commandAction(Command c, Displayable s) {
        // when user clicks on the "send" button
        if (c == sendCommand) {
            // retrieve the Web URL that user entered
            String urlstring = requestField.getString();

            // send a HEAD request to Web server
            String resultstring = "";
            try{
                resultstring = sendHeadRequest(urlstring);
            } catch (IOException e) {
                resultstring = "ERROR";
            }

            // display the header information retrieved from Web server
            resultScreen = new Form("HEAD Result:");
            resultField = new StringItem(null, resultstring);
            resultScreen.append(resultField);
            resultScreen.addCommand(backCommand);
            resultScreen.setCommandListener(this);
            myDisplay.setCurrent(resultScreen);
        } else if (c == backCommand) {
            // do it all over again
            requestField.setString(defaultURL);
            myDisplay.setCurrent(mainScreen);
        }
    }
```

LISTING 9.8   Continued

```
// send a HEAD request to Web server
public String sendHeadRequest(String urlstring) throws IOException {
    HttpConnection hc = null;
    InputStream is = null;
    String message = "";
    try {
        // open up an HttpConnection with the Web server
        hc = (HttpConnection) Connector.open(urlstring);
        // set request method to HEAD
        hc.setRequestMethod(HttpConnection.HEAD);
        // obtain an InputStream from the HttpConnection
        is = hc.openInputStream();
        // retrieve the value pairs of HTTP header information
        int i = 1;
        String key = "";
        String value = "";
        while ((value = hc.getHeaderField(i)) != null) {
            key = hc.getHeaderFieldKey(i++);
            message = message + key + ":" + value + "\n";
        }
    } finally {
        if (hc != null) hc.close();
        if (is != null) is.close();
    }
    return message;
    }
}
```

Figure 9.11 shows a screenshot of all the header information retrieved from a Web server.

Several additional methods are available in HttpConnection for retrieving header information: getLength, getType, getEncoding, getResponseCode, getResponseMessage, getHeaderFieldInt, and getHeaderFieldDate.

Using the POST Request Method with HttpConnection

To send an HTTP request using the POST method, both InputStream and OutputStream have to be obtained from the HttpConnection. InputStream will be used to retrieve the responses from the Web server. OutputStream will be used to send the data separately via a stream (in our examples, the data to be sent is request=gettimestamp).

The following MIDlet application is very similar to HttpGET.java, except that the request being sent is a POST request. The Web URL is

```
http://64.28.105.110/servlets/webyu/Chapter9Servlet
```

9

BASIC NETWORK
PROGRAMMING IN
J2ME MIDP

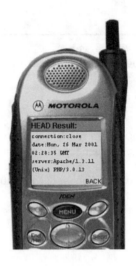

FIGURE 9.11

Header information retrieved by the program HttpHEAD.java.

The Java servlet Chapter9Servlet will accept this request, get the local current time, and send it back to the client. Notice that in this POST request, the data to be sent request=gettimestamp is no longer part of the URL. It will be sent to Web server separately once the HTTP connection is established.

Listing 9.9 demonstrates how to send a POST request to a Web server using HttpConnection.

LISTING 9.9   HttpPOST.java

```
/**
 * This MIDlet application demonstrates how to establish
 * an HttpConnection and use it to send a POST request
 * to a Web server.
 */
import javax.microedition.midlet.*;
import javax.microedition.lcdui.*;
import javax.microedition.io.*;
import java.io.*;

public class HttpPOST extends MIDlet
implements CommandListener  {
    // A default URL is used. User can change it from the GUI.
    private static String defaultURL =
    "http://64.28.105.110/servlets/webyu/Chapter9Servlet";
    // GUI component for entering a Web URL
    private Display myDisplay = null;
```

LISTING 9.9 Continued

```java
private Form mainScreen;
private TextField requestField;
// GUI component for displaying server responses.
private Form resultScreen;
private StringItem resultField;
// the "send" button used on mainScreen
Command sendCommand = new Command("SEND", Command.OK, 1);
// the "back" button used on resultScreen
Command backCommand = new Command("BACK", Command.OK, 1);

public HttpPOST(){
    // initialize the GUI components
    myDisplay = Display.getDisplay(this);
    mainScreen = new Form("Type in a URL:");
    requestField =
    new TextField(null, defaultURL, 100, TextField.URL);
    mainScreen.append(requestField);
    mainScreen.addCommand(sendCommand);
    mainScreen.setCommandListener(this);
}

public void startApp() {
    myDisplay.setCurrent(mainScreen);
}

public void pauseApp() {
}

public void destroyApp(boolean unconditional) {
    // help Garbage Collector
    Display myDisplay = null;
    mainScreen = null;
    requestField = null;
    resultScreen = null;
    resultField = null;
}

public void commandAction(Command c, Displayable s) {
    // when user clicks on the "send" button
    if (c == sendCommand) {
        // retrieve the Web URL that user entered
        String urlstring = requestField.getString();
        // send a POST request to Web server
        String resultstring = "";
```

LISTING 9.9 Continued

```
        try {
            resultstring = sendPostRequest(urlstring);
        } catch (IOException e) {
            resultstring = "ERROR";
        }

        // display the message received from Web server
        resultScreen = new Form("POST Result:");
        resultField  = new StringItem(null, resultstring);
        resultScreen.append(resultField);
        resultScreen.addCommand(backCommand);
        resultScreen.setCommandListener(this);
        myDisplay.setCurrent(resultScreen);
    } else if (c == backCommand) {
        // do it all over again
        requestField.setString(defaultURL);
        myDisplay.setCurrent(mainScreen);
    }
}
// send a POST request to Web server
public String sendPostRequest(String urlstring) throws IOException {
    HttpConnection hc = null;
    DataInputStream dis = null;
    DataOutputStream dos = null;
    String message = "";
    // the request body
    String requeststring = "request=gettimestamp";
    try {
        // an HttpConnection with both read and write access
        hc = (HttpConnection)
        Connector.open(urlstring, Connector.READ_WRITE);
        // set the request method to POST
        hc.setRequestMethod(HttpConnection.POST);
        // obtain DataOutputStream for sending the request string
        dos = hc.openDataOutputStream();
        byte[] request_body = requeststring.getBytes();
        // send request string to Web server
        for (int i = 0; i < request_body.length; i++) {
            dos.writeByte(request_body[i]);
        }
        // flush it out
        dos.flush();
        // obtain DataInputStream for receiving server responses
        dis = new DataInputStream(hc.openInputStream());
```

Listing 9.9 Continued

```
                // retrieve the responses from Web server
                int ch;
                while ((ch = dis.read()) != -1) {
                    message = message + (char) ch;
                }
            } finally {
                // free up i/o streams and http connection
                if (hc != null) hc.close();
                if (dis != null) dis.close();
                if (dos != null) dos.close();
            }
            return message;
    }
}
```

When the sample program HttpPOST.java runs successfully, it should generate the same result as shown in Figure 9.9.

Server-Side Handling of GET and POST Requests

The requests sent by both HttpGET.java and HttpPOST.java are handled by a single Java servlet Chapter9Servlet on www.webyu.com. The responses to these requests are identical even though they are handled differently inside the servlet.

Network programming with J2ME typically involves both client and server programs. Due to the limited resources available on wireless, most of J2ME clients are thin clients. This means that complex business logic and heavy computation will be left to the servers. Server-side programming is as important as client-side programming, if not more so. It is beneficial to understand how HTTP's GET and POST requests are handled on the Web server side.

Listing 9.10 is the Java servlet that handles the HTTP requests sent by HttpGET.java and HttpPOST.java.

Listing 9.10 Chapter9Servlet.java

```
/**
 * Chapter9Servlet is a Java servlet running at
 * http://www.webyu.com/servlets/webyu/Chatper9Servlet.
 * It responds to both GET and POST requests. The request
 * message must be "request=gettimestamp". The response
 * message is a current timestamp.
 */
import java.util.*;
import javax.servlet.*;
```

LISTING 9.10   Continued

```java
import javax.servlet.http.*;
import java.io.*;
public class Chapter9Servlet extends HttpServlet{

    public void init (ServletConfig config)
    throws ServletException {
        super.init(config);
    }

    // doGet will be called when a GET request is received.
    public void doGet (HttpServletRequest request,
    HttpServletResponse response)
    throws ServletException, IOException {
        // get field value in the query string
        String value = request.getParameter("request");
        // turn auto flush on
        PrintWriter out = new PrintWriter(
        response.getOutputStream(), true);
        // call getResult to get the current timestamp
        String message = getResult(value);
        // send an HTML response back to the client
        response.setContentType("text/html");
        response.setContentLength(message.length());
        out.println(message);
    }

    // doPost will be called when a POST request is received.
    public void doPost (HttpServletRequest request,
    HttpServletResponse response)
    throws ServletException, IOException {
        String name = "";
        String value = "";
        // parse out the value pair from the POST body
        // the expected string is "request=gettimestamp"
        try {
            BufferedReader br = request.getReader();
            String line;
            String requeststring = "";
            while (( line = br.readLine()) != null) {
                requeststring = requeststring + line;
            }
            StringTokenizer sTokenizer =
            new StringTokenizer(requeststring, "=");
            if (sTokenizer.hasMoreTokens())
```

LISTING 9.10 Continued

```
                name = (String) sTokenizer.nextToken();
            if (sTokenizer.hasMoreTokens())
                value = (String) sTokenizer.nextToken();
        } catch (Exception e) {
            System.err.println(e);
        }
        // turn auto flush on
        PrintWriter out =
        new PrintWriter(response.getOutputStream(), true);
        String message = getResult(value);
        response.setContentType("text/html");
        response.setContentLength(message.length());
        out.println(message);
    }


    //get current timestamp and put it into HTML format
    public String getResult(String method) {
        String message = "";
        // if the query string value is "gettimestamp"
        //then current local timestamp is returned
        if ( method.equals("gettimestamp") ) {
            TimeZone timezone = TimeZone.getDefault();
            Calendar calendar = Calendar.getInstance(timezone);
            String local_time = calendar.getTime().toString();
            message = message + "<html><head><title>" +
            local_time + "</title></head>\n";
            message = message +
            "<body>Web Server's Local Time is <br>\n";
            message = message + local_time + "</body></html>\n";
        } else {
            // otherwise, an error message is returned
            message = message +
            "<html><head><title>Error</title></head>\n";
            message = message +
            "<body>Unrecoganized Method Name</body></html>\n";
        }
        return message;
    }
}
```

In Chapter9Servlet.java, the doGet() method is called when GET requests are received, and the doPost() method is called when POST requests are received. In the doGet() method, the environment variable request is retrieved by calling the getParameter("request") method. While in the doPost() method, the data chunk request=timestamp is retrieved via a

`BufferedReader`. Compiling and running this server program requires Java servlet and Web server knowledge and is beyond the scope of this book. For more information about Java servlets, please visit Sun's Java Web site at `http://www.javasoft.com`.

Summary

This chapter discussed the basics of network programming in J2ME using the CLDC and MIDP networking class libraries, explained the concept of the Generic Connection framework and its connection interfaces, and explained the mandatory class `HttpConnection` in MIDP. It then used sample MIDlet applications to demonstrate how to use socket, datagram, and http communications with your wireless applications.

Using XML in Wireless Applications

IN THIS CHAPTER

Overview

In recent years, the Extensible Markup Language (XML) has been adopted by more and more businesses as an industry standard for data exchange and data sharing. XML provides a system-independent standard format for specifying the information exchanged over networks and between applications.

The concept of XML is fairly simple, but the effectiveness it brings to the distributed computing world is tremendous. It revolutionizes the ways in which companies conduct business online, from Internet content delivery (wired or wireless) to electronic commerce to enterprise computing.

From a developer's perspective, Java makes your application portable among different platforms, and XML makes your data portable among different applications. These languages make our lives easier.

Wireless devices give developers a viable mobile platform to develop applications for consumers and businesses. Most of these wireless applications are not standalone. They need to exchange and share data over the wireless network with other applications including corporate databases, message-oriented middlewares, or other back-end business applications. Using XML in your wireless applications may dramatically reduce development costs and efforts while improving interoperability of your data and the flexibility of your programs.

> **NOTE**
>
> Recently, a special-interest group was formed among major players in the wireless device and PDA space. Its members include Nokia, Palm, Motorola, IBM, and others. The purpose of this group is to come up a vendor-neutral standard based on XML for synchronizing user data such as address books and appointments between wireless devices from different vendors and across different Internet data repository servers. The standard is SyncML (`http://www.syncml.org`). In Chapter 12, "Data Synchronization for Wireless Applications," we will show you an example of how to perform data synchronization between a MIDlet application and an Internet data repository using SyncML.

Transmitting, storing, and parsing XML data may not be an issue for traditional applications running on desktops and servers, but they can become an issue for J2ME developers who are dealing with the CPU, memory, and network bandwidth constraints of wireless devices. So, you should use XML only when it makes sense.

XML parsing creates extra CPU load and memory/storage overhead. Choosing an XML parser for your wireless application is a balance of functionality, performance, and storage overhead. A good XML parser for J2ME should be small yet robust.

Before we get into the details of individual XML parsers, the following section takes a look at XML parsing in general and how it has been used in traditional applications.

XML and Parsing XML Documents

An XML document is a *tagged* data file. The tags in an XML document define the structures and boundaries of the embedded data elements. The syntax of the tags is very similar to that of HTML. Parsing XML simply means retrieving data from an XML document based on its meaning and structure.

Listing 10.1 is a sample XML document that contains a mail message. We will use this sample XML document as the data source for all the sample programs in this chapter. This file is located at `http://www.webyu.com/book/mail.xml`.

LISTING 10.1   `mail.xml`

```
<?xml version="1.0"?>
<!DOCTYPE mail SYSTEM "http://www.webyu.com/book/mail.dtd" [
  <!ENTITY from   "yfeng@webyu.com">
  <!ENTITY to     "somebody@somewhere.com">
  <!ENTITY cc     "jzhu@webyu.com">
]>
<mail>
  <From>  &from;    </From>
  <To>    &to;      </To>
  <Cc>    &cc;      </Cc>
  <Date>Fri, 12 Jan 2001 10:21:56 -0600</Date>
  <Subject>XML Parsers for J2ME MIDP</Subject>
  <Body language="english">
  Ælfred, NanoXML and TinyXML are the three small-foot-print
  XML parsers that are suitable for J2ME MIDP applications.
  The sizes of these parsers range from 10K to 30K, which fit
  with memory budget of MIDP devices.
  <Signature>
  ----------------------------------------------------------
  Yu Feng
  &from;
  http://www.webyu.com
  </Signature>
  </Body>
</mail>
```

In general, there are four main components associated with an XML document: elements, attributes, entities, and DTDs.

An *element* is something that describes a piece of data. An element is comprised of markup tags and the element's content. The following is an element in Listing 10.1:

```
<Subject>XML Parsers for J2ME MIDP</Subject>
```

It contains a start tag `<Subject>`, the content `XML Parsers for J2ME MIDP`, and an end tag `</Subject>`.

An *attribute* is used in an element to provide additional information about the element. It usually resides inside the start tag of an element. In the following example, `language` is an attribute of the element `Body` that describes the language used in the message body.

```
<Body language="english">
```

An *entity* is a virtual storage of a piece of data (either text data or binary data) that you can reference in an XML document. Entities can be further categorized into internal entities and external entities. An internal entity is defined inside an XML document and doesn't reference any outside content. For example, `from` is an internal entity defined in Listing 10.1:

```
<!ENTITY from  "yfeng@webyu.com">
```

The entity `from` is later on referenced in the XML document as `&from;`. When the XML document is parsed, the parser simply replaces the entity with its actual value `yfeng@webyu.com`.

An external entity refers to content outside an XML document. Its content is usually a filename or a URL proceeded with `SYSTEM` or `PUBLIC` identifier. The following is an example of an external entity `iconimage` that references to a local file called `icon.png`:

```
<!ENTITY iconimage SYSTEM "icon.png" NDATA png>
```

A *Document Type Definition (DTD)* is an optional portion of XML that defines the allowable structure for a particular XML document. Think of DTD as the roadmap and rulebook of the XML document. Listing 10.2 shows the DTD definition for the `mail.xml` shown in Listing 10.1.

LISTING 10.2   `mail.dtd`

```
<!ELEMENT mail    (From,
                   To,
                   Cc,
                   Date,
                   Subject,
                   Body)>
<!ELEMENT From         (#PCDATA)>
<!ELEMENT To           (#PCDATA)>
```

LISTING 10.2 Continued

```
<!ELEMENT Cc          (#PCDATA)>
<!ELEMENT Date        (#PCDATA)>
<!ELEMENT Subject     (#PCDATA)>
<!ELEMENT Signature   (#PCDATA)>
<!ELEMENT Body        (#PCDATA|Signature)+>
```

This DTD basically says that the element mail contains six sub-elements: From, To, Cc, Date, Subject, and Body. The term #PCDATA refers to the "Parsed Character Data," which indicates that an element can contain only text. The last line of the DTD definition indicates that the element Body could contain mixed contents that include text, sub-element Signature, or both.

Event-based XML Parser Versus Tree-based XML Parser

Two types of interfaces are available for parsing XML documents: the event-based interface and the tree-based interface.

An event-based XML parser reports parsing events directly to the application through callback methods. It provides a serial-access mechanism for accessing XML documents. Applications that use a parser's event-based interface need to implement the interface's event handlers to receive parsing events.

The Simple API for XML (SAX) is an industry standard event-based interface for XML parsing. The SAX 1.0 Java API defines several callback methods in one of its interface classes. The applications need to implement these callback methods to receive parsing events from the parser. For example, the startElement() is one of the callback methods. When a SAX parser reaches the start tag of an element, the application that implements the parser's startElement() method will receive the event, and also receive the tag name through one of the method's parameters.

A tree-based XML parser reads an entire XML document into an internal tree structure in memory. Each node of the tree represents a piece of data from the original document. It allows an application to navigate and manipulate the parsed data quickly and easily.

The Document Object Model (DOM) is an industry standard tree-based interface for XML parsing. A DOM parser can be very memory- and CPU-intensive because it keeps the whole data structure in memory. A DOM parser may become a performance issue for your wireless applications, especially when the XML document to be parsed is large and complex.

In general, SAX parsers are faster and consume less CPU and memory than DOM parsers. But the SAX parsers allow only serial access to the XML data. DOM parsers' tree-structured data

10

USING XML IN WIRELESS APPLICATIONS

is easier to access and manipulate. SAX parsers are often used by Java servlets or network-oriented programs to transmit and receive XML documents in a fast and efficient fashion. DOM parsers are often used for manipulating XML documents.

For traditional Java applications, several Java-based XML parsers are available from different software vendors, such as Sun, IBM, and Microsoft. For example, Sun's Java API for XML Processing (JAXP) package defines both SAX and DOM APIs. These XML parsers provide a rich set of features for dealing with XML data within enterprise applications. But these parsers are too big for J2ME MIDP applications. The total size of JAXP is about 140KB. It doesn't fit on the J2ME MIDP devices that only have a storage budget of a few hundred kilobytes.

However, several small-footprint Java-based XML parsers are good candidates for wireless applications. Their code is small, their performance is robust, and they're very functional.

The following sections take a look at three small-footprint XML parsers: the TinyXML parser, the NanoXML parser, and the Ælfred parser. Using these XML parsers generally creates a storage overhead of 10KB to 30KB. Each parser has its own pros and cons. You will see how to evaluate them based on three criteria: functionality, performance, and code size.

XML Parsers for Wireless Applications

The TinyXML, NanoXML, and Ælfred parsers are all Java based. They were originally designed for use with embedded Java applications or Java applets. With some modifications, they should be able to fit in the J2ME MIDP's resource-constrained environment.

Because all three XML parsers were originally written in J2SE, they must be ported to J2ME MIDP before they can be used with MIDlet applications. Some of the J2ME porting work has already been done by other developers; we collected those porting efforts, made some additional modifications, and repackaged them in a way that can be more easily presented to you.

One of the goals of this book is to give you, as a J2ME MIDP developer, a jump-start on your development efforts. Toward this end, several sample programs that use these parsers are also listed and explained in this chapter.

There are pros and cons associated with using each of these parsers. You must evaluate them individually and use whichever is best suited for your applications. They are all open-source packages, so you can customize them to fit your own development needs as long as the license agreement is met.

Choosing the right XML parser for your application should be based on its functionality, code size, and performance. The following sections compare the three parsers in those areas, and also look at their license differences.

Functionality

All three parsers are non-validating parsers. TinyXML and Ælfred support XML DTD definitions, but NanoXML doesn't. TinyXML and Ælfred support both internal and external entities, but NanoXML doesn't.

All three parsers come with event-based interfaces. NanoXML has a SAX 1.0–compliant event-based interface. TinyXML's event-based interface is proprietary and doesn't support SAX 1.0. Ælfred provides both a proprietary event-based interface and a SAX 1.0–compliant interface.

None of the parsers support the standard DOM interface. However, NanoXML and TinyXML both provide a simple tree-based interface. Ælfred is solely event-based; it doesn't have a tree-based interface.

Code Size

In J2ME MIDP environment, developers must constantly be aware of the CPU and memory usage of their applications. Using XML parsers along with your applications creates a storage overhead of 10KB to 30KB, as shown in Table 10.1. (`sax10_midp.jar` contains the J2ME version of SAX1.0 Java API.)

TABLE 10.1   Comparison of the Parsers' Code Sizes

Package(s)	File(s) to be Included	Size (JAR Compressed)
TinyXML's proprietary event-based interface	`tinyxml_event.jar`	10KB
TinyXML's proprietary tree-based interface	`tinyxml_tree.jar`	14KB
NanoXML's proprietary tree-based interface	`nanoxml_tree.jar`	9KB
NanoXML's SAX interface	`nanoxml_sax.jar +` `sax10_midp.jar`	21KB
Ælfred's proprietary event-based interface	`aelfred_event.jar`	18KB
Ælfred's SAX interface	`aelfred_sax.jar +` `sax10_midp.jar`	30KB

The code sizes shown in Table 10.1 are the sizes of compressed JAR files. A Java obfuscator can be used to further reduce the size of these packages.

Using a standard SAX 1.0 interface with these parsers adds about 10K storage overhead on top of existing code (that's the size of SAX 1.0 Java interface); however, using a standard interface offers certain advantages. Your programs will be less reliant on an individual parser, and will therefore be more portable. You'll see an actual example to illustrate this point later in the chapter.

Performance

In general, event-driven interfaces offer better performance than tree-based interfaces because they consume less CPU and memory. However, tree-based interfaces are easier to use because the parsed data is already in a tree-structure.

If you are interested in benchmarking the actual performance of these parsers, you can run the sample code with each parser to parse the same set of XML data and monitor their CPU consumption and memory usage.

Licenses

All three parsers are free, which means they are open-source licensed. Developers have full access to the source code and can modify it for their own use. But make sure that your packaging complies with the individual license agreements.

Generally speaking, Ælfred and NanoXML are under a looser license for commercial and non-commercial use. TinyXML is under a GPL license, which a little more restrictive than the other two.

SAX 1.0 Java API For J2ME MIDP

```
Author: David Megginson
Original Web URL: http://www.megginson.com/SAX/SAX1/index.html
Last package release date:    May 11, 1998
Last release version:    1.0
License agreement:    Free for both commercial and non-commercial use.
```

SAX is a standard interface for event-based XML parsing, initiated and maintained by David Megginson (who is also the author of the Ælfred parser). The SAX API specification was developed collaboratively by the members of the XML-DEV mailing list. The SAX API provides a standard way of dealing with XML documents and has been adopted by most XML parser implementations.

The SAX 1.0 API basically defines a number of standard interfaces that every SAX-compliant parser must support. For example, all SAX parsers must support eight callback methods defined in SAX's DocumentHandler interface. These callback methods are startDocument(), endDocument(), startElement(), endElement(), characters(), ignorableWhitespace(), processingInstruction(), and setDocumentLocator(). The applications that implement these methods will receive parsing events and parsed data from the parser while the XML document is being processed.

The benefit of using standards is that it makes your code portable, the same thing is true with using the SAX API. The following example shows how to plug a different SAX parser into your program without modifying source code. Your code is no longer parser dependent.

The first sample program uses NanoXML's SAX interface:

```
try {
    Parser parser = ParserFactory.makeParser(
      "nanoxml.sax.SAXParser");
    DemoHandler myHandler = new DemoHandler();
    parser.setDocumentHandler(myHandler);
    parser.parse(urlstring);
    resultString = myHandler.getResultString();
} catch (Exception e) {
    System.out.println(e);
}
```

The second sample program uses Ælfred's SAX interface:

```
try {
    Parser parser = ParserFactory.makeParser(
      "com.microstar.xml.SAXDriver");
    DemoHandler myHandler = new DemoHandler();
    parser.setDocumentHandler(myHandler);
    parser.parse(urlstring);
    resultString = myHandler.getResultString();
} catch (Exception e) {
    System.out.println("startApp: " + e);
}
```

The only difference between the two sample programs is the parameter string inside the ParserFactory.makeParser() method. The parameter string indicates which parser to use. To make the code more portable, the value of the parameter string can be placed in a resource file or set as a system property, and be read into the application at runtime.

Since both the NanoXML parser and the Ælfred parser provide optional SAX adapters to support SAX 1.0, it is worthwhile to spend some effort porting the original SAX 1.0 Java API to J2ME MIDP.

Porting the original SAX 1.0 Java API (written in J2SE) to J2ME is very straightforward. java.util.locale is the only class that needs to be ported to J2ME. For simplicity, an empty

10

USING XML IN
WIRELESS
APPLICATIONS

class `java.util.locale` is created for the package. Because there is nothing in the simulated `java.util.locale` class, the original use of `locale` is no longer supported in our J2ME version of the SAX 1.0 Java API. To use the SAX API in your program, make sure `sax10_midp.jar` is included in the Java class path.

The drawback to using the SAX interface in your MIDP application is that you have to include `sax10_midp.jar`, the SAX 1.0 Java API package, which is about 10KB in size. You can find more information about the SAX 1.0 API at `http://www.megginson.com/SAX/SAX1/index.html`.

TinyXML Parser for J2ME MIDP

Author: Tom Gibara
Original Web URL: http://gibaradunn.srac.org/tiny/index.shtml
Last package release date: January 2, 2000
Last release version: 0.7
License agreement: GPL http://www.fsf.org/copyleft/gpl.html

Christian Sauer has ported a J2ME version of TinyXML (you can find more information at `http://www.kvmworld.com/Articles/TinyXML.shtml`). The TinyXML package used in this book is a combination of Christian's contribution and some modifications we made to preserve the structures and features of the original TinyXML parser.

TinyXML is a non-validating parser. It supports both UTF-8 and UTF-16 encoding in XML documents. It also supports DTD and internal/external entities. It consists of two sets of interfaces: a non-SAX event-based interface and a simple tree-based interface. For convenience, the class files for the event-based interface are all included in `tinyxml_event.jar`. The class files for the tree-based interface are all included in `tinyxml_tree.jar`.

`tinyxml_event.jar` contains the class files of the following Java files:

- `gd/xml/CharacterUtility.java`: Christian Sauer wrote the two static methods `isLetter()` and `isLetterOrDigit()` to replace the equivalent methods in the `Character` class that are not available in J2ME.
- `gd/xml/XMLReader.java`: Defines input/output utility methods for XML parsing.
- `gd/xml/ParseException.java`: Defines the exception for errors generated by the parser.
- `gd/xml/XMLResponder.java`: Defines the interface of all event callback methods.
- `gd/xml/XMLParser.java`: Defines XML parser logic.

`tinyxml_tree.jar` contains all the class files in `tinyxml_event.jar` plus four additional class files of the following Java files:

- `gd/xml/tiny/ParsedXML.java`: Defines the interface of a tree node for storing an element of the parsed XML data.

- `gd/xml/tiny/ParseNode.java`: Implements the `ParsedXML` interface and defines a tree node to store an element of the parsed XML data.

- `gd/xml/tiny/TinyParser.java`: Defines a wrapper class around `XMLParser` to support the tree-based interface.

- `gd/xml/tiny/TinyResponder.java`: Implements the `XMLResponder`'s callback methods to construct the tree structure out of the parsed XML data.

An Example of Using TinyXML's Event-based Interface

To use TinyXML's event-based interface, you need to include the package `tinyxml_event.jar` in your Java class path. You also must implement all the callback methods defined in the `XMLResponder` interface to receive parsing events from the parser.

The following sample application illustrates how to use TinyXML's event-based interface. Our example contains two Java files: `DemoEventResponder.java` (which implements the `XMLResponder` interface) and `tinyEventDemo.java` (a J2ME MIDlet). The XML data source is shown in Listing 10.1 and Listing 10.2.

LISTING 10.3   `DemoEventResponder.java`

```
import javax.microedition.io.*;
import java.util.*;
import java.io.*;
// include TinyXML's event-based interface
import gd.xml.*;

public class DemoEventResponder implements XMLResponder {

    private InputStream is;
    private InputConnection ic;
    private InputStream is_sysid;
    private InputConnection ic_sysid;
    private String prefix;
    private StringBuffer resultStringBuffer;

    public DemoEventResponder(String _url) throws ParseException {
        prefix = "> ";
        resultStringBuffer = new StringBuffer();
```

10

LISTING 10.3   Continued

```java
    try {
        ic = (InputConnection) Connector.open(_url);
        is = ic.openInputStream();
    } catch (IOException ioex) {
        throw new ParseException(
            "Failed to open http connection: " + ioex);
    }
}

public String getResultString() {
    return resultStringBuffer.toString();
}

public void closeConnection() {
    try { if (ic != null) ic.close(); }
    catch (Exception ignored) {}

    try { if (is != null) is.close(); }
    catch (Exception ignored) {}

    try { if (ic_sysid != null) ic_sysid.close(); }
    catch (Exception ignored) {}

    try { if (is_sysid != null) is_sysid.close(); }
    catch (Exception ignored) {}
}

public void recordNotationDeclaration(
  String name,String pubID,String sysID)
  throws ParseException {
    System.out.print(prefix+"!NOTATION: "+name);
    resultStringBuffer.append(prefix+"!NOTATION: "+name);
    if (pubID!=null)
    {
        System.out.print("  pubID = "+pubID);
        resultStringBuffer.append("  pubID = "+pubID);
    }
    if (sysID!=null)
    {
        System.out.print("  sysID = "+sysID);
        resultStringBuffer.append("  sysID = "+sysID);
    }
    System.out.println("");
```

LISTING 10.3   Continued

```
        resultStringBuffer.append("\n");
    }

    public void recordEntityDeclaration(String name, String value,
      String pubID, String sysID, String notation)
      throws ParseException {
        System.out.print(prefix+"!ENTITY: "+name);
        resultStringBuffer.append(prefix+"!ENTITY: "+name);
        if (value!=null)
        {
            System.out.print("  value = "+value);
            resultStringBuffer.append("  value = "+value);
        }
        if (pubID!=null)
        {
            System.out.print("  pubID = "+pubID);
            resultStringBuffer.append("  pubID = "+pubID);
        }
        if (sysID!=null)
        {
            System.out.print("  sysID = "+sysID);
            resultStringBuffer.append("  sysID = "+sysID);
        }
        if (notation!=null)
        {
            System.out.print("  notation = "+notation);
            resultStringBuffer.append("  notation = "+notation);
        }
        System.out.println("");
        resultStringBuffer.append("\n");
    }

    public void recordElementDeclaration(String name, String content)
    throws ParseException {
        System.out.print(prefix+"!ELEMENT: "+name);
        resultStringBuffer.append(prefix+"!ELEMENT: "+name);
        System.out.println("  content = "+content);
        resultStringBuffer.append("  content = "+content + "\n");
    }

    public void recordAttlistDeclaration(String element, String attr,
    boolean notation, String type, String defmod, String def)
    throws ParseException {
        System.out.print(prefix+"!ATTLIST: "+element);
        resultStringBuffer.append(prefix+"!ATTLIST: "+element);
```

LISTING 10.3 Continued

```java
        System.out.print("  attr = "+attr);
        resultStringBuffer.append("  attr = "+attr);
        System.out.print(
            "  type = " + ((notation) ? "NOTATIONS " : "") + type);
        resultStringBuffer.append(
            "  type = " + ((notation) ? "NOTATIONS " : "") + type);
        System.out.print("  def. modifier = "+defmod);
        resultStringBuffer.append("  def. modifier = "+defmod);
        System.out.println( (def==null) ? "" : "  def = "+notation);
        resultStringBuffer.append(
            (def==null) ? "\n" : "  def = "+notation + "\n");
    }

    public void recordDoctypeDeclaration(
      String name,String pubID,String sysID)
      throws ParseException {
        System.out.print(prefix+"!DOCTYPE: "+name);
        resultStringBuffer.append(prefix+"!DOCTYPE: "+name);
        if (pubID!=null)
        {
            System.out.print("  pubID = "+pubID);
            resultStringBuffer.append("  pubID = "+pubID);
        }
        if (sysID!=null)
        {
            System.out.print("  sysID = "+sysID);
            resultStringBuffer.append("  sysID = "+sysID);
        }
        System.out.println("");
        resultStringBuffer.append("\n");
        prefix = "";
    }

    public void recordDocStart() {
        System.out.println("Parsing began");
        resultStringBuffer.append("Parsing began\n");
    }

    public void recordDocEnd() {
        System.out.println("");
        resultStringBuffer.append("\n");
        System.out.println("Parsing finished without error");
```

LISTING 10.3   Continued

```
        resultStringBuffer.append("Parsing finished without error\n");
    }

    public void recordElementStart(String name, Hashtable attr)
    throws ParseException {
        System.out.println(prefix+"ELEMENT: "+name);
        resultStringBuffer.append(prefix+"ELEMENT: "+name +"\n");
        if (attr!=null) {
            Enumeration e = attr.keys();
            System.out.print(prefix);
            resultStringBuffer.append(prefix);
            String conj = "ATTR: ";
            while (e.hasMoreElements()) {
                Object k = e.nextElement();
                System.out.print(conj+k+" = "+attr.get(k));
                resultStringBuffer.append(conj+k+" = "+attr.get(k));
                conj = ", ";
            }
            System.out.println("");
            resultStringBuffer.append("\n");
        }
        prefix = prefix+"  ";
    }

    public void recordElementEnd(String name) throws ParseException {
        prefix = prefix.substring(2);
    }

    public void recordPI(String name, String pValue) {
        System.out.println(prefix+"*"+name+" PI: "+pValue);
        resultStringBuffer.append(prefix+"*"+name+" PI: "+pValue + "\n");
    }

    public void recordCharData(String charData) {
        System.out.println(prefix+charData);
        resultStringBuffer.append(prefix+charData + "\n");
    }

    public void recordComment(String comment) {
        System.out.println(prefix+"*Comment: "+comment);
        resultStringBuffer.append(prefix+"*Comment: "+comment + "\n");
    }
```

LISTING 10.3   Continued

```java
    public InputStream getDocumentStream() throws ParseException {
        return is;
    }

    public InputStream resolveExternalEntity(
      String name,String pubID,String sysID)
      throws ParseException {
        if (sysID!=null) {
            try {
                ic_sysid = (InputConnection) Connector.open(sysID);
                is_sysid = ic_sysid.openInputStream();
                return is_sysid;
            }
            catch (IOException e) {
                throw new ParseException("Failed to open http connection: "
                + sysID);
            }
        }
        else return null;
    }

    public InputStream resolveDTDEntity(
      String name, String pubID, String sysID)
      throws ParseException {
        return resolveExternalEntity(name, pubID, sysID);
    }
}
```

DemoEventResponder.java implements all 15 callback methods defined in TinyXML's event-based interface XMLResponder. These callback methods basically are implemented with a number of print statements that print out the contents received from the parser while the XML document is being processed. The callback methods defined in XMLResponder are similar to the ones defined in the SAX API. For example, recordElementStart(), recordElementEnd(), and recordCharData() are very similar to the SAX API's startElement(), endElement(), and characters() methods.

The program in Listing 10.4 is a J2ME MIDlet application that reads XML data from http://www.webyu.com/book/mail.xml by instantiating a DemoEventResponder object myResponder = new DemoEventResponder(urlstring);, parses the data using the TinyXML parser by calling xp.parseXML(myResponder);, and uses the DemoEventResponder callbacks to print the parsing results.

LISTING 10.4   tinyEventDemo.java

```java
import java.io.*;
import java.util.*;
import java.lang.String;
import javax.microedition.io.*;
import javax.microedition.lcdui.*;
import javax.microedition.midlet.*;
import gd.xml.*;

public class tinyEventDemo extends MIDlet implements CommandListener {

    private String url;
    private DemoEventResponder myResponder;

    // GUI component for user to enter url for the xml document
    private Display myDisplay = null;
    private Form mainScreen;
    private TextField requestField;

    // GUI component for displaying xml data content
    private Form resultScreen;
    private StringItem resultField;

    // the "send" button used on mainScreen
    Command sendCommand = new Command("SEND", Command.OK, 1);
    // the "back" button used on resultScreen
    Command backCommand = new Command("BACK", Command.OK, 1);

    public tinyEventDemo() {
        // default url
        url = "http://www.webyu.com/book/mail.xml";

        // initializing the GUI components for entering url
        // for the xml document
        myDisplay = Display.getDisplay(this);
        mainScreen = new Form("Type in a URL:");
        requestField =
        new TextField(null, url,
        100, TextField.URL);
        mainScreen.append(requestField);
        mainScreen.addCommand(sendCommand);
        mainScreen.setCommandListener(this);
    }
```

LISTING 10.4 Continued

```java
public void startApp() throws MIDletStateChangeException {
    myDisplay.setCurrent(mainScreen);
}

public void pauseApp() {
}

public void destroyApp(boolean unconditional) {
    myResponder.closeConnection();
}

public void commandAction(Command c, Displayable s) {

    // when user clicks on "send" button on mainScreen
    if (c == sendCommand) {

        // retrieving the web url that user entered
        String urlstring = requestField.getString();

        String resultstring = "";

        try {
            myResponder = new DemoEventResponder(urlstring);
            XMLParser xp = new XMLParser();
            xp.parseXML(myResponder);
            resultstring = myResponder.getResultString();
        } catch (ParseException e) {
            System.out.println(e);
        }

        // displaying the page content retrieved from web server
        resultScreen = new Form("XML Result:");
        resultField  =
        new StringItem(null, resultstring);
        resultScreen.append(resultField);
        resultScreen.addCommand(backCommand);
        resultScreen.setCommandListener(this);
        myDisplay.setCurrent(resultScreen);

    } else if (c == backCommand) {

        // do it all over again
        requestField.setString(url);
```

LISTING 10.4   Continued

```
        myDisplay.setCurrent(mainScreen);
    }
  }
}
```

Figures 10.1 and 10.2 show the `tinyEventDemo` program.

FIGURE 10.1
Entering the Web URL for the XML data to be parsed.

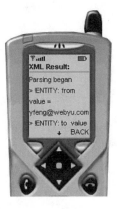

FIGURE 10.2
Display for the parsed XML data elements.

The actual command-line output from this program is as follows:

```
Parsing began
> !ENTITY: from  value = yfeng@webyu.com
> !ENTITY: to  value = somebody@somewhere.com
> !ENTITY: cc  value = jzhu@webyu.com
> !ELEMENT: mail  content = (From,
                    To,
                    Cc,
                    Date,
                    Subject,
                    Body)
> !ELEMENT: From  content = (#PCDATA)
> !ELEMENT: To  content = (#PCDATA)
> !ELEMENT: Cc  content = (#PCDATA)
> !ELEMENT: Date  content = (#PCDATA)
> !ELEMENT: Subject  content = (#PCDATA)
> !ELEMENT: Signature  content = (#PCDATA)
> !ELEMENT: Body  content = (#PCDATA|Signature)+
> !DOCTYPE: mail  sysID = http://www.webyu.com/book/mail.dtd
ELEMENT: mail
  ELEMENT: From
    yfeng@webyu.com
  ELEMENT: To
    somebody@somewhere.com
  ELEMENT: Cc
    jzhu@webyu.com
  ELEMENT: Date
    Fri, 12 Jan 2001 10:21:56 -0600
  ELEMENT: Subject
    XML Parsers for J2ME MIDP
  ELEMENT: Body
  ATTR: language = english
    Ælfred, NanoXML and TinyXML are the three small-foot-print
        XML parsers that are suitable for J2ME MIDP applications.
        The sizes of these parsers range from 10K to 30K, which fit
        with memory budget of MIDP devices.

    ELEMENT: Signature
    - - - - - - - - - - - - - - - - - - - - - - - - - - - - - - - - - - - - - - - - - - - - - - - - - - - - - - - - -
        Yu Feng
        yfeng@webyu.com
        http://www.webyu.com
Parsing finished without error
```

By looking at the output, you can verify two things quickly:

- TinyXML supports DTD and mixed content. The DTD definition
  `http://www.webyu.com/book/mail.dtd` is parsed correctly, and the sub-element
  `<Signature>` inside `<Body>` is parsed out correctly based on the DTD definition.

- TinyXML supports entities. The entities `from`, `to`, and `cc` are parsed correctly and used
  to substitute `&from;`, `&to;`, and `&cc;` with their actual contents.

An Example of Using TinyXML's Tree-based Interface

To use TinyXML's tree-based interface, first you must make sure the package
`tinyxml_tree.jar` is included in your Java class path. Unlike using the event-based interface,
there is no need to implement the callback methods in `XMLResponder` in order to use the tree-
based interface. The callback methods are already implemented in TinyXML's `TinyResponder`
class for constructing the tree structure out of parsed XML data.

The sample application in Listing 10.5 illustrates how to use TinyXML's tree-based interface.
The same data source `mail.xml` from Listing 10.1 is used in this example. The parser takes
`url` as input and returns a tree structure root: `root = TinyParser.parseXML(url);`. Because
the parsed result is stored in a tree structure, a recursive method `displayNode()` is used to display the content stored in the tree structure.

LISTING 10.5   `tinyTreeDemo.java`

```java
import java.io.*;
import java.util.*;
import java.lang.String;
import javax.microedition.io.*;
import javax.microedition.lcdui.*;
import javax.microedition.midlet.*;
import gd.xml.*;
import gd.xml.tiny.*;

public class tinyTreeDemo extends MIDlet
  implements CommandListener {

    private String url;
    private ParsedXML root;

    // GUI component for user to enter url for the xml document
    private Display myDisplay = null;
    private Form mainScreen;
    private TextField requestField;
```

Listing 10.5 Continued

```java
// the "send" button used on mainScreen
Command sendCommand = new Command("SEND", Command.OK, 1);

public tinyTreeDemo() {
    url = "http://www.webyu.com/book/mail.xml";

    // initializing the GUI components for entering url
    // for the xml document
    myDisplay = Display.getDisplay(this);
    mainScreen = new Form("Type in a URL:");
    requestField =
    new TextField(null, url,
    100, TextField.URL);
    mainScreen.append(requestField);
    mainScreen.addCommand(sendCommand);
    mainScreen.setCommandListener(this);
}

public void startApp() throws MIDletStateChangeException {
    myDisplay.setCurrent(mainScreen);
}

public void pauseApp() {
}

public void destroyApp(boolean unconditional) {
}

public void commandAction(Command c, Displayable s) {

    // when user clicks on "send" button on mainScreen
    if (c == sendCommand) {

        // retrieving the web url that user entered
        String urlstring = requestField.getString();
        try {
            root = TinyParser.parseXML(url);
            displayNode(root);
        } catch (ParseException e) {
            System.err.println("startApp: " + e);
        }
    }
}

private void displayNode(ParsedXML px) {
```

Listing 10.5 Continued

```
        //choose name
        String nodeName = px.getTypeName();
        if (px.getName()!=null)
            nodeName += " <" + px.getName() + ">";
        String nodeContent = px.getContent();
        if (nodeContent==null) nodeContent = "";
        System.out.print(nodeName + ":");
        System.out.println(nodeContent);

        //add subtrees
        Enumeration e;

        //add attributes
        e = px.attributes();
        if (e.hasMoreElements()) {
            System.out.print("attribute:");
            while (e.hasMoreElements()) {
                String attrName = (String)e.nextElement();
                System.out.println(
                    attrName+ ":" +px.getAttribute(attrName) );
            }
        }

        e = px.elements();
        if (e.hasMoreElements()) {
            while (e.hasMoreElements())
                displayNode((ParsedXML)e.nextElement());
        }
    }
}
```

The actual command-line output from this program basically generates the same output as
`tinyTreeDemo`:

```
root:
tag <mail>:
tag <From>:
text:yfeng@webyu.com
tag <To>:
text:somebody@somewhere.com
tag <Cc>:
text:jzhu@webyu.com
tag <Date>:
```

```
text:Fri, 12 Jan 2001 10:21:56 -0600
tag <Subject>:
text:XML Parsers for J2ME MIDP
tag <Body>:
attribute:language:english
text:Ælfred, NanoXML and TinyXML are the three small-foot-print
    XML parsers that are suitable for J2ME MIDP applications.
    The sizes of these parsers range from 10K to 30K, which fit
    with memory budget of MIDP devices.

tag <Signature>:
text:------------------------------------------------------------
        Yu Feng
        yfeng@webyu.com
        http://www.webyu.com
```

You can find more information about the TinyXML parser at `http://gibaradunn.srac.org/tiny/index.shtml`.

NanoXML Parser for J2ME MIDP

```
Author: Marc De Scheemaecker
Original Web URL: http://nanoxml.sourceforge.net/index.html
Last package release date: November 29, 2000
Last release version:    1.6.7
License agreement: zlib/libpng,
http://www.opensource.org/licenses/zlib-license.html
```

Eric Giguere has ported NanoXML to J2ME (you can find more information at `http://www.ericgiguere.com/microjava/cldc_xml.html`). The NanoXML package used in this book is a combination of Eric Giguere's contribution and some modifications we made to the parser's SAX adapter.

NanoXML is a non-validating XML parser. It contains two sets of interfaces: a simple tree-based interface and a SAX 1.0–compliant event-based interface.

NanoXML doesn't support DTD and entities, and it doesn't support mixed content either. You can see these limitations from the output of the sample programs in this section.

For convenience, the class files for the NanoXML simple tree-based interface are included in `nanoxml_tree.jar`. The class files for the SAX interface are included in `nanoxml_sax.jar`.

nanoxml_tree.jar contains the class files of the following Java files:

- nanoxml/XMLElement.java: Implements the XML parser functionality. Ported to J2ME by Eric Giguere.

- nanoxml/XMLParseException.java: Defines the exception for errors generated by the parser.

nanoxml_sax.jar contains all the class files in nanoxml_tree.jar and the class files of the following Java files to support SAX 1.0 API:

- nanoxml/sax/SAXLocator.java: Implements the Locator interface in SAX 1.0 Java API.

- nanoxml/sax/SAXParser.java: The SAX adapter of NanoXML parser.

An Example of Using NanoXML's Tree-based Interface

To use NanoXML's tree-based interface, nanoxml_tree.jar must be included in your Java class path.

The sample application in Listing 10.6 (nanoTreeDemo.java) illustrates how to use NanoXML's tree-based interface. The XML data source is shown in Listing 10.1 and Listing 10.2. The program reads the XML document for the URL and passes the whole content of the document as a big string to the parser: foo.parseString(xml.toString(), 0);. foo itself is a tree-structure that contains all the parsed data. A recursive method displayTree() is used to display the content stored in the tree structure.

LISTING 10.6   nanoTreeDemo.java

```
import java.io.*;
import java.util.*;
import java.lang.String;
import javax.microedition.io.*;
import javax.microedition.lcdui.*;
import javax.microedition.midlet.*;
import nanoxml.*;

public class nanoTreeDemo extends MIDlet implements CommandListener {

    private String url;

    // for output display
    private StringBuffer resultStringBuffer;

    // GUI component for user to enter url for the xml document
    private Display myDisplay = null;
```

LISTING 10.6   Continued

```java
private Form mainScreen;
private TextField requestField;

// GUI component for displaying xml data content
private Form resultScreen;
private StringItem resultField;

// the "send" button used on mainScreen
Command sendCommand = new Command("SEND", Command.OK, 1);
// the "back" button used on resultScreen
Command backCommand = new Command("BACK", Command.OK, 1);

public nanoTreeDemo() {
    // default url
    url = "http://www.webyu.com/book/mail.xml";

    resultStringBuffer = new StringBuffer();

    // initializing the GUI components for entering url
    // for the xml document
    myDisplay = Display.getDisplay(this);
    mainScreen = new Form("Type in a URL:");
    requestField =
    new TextField(null, url,
    100, TextField.URL);
    mainScreen.append(requestField);
    mainScreen.addCommand(sendCommand);
    mainScreen.setCommandListener(this);
}

public void startApp() throws MIDletStateChangeException {

    myDisplay.setCurrent(mainScreen);
}

public void pauseApp() {
}

public void destroyApp(boolean unconditional) {
}

public void commandAction(Command c, Displayable s) {
```

LISTING 10.6 Continued

```
// when user clicks on "send" button on mainScreen
if (c == sendCommand) {

    // retrieving the web url that user entered
    String urlstring = requestField.getString();

    InputConnection ic = null;
    InputStream is = null;

    StringBuffer xml = new StringBuffer();
    try {
        ic = (InputConnection) Connector.open(url);
        is = ic.openInputStream();
        int ch;
        while ( (ch = is.read()) != -1) {
            xml.append((char) ch);
        }
    } catch (IOException e) {
    } finally {
        try { if (ic!=null) ic.close(); }
        catch (Exception e) {}
        try { if (is!=null) is.close(); }
        catch (Exception e) {}
    }

    try {

        XMLElement foo = new XMLElement();
        foo.parseString(xml.toString(), 0);
        displayTree(foo);

        System.out.println("");
        System.out.println(
          "---------original XML--------------------");
        System.out.println(foo);
        System.out.println(
          "---------original XML--------------------");

    } catch (Exception e) {
        System.err.println(e);
    }

    // displaying the page content retrieved from web server
    resultScreen = new Form("XML Result:");
    resultField  =
```

LISTING 10.6   Continued

```
                new StringItem(null, resultStringBuffer.toString());
                resultScreen.append(resultField);
                resultScreen.addCommand(backCommand);
                resultScreen.setCommandListener(this);
                myDisplay.setCurrent(resultScreen);

            } else if (c == backCommand) {

                // do it all over again
                requestField.setString(url);
                myDisplay.setCurrent(mainScreen);
            }
        }

    public void displayTree(XMLElement node) {
        if ( node.getTagName() != null )
        {
            System.out.println("<" + node.getTagName() + ">");
            resultStringBuffer.append(
              "<" + node.getTagName() + ">\n");
        }

        if ( node.getContents() != null )
        {
            System.out.println("    contents: " + node.getContents());
            resultStringBuffer.append(
              "    contents: " + node.getContents() + "\n");
        }

        Enumeration enum = node.enumerateChildren();
        while (enum.hasMoreElements()) {
            XMLElement bar = (XMLElement)(enum.nextElement());
            displayTree(bar);
        }
    }
}
```

The actual command-line output from nanoTreeDemo is as follows:

```
<mail>
<From>
    contents:    &from;
<To>
    contents:    &to;
```

```
<Cc>
    contents:      &cc;
<Date>
    contents: Fri, 12 Jan 2001 10:21:56 -0600
<Subject>
    contents: XML Parsers for J2ME MIDP
<Body>
    contents:
        Ælfred, NanoXML and TinyXML are the three small-foot-print
        XML parsers that are suitable for J2ME MIDP applications.
        The sizes of these parsers range from 10K to 30K, which fit
        with memory budget of MIDP devices.
        <Signature>
        ------------------------------------------------------------
        Yu Feng
        &from;
        http://www.webyu.com
        </Signature>
```

Because NanoXML doesn't support DTD and entities, the DTD definition is ignored and as a result the sub-element <Signature> is treated as part of the <Body> contents. The entities from, to and cc are not substituted correctly either in the result.

An Example of Using NanoXML's SAX Interface

The following sample application illustrates how to use NanoXML's SAX interface. Because NanoXML supports SAX 1.0 Java API, both nanoxml_sax.jar and sax10_midp.jar must be included in your Java class path.

To use the SAX 1.0 API, you need to implement all the callback methods defined in the DocumentHandler interface. You can also extend the convenience class HandlerBase when you need to only implement part of the interface. The HandlerBase class implements the default behavior of the DocumentHandler interface. Both DocumentHandler and HandlerBase can be found in the SAX 1.0 Java API.

The example in Listings 10.7 and 10.8 consists of two files: DemoHandler.java and nanoSaxDemo.java. DemoHandler extends SAX API's convenience class HandlerBase and overrides its getResultString(), startDocument(), endDocument(), resolveEntiry(), startElement(), endElement(), characters(), and processingInstruction() methods. nanoSaxDemo reads the XML data from a Web server and calls NanoXML parser to parse the data.

10

LISTING 10.7   DemoHandler.java

```java
import org.xml.sax.*;
import org.xml.sax.helpers.*;
import java.io.Reader;

public class DemoHandler extends HandlerBase {

    private StringBuffer resultStringBuffer;

    public DemoHandler() {
        resultStringBuffer = new StringBuffer();
    }

    public String getResultString() {
        return resultStringBuffer.toString();
    }

    public void startDocument ()
    throws SAXException
    {
        System.out.println("Start parsing document >>>>");
    }

    public void endDocument ()
    throws SAXException
    {
        System.out.println("Finish parsing document <<<<");
    }

    public InputSource resolveEntity (
      String publicId, String systemId)
      throws SAXException
    {
        return new InputSource(systemId);
    }

    public void startElement (
      String elname, AttributeList attributes)
      throws SAXException
    {
        System.out.println(" <" + elname + ">");
        AttributeListImpl myatts =
          new AttributeListImpl(attributes);
        if ( myatts.getLength() > 0 ) {
            System.out.print("  Attribute:\t");
            resultStringBuffer.append("  Attribute:");
```

LISTING 10.7   Continued

```java
            for (int i = 0; i < myatts.getLength(); i++)
            {
                System.out.print(myatts.getName(i) + ":");
                resultStringBuffer.append(
                  myatts.getName(i) + ":");
                System.out.println(myatts.getValue(i));
                resultStringBuffer.append(
                  myatts.getValue(i) + "\n");
            }
        }
    }

    public void endElement (String elname)
    throws SAXException
    {
        System.out.println(" END <" + elname + ">");
        resultStringBuffer.append(" END <" + elname + ">\n");
    }

    public void characters (char ch[], int start, int length)
    throws SAXException
    {
        String contents = new String(ch, start, length);
        System.out.println("  Contents:\t" + contents);
        resultStringBuffer.append(
          "  contents:" + contents + "\n");
    }

    public void processingInstruction (String target, String data)
    throws SAXException
    {
        System.out.println("PI:");
        System.out.println("target:" + target);
        System.out.println("data:" + data);
    }
}
```

LISTING 10.8   nanoSaxDemo.java

```java
import java.io.*;
import java.util.*;
import java.lang.String;
import javax.microedition.io.*;
import javax.microedition.lcdui.*;
```

Listing 10.8 Continued

```java
import javax.microedition.midlet.*;
import nanoxml.sax.*;
import org.xml.sax.*;
import org.xml.sax.helpers.*;

public class nanoSaxDemo extends MIDlet
  implements CommandListener {

    private String url;

    // GUI component for user to enter url for the xml document
    private Display myDisplay = null;
    private Form mainScreen;
    private TextField requestField;

    // GUI component for displaying xml data content
    private Form resultScreen;
    private StringItem resultField;

    // the "send" button used on mainScreen
    Command sendCommand = new Command("SEND", Command.OK, 1);
    // the "back" button used on resultScreen
    Command backCommand = new Command("BACK", Command.OK, 1);

    public nanoSaxDemo() {
        // deault url
        url = "http://www.webyu.com/book/book.xml";

        // initializing the GUI components for entering url
        // for the xml document
        myDisplay = Display.getDisplay(this);
        mainScreen = new Form("Type in a URL:");
        requestField =
        new TextField(null, url,
        100, TextField.URL);
        mainScreen.append(requestField);
        mainScreen.addCommand(sendCommand);
        mainScreen.setCommandListener(this);
    }

    public void startApp() throws MIDletStateChangeException {

        myDisplay.setCurrent(mainScreen);
    }
```

LISTING 10.8   Continued

```java
public void pauseApp() {
}

public void destroyApp(boolean unconditional) {
}

public void commandAction(Command c, Displayable s) {

    // when user clicks on "send" button on mainScreen
    if (c == sendCommand) {

        // retrieving the web url that user entered
        String urlstring = requestField.getString();

        String resultString = "";

        try {

            Parser parser =
              ParserFactory.makeParser("nanoxml.sax.SAXParser");
            DemoHandler myHandler = new DemoHandler();
            parser.setDocumentHandler(myHandler);
            parser.parse(urlstring);
            resultString = myHandler.getResultString();

        } catch (Exception e) {
            System.err.println(e);
        }

        // displaying the page content retrieved from web server
        resultScreen = new Form("XML Result:");
        resultField  =
        new StringItem(null, resultString);
        resultScreen.append(resultField);
        resultScreen.addCommand(backCommand);
        resultScreen.setCommandListener(this);
        myDisplay.setCurrent(resultScreen);

    } else if (c == backCommand) {
        // do it all over again
        requestField.setString(url);
        myDisplay.setCurrent(mainScreen);
    }
}
}
```

The actual command-line output from `nanoSaxDemo` is as follows:

```
Start parsing document >>>>
 <mail>
 <From>
  Contents:         &from;
 END <From>
 <To>
  Contents:         &to;
 END <To>
 <Cc>
  Contents:         &cc;
 END <Cc>
 <Date>
  Contents:      Fri, 12 Jan 2001 10:21:56 -0600
 END <Date>
 <Subject>
  Contents:      XML Parsers for J2ME MIDP
 END <Subject>
 <Body>
  Attribute:     LANGUAGE:english
  Contents:
     Ælfred, NanoXML and TinyXML are the three small-foot-print
     XML parsers that are suitable for J2ME MIDP applications.
     The sizes of these parsers range from 10K to 30K, which fit
     with memory budget of MIDP devices.
     <Signature>
     -----------------------------------------------------------
     Yu Feng
     &from;
     http://www.webyu.com
     </Signature>

 END <Body>
 END <mail>
Finish parsing document <<<<
```

You can find more information about the NanoXML parser at `http://nanoxml.sourceforge.net/index.html`.

Ælfred Parser for J2ME MIDP

```
Author: David Megginson
Original Web URL: http://www.microstar.com/aelfred.html
Last package release date: July 2, 1998
```

Last release version: 1.2
License agreement: Free for both commercial and non-commercial use.
Please see the original package for the actual license agreement.

The Ælfred parser was written by David Megginson, who also maintains the SAX APIs. The parser is named for the Saxon king Ælfred. Here is an interesting quote from the author:

> "Ælfred the Great was king of Wessex, and at least nominally of all England, at the time of his death in 899AD. Ælfred introduced a wide-spread literacy program in the hope that his people would learn to read English, at least, if Latin was too difficult for them. This Ælfred hopes to bring another sort of literacy to Java, using XML, at least, if full SGML is too difficult. The initial "AE" ("Æ" in ISO-8859-1) is also a reminder that XML is not limited to ASCII."

Jun Fujisawa has ported Ælfred to Palm KVM (you can find more information at `http://fujisawa.org/palm/`). However, the source code of this port is not available to the public. The Ælfred parser used in this book is version modified by the authors. The two main modifications to the original source code simulate the unsupported J2SE classes and change J2SE networking to J2ME networking.

Ælfred is a fast, non-validating XML parser. It contains two sets of event-based interfaces: a proprietary event-based interface and a SAX 1.0–compliant interface. It supports DTD and entities and has the capability of handling international encoding.

For convenience, the class files for the proprietary event-based interface are included in `aelfred_event.jar`. The class files for the SAX interface are included in `aelfred_sax.jar`.

`aelfred_event.jar` contains the class files of the following Java programs:

- `com/microstar/xml/HandlerBase.java`: A convenience class that implements the `XmlHandler` interface. If users don't want to implement all the methods from `XmlHandler`, they can simply extend from this base class and only implement a subset of callback methods.

- `com/microstar/xml/XmlHandler.java`: An interface that defines the event-driven callback methods that must be implemented by applications that use the Ælfred parser. This interface is very similar to the `DocumentHandler` interface defined in the SAX 1.0 Java API.

- `com/microstar/xml/XmlException.java`: Defines the exception for errors generated by the parser.

- `com/microstar/xml/XmlParser.java`: Defines the XML parser that parses XML documents and generates parsing events through callbacks.

`aelfred_sax.jar` contains all the class files in `aelfred_event.jar` and the class file of the SAX adapter for the Ælfred parser, `com/microstar/xml/SAXDriver.java`. `SAXDriver.java` implements the SAX 1.0 Java interfaces.

An Example of Using Ælfred's Proprietary Event-based Interface

To use Ælfred's proprietary event-based interface, `aelfred_event.jar` must be included in your Java class path.

The sample programs in Listings 10.9 and 10.10 show how to use Ælfred's proprietary event-based interface, which can be roughly described as a simplified SAX interface. The example consists of two files: `DemoEventHandler.java` and `aelfredEventDemo.java`. `DemoEventHandler.java` implements all the callback methods defined in Ælfred's `XMLHandler` interface. These callback methods are very similar to SAX's callback methods, a lot of them even share the same method names. `aelfredEventDemo.java` is a MIDlet application that calls the Ælfred parser. The XML data source is shown in Listing 10.1 and Listing 10.2.

LISTING 10.9   `DemoEventHandler.java`

```java
import java.io.InputStream;
import java.io.Reader;
import javax.microedition.io.*;

import com.microstar.xml.XmlHandler;
import com.microstar.xml.XmlParser;

public class DemoEventHandler implements XmlHandler {

    public XmlParser parser;
    private StringBuffer resultStringBuffer;

    public String getResultString() {
        return resultStringBuffer.toString();
    }

    public DemoEventHandler() {
        resultStringBuffer = new StringBuffer();
    }

    public Object resolveEntity (
      String publicId, String systemId)
    {
        System.out.println("Resolving entity: pubid="
          + publicId + ", sysid=" + systemId);
        resultStringBuffer.append("Resolving entity: pubid="
          + publicId + ", sysid=" + systemId + "\n");
```

LISTING 10.9 Continued

```
        return null;
    }

    public void startExternalEntity (String systemId)
    {
        System.out.println(
          "Starting external entity:  " + systemId);
        resultStringBuffer.append(
          "Starting external entity:  " + systemId + "\n");
    }

    public void endExternalEntity (String systemId)
    {
        System.out.println(
          "Ending external entity:  " + systemId);
        resultStringBuffer.append(
          "Ending external entity:  " + systemId + "\n");
    }

    public void startDocument ()
    {
        System.out.println("Start parsing document >>>>");
        resultStringBuffer.append("Start parsing document >>>>\n");
    }

    public void endDocument ()
    {
        System.out.println("Finish parsing document <<<<");
        resultStringBuffer.append("Finish parsing document <<<<\n");
    }

    public void doctypeDecl (String name,
    String pubid, String sysid)
    {
        System.out.println("Doctype declaration:  " + name
          + ", pubid=" + pubid + ", sysid=" + sysid);
        resultStringBuffer.append("Doctype declaration:  "
          + name + ", pubid=" +  pubid + ", sysid=" + sysid + "\n");
    }

    public void attribute (String name, String value,
    boolean isSpecified)
    {
        System.out.print("  Attribute:\t" + name + ":" + value);
        resultStringBuffer.append(
```

LISTING 10.9 Continued

```java
                " Attribute:\t" + name + ":" + value);
    }

    public void startElement (String name)
    {
        System.out.println(" <" + name + ">\n");
        resultStringBuffer.append(" <" + name + ">\n");
    }

    public void endElement (String name)
    {
        System.out.println(" END <" + name + ">");
        resultStringBuffer.append(" END <" + name + ">\n");
    }

    public void charData (char ch[], int start, int length)
    {
        String contents = new String(ch, start, length);
        System.out.println("  Contents:\t" + contents);
        resultStringBuffer.append("  contents:" + contents + "\n");
    }

    public void ignorableWhitespace (char ch[],
    int start, int length)
    {
    }

    public void processingInstruction (String target,
    String data)
    {
    }

    public void error (String message,
    String url, int line, int column)
    {
        System.out.println("FATAL ERROR: " + message);
        System.out.println("  at " + url.toString() + ": line "
          + line + " column " + column);
        throw new Error(message);
    }

    void doParse (String url)
    throws java.lang.Exception
    {
```

LISTING 10.9   Continued

```java
        parser = new XmlParser();
        parser.setHandler(this);
        parser.parse(url, null, (String)null);
    }

    String escape (char ch[], int length)
    {
        StringBuffer out = new StringBuffer();
        for (int i = 0; i < length; i++) {
            switch (ch[i]) {
                case '\\':
                    out.append("\\\\");
                    break;
                case '\n':
                    out.append("\\n");
                    break;
                case '\t':
                    out.append("\\t");
                    break;
                case '\r':
                    out.append("\\r");
                    break;
                case '\f':
                    out.append("\\f");
                    break;
                default:
                    out.append(ch[i]);
                    break;
            }
        }
        return out.toString();
    }
}
```

LISTING 10.10   aelfredEventDemo.java

```java
import java.io.*;
import java.lang.String;
import javax.microedition.io.*;
import javax.microedition.lcdui.*;
```

10

USING XML IN
WIRELESS
APPLICATIONS

LISTING 10.10   Continued

```java
import javax.microedition.midlet.*;
import com.microstar.xml.*;

public class aelfredEventDemo extends MIDlet implements CommandListener {

    private String url;

    // GUI component for user to enter url for the xml document
    private Display myDisplay = null;
    private Form mainScreen;
    private TextField requestField;

    // GUI component for displaying xml data content
    private Form resultScreen;
    private StringItem resultField;

    // the "send" button used on mainScreen
    Command sendCommand = new Command("SEND", Command.OK, 1);
    // the "back" button used on resultScreen
    Command backCommand = new Command("BACK", Command.OK, 1);

    public aelfredEventDemo() {
        url = "http://www.webyu.com/book/mail.xml";

        // initializing the GUI components for entering url for the xml document
        myDisplay = Display.getDisplay(this);
        mainScreen = new Form("Type in a URL:");
        requestField =
          new TextField(null, url,
          100, TextField.URL);
        mainScreen.append(requestField);
        mainScreen.addCommand(sendCommand);
        mainScreen.setCommandListener(this);
    }

    public void startApp() throws MIDletStateChangeException {

        myDisplay.setCurrent(mainScreen);
    }

    public void pauseApp() {
    }
```

LISTING 10.10   Continued

```java
public void destroyApp(boolean unconditional) {
}

public void commandAction(Command c, Displayable s) {

    // when user clicks on "send" button on mainScreen
    if (c == sendCommand) {

        // retrieving the web url that user entered
        String urlstring = requestField.getString();

        String resultString = "";

        try {
            XmlParser parser = new XmlParser();
            DemoEventHandler myHandler = new DemoEventHandler();
            parser.setHandler(myHandler);
            parser.parse(urlstring, (String) null, (String) null);
            resultString = myHandler.getResultString();
        } catch (Exception e) {
            System.err.println("startApp: " + e);
        }

        // displaying the page content retrieved from web server
        resultScreen = new Form("XML Result:");
        resultField  =
          new StringItem(null, resultString);
        resultScreen.append(resultField);
        resultScreen.addCommand(backCommand);
        resultScreen.setCommandListener(this);
        myDisplay.setCurrent(resultScreen);

    } else if (c == backCommand) {
        // do it all over again
        requestField.setString(url);
        myDisplay.setCurrent(mainScreen);
    }
}
}
```

The output of `aelfredEventDemo` is as follows:

```
Start parsing document >>>>
Resolving entity: pubid=null, sysid=http://www.webyu.com/book/mail.xml
Starting external entity:  http://www.webyu.com/book/mail.xml
```

```
Resolving entity: pubid=null, sysid=http://www.webyu.com/book/mail.dtd
Starting external entity:  http://www.webyu.com/book/mail.dtd
Ending external entity:  http://www.webyu.com/book/mail.dtd
Doctype declaration:  mail, pubid=null,
sysid=http://www.webyu.com/book/mail.dtd
 <mail>
 <From>
  Contents:         yfeng@webyu.com
 END <From>
 <To>
  Contents:           somebody@somewhere.com
 END <To>
 <Cc>
  Contents:         jzhu@webyu.com
 END <Cc>
 <Date>
  Contents:      Fri, 12 Jan 2001 10:21:56 -0600
 END <Date>
 <Subject>
  Contents:     XML Parsers for J2ME MIDP
 END <Subject>
  Attribute:     language:english <Body>
  Contents:
     Ælfred, NanoXML and TinyXML are the three small-foot-print
     XML parsers that are suitable for J2ME MIDP applications.
     The sizes of these parsers range from 10K to 30K, which fit
     with memory budget of MIDP devices.
 <Signature>
  Contents:
     -----------------------------------------------------------
     Yu Feng
     yfeng@webyu.com
     http://www.webyu.com
 END <Signature>
  Contents:
 END <Body>
 END <mail>
Ending external entity:  http://www.webyu.com/book/mail.xml
Finish parsing document <<<<
```

Similar to the output generated by TinyXML, the DTD and entities are parsed and used correctly in this sample.

An Example of Using Ælfred's SAX Interface

To use Ælfred's SAX interface, both `aelfred_sax.jar` and `sax10_midp.jar` must be included
in your Java class path.

The sample program contains two Java files: `DemoHandler.java` and `aelfredSaxDemo.java`. `DemoHandler.java` is the same as Listing 10.7, and `aelfredSaxDemo.java` is almost identical to Listing 10.8 (`nanoSaxDemo.java`). The only difference between the two programs is that `nanoSaxDemo.java` (Listing 10.8) uses

```
Parser parser = ParserFactory.makeParser("nanoxml.sax.SAXParser");
```

and `aelfredSaxDemo.java` uses

```
Parser parser = ParserFactory.makeParser("com.microstar.xml.SAXDriver");
```

You should have figured out by now why this happens. It shows the benefit of using the standard SAX interface. The SAX API acts as a dashboard for XML parsers: The parsers from different vendors can be easily swapped in and out from an application without extra coding.

Here is the output from the `aelfredSaxDemo`:

```
Start parsing document >>>>
 <mail>
 <From>
  Contents:        yfeng@webyu.com
 END <From>
 <To>
  Contents:        somebody@somewhere.com
 END <To>
 <Cc>
  Contents:        jzhu@webyu.com
 END <Cc>
 <Date>
  Contents:     Fri, 12 Jan 2001 10:21:56 -0600
 END <Date>
 <Subject>
  Contents:     XML Parsers for J2ME MIDP
 END <Subject>
 <Body>
  Attribute:     language:english
  Contents:
     Ælfred, NanoXML and TinyXML are the three small-foot-print
     XML parsers that are suitable for J2ME MIDP applications.
     The sizes of these parsers range from 10K to 30K, which fit
     with memory budget of MIDP devices.

 <Signature>
  Contents:
     ----------------------------------------------------------
     Yu Feng
     yfeng@webyu.com
     http://www.webyu.com
```

```
END <Signature>
 Contents:

END <Body>
END <mail>
endDoc
Finish parsing document <<<<
```

You can find more information about the Ælfred parser at http://www.microstar.com/
aelfred.html.

> **NOTE**
>
> One thing we didn't show in this chapter is the actual CPU and memory consumption
> of the three parsers we've discussed. You should be able to run the sample programs
> against your own XML data to get a performance benchmark and decide for yourself
> which parser is more suitable for your application. Roughly speaking, the NanoXML
> and TinyXML parsers consume half amount of the memory that Ælfred parser con-
> sumes, and the TinyXML parser runs a little faster than the NanoXML and Ælfred
> parsers against our sample XML documents.

Summary

This chapter discussed three small-footprint XML parsers. TinyXML is a fairly small and fast
parser with an event-based interface at 10KB and a tree-based interface at 14KB. Because it is
licensed under GPL, certain restrictions apply for both commercial and non-commercial uses.
You should consult with the license agreement before packaging and distributing it with your
applications.

NanoXML has a simple tree-based interface that takes up only 9KB. This interface is simple
and easy to use, but it may not be suitable for parsing large XML files in the memory-
constrained environment. Some of the features, such as DTD support and entities, are not
supported by the NanoXML parser.

The event-based interfaces make Ælfred a fast XML parser. It supports a more complete set of
XML features than the other two parsers, but this parser is the biggest in size. The code size of
the proprietary event-based interface is about 18KB, and the size of the SAX compliant interface is about 30KB including the SAX 1.0 Java API.

In addition to the three XML parsers shown in this chapter, several other XML parsers (such as
the kXML parser) might be good candidates for J2ME MIDP applications. You can find more
information about kXML at http://www.kxml.de.

A Complete Example: MotoShop

IN THIS CHAPTER

MotoShop

So far, you have studied three major aspects of J2ME MIDP programming: the Graphical User Interface, network programming, and XML data exchange. Now it's time to take a look at a real-world example. This chapter examines a mobile commerce application: MotoShop. MotoShop is a client/server application that allows the user to comparison-shop for books via cell phone. The client component of MotoShop is a J2ME MIDlet program running on cell phones or two-way pagers. The server component is a Java servlet running on a Web server on the Internet.

The original version of MotoShop is the grand-prize winner of the J2ME Developer Contest held by Motorola in San Diego, California in August, 2000. The code example in this chapter is a modified version of MotoShop, which has a cleaner user interface, a better network communication mechanism, and a new data exchange format: XML.

To understand how you'd use MotoShop, imagine yourself sitting in a bookstore on a Saturday afternoon, enjoying a cup of coffee and browsing interesting books. You find a brand-new book on wireless J2ME programming that you want to buy. But before you make the purchase, you want to be sure you're getting the best price—you know it is usually cheaper to buy books online. You take out your cell phone, start the MotoShop application, enter the book's ISBN number, and get the prices instantly from various online bookstores, such as Amazon.com and borders.com. You can save money by buying the book from Amazon.com, and it will be delivered to you by next Monday.

System Architecture

The architecture of the client and server are illustrated in Figure 11.1.

As shown in Figure 11.1, MotoShop's client program is a MIDlet that runs on cell phones. The MIDlet takes the ISBN number that the user enters, sends a search request to MotoShop's search server via an http connection over a wireless network, receives the search results sent back from the search server, and displays them on the phone. (The search is not limited to the ISBN number; users can search books by keywords as well.) Once a search request is received, the search server simultaneously queries several online bookstores for price and book information. The search results are sent back to the client in XML format.

The client program contains four Java files:

- `MotoShop.java`—MotoShop is the main MIDlet program that users interact with.

- `BookHandler.java`—BookHandler extends the SAX 1.0 API's HandlerBase class. It is used in conjunction with the Ælfred XML parser to parse the search results received from the search server.

- `Book.java`—`Book.java` defines a book object that contains author, title, publisher, and price information.

- `Pair.java`—A `Pair` contains two fields: the name of a book site and its book price.

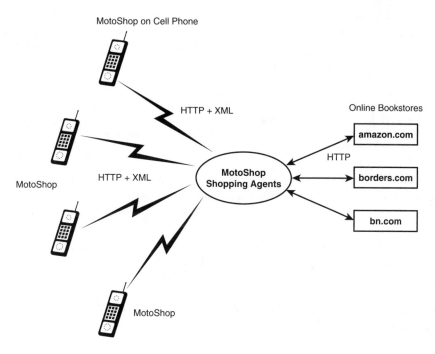

FIGURE 11.1

MotoShop system architecture.

The server program contains two Java files:

- `MotoShopServer.java`, a Java servlet program that receives search requests from the MIDlet client, calls the search routine to perform book search, and sends the search results back to the client in XML format.

- `BookSearch.java`, a Java file that provides the search routine to query book information and prices from various online bookstores.

The following sections show you the actual programs in the following order: GUI, networking, XML handling, and the server program.

The Graphical User Interface of MotoShop

We originally developed MotoShop with the MotoSDK (release 0.5). It was installed and tested on a pre-release Motorola iDEN3000 handset (code name: Condor). However, the Motorola MIDP implementation has been a work in progress for the past couple of months. The GUI APIs have changed considerably, as the implementation becomes more compliant with the MIDP 1.0 specifications. The program shown in this chapter is modified from the original version of MotoShop. We have tested it under both MotoSDK 0.7 (the latest) and Sun's reference MIDP.

MotoShop's Five Screens

The graphical user interface of the MotoShop client is fairly simple. The application contains five basic screens: `mainMenu`, `keywordScreen`, `isbnScreen`, `resultScreen`, and `detailScreen`. The application starts with the `mainMenu`, where users choose to search books either by keywords or by ISBN numbers. Users enter search keywords on the `keywordScreen` and enter the book's ISBN number on the `isbnScreen`. If the book search is based on ISBN number, the search results consist of only one book or none if ISBN is incorrect. If the book search is based on keywords, the search results often consist of multiple books instead of just one book. The titles of these books are displayed on the `resultScreen`. Users then select the book title to see the detail information.

Figures 11.2 through 11.5 are taken from MotoShop running under Sun's MIDP reference implementation.

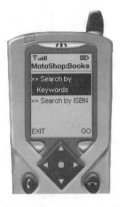

FIGURE 11.2

The `mainMenu`.

A Complete Example: MotoShop

CHAPTER 11

383

11

A COMPLETE
EXAMPLE:
MOTOSHOP

FIGURE 11.3

The keywordScreen.

FIGURE 11.4

The isbnScreen.

FIGURE 11.5

The resultScreen.

Figure 11.6 shows the upper part of the detailScreen. If you scroll down, you can see the lower part of the screen, which is shown in Figure 11.7.

FIGURE 11.6
The detailScreen *(1).*

FIGURE 11.7
The detailScreen *(2).*

Figure 11.8 shows the program flow of the MotoShop application. The mainDisplay.setCurrent() method is called to toggle from one screen to another among the five screens. For example, when the user navigates from mainMenu to keywordScreen, mainDisplay.setCurrent(keywordScreen) is called. The user's click and selection actions on the screens are handled in the commandAction() method.

The book list sent back from the search server is in XML format. Before the book list can be displayed on the resultScreen, it has to be parsed by an XML parser. We will talk more about this process in the section "XML Data Exchange in MotoShop" later in this chapter.

A Complete Example: MotoShop

CHAPTER 11

385

11

A COMPLETE
EXAMPLE:
MOTOSHOP

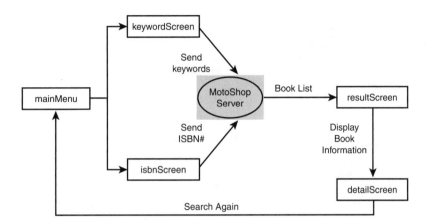

FIGURE 11.8

MotoShop program flow.

Listing 11.1 contains the code for MotoShop's client component.

LISTING 11.1 MotoShop.java

```java
import java.util.*;
import java.io.*;
import javax.microedition.lcdui.*;
import javax.microedition.midlet.*;
import javax.microedition.io.*;
import org.xml.sax.*;
import org.xml.sax.helpers.*;

public class MotoShop extends MIDlet
implements CommandListener {
    // Main display
    private Display mainDisplay;
    private Command motoshop_HOME =
    new Command("MAIN", Command.OK, 1);
    // the SUBMIT button used on the keywordScreen and isbnScreen
    private Command motoshop_SUBMIT =
    new Command("SUBMIT", Command.OK, 1);

    // Vector for storing the search results
    private Vector bookList;
    private Book currBook;

    // the mainMenu Screen and its commands
    List mainMenu;
```

LISTING 11.1 Continued

```java
private Command mm_GO =
new Command("GO", Command.OK, 1);
private Command mm_EXIT =
new Command("EXIT", Command.OK, 1);

// the keywordScreen
Form keywordScreen;
TextField keywordField;

// the isbnScreen
Form isbnScreen;
TextField isbnField;

// the resultScreen and its command
List resultScreen;
private Command rs_SELECT =
new Command("SELECT", Command.OK, 1);

// the detailScreen and its command
Form detailScreen;
private Command ds_BACK =
new Command("BACK", Command.OK, 1);

public MotoShop() {
    initMainMenuScreen();
    mainDisplay = Display.getDisplay(this);
}

public void startApp()
throws MIDletStateChangeException {
    mainDisplay.setCurrent(mainMenu);
}

public void pauseApp() {
}

public void destroyApp(boolean unconditional) {
}

// Initialize the "mainMenu" screen
void initMainMenuScreen() {
    mainMenu = new List("MotoShop:Books", List.IMPLICIT);
    mainMenu.append(">> Search by Keywords", null);
    mainMenu.append(">> Search by ISBN", null);
```

A Complete Example: MotoShop

CHAPTER 11

387

11

A COMPLETE
EXAMPLE:
MOTOSHOP

LISTING 11.1 Continued

```
        mainMenu.setCommandListener(this);
        mainMenu.addCommand(mm_GO);
        mainMenu.addCommand(mm_EXIT);
    }

    // Initialize the "keywordScreen" screen
    void initKeywordScreen() {
        keywordScreen = new Form("MotoShop:Books");
        keywordField =
        new TextField(
        "Enter keyword(s):", "java xml", 20, TextField.ANY);
        keywordScreen.append(keywordField);
        keywordScreen.append("Example: java xml");
        keywordScreen.setCommandListener(this);
        keywordScreen.addCommand(motoshop_SUBMIT);
        keywordScreen.addCommand(motoshop_HOME);
    }

    // Initialize the "isbnScreen" screen
    void initIsbnScreen() {
        isbnScreen = new Form("MotoShop:Books");
        isbnField = new TextField(
        "Enter ISBN#:", "1565924878", 10, TextField.NUMERIC);
        isbnScreen.append(isbnField);
        isbnScreen.append("Example: 1565924878");
        isbnScreen.setCommandListener(this);
        isbnScreen.addCommand(motoshop_SUBMIT);
        isbnScreen.addCommand(motoshop_HOME);
    }

    // Initialize the "resultScreen" screen
    void initResultScreen(Vector _bookList) {
        resultScreen = new List("Search Results:", List.IMPLICIT);
        Enumeration e = _bookList.elements();
        while (e.hasMoreElements())
        resultScreen.append(
        ">" + ((Book) e.nextElement()).getTitle(), null);
        resultScreen.setCommandListener(this);
        resultScreen.addCommand(rs_SELECT);
        resultScreen.addCommand(motoshop_HOME);
    }

    // Initialize the "detailScreen" screen
    void initDetailScreen(Book _currBook) {
```

LISTING 11.1   Continued

```java
        detailScreen = new Form("Detail Info:");
        detailScreen.append(
        "Title: " + _currBook.getTitle() + "\n");
        detailScreen.append(
        "Author: " + _currBook.getAuthor() + "\n");
        detailScreen.append(
        "Publisher: " + _currBook.getPublisher() + "\n");
        Vector priceList = _currBook.getPrices();
        for (int i = 0; i < priceList.size(); i++) {
            Pair price = (Pair) priceList.elementAt(i);
            detailScreen.append("> " + price.getSiteName() + "\n");
            detailScreen.append("    " + price.getPrice() + "\n");
        }
        detailScreen.addCommand(motoshop_HOME);
        detailScreen.addCommand(ds_BACK);
        detailScreen.setCommandListener(this);
    }

    // Command action handling
    public void commandAction(
    Command command, Displayable display) {
        Screen screen = (Screen) display;
        if (command == motoshop_HOME) {
            mainDisplay.setCurrent(mainMenu);
        } else if ( screen == mainMenu) {
            if ( command == mm_GO ) {
                // the keywordScreen is selected
                if (mainMenu.getSelectedIndex() == 0 ) {
                    initKeywordScreen();
                    mainDisplay.setCurrent(keywordScreen);
                    // the isbnScreen is selected
                } else if (mainMenu.getSelectedIndex() == 1 ) {
                    initIsbnScreen();
                    mainDisplay.setCurrent(isbnScreen);
                }
                // terminate the MotoShop MIDlet
            } else if ( command == mm_EXIT ) {
                destroyApp(false);
                notifyDestroyed();
            }
        } else if ( screen == keywordScreen) {
            if ( command == motoshop_SUBMIT ) {
                String requestString = keywordField.getString();
                if ( !requestString.equals("") ) {
```

LISTING 11.1 Continued

```
                        String queryString = "keyword=yes";
                        try {
                            // Send keyword search request to server
                            bookList = searchBooks(queryString, requestString);
                            // Display search results
                            initResultScreen(bookList);
                            mainDisplay.setCurrent(resultScreen);
                        } catch (IOException ioe) {
                            System.out.println("IO Error:" + ioe.toString());
                        }
                    }
                }
            } else if ( screen == isbnScreen) {
                if ( command == motoshop_SUBMIT) {
                    String requestString = isbnField.getString();
                    if ( !requestString.equals("") ) {
                        String queryString = "isbn=yes";
                        try {
                            // Send isbn search request to server
                            bookList = searchBooks(queryString, requestString);
                            // Display search results
                            initResultScreen(bookList);
                            mainDisplay.setCurrent(resultScreen);
                        } catch (IOException ioe) {
                            System.out.println("IO Error:" + ioe.toString());
                        }
                    }
                }
            } else if ( screen == resultScreen) {
                // A book is selected
                if ( command == rs_SELECT) {
                    int index = resultScreen.getSelectedIndex();
                    if ( index != -1) {
                        currBook = (Book) bookList.elementAt(index);
                        String requestString = currBook.getIsbn();
                        // if there is no pricing information on this book
                        // then use the book39s ISBN number to retrieve
                        // pricing information on the selected book
                        if (currBook.getPrices().size() == 0) {
                            String queryString = "isbn=yes";
                            try {
                                Vector tmpBookList =
                                searchBooks(queryString, requestString);
                                if (tmpBookList.size() > 0)
```

LISTING 11.1   Continued

```
                                    currBook = (Book) tmpBookList.elementAt(0);
                                    bookList.setElementAt(currBook, index);
                               } catch (IOException ioe) {
                                    System.out.println("IO Error:" + ioe.toString());
                               }
                          }
                          // Display book detail information
                          initDetailScreen(currBook);
                          mainDisplay.setCurrent(detailScreen);
                     } else {
                          mainDisplay.setCurrent(mainMenu);
                     }
                }
          } else if ( screen == detailScreen) {
                if ( command == ds_BACK) {
                     mainDisplay.setCurrent(resultScreen);
                }
          }
     }
}

private Vector searchBooks (
String queryString, String searchString) throws IOException {
     // the base URL of MotoShop39s search server
     String baseURL =
     "http://www.webyu.com/servlets/webyu/MotoShopServer?";
     // Vector used for storing search results
     Vector bookList = null;
     // I/O streams used for communicating with server
     HttpConnection hc = null;
     InputStream is = null;
     DataOutputStream os = null;
     try {
          // append the queryString to baseURL
          String urlString = baseURL + queryString;
          // need both read and write access
          hc = (HttpConnection)
          Connector.open(urlString, Connector.READ_WRITE);
          // set the request method to POST
          hc.setRequestMethod(HttpConnection.POST);

          // use the outputstream os to send the requestString
          os = hc.openDataOutputStream();
          byte[] searchStringBody = searchString.getBytes();
          for (int i = 0; i < searchStringBody.length; i++)
```

LISTING 11.1   Continued

```
            os.writeByte(searchStringBody[i]);
            os.flush();
            os.close();

            // use the inputstream to read the server39s response
            is = hc.openInputStream();
            // use the Aelfred XML parser to parse the response
            try {
                Parser parser =
                ParserFactory.makeParser("com.microstar.xml.SAXDriver");
                // BookHandler parses the XML string returned from server
                // and returns the results in a Vector
                BookHandler myHandler = new BookHandler();
                parser.setDocumentHandler(myHandler);
                InputSource inputSource = new InputSource(is);
                // start XML parsing
                parser.parse(inputSource);
                bookList = myHandler.getBooks();
            } catch (Exception se) {
                System.err.println("XML Error:" + se);
            }
        } finally {
            // freeing up i/o streams and http connection
            if (hc != null) hc.close();
            if (is != null) is.close();
            if (os != null) os.close();
        }
        return bookList;
    }
}
```

Several methods are defined in this MIDlet:

- The initMainMenuScreen() method initializes the mainMenu screen with two search options: Search By Keywords and Search By ISBN.

- The initKeywordScreen() method initializes the keywordScreen with a text input field where the user can enter search keyword(s).

- The initIsbnScreen() method initializes the isbnScreen with a text input field where the user can enter an ISBN number.

- The initResultScreen() method takes a Vector of book objects as a parameter and uses it to initialize the resultScreen with the book titles.

- The `initDetailScreen()`method takes a book object as a parameter and uses it to initialize the `detailScreen` with the book's title, author, publisher, and price quotes from various online bookstores.

- The `commandAction()` method handles all the user's interactions with the MIDlet and is responsible for switching from one screen to the next based on the user's key events.

- The `searchBooks()` method is responsible for sending search requests to the MotoShop's server program. It also receives the search results in XML format from the server, calls the Ælfred parser via its SAX interface to parse the search results, constructs a list of book objects using the parsed data, and returns the list of book objects in a `Vector`.

Network Communication in MotoShop

Datagrams were the only communication mechanism supported by Motorola's MIDP (release 0.5) at the time we developed MotoShop in June, 2000. We had no choice but to use datagrams for the remote communication between the client and the server. The original search engine program was developed as a background process that listened to a specific port preset in both the client and server code.

Because support for datagrams is not guaranteed on MIDP devices, using datagrams could potentially cause portability issues for your applications. For this reason, you should always consider http communication first when you're developing network-related J2ME applications. It is guaranteed to be available on MIDP cell phones and pagers. Plus, http is the most common network protocol used on the Internet; using http communication in your programs could mean less trouble in dealing with firewalls, because http's well-known port 80 is the least likely port to be blocked by firewalls.

In the current version of MotoShop, datagrams are replaced by the http connection. The old Java search engine is replaced by a Java servlet running on an Apache Web server with a JServ servlet engine.

Http Communications in MotoShop

Listing 11.2 shows the `searchBooks()` method in `MotoShop.java` that is responsible for sending requests to the server and receiving responses from the server. All the http connection-related code is highlighted in the code listing.

LISTING 11.2   The `searchBooks()` Method in `MotoShop.java`

```
private Vector searchBooks (
    String queryString, String searchString) throws IOException {
        // the base URL of MotoShop39s search server
        String baseURL =
```

A Complete Example: MotoShop

CHAPTER 11

393

11

A COMPLETE
EXAMPLE:
MOTOSHOP

LISTING 11.2 Continued

```
    "http://www.webyu.com/servlets/webyu/MotoShopServer?";
    // Vector used for storing search results
    Vector bookList = null;
    // I/O streams used for communicating with server
    HttpConnection hc = null;
    InputStream is = null;
    DataOutputStream os = null;
    try {
        // append the queryString to baseURL
        String urlString = baseURL + queryString;
        // need both read and write access
        hc = (HttpConnection)
        Connector.open(urlString, Connector.READ_WRITE);
        // set the request method to POST
        hc.setRequestMethod(HttpConnection.POST);

        // use the outputstream os to send the requestString
        os = hc.openDataOutputStream();
        byte[] searchStringBody = searchString.getBytes();
        for (int i = 0; i < searchStringBody.length; i++)
        os.writeByte(searchStringBody[i]);
        os.flush();
        os.close();

        // use the inputstream to read the server39s response
        is = hc.openInputStream();
        // use the Aelfred XML parser to parse the response
        try {
            Parser parser =
            ParserFactory.makeParser("com.microstar.xml.SAXDriver");
            // BookHandler parses the XML string returned from server
            // and returns the results in a Vector
            BookHandler myHandler = new BookHandler();
            parser.setDocumentHandler(myHandler);
            InputSource inputSource = new InputSource(is);
            // start XML parsing
            parser.parse(inputSource);
            bookList = myHandler.getBooks();
        } catch (Exception se) {
            System.err.println("XML Error:" + se);
        }
    } finally {
        // freeing up i/o streams and http connection
        if (hc != null) hc.close();
```

LISTING 11.2   Continued

```
        if (is != null) is.close();
        if (os != null) os.close();
    }
    return bookList;
}
```

When the client program is ready to send a request, an `HttpConnection hc` is established with the Web server where the server program is running:

```
hc = (HttpConnection)
        Connector.open(urlString, Connector.READ_WRITE);
```

`hc` is opened with the `READ_WRITE` flag, which indicates that this connection will be used for both sending messages to and receiving messages from the Web server. The `urlString` is a concatenation of the `baseURL` and the query string.

> **NOTE**
>
> The query string method is an explicit and easy way of passing a simple message from a client to a Web server. However, if a query string contains character whitespace, "&", or "/", the URL string must be encoded before it can be used.
>
> In J2SE, encoding a URL can be done easily by using the `encode()` method in the `URL` class. However, this method is not available in J2ME; you have to write your own encoding functions. In this case, you should consider using the http `POST` method, as we do to pass the search string to the server. The size of the contents you pass to the server is unlimited.

The `baseURL` `"http://www.webyu.com/servlets/webyu/MotoShopServer?"` is the URL of MotoShop's search engine. The query string indicates the search types: `"keyword=yes"` if the request is a keyword-based search or `"isbn=yes"` if the request is an ISBN-based search. The search engine's Java servlet will parse out the query string from the URL and perform searches accordingly.

In the `bookSearch()` method, a `DataOutputStream os` is opened for sending the search string. The search string can be either an ISBN number or search keywords, based on the search type. If the search request is keyword-based, the search string is the actual search keywords. If the search request is ISBN-based, the search string is the ISBN number. The string is transformed into a byte array and sent byte by byte via the `DataOutputStream os` to the server program. The http `POST` method is used:

```
hc.setRequestMethod(HttpConnection.POST);
```

If the search succeeds, an XML string that contains a list of books will be sent back from the server program. The `InputStream` is opened for receiving the XML string of a list of books:

```
is = hc.openInputStream();
```

The `InputStream` is then passed to an XML parser that reads and parses the contents of this XML string.

After the request-response communication is finished, all the I/O streams and the http connection should be freed up immediately. The `finally` block is a good place to perform the cleanups.

XML Data Exchange in MotoShop

In the original version of MotoShop, the search results are not in XML format. Instead, they appear like this:

```
"^^Java and XML^^Brett McLaughlin^^^^$31.96^^amazon.com^^$27.96^^bn.com..."
```

The first field, `Java and XML`, is the title of the book; the second field, `Brett McLaughlin`, is the author name; and so on. The string `^^` is used as the delimiter between the fields. The client program has to parse out these fields one by one. The parsing logic must be hard-coded in the program. This process is very cumbersome and unreliable.

XML would be a good fit for this type of data exchange. Equipped with the three XML parsers described in Chapter 10, "Using XML in Wireless Applications," we can replace the old message format with the standard XML format.

Here's an example of the search results sent back from the search engine:

```
<BOOKLIST>
<BOOK>
<TITLE>Java and XML</TITLE>
<AUTHOR>Brett McLaughlin</AUTHOR>
<PUBLISHER>O'Reilly</PUBLISHER>
<ISBN>1565924878</ISBN>
<SITENAME>borders.com</SITENAME>
<PRICE>$31.99</PRICE>
<SITENAME>bn.com</SITENAME>
<PRICE>$31.96</PRICE>
<SITENAME>amazon.com</SITENAME>
<PRICE>$27.96</PRICE>
</BOOK>
</BOOKLIST>
```

The XML parser used in our application is the Ælfred parser. A list of `Book` objects, `bookList`, is constructed based on the parsed data. The construction of the `Book` objects is handled through three callback methods defined in `BookHandler.java`, which is shown in Listing 11.3.

LISTING 11.3 BookHandler.java

```java
import java.util.*;
import java.io.*;
import org.xml.sax.*;

public class BookHandler extends HandlerBase {
    // the Vector used for storing search results
    private Vector bookList;
    // the current element being processed
    private String currTag;
    // the current Book object being constructed
    private Book currBook;
    private Pair currPricePair;

    BookHandler() {
        bookList = new Vector();
    }

    public Vector getBooks() {
        return bookList;
    }

    public void startElement (
    String name, AttributeList attributes)
    throws SAXException {
        currTag = name;
        if (currTag.equals("BOOK"))
        currBook = new Book();
        else if (currTag.equals("SITENAME"))
        currPricePair = new Pair();
        System.out.println("Start:<" + name + ">");
    }

    public void endElement (String name)
    throws SAXException {
        currTag = name;
        if (currTag.equals("BOOK"))
        bookList.addElement(currBook);
        else if (currTag.equals("PRICE"))
        currBook.addPricePair(currPricePair);
```

A Complete Example: MotoShop

CHAPTER 11

397

11

A COMPLETE
EXAMPLE:
MOTOSHOP

LISTING 11.3   Continued

```
        System.out.println("End:<" + name + ">");
    }

    public void characters (char ch[], int start, int length)
    throws SAXException {
        String contents = new String(ch, start, length);
        // populate the fields of current Book with parsed data
        if (currTag.equals("TITLE"))
        currBook.setTitle(contents);
        else if (currTag.equals("AUTHOR"))
        currBook.setAuthor(contents);
        else if (currTag.equals("PUBLISHER"))
        currBook.setPublisher(contents);
        else if (currTag.equals("ISBN"))
        currBook.setIsbn(contents);
        else if (currTag.equals("SITENAME"))
        currPricePair.setSiteName(contents);
        else if (currTag.equals("PRICE"))
        currPricePair.setPrice(contents);
    }
}
```

BookHandler derives from HandlerBase, the convenience class that implements the callback interface DocumentHandler in the SAX 1.0 Java API.

XML Callbacks

As mentioned in Chapter 10, each XML element has three callbacks: startElement(), characters(), and endElement(). When the parser reaches the start tag of an XML element, the startElement() method is called. The tag name and attributes are passed to the application by the parameters name and attributes. Similarly, the endElement() method is called when the parser reaches the end tag of an XML element. The method characters() is called when the parsers parses the character contents of the element. The contents is passed to the application by the parameter ch[]. The characters() method, ch[] is a character array, start is the starting index of the array, and length is the length of the contents in the character array.

Because SAX-compliant parsers are event-based parsers, they do not keep track of their current position in the XML document. currTag is used to make up for these memory lapses. It remembers the tag name that the parser is currently dealing with. If the value of currTag is "BOOK" when the startElement() method is called, it indicates that a new data block for a Book object is being parsed; therefore, a new Book object currBook is created. The currBook's fields are then populated by the characters() method. If the value of currTag is "BOOK" when the endElement() method is called, it indicates that the parser has finished receiving all the field values for currBook. The currBook is then added to the bookList. New currBook objects will be created and added to the bookList until the parser reaches the end of the XML data.

Using the Ælfred XML Parser

The highlighted lines in Listing 11.4 show how the Ælfred XML parser and its SAX interface are used in our program. Because the XML data transferred between the client program and the server program is fairly simple and small, any one of the three parsers examined in Chapter 10 should work. We chose the Ælfred parser for MotoShop just because it is our personal favorite. In addition, its SAX interface makes our application more portable; later on, if we decide to replace the Ælfred parser with another SAX-compliant parser, we can do so easily without extra code changes.

First, the parser is instantiated by

```
Parser parser =
  ParserFactory.makeParser("com.microstar.xml.SAXDriver");
```

The ParserFactory class can be found in the org.xml.helpers package that comes with the SAX API. It allows applications to allocate a SAX parser dynamically at runtime based either on the value of the org.xml.sax.parser system property or on a string containing the class name.

A SAX InputSource object is constructed from the InputStream is and passed to the Ælfred parser. The parser then reads the XML contents and calls the callback methods defined in the BookHandler to construct the bookList.

LISTING 11.4   The XML Parser Used by MotoShop

```
private Vector searchBooks (
    String queryString, String searchString) throws IOException {
        // the base URL of MotoShop39s search server
        String baseURL =
        "http://www.webyu.com/servlets/webyu/MotoShopServer?";
        // Vector used for storing search results
        Vector bookList = null;
        // I/O streams used for communicating with server
        HttpConnection hc = null;
        InputStream is = null;
        DataOutputStream os = null;
        try {
```

LISTING 11.4   Continued

```java
        // append the queryString to baseURL
        String urlString = baseURL + queryString;
        // need both read and write access
        hc = (HttpConnection)
        Connector.open(urlString, Connector.READ_WRITE);
        // set the request method to POST
        hc.setRequestMethod(HttpConnection.POST);

        // use the outputstream os to send the requestString
        os = hc.openDataOutputStream();
        byte[] searchStringBody = searchString.getBytes();
        for (int i = 0; i < searchStringBody.length; i++)
        os.writeByte(searchStringBody[i]);
        os.flush();
        os.close();

        // use the inputstream to read the server39s response
        is = hc.openInputStream();
        // use the Aelfred XML parser to parse the response
        try {
            Parser parser =
            ParserFactory.makeParser("com.microstar.xml.SAXDriver");
            // BookHandler parses the XML string returned from server
            // and returns the results in a Vector
            BookHandler myHandler = new BookHandler();
            parser.setDocumentHandler(myHandler);
            InputSource inputSource = new InputSource(is);
            // start XML parsing
            parser.parse(inputSource);
            bookList = myHandler.getBooks();
        } catch (Exception se) {
            System.err.println("XML Error:" + se);
        }
    } finally {
        // freeing up i/o streams and http connection
        if (hc != null) hc.close();
        if (is != null) is.close();
        if (os != null) os.close();
    }
    return bookList;
}
```

The `Book` and `Pair` Objects

The `Book` object is defined in `Book.java` (shown in Listing 11.5) for storing the information about a book. It contains member variables for the author name, the book title, the ISBN number, the publisher, and the prices. The quoted prices from online bookstores are stored in a `Vector` of `Pair` objects. The `Pair` object is defined in `Pair.java` (shown in Listing 11.6).

LISTING 11.5   `Book.java`

```java
import java.util.*;

public class Book {
    String title;
    String author;
    String publisher;
    String isbn;
    Vector prices;

    Book() {
        prices = new Vector();
    }

    void setTitle(String title) {
        this.title = title;
    }

    void setIsbn(String isbn) {
        this.isbn = isbn;
    }

    void setAuthor(String author) {
        this.author = author;
    }

    void setPublisher(String publisher) {
        this.publisher = publisher;
    }

    void addPricePair(Pair _pricePair) {
        prices.addElement(_pricePair);
    }

    String getTitle() {
        return title;
    }
```

LISTING 11.5 Continued

```java
    String getIsbn() {
        return isbn;
    }

    String getAuthor() {
        return author;
    }

    String getPublisher() {
        return publisher;
    }

    Vector getPrices() {
        return prices;
    }

    Pair getPricePair(int index) {
        return (Pair) prices.elementAt(index);
    }
}
```

`Pair.java` defines a value pair for storing the name of an online bookstore and the book price quoted from that online bookstore.

LISTING 11.6 `Pair.java`

```java
public class Pair {
    String sitename;
    String price;

    void setSiteName(String sitename) {
        this.sitename = sitename;
    }

    void setPrice(String price) {
        this.price = price;
    }

    String getSiteName() {
        return sitename;
    }

    String getPrice() {
        return price;
    }
}
```

MotoShop's Server Program

The original search engine of MotoShop is a background Java program running on a server connected to the Internet. It responds to the datagram requests through a preset port. Because we chose to use the http communication in our modified version, MotoShop's server program is changed to a Java servlet running on an Apache Web server with a JServ servlet engine.

The client program sends two pieces of information to the server program. The first piece of information is sent via the query string embedded in the URL: keyword=yes. The second piece of information is the actual search string sent via the http POST action.

The query string is the characters after the "?" in a URL. For example, keyword=yes is the query string in the following URL:

```
"http://www.webyu.com/servlets/MotoShopServer?keyword=yes"
```

There are two potential fields in this query string: keyword and isbn. In the Java servlet program, the value of a field in the query string can be retrieved by using the getParameter() method:

```
request.getParameter("keyword");
```

The search string is sent to the server program by the MIDlet client using the http POST method. To read the search string, a BufferedReader br is opened in the Java servlet:

```
BufferedReader br = request.getReader();
```

The content is read in by the readLine() method.

When the server program receives a keyword search request, the keyword search is started:

```
bookList = BookSearch.search("KEYWORD", requestString);
```

When the server program receives an ISBN search request, the ISBN search routine is started:

```
bookList = BookSearch.search("ISBN", requestString);
```

Listing 11.7 shows the Java servlet used in the search engine.

LISTING 11.7   MotoShopServer.java

```
/**
 * MotoShopServer.java is a Java servlet running on a Apache
 * Web server with a JServ servlet engine.
 * Once the servlet receives a search request from
 * MotoShop's MIDlet client, it then calls the search routine
 * BookSearch.search() to perform book search based on the request
 * type: either a keyword search or an ISBN search.
```

LISTING 11.7   Continued

```java
 * The search results are then sent back to MotoShop
 * client in XML format.
 */
import java.io.*;
import java.util.*;
import javax.servlet.*;
import javax.servlet.http.*;

public class MotoShopServer extends HttpServlet{

    public void init (ServletConfig config)
    throws ServletException {
        super.init(config);
    }

    // the doPost() method handles all the POST requests
    // received by the Java servlet
    public void doPost (
    HttpServletRequest request, HttpServletResponse response)
    throws ServletException, IOException {
        // Get the fields from the query string
        String keyword_flag = request.getParameter("keyword");
        String isbn_flag  = request.getParameter("isbn");

        // Get the request string sent by MotoShop client
        String requestString = "";
        try {
            BufferedReader br = request.getReader();
            requestString = br.readLine();
        } catch (Exception e) {
            System.err.println(e);
        }

        // The BookSearch.search() queries various online
        // bookstores to get price and book information.
        Vector bookList = null;
        StringBuffer messageBuffer = new StringBuffer();
        if ( keyword_flag != null ) {
            if ( keyword_flag.equalsIgnoreCase("YES"))
            bookList = BookSearch.search("KEYWORD", requestString);
        } else if ( isbn_flag != null ) {
            if ( isbn_flag.equalsIgnoreCase("YES"))
```

LISTING 11.7   Continued

```java
                bookList = BookSearch.search("ISBN", requestString);
        }

        // Construct the XML response string from the search results
        if ( bookList != null ) {
            messageBuffer.append("<BOOKLIST>");
            // Retrieving book information
            for (int i = 0; i < bookList.size(); i++) {
                messageBuffer.append("<BOOK>");
                Book book = (Book) bookList.elementAt(i);
                Vector prices = book.getPrices();
                messageBuffer.append(
                "<TITLE>" + book.getTitle() + "</TITLE>");
                messageBuffer.append(
                "<AUTHOR>" + book.getAuthor() + "</AUTHOR>");
                messageBuffer.append(
                "<ISBN>" + book.getIsbn() + "</ISBN>");
                messageBuffer.append(
                "<PUBLISHER>" + book.getPublisher() + "</PUBLISHER>");
                // Retrieving price information
                for (int j = 0; j < prices.size(); j++) {
                    Pair price = (Pair) prices.elementAt(j);
                    messageBuffer.append(
                    "<SITENAME>" + price.getSiteName() + "</SITENAME>");
                    messageBuffer.append(
                    "<PRICE>" + price.getPrice() + "</PRICE>");
                }
                messageBuffer.append("</BOOK>");
            }
            messageBuffer.append("</BOOKLIST>");
        } else {
            messageBuffer.append("<ERROR>No Book Found</ERROR>");
        }

        // send the response back to client
        PrintWriter out =
        new PrintWriter(response.getOutputStream(), true);
        response.setContentType("text/html");
        out.println(messageBuffer);
    }
}
```

The actual search routine is implemented in the class BookSearch.java. It is not shown here because it is proprietary and outside the scope of J2ME programming. If you would like to compile the `MotoShopServer.java` program, just comment out the two lines where the `BookSearch.search()` method is called in the program.

Summary

In this chapter, we used MotoShop as an example to demonstrate how to design GUI components, handle GUI events, parse XML data, and transfer XML data over an http connection in a wireless application using J2ME MIDP.

We also demonstrated the comparison-shopping capability of an m-commerce application. Similar functionality can be extended to other areas as well, such as travel reservations, music CDs, auctions, or even business-to-business markets. The application will be most useful with purchasing agents that can make the purchase on behalf of users from online stores with the personal information stored on the devices.

Data Synchronization for
Wireless Applications

IN THIS CHAPTER

Overview

Mobile communication device users enjoy the convenience of accessing information anywhere at anytime. However, the information they want may not always be on the device they carry. Their cell phones need the phone numbers on their PDAs, and the really important e-mail is always on the corporate server. Users want ubiquitous access to information and applications from the device at hand, plus they want to access and update this information on-the-fly.

Mobile users may not want to be constantly connected to a network and data stored over the network, especially if they have to pay for the airtime by the minute. They want to retrieve data from the network and store it on the mobile device, where they can access and manipulate it locally. Periodically, they can reconnect with the network to send any local changes back to the networked data repository, and learn about updates made to the data over the network while the device was disconnected. Occasionally, they also need to resolve conflicts between the updates made to the two copies. This reconciliation operation—where updates are exchanged and conflicts are resolved—is known as *data synchronization*.

Data stored on many different types of devices must be able to be synchronized, as shown in Figure 12.1. A proliferation of different proprietary data synchronization protocols exists for mobile devices. But they are incompatible with each other. Users using one kind of device may not be able to synchronize data with other kinds of devices, which causes a lot of inconvenience for the users.

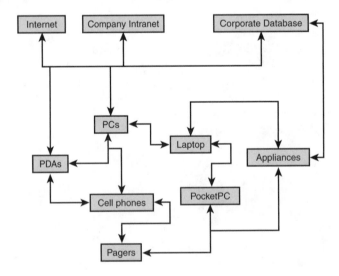

Figure 12.1

A universe of data to be synchronized.

To achieve universal synchronization, the following two requirements must be fulfilled:

- Synchronization servers must support synchronization with any mobile devices
- Mobile devices must be able to synchronize with any networked data

This chapter discusses a new open standard for universal data synchronization: SyncML. It then looks at data synchronization with J2ME MIDP. At the end of the chapter, you will see how to implement SyncML in J2ME MIDP applications.

SyncML

Over the last year, IBM, Lotus, Motorola, Nokia, Palm, Psion, and Starfish Software created a consortium to develop an open standard protocol for data synchronization: Synchronization Markup Language (SyncML). Since the release of the SyncML 1.0 specification at the end of last year, more than 600 companies have signed on to support SyncML.

SyncML is an XML-based standard. With SyncML, networked information can be synchronized with any mobile device, and mobile information can be synchronized with any networked applications. Using SyncML, any personal information, such as e-mail, calendars, to-do lists, and contact information will be consistent, accessible, and up to date, no matter where the information is stored. The data sources of synchronization include the sync server, corporate databases, and data stored on consumer service, PC, and mobile devices.

SyncML messages are represented in XML format. The MIME type, which is the industry standard for identifying different content types sent over the Internet, is registered for SyncML messages. The cleartext XML representation for SyncML messages is identified with MIME type `application/vnd.syncml-xml`. The WBXML binary representation for SyncML messages is identified with MIME type `application/vnd.synchml-wbxml`.

SyncML Protocols

SyncML consists of two parts: the SyncML representation protocol and the SyncML sync protocol. They both are based on the SyncML syntax. The sample program in this chapter primarily will demonstrate the features of the representation protocol.

The SyncML representation protocol focuses on organizing the data contents of the synchronization. It defines methods for uniquely naming and identifying records. It also defines the XML document type used to represent a SyncML message, such as common protocol commands and message containers. Synchronization command elements include `Add`, `Alert`, `Atomic`, `Copy`, `Delete`, `Exec`, `Get`, `Map`, `Replace`, `Search`, `Sequence`, and `Sync`.

The sync protocol focuses on managing the session operations of the synchronization. It defines the message flow between a SyncML client and server during a data synchronization session. The types of synchronization include one-way sync from the client only, one-way sync from the server only, two-way sync, and server alerted sync. This protocol also defines how to challenge authentication, how to initiate a synchronization session, and how to resolve conflicts.

SyncML messages can be transported over a wireless network using HTTP; Wireless Session Protocol (WSP), which is part of the WAP protocol suite; or Object Exchange protocol (OBEX) for local connectivity.

The SyncML protocol holds the promise of universal synchronization—and its commerce implications in the future could be even more revolutionary for mobile computing. You can find more information about SyncML at `http://www.syncml.org`.

Data Synchronization in J2ME MIDP

J2ME opens a door for Java developers to develop applications using one language that can run on all types of devices. This was never possible before Java.

We not only want our applications to run on as many devices as possible, we also want our data to be interoperable with as many devices as possible. It is very costly to have your application support many different synchronization technologies and protocols. It also increases the complexity of the resulting product. The added complexity of the networked data repository can create a barrier to installation and adoption by service providers. SyncML makes possible unified data synchronization among a more diverse set of devices and networked data.

HTTP Network Transport Protocol

Because all MIDP devices are required to support the HTTP protocol, it is a natural candidate to be the network transport protocol used in data synchronization between MIDP devices and sync servers.

Once an HTTP connection is established, one or more SyncML messages can be sent to the server by the SyncML client in the body of HTTP requests or received from the server in the body of HTTP responses.

The POST method is used to transfer the SyncML message in an HTTP request. The following information needs to be specified in a HTTP header:

- Cache control—Used to control the caching mechanisms in the request/response chain between the HTTP client and the HTTP server.
- Accepted date type—Used to specify which MIME types are acceptable in the response message.

- Accepted character set—Used to specify which character sets are acceptable in the response message.

- Transfer-encoding—Used to indicate what type of transformation has been applied to the message body.

- Authorization information—Used by an HTTP client to authenticate itself to the HTTP server.

- User agent—Used to identify the type of user agent originating the request.

The following is a sample HTTP header used in SyncML data synchronization:

```
POST ./servlet/syncit HTTP/1.1
Host: www.datasync.org
Accept: application/vnd.syncml-xml
Accept-Charset: utf-8
Accept-Encodings: chunked
Authorization: Basic QWxhZGRpbjpwcGVuIHNlc2FtZQ==
Content-Type: application/vnd.syncml-xml; charset="utf-8"
User-Agent: MIDP sync product
Content-Length: 1023
Cache-Control: no-store
Transfer-Encoding: chunked
```

Synchronizing a Calendar

The data synchronization protocol synchronizes networked data with many different devices, including handheld computers, mobile phones, automotive computers, and desktop PCs. Many types of data need to be synchronized including e-mail, calendar, contacts, bank accounts, company files and documents, product information, customer information, product prices, and so on. For example, a user could read his calendar from either a handheld or a mobile phone, and still maintain a consistent, updated record of which messages had been read. SyncML can be used to synchronize calendar information between MIDP devices and an Internet sync server. The calendar format used in SyncML is based on vCalendar version 1.0.

NOTE

vCalendar is an exchange format for personal scheduling information. It is an open specification based on industry standards such as the x/Open and XAPIA Calendaring and Scheduling API (CSA), the ISO 8601 international date and time standard, and the related MIME e-mail standards. It is applicable to a wide variety of calendaring and scheduling products and is useful in exchanging information across a broad range of transport methods. vCalendar is receiving wide industry adoption. You can find more information on vCalendar at http://www.imc.org/pdi/.

The following is an appointment example in vCalendar format:

```
BEGIN:VCALENDAR
VERSION:1.0
BEGIN:VEVENT
DTSTART:20000509T063000Z
DTEND:20000509T073000Z
SUMMARY:SyncML Briefing
DESCRIPTION;ENCODING=QUOTED-PRINTABLE:John Smith is =
 the presenter.=0D=0ASyncML is the topic.
CLASS:PUBLIC
CATEGORIES:APPOINTMENT
AALARM:20000509T061500Z
END:VEVENT
END:VCALENDAR
```

This vCalendar specifies that an appointment begins at 6:30 a.m. on May 9, 2000 and ends at 7:30 a.m. The subject of the appointment is "SyncML briefing." However, the calendar data format used by wireless applications or synchronization servers doesn't have to be the vCalendar format. If a data field of vCalendar is not supported in the local representation, the field will be ignored. When a SyncML message is generated, the fields that are only supported in the local format will not be included in the vCalendar object. The following is a SyncML message sent from a sync server to a sync client:

```
<SyncML>
    <SyncHdr>
    <VerDTD>1.0</VerDTD>
    <VerProto>SyncML/1.0</VerProto>
    <SessionID>1</SessionID>
    <MsgID>2</MsgID>
    <Target><LocURI>my_phone</LocURI></Target>
    <Source>
       <LocURI>http://www.webyu.com/servlets/samsbook</LocURI>
    </Source>
    </SyncHdr>
    <SyncBody>
      <Sync>
        <CmdID>1</CmdID>
        <Target><LocURI>CalendarDB</LocURI></Target>
        <Source><LocURI>samsbook.nsf</LocURI></Source>
        <!--Add a new record to the CalendarDB, record ID 2021 -->
        <Add>
          <CmdID>4</CmdID>
          <Meta><mi:Type>text/x-vCalendar</mi:Type></Meta>
          <Item>
            <Source><LocURI>2021</LocURI></Source>
```

Data Synchronization for Wireless Applications

CHAPTER 12

413

12

DATA
SYNCHRONIZATION
FOR WIRELESS

```
          <Data><!--The vCalendar data would be placed here.-->
            BEGIN:VCALENDAR
            VERSION:1.0
            BEGIN:VEVENT
            DTSTART:20010510T063000Z
            DTEND:20010510T073000Z
            SUMMARY:SyncML Test Checkpoint DB002021
            DESCRIPTION;ENCODING=QUOTED-PRINTABLE:John =
                Smith is still the presenter.=0D=0ASyncML =
                is the topic.
            CLASS:PUBLIC
            CATEGORIES:APPOINTMENT
            AALARM:20010510T061500Z
            END:VEVENT
            END:VCALENDAR
          </Data>
        </Item>
      </Add>
      <!--Delete a record, record ID 2022 -->
      <Delete>
        <CmdID>5</CmdID>
        <Meta><mi:Type>text/x-vCalendar</mi:Type></Meta>
        <Item>
          <Source><LocURI>2022</LocURI></Source>
        </Item>
      </Delete>
    </Sync>
  </SyncBody>
</SyncML>
```

This SyncML message contains two components: the SyncML header (SyncHdr) and the SyncML body (SyncBody). The SyncML header specifies routing and versioning information about the SyncML message. The SyncML body is a container for one or more SyncML Commands. The SyncHdr identifies the revisioning, the source, and the target of the data contents. The source is an Internet data repository at http://www.webyu.com/servlets/ samsbook. The target is a cell phone labeled "my phone." The SyncBody specifies the contents of the synchronization including the sync commands and data items. In this example, the target of this SyncBody is CalendarDB and the source is samsbook.nsf. The SyncBody contains two sync operations: Add and Delete.

Within the Add operation, a new record with source record id 2021 will be added to the target calendar database CalendarDB on the cell phone. In this example, only one record is added. The actual appointment data is represented in vCalendar format enclosed in a Data tag. The Delete operation is simple in this case. One record with target record id 2022 needs to be deleted.

Sample Implementation of SyncML: Mobile Scheduler

This section looks at how to extend the MobileScheduler application you worked on in Chapter 8, "Persistent Storage," to perform data synchronization with a test sync server. In this example, you will use SyncML as the data exchange protocol. The network protocol used in the example is the HTTP protocol. The synchronization involves two sync agents: one running on a MIDP device and one running on the sync server as depicted in Figure 12.2.

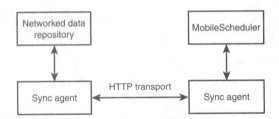

FIGURE 12.2
The Mobile Scheduler data synchronization system.

Sync Agent

Fully implementing SyncML is too lengthy and is not the intention of this chapter. The sync agents shown in this chapter implement only a subset of SyncML's functionality. The sync agents are almost identical at the client and server. Both client and server interact with the sync agent to make synchronization modifications.

In this example, you will only implement synchronization commands: Add, Delete, Sync, and Update. No conflicts or synchronization results will be checked. Authentication is not checked either.

Listing 12.1 shows the subset of SyncML markup language definitions used in this example.

LISTING 12.1 syncml_subset.dtd

```
<!--Copyright NoticeCopyright Notice
Copyright (c) Ericsson, IBM, Lotus, Matsushita Communication IndustrialCo.,
LTD, Motorola, Nokia, Palm, Inc., Psion, Starfish Software (2000).
All Rights Reserved.

Implementation of all or part of any Specification may require licenses under
third party intellectual property rights, including without limitation, patent
rights (such a third party may or may not be a Supporter). The Sponsors of the
```

LISTING 12.1 Continued

Specification are not responsible and shall not be held responsible in any
manner for identifying or failing to identify any or all such third party
intellectual property rights.

THIS DOCUMENT AND THE INFORMATION CONTAINED HEREIN ARE PROVIDED ON AN
"AS IS" BASIS WITHOUT WARRANTY OF ANY KIND AND ERICSSON, IBM, LOTUS,
MATSUSHITA COMMUNICATION INDUSTRIAL CO. LTD, MOTOROLA, NOKIA, PALM INC., PSION,
STARFISH SOFTWARE AND ALL OTHER SYNCML SPONSORS DISCLAIM ALL WARRANTIES,
EXPRESS OR IMPLIED, INCLUDING BUT NOT LIMITED TO ANY WARRANTY THAT THE USE OF
THE INFORMATION HEREIN WILL NOT INFRINGE ANY RIGHTS OR ANY IMPLIED WARRANTIES
OF MERCHANTABILITY OR FITNESS FOR A PARTICULAR PURPOSE. IN NO EVENT SHALL
ERICSSON, IBM, LOTUS, MATSUSHITA COMMUNICATION INDUSTRIAL CO., LTD, MOTOROLA,
NOKIA, PALM INC., PSION, STARFISH SOFTWARE OR ANY OTHER SYNCML SPONSOR BE
LIABLE TO ANY PARTY FOR ANY LOSS OF PROFITS, LOSS OF BUSINESS, LOSS OF USE OF
DATA, INTERRUPTION OF BUSINESS, OR FOR DIRECT, INDIRECT, SPECIAL OR EXEMPLARY,
INCIDENTAL, PUNITIVE OR CONSEQUENTIAL DAMAGES OF ANY KIND IN CONNECTION WITH
THIS DOCUMENT OR THE INFORMATION CONTAINED HEREIN, EVEN IF ADVISED OF THE
POSSIBILITY OF SUCH LOSS OR DAMAGE.

The above notice and this paragraph must be included on all copies of this
document that are made. -->
<!-- This DTD defines the SyncML DTD. The document type defines a common format
for representing data sychronization protocol data units.
This DTD is to be identified by the URI string "syncml:syncml".
Single element types from this name space can be referenced as follows:
    <element   xmlns='syncml:syncml'>blah, blah</element>
-->
<!-- Root or Document Element and -->
<!ELEMENT SyncML (SyncHdr, SyncBody)>
<!ELEMENT SyncHdr (VerDTD, VerProto, SessionID, MsgID, Target, Source)>
<!ELEMENT SyncBody (Sync)+>
<!-- Value must be one of "Add" | "Delete" | "Update". -->
<!ELEMENT Cmd (#PCDATA)>
<!-- Sync message unique identifier for command -->
<!ELEMENT CmdID (#PCDATA)>
<!-- Reference to command identifier -->
<!ELEMENT CmdRef (#PCDATA)>
<!-- Location displayable name -->
<!ELEMENT LocName (#PCDATA)>
<!-- Location URI -->
<!ELEMENT LocURI (#PCDATA)>
<!-- SyncML Message ID -->
<!ELEMENT MsgID (#PCDATA)>
<!-- Reference to a SyncML Message ID -->

12

DATA SYNCHRONIZATION FOR WIRELESS

LISTING 12.1 Continued

```
<!ELEMENT MsgRef (#PCDATA)>
<!-- SyncML session identifier -->
<!ELEMENT SessionID (#PCDATA)>
<!-- Source location -->
<!ELEMENT Source (LocURI, LocName?)>
<!ELEMENT SourceRef (#PCDATA)>
<!-- Target location information -->
<!ELEMENT Target (LocURI, LocName?)>
<!ELEMENT TargetRef (#PCDATA)>
<!-- SyncML specificaiton major/minor version info. -->
<!-- For this version of the DTD, the value is "1.0" -->
<!ELEMENT VerDTD (#PCDATA)>
<!-- Data sync protocol major/minor version -->
<!-- For example, "xyz/1.0" -->
<!ELEMENT VerProto (#PCDATA)>
<!-- Synchronization data elements -->
<!-- Item element type -->
<!ELEMENT Item (Target?, Source?, Data?)>
<!-- Actual data content -->
<!ELEMENT Data (#PCDATA)>
<!-- SyncML Commands -->
<!-- Add operation. -->
<!ELEMENT Add (CmdID, Item+)>
<!-- Delete operation. -->
<!ELEMENT Delete (CmdID, Item+)>
<!-- Update operation. -->
<!ELEMENT Update (CmdID, Item+)>
<!-- Synchronize Operation. -->
<!ELEMENT Sync (CmdID, Target?, Source?, (Add | Delete | Update)*)>
<!-- End of DTD Definition -->
```

You can download the complete DTD file for SyncML's representation protocol at
http://www.syncml.org/docs/syncml_represent_v10_20001207.dtd.

Data Representation

The data format for storing calendar information in MobileScheduler is different from
vCalendar format. We refer to the data format for storing data on MIPD devices as *internal
data format*, and we refer to the vCalendar format as *external data format*. By separating the
two formats, the application will have a better chance to incorporate any future changes made
to them. Listing 12.2 is the class for representing the external data format.

LISTING 12.2   CalendarItem.java

```java
import java.util.*;
import java.io.*;

/* for simplicity we assume we only deal with one server.
 * Thus, we do not need to store server_id.
 */
public class CalendarItem {
    Location target;    //local id
    Location source;    //remote id
    String start;
    String end;
    String summary;
    String description;
    String categories;
    String c_class;
    String alarm;

    // Set the default values
    public CalendarItem() {
        target=null;
        source=null;
        start = null;
        end = null;
        summary = null;
        description = null;
        categories = null;
        c_class = null;
        alarm = null;
    }

    public CalendarItem(Appointment app, SynchOption so) {
        this();
        source=new Location("calendarDB",
                            String.valueOf(app.getId()));
        target=new Location(so.getUrl()+":"+so.getUser(),
                            app.getRemoteId());
        start= toTimeString(app.getTime());
        end=toTimeString(app.getTime()+app.getLength()*60000);
        summary= app.getSubject();
    }

    private long fromTimeString(String str) {
        Calendar cal= Calendar.getInstance();
```

LISTING 12.2   Continued

```java
            //year
            cal.set(cal.YEAR, Integer.parseInt(str.substring(0,4)));
            //month
            cal.set(cal.MONTH, Integer.parseInt(str.substring(4,6))-1);
            //day
            cal.set(cal.DAY_OF_MONTH,
                    Integer.parseInt(str.substring(6,8)));
            //hour
            cal.set(cal.HOUR_OF_DAY,
                    Integer.parseInt(str.substring(9,11)));
            //minute
            cal.set(cal.MINUTE, Integer.parseInt(str.substring(11,13)));
            //second and millisecond
            cal.set(cal.SECOND, 0);
            cal.set(cal.MILLISECOND, 0);

            return cal.getTime().getTime();
        }

        private String toTimeString(long t) {
            StringBuffer sb= new StringBuffer();
            Calendar cal= Calendar.getInstance();
            cal.setTime(new Date(t));
            //year
            sb.append(cal.get(cal.YEAR));
            //month
            int m=cal.get(cal.MONTH)+1;
            if(m<10) sb.append(0);
            sb.append(m);
            //day
            int d=cal.get(cal.DAY_OF_MONTH);
            if(d<10) sb.append(0);
            sb.append(d);
            //mark it as UTC
            sb.append('T');
            //hour
            int h=cal.get(cal.HOUR_OF_DAY);
            if(h<10) sb.append(0);
            sb.append(h);
            //minute
            int min=cal.get(cal.MINUTE);
            if(min<10) sb.append(0);
            sb.append(min);
            //add second
```

LISTING 12.2   Continued

```
        sb.append("00Z");

        return sb.toString();
    }

    String getAlarm() {
        return alarm;
    }
    String getCategories() {
        return categories;
    }
    String getC_Class() {
        return c_class;
    }
    String getDescription() {
        return description;
    }
    String getEnd() {
        return end;
    }
    long getEndLong() {
        return fromTimeString(end);
    }
    String getStart() {
        return start;
    }
    long getStartLong() {
        return fromTimeString(start);
    }
    String getSummary() {
        return summary;
    }
    Location getTarget() {
        return target;
    }
    Location getSource() {
        return source;
    }
    void setAlarm(String _alarm) {
        alarm = _alarm;
    }
    void setCategories(String _categories) {
        categories = _categories;
    }
```

LISTING 12.2   Continued

```java
    void setC_Class(String _cclass) {
        c_class = _cclass;
    }
    void setDescription(String _description) {
        description = _description;
    }
    void setEnd(String _end) {
        end = _end;
    }
    void setStart(String _start) {
        start = _start;
    }
    void setSummary(String _summary) {
        summary = _summary;
    }
    void setTarget(Location _target) {
        target = _target;
    }
    void setSource(Location _source) {
        source=_source;
    }

    //set data from vCalendar data
    void setData(String _data) {
        int startIndex = 0;
        int endIndex = 0;
        int len = _data.length();
        while ((endIndex = data.indexOf('\n', startIndex)) != -1) {
            String aline = _data.substring(startIndex,
                                          endIndex).trim();
            if (aline.startsWith("DTSTART"))
                start = aline.substring(aline.indexOf(":")+1);
            else if (aline.startsWith("DTEND"))
                end = aline.substring(aline.indexOf(":")+1);
            else if (aline.startsWith("SUMMARY"))
                summary = aline.substring(aline.indexOf(":")+1);
            else if (aline.startsWith("DESCRIPTION"))
                description = aline.substring(aline.indexOf(":")+1);
            else if (aline.startsWith("CLASS"))
                c_class = aline.substring(aline.indexOf(":")+1);
            else if (aline.startsWith("CATEGORIES"))
                categories = aline.substring(aline.indexOf(":")+1);
            else if (aline.startsWith("AALARM"))
                alarm = aline.substring(aline.indexOf(":")+1);
```

LISTING 12.2   Continued

```
            startIndex = endIndex + 1;
        }
    }

    //output the item to SynchML string
    public String toSyncML() {
        StringBuffer sb = new StringBuffer("<Item>");
        sb.append("<Source><LocURI>").append(source.getLocUri())
          .append("</LocURI></Source>");
        sb.append("<Data>");
        sb.append("BEGIN:VCALENDAR\n");
        sb.append("VERSION:1.0\n");
        sb.append("BEGIN:VEVENT\n");
        sb.append("DTSTART:").append(start).append("\n");
        sb.append("DTEND:").append(end).append("\n");
        sb.append("SUMMARY:").append(summary).append("\n");

        if(description!=null) {
            sb.append("DESCRIPTION;ENCODING=QUOTED-PRITABLE:")
              .append(description).append("\n");
        }
        if(c_class!=null) {
            sb.append("CLASS:").append(c_class).append("\n");
        }
        if(c_class!=null) {
            sb.append("CLASS:").append(c_class).append("\n");
        }
        if(categories!=null) {
            sb.append("CATEGORIES:").append(categories)
              .append("\n");
        }
        if(alarm!=null) {
            sb.append("ALARM:").append(alarm).append("\n");
        }
        sb.append("END:VEVENT\n");
        sb.append("END:VCALENDAR\n");
        sb.append("</Data>");
        sb.append("</Item>");

        return sb.toString();
    }
}
```

The Location class used in CalendarItem is defined in Listing 12.3.

LISTING 12.3 Location.java

```java
public class Location {
    String locuri;
    String locname;

    public Location () {
        locuri=null;
        locname=null;
    }
    public Location (String name, String uri) {
        locname=name;
        locuri=uri;
    }
    String getLocUri() {
        return locuri;
    }
    String getLocName() {
        return locname;
    }
    void setLocUri(String _locuri) {
        locuri = _locuri;
    }
    void setLocName(String _locname) {
        locname = _locname;
    }
}
```

A data field of the internal data format that is not supported in the external data format, such as Appointment's location, is ignored when a CalendarItem object is created. The reverse is also true when an Appointment object of the internal data format is created. For example, CalendarItem's c_class and categories fields are ignored. To support synchronization, two data fields (remoteID and attribute) are added to the Appointment class. Listing 12.4 shows this modification of the Appointment class.

LISTING 12.4 Appointment.java

```java
/*
 * Appointment.java
 *
 */

import java.util.Calendar;
import java.util.Date;
import java.util.Vector;
```

LISTING 12.4 Continued

```java
import java.io.DataInputStream;
import java.io.DataOutputStream;
import java.io.ByteArrayInputStream;
import java.io.ByteArrayOutputStream;
import javax.microedition.rms.*;


public class Appointment  {
    private int  id;
    private String remoteId;   //identifier on remove synch server
    private long time;
    private int length;
    private String location;
    private String subject;
    private String attribute; //possible value "dirty", "delete"

    public Appointment () {
        id=0;
        remoteId="";
        time=0;
        length=0;
        location="";
        subject="";
        attribute="";
    }

    public Appointment(Date date) {
        this();
        time=date.getTime();
        length=30;
    }

    public Appointment(int _id,long _time, int _length,
                       String _location, String _subject) {
        this();
        id=_id;
        time=_time;
        length=_length;
        location=_location;
        subject=_subject;
        //set attribute
        attribute="dirty";
    }

    public Appointment (int _id, byte[] rec) {
        this();
```

LISTING 12.4   Continued

```
        id=_id;
        init_app(rec);
    }

    public Appointment (CalendarItem item) {
        this();
        if(item.getTarget() !=null &&
           item.getTarget().getLocUri()!=null) {
            id=Integer.parseInt(item.getTarget().getLocUri());
        }
        if(item.getSource() !=null &&
           item.getSource().getLocUri()!=null) {
            remoteId=item.getSource().getLocUri();
        }
        if(item.getStart()!=null) {
            time=item.getStartLong();
        }
        if(item.getEnd()!=null) {
            length=(int)(item.getEndLong()-time)/60000;
        }
        if(item.getSummary()!=null) {
            subject=item.getSummary();
        }
    }

    public void init_app(byte[] rec) {
        // parse the record
        ByteArrayInputStream bais= new ByteArrayInputStream(rec);
        DataInputStream dis= new DataInputStream(bais);
        try {
            remoteId=dis.readUTF();
            time=dis.readLong();
            length=dis.readInt();
            location=dis.readUTF();
            subject=dis.readUTF();
            attribute=dis.readUTF();
        }catch(Exception e){}
    }

    public byte[] toBytes() {
        byte data[]=null;
        try {
            ByteArrayOutputStream baos= new ByteArrayOutputStream();
            DataOutputStream dos= new DataOutputStream(baos);
```

LISTING 12.4 Continued

```
            dos.writeUTF(remoteId);
            dos.writeLong(time);
            dos.writeInt(length);
            dos.writeUTF(location);
            dos.writeUTF(subject);
            dos.writeUTF(attribute);
            data=baos.toByteArray();

            baos.close();
            dos.close();
        }catch(Exception e) {}
        return data;
    }

    public String getTimeString() {
        StringBuffer sb= new StringBuffer();
        Calendar cal= Calendar.getInstance();
        cal.setTime(new Date(time));
        sb.append(cal.get(Calendar.MONTH)+1).append("/");
        sb.append(cal.get(Calendar.DAY_OF_MONTH)).append("/");
        sb.append(cal.get(Calendar.YEAR)).append(" ");
        sb.append(cal.get(Calendar.HOUR_OF_DAY)).append(":");
        if(cal.get(Calendar.MINUTE)<10) sb.append(0);
        sb.append(cal.get(Calendar.MINUTE));

        return sb.toString();
    }
    public int  getId() {return id;}
    public void setId(int _id) { id=_id;}
    public String getRemoteId() {return remoteId;}
    public void setRemoteId(String _remoteId) {remoteId=_remoteId;}
    public long getTime() {return time;}
    public  void setTime(long _time){time=_time;}
    public int  getLength(){return length;}
    public void setLength(int _length) {length=_length;}
    public String getLocation() {return location;}
    public void setLocation(String _location){location=_location;}
    public String getSubject() {return subject;}
    public void setSubject(String _subject) {subject=_subject;}
    public String getAttribute() {return attribute;}
    public void setAttribute(String _attribute) {
    attribute = _attribute;
    }
}
```

Data Flow

The data flow of synchronization consists of many steps, as shown in Figure 12.3. We'll describe these steps in the following sections.

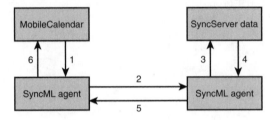

FIGURE 12.3
The data flow in a synchronization session.

Step 1: Collecting Data to be Synced On MIDP Devices

Before the client sync agent initiates a sync session with a sync server, it collects all calendar items that need to be synchronized. The items include newly created items for the Add operation, recently modified items for the Update operation, and items that the user wants to delete. Each item associates with a SyncML operation. The item and its associated SyncML operation are collectively represented by the SyncOperation class in Listing 12.5.

LISTING 12.5   SyncOperation.java

```java
import java.util.*;

public class SyncOperation {
    String command_id;
    String command;
    Vector items;

    SyncOperation(String _command) {
        command_id = null;
        command = _command;
        items = new Vector();
    }

    public String toSyncML() {
        StringBuffer sb = new StringBuffer();
        sb.append("<").append(command).append(">");
        sb.append("<CmdID>").append(command_id).append("</CmdID>");
        sb.append("<Meta><mi:Type>text/x-vCalendar</mi:Type></Meta>");
        for(Enumeration e = items.elements(); e.hasMoreElements(); ) {
```

LISTING 12.5   Continued

```
            CalendarItem calItem= (CalendarItem) e.nextElement();
            sb.append(calItem.toSyncML());
        }
        return sb.toString();
    }

    void addItem(CalendarItem _item) {
        items.addElement(_item);
    }
    String getCommand() {
        return command;
    }
    String getCommandId() {
        return command_id;
    }
    Vector getItems() {
        return items;
    }
    void setCommand(String _command) {
        command = _command;
    }
    void setCommandId(String _command_id) {
        command_id = _command_id;
    }
}
```

Sync operations are collected into a SyncOperations object, as shown in Listing 12.6.

LISTING 12.6   SyncOperations.java

```
import java.util.*;

public class SyncOperations extends Vector {
    String commandid;
    Location source;
    Location target;

    // Set the default values
    public SyncOperations() {
        super();
        commandid = null;
        source = null;
```

LISTING 12.6 Continued

```java
            target = null;
    }

    public String toSyncML() {
        StringBuffer sb = new StringBuffer();
        sb.append("<CmdID>").append(commandid).append("</CmdID>");
        sb.append("<Target><LocRUI>").append(target.getLocUri())
          .append("</LocRUI></Target>");
        sb.append("<Source><LocRUI>").append(source.getLocUri())
          .append("</LocRUI></Source>");
        for(Enumeration e= this.elements(); e.hasMoreElements(); ) {
            SyncOperation item = (SyncOperation) e.nextElement();
            sb.append(item.toSyncML());
        }
        return sb.toString();
    }

    String getCommandId() {
        return commandid;
    }
    Location getSource() {
        return source;
    }
    Location getTarget() {
        return target;
    }
    void setCommandId(String _commandid) {
        commandid = _commandid;
    }
    void setSource(Location _source) {
        source = _source;
    }
    void setTarget(Location _target) {
        target = _target;
    }
}
```

The sync operations are converted a SyncML message using the `toSyncML()` method of
`SyncOperations` and `SyncOperation`. Each SyncML message has a header that contains ses-
sionid, source, target locations, and authentication information. The header of a SyncML message is represented by a `SyncHeader` object, as shown in Listing 12.7.

LISTING 12.7   SyncHeader.java

```java
/* SyncHeader is used for storing Header information
 */
public class SyncHeader {
    String sessionid;
    String msgid;
    String msgref;
    Location source;
    String sourceref;
    Location target;
    String targetref;
    String verdtd;
    String verproto;
    String user;
    String passwd;

    // Set the default values
    public SyncHeader() {
        sessionid = null;
        msgid = null;
        msgref = null;
        source = null;
        sourceref = null;
        target = null;
        targetref = null;
        verdtd = null;
        verproto = null;
        user=null;
        passwd=null;
    }

    public void setDefault(SynchOption so) {
        sessionid=Integer.toString(1);
        msgid=Integer.toString(1);
        verdtd="1.0";
        verproto="SynchML/1.0";
        target= new Location();
        target.setLocUri(so.getUrl());
        source = new Location();
        source.setLocUri("my_phone");
        user=so.getUser();
        passwd=so.getPasswd();
    }

    public String toString() {
        StringBuffer sb= new StringBuffer();
```

LISTING 12.7   Continued

```java
        sb.append("<SyncHdr>");
        sb.append("<VerDTD>").append(verdtd).append("</VerDTD>");
        sb.append("<SessionID>").append(sessionid)
          .append("</SessionID>");
        sb.append("<MsgID>").append(msgid).append("<MsgID>");
        sb.append("<Target>");
        sb.append("<LocURI>").append(target.getLocUri())
          .append("</LocURI>");
        sb.append("</Target>");
        sb.append("<Source>");
        sb.append("<LocURI>").append(source.getLocUri())
          .append("</LocURI>");
        sb.append("</Source>");
        sb.append("<Cred>");
        sb.append("<Data>").append(user).append(":").append(passwd)
          .append("</Data>");
        sb.append("</Cred>");
        sb.append("</SyncHdr>");

        return sb.toString();
    }

    String getMsgId() {
        return msgid;
    }
    String getMsgRef() {
        return msgref;
    }
    String getSessionId() {
        return sessionid;
    }
    Location getSource() {
        return source;
    }
    String getSourceRef() {
        return sourceref;
    }
    Location getTarget() {
        return target;
    }
    String getTargetRef() {
        return targetref;
    }
    String getVerDTD() {
```

LISTING 12.7   Continued

```
        return verdtd;
    }
    String getVerProto() {
        return verproto;
    }
    void setMsgId(String _msgid) {
        msgid = _msgid;
    }
    void setMsgRef(String _msgref) {
        msgref = _msgref;
    }
    void setSessionId(String _sessionid) {
        sessionid = _sessionid;
    }
    void setSource(Location _source) {
        source = _source;
    }
    void setSourceRef(String _sourceref) {
        sourceref = _sourceref;
    }
    void setTarget(Location _target) {
        target = _target;
    }
    void setTargetRef(String _targetref) {
        targetref = _targetref;
    }
    void setVerDTD(String _verdtd) {
        verdtd = _verdtd;
    }
    void setVerProto(String _verproto) {
        verproto = _verproto;
    }
}
```

Step 2: Sending SyncML Messages to Sync Servers

After obtaining all the sync operations that the client wants the sync server to perform, the client sync agent establishes an HTTP connection with the sync server. It then passes the SyncML message in an HTTP request to the sync server.

Step 3: Updating Data on Sync Servers

The sync agent on the server side extracts the SyncML operations and updates the data on the sync server accordingly.

Step 4: Collecting Data to be Synced on Servers

The server sync agent collects information that needs to be passed to the client and converts it into a SyncML message. This message is sent in the HTTP response.

Step 5: Extracting SyncML Operations

The client sync agent waits for a server response after sending a request to the server until it reads an HTTP response that contains a SyncML message. A SAX XML parser (discussed in Chapter 10, "Using XML in Wireless Applications") is used to parse the SyncML message and extract SyncML operations. The SyncML handler is defined in Listing 12.8.

LISTING 12.8   SyncMLHandler.java

```java
import java.util.*;
import java.io.*;
import org.xml.sax.*;

/* this version of SyncML handler supports three
 * sync operations: Add, Delete, Update
 */
public class SyncMLHandler extends HandlerBase {

    // the Vector used for storing SyncOperations
    private SyncOperations operationList;
    // the current XML element being processed
    private String currTag;
    //the type of item (vcard or vcalendar)
    private String miType;
    // the current CalendarItem being parsed
    private CalendarItem currItem;
    // the current SyncOperation object being constructed
    private SyncOperation currOperation;
    // XML element tracker
    private Stack elementStack;
    // syncHeader
    private SyncHeader syncHeader;
    // source
    private Location currSource;
    // target
    private Location currTarget;

    SyncMLHandler() {
        elementStack = new Stack();
        syncHeader = new SyncHeader();
        operationList = new SyncOperations();
    }
```

LISTING 12.7   Continued

```java
public SyncOperations getOperations() {
    return operationList;
}
public void startElement (String name, AttributeList attributes)
        throws SAXException {
    currTag = name;
    if (currTag.equals("SyncHdr")) {
        elementStack.push(currTag);
    } else if (currTag.equals("SyncBody")) {
        elementStack.push(currTag);
    } else if (currTag.equals("Sync")) {
        elementStack.push(currTag);
    } else if (currTag.equals("Add") ||
                currTag.equals("Delete") ||
                currTag.equals("Update")){
        currOperation = new SyncOperation(currTag);
        elementStack.push(currTag);
    } else if (currTag.equals("Item")) {
        currItem = new CalendarItem();
        elementStack.push(currTag);
    } else if (currTag.equals("Source")) {
        currSource = new Location();
        elementStack.push(currTag);
    } else if (currTag.equals("Target")) {
        currTarget = new Location();
        elementStack.push(currTag);
    }
}
public void endElement (String name)
        throws SAXException {
    currTag = name;
    if (currTag.equals("SyncHdr")) {
        Object tmp = elementStack.pop();
    } else if (currTag.equals("SyncBody")) {
        Object tmp = elementStack.pop();
    } else if (currTag.equals("Sync")) {
        Object tmp = elementStack.pop();
    } else if (currTag.equals("Add") ||
                currTag.equals("Delete") ||
                currTag.equals("Update")) {
        Object tmp =  elementStack.pop();
        operationList.addElement(currOperation);
        currOperation = null;
```

12

**DATA
SYNCHRONIZATION
FOR WIRELESS**

LISTING 12.8 Continued

```java
            } else if (currTag.equals("Item")) {
                Object tmp= elementStack.pop();
                if(miType.equals("text/x-vCalendar")) {
                    currOperation.addItem(currItem);
                }
                currItem = null;
            } else if (currTag.equals("Source")) {
                Object tmp = elementStack.pop();
                String parent = (String) elementStack.peek();
                if (parent.equals("SyncHdr"))
                    syncHeader.setSource(currSource);
                else if (parent.equals("Item"))
                    currItem.setSource(currSource);
                else if (parent.equals("Sync"))
                    operationList.setSource(currSource);

                currSource = null;
            } else if (currTag.equals("Target")) {
                Object tmp = elementStack.pop();
                String parent = (String) elementStack.peek();
                if (parent.equals("SyncHdr"))
                    syncHeader.setTarget(currTarget);
                else if (parent.equals("Item"))
                    currItem.setTarget(currTarget);
                else if (parent.equals("Sync"))
                    operationList.setTarget(currTarget);
                currTarget = null;
            }
            currTag = "NULL";
        }
        public void characters (char ch[], int start, int length)
                throws SAXException {
            if (!currTag.equals("NULL")) {
                String contents = new String(ch, start, length);
                // populate the fields of current Book with parsed data
                if (currTag.equals("SessionID")) {
                    syncHeader.setSessionId(contents);
                } else if (currTag.equals("MsgID")) {
                    syncHeader.setMsgId(contents);
                } else if (currTag.equals("MsgRef")) {
                    syncHeader.setMsgRef(contents);
                } else if (currTag.equals("VerDTD")) {
                    syncHeader.setVerDTD(contents);
                } else if (currTag.equals("VerProto")) {
```

LISTING 12.8 Continued

```
                syncHeader.setVerProto(contents);
        } else if (currTag.equals("mi:Type")) {
            miType=contents;
        } else if (currTag.equals("Data")) {
            //we only implement vcalendar here. Ignore vcard
            if(miType.equals("text/x-vCalendar")) {
                currItem.setData(contents);
            }
        } else if (currTag.equals("LocURI")) {
            String parent = (String) elementStack.peek();
            if (parent.equals("Source"))
                currSource.setLocUri(contents);
            else if (parent.equals("Target"))
                currTarget.setLocUri(contents);
        } else if (currTag.equals("LocName")) {
            String parent = (String) elementStack.peek();
            if (parent.equals("Source"))
                currSource.setLocName(contents);
            else if (parent.equals("Target"))
                currTarget.setLocName(contents);
        } else if (currTag.equals("CmdID")) {
            String parent = (String) elementStack.peek();
            if (parent.equals("Sync"))
                operationList.setCommandId(contents);
            else if (parent.equals("Add") ||
                    parent.equals("Delete") ||
                    parent.equals("Update"))
                currOperation.setCommandId(contents);
        }
    }
}
public SyncOperations getOperationList() {
    return operationList;
}
}
```

Step 6: Updating Client Data

At last, the client sync agent updates the Mobile Calendar information according to the extracted SyncML operations.

Steps 3 and 4 are functions of a sync server. The sync server can be implemented using a Java servlet; this implementation is out of the scope of this chapter.

12

**DATA
SYNCHRONIZATION
FOR WIRELESS**

Steps, 1, 2, 5, and 6 are functions of a client sync agent. They are implemented in
SyncAgent.java, shown in Listing 12.9.

LISTING 12.9   SyncAgent.java

```java
import java.io.*;
import java.util.*;
import javax.microedition.midlet.*;
import javax.microedition.io.*;
import org.xml.sax.*;
import org.xml.sax.helpers.*;

public class SyncAgent {
    SyncOperations  toServer;
    SyncOperations fromServer;
    CalendarDB      calendarDB;
    SynchOption     so;

    public SyncAgent(CalendarDB calDB, SynchOption s) {
        calendarDB= calDB;
        so=s;
    }

    public boolean startSync() {
        boolean success=false;
        HttpConnection hc = null;
        DataInputStream dis = null;
        OutputStream os = null;

        try {
            hc = (HttpConnection)
            Connector.open(so.getUrl(), Connector.READ_WRITE);
            hc.setRequestMethod(HttpConnection.POST);

            StringBuffer sb= new StringBuffer("<SyncML>");
            //create SyncHeader
            SyncHeader syncHdr= new SyncHeader();
            syncHdr.setDefault(so);
            sb.append(syncHdr.toString());
            //create syncBody
            sb.append("<SyncBody>");
            sb.append("<sync>");
            int cmdid=1;
            toServer=calendarDB.getToSync(cmdid);
            toServer.setSource(new Location("","CalendarDB"));
            toServer.setTarget(new Location("",so.getUser()+".nsf"));
```

LISTING 12.9   Continued

```
sb.append(toServer.toSyncML());
sb.append("</Sync>");
//end
sb.append("<Final/>");
sb.append("</SyncBody>");
sb.append("</SyncML>");

os = hc.openOutputStream();
os.write(sb.toString().getBytes());
os.flush();
os.close();

/* clear the attribute of local copies if the operation
 * is Add or Update. Physically delete the local copy if
 * the operation is Delete.
 */
for(Enumeration e = toServer.elements();
    e.hasMoreElements(); ) {
    SyncOperation syncOp = (SyncOperation) e.nextElement();
    Vector items = syncOp.getItems();
    for(Enumeration eo = items.elements();
        eo.hasMoreElements();){
        CalendarItem calItem =
            (CalendarItem) eo.nextElement();
        Appointment app=calendarDB.getAppointmentById(
            Integer.parseInt(
                calItem.getSource().getLocUri()));
        app.setAttribute("");
        if(syncOp.getCommand().equals("Delete")) {
            calendarDB.delete(app);
        }
        else if(syncOp.getCommand().equals("Add") ||
            syncOp.getCommand().equals("Update")) {
            calendarDB.update(app);
        }
    }
}

dis = hc.openDataInputStream();
//dis = new DataInputStream(new
    ByteArrayInputStream(data.getBytes()));

//set xml parser
Parser parser =
```

LISTING 12.9   Continued

```
                ParserFactory.makeParser("com.microstar.xml.SAXDriver");
        SyncMLHandler syncmlHandler = new SyncMLHandler();
        parser.setDocumentHandler(syncmlHandler);

        //get all the operations
        InputSource inputSource = new InputSource(dis);
        parser.parse(inputSource);
        fromServer = syncmlHandler.getOperationList();

        // print out parsing results
        System.out.println("operationList_size:" +
                            fromServer.size());
        System.out.println("operationList_commandid:" +
                            fromServer.getCommandId());
        Location loc1;
        if ( (loc1 = fromServer.getSource())!= null )
           System.out.println("operationList_sourcelocuri:" +
                                loc1.getLocUri());
        if ( (loc1 = fromServer.getTarget())!= null )
           System.out.println("operationList_targetlocuri:" +
                                loc1.getLocUri());
        Enumeration e = fromServer.elements();

        // print out sync operations
        while (e.hasMoreElements()) {
            SyncOperation syncOperation =
                   (SyncOperation) e.nextElement();
            System.out.println(" command:" +
                                syncOperation.getCommand());
            System.out.println(" command_id:" +
                                syncOperation.getCommandId());
            Vector items = syncOperation.getItems();

            // print out data items in operations
            for (int i = 0; i < items.size(); i++) {
                CalendarItem item =
                    (CalendarItem) items.elementAt(i);
                if(syncOperation.getCommand().equals("Add")) {
                    /* we need map operation to complete this
                     * operation. Without it, we will synch this
                     * record later to pass local id to server.
                     */

                    calendarDB.mark4Synch(new Appointment(item));
                }
```

LISTING 12.9   Continued

```
                else if(syncOperation.getCommand()
                        .equals("Delete")) {
                    Appointment app = new Appointment(item);
                    app.setId(calendarDB.findIdByRemoteId(app));
                    calendarDB.delete(app);
                }
                else if(syncOperation.getCommand()
                        .equals("Update")) {
                    Appointment app = new Appointment(item);
                    app.setId(calendarDB.findIdByRemoteId(app));
                    calendarDB.update(app);
                }
                System.out.println("  item_summary:" +
                                    item.getSummary());
                System.out.println("  item_description:" +
                                    item.getDescription());
                System.out.println("  item_start:" +
                                    item.getStart());
                System.out.println("  item_end:" + item.getEnd());
            }
        }
        success=true;
    } catch (IOException ie) {
        System.err.println("IO Error:" + ie);
    } catch (SAXException se) {
        System.err.println("XML Error:" + se);
    } catch (Exception e) {
        System.err.println("Other Error:" + e);
    } finally {
        // freeing up i/o streams and http connection
        try { if (hc != null) hc.close();
        } catch (IOException ignored) {}
        try { if (dis != null) dis.close();
        } catch (IOException ignored) {}
        try { if (os != null) os.close();
        } catch (IOException ignored) {}
    }
    return success;
}
}
```

Linking with the Rest of the MobileScheduler Functions

The synchronization function is added to the main menu of the MobileScheduler application. When appointments are listed, appointments that need to be synced are marked with an asterisk (*), and appointments that are deleted locally are marked with a letter *d*. The updated Scheduler.java appears in Listing 12.10.

LISTING 12.10   Scheduler.java

```java
import java.util.Calendar;
import java.util.Vector;
import javax.microedition.midlet.*;
import javax.microedition.lcdui.*;

public class Scheduler extends MIDlet implements CommandListener{
    private Calendar        calendar;
    private List            menu;
    private AppointmentForm appForm=null;
    private List            appList=null;
    private SynchOptionForm soForm=null;
    private MyCalendar       mycalendar=null;
    private String[]         options={"Add Appointment",
                                "Retrieve Appointments",
                                "Synch Setup",
                                "Start sync",
                                "Calendar view"};

    private Display         display;
    private Command         backCommand= new Command("Back",
                                        Command.BACK, 1);
    private Command         exitCommand = new Command("Exit",
                                        Command.EXIT, 1);

    private CalendarDB      calendarDB;
    private Vector          apps;
    private SynchOption     so;
    public Scheduler() {
        //create an implicit choice list, and use it as start menu
        menu= new List("Scheduler", List.IMPLICIT,options,null);
        menu.addCommand(exitCommand);
        menu.setCommandListener(this);

        //get a calendar
        calendar=Calendar.getInstance();
```

LISTING 12.10   Continued

```
        calendarDB = new CalendarDB();
        so = new SynchOption();

        //retrieve display
        display=Display.getDisplay(this);
    }
    public void startApp() throws MIDletStateChangeException {
        display.setCurrent(menu);
    }

    /**
     * Pause the MIDlet
     */
    public void pauseApp() {
    }

    /**
     * Called by the framework before the application is unloaded
     */
    public void destroyApp(boolean unconditional) {
        //clear everything
        menu= null;
        calendar=null;
        display=null;
        appForm = null;
        appList =null;
        apps=null;
        soForm = null;
        mycalendar=null;
    }

    public void commandAction(Command c, Displayable d) {
        if(d==menu && c==List.SELECT_COMMAND) {
            switch(menu.getSelectedIndex()) {
            case 0: //Add appointment
                //create a new appointment from
                appForm = new AppointmentForm(display, menu,
                                              calendarDB);
                appForm.setAppointment(new
                             Appointment(calendar.getTime()));
                display.setCurrent(appForm);
                break;
            case 1: //retrieve appointments
                //create an appointment list
```

12

DATA SYNCHRONIZATION FOR WIRELESS

LISTING 12.7   Continued

```java
        appList = new List("Appointments", List.IMPLICIT);
        appList.addCommand(backCommand);
        appList.setCommandListener(this);

        //retrieve all the appointments
        apps= calendarDB.retrieveAll();
        for(int i=0; i<apps.size(); i++) {
            Appointment app= (Appointment) apps.elementAt(i);
            StringBuffer sb = new StringBuffer();
            if (app.getAttribute().equals("dirty")) {
                sb.append("* ");
            }
            else if(app.getAttribute().equals("delete")) {
                sb.append("d ");
            }
            else {
                sb.append("  ");
            }
            sb.append(app.getTimeString()).append(" ")
              .append(app.getSubject());
            appList.append(sb.toString(),null);
        }
        display.setCurrent(appList);
        break;
    case 2: //synchronization set up
        if(soForm==null) {
            //synchsetting
            soForm = new SynchOptionForm(display,menu,so);
        }
        display.setCurrent(soForm);
        break;
    case 3: //start synch
        Alert alert = new Alert ("Sync Info.");
        alert.setTimeout(Alert.FOREVER);
        if(new SyncAgent(calendarDB, so).startSync()) {
            alert.setString("Success!");
        }
        else {
            alert.setString("Failed!");
        }
        display.setCurrent(alert,menu);
        break;
```

LISTING 12.7   Continued

```
            case 4: // calendar view
                if(mycalendar==null) {
                    //mycalendar
                    mycalendar= new MyCalendar(display, menu,
                                                calendar);
                }
                display.setCurrent(mycalendar);
                break;
            default:
            }
        }
        else if(d==menu && c==exitCommand ) {
            calendarDB.close();
            destroyApp(true);
            notifyDestroyed();
        }
        else if(d==appList) {
            if(c==List.SELECT_COMMAND) {
                //create a new appointment from
                appForm = new AppointmentForm(display, menu,
                                                calendarDB);
                appForm.setAppointment(
                  (Appointment)apps.elementAt(
                      appList.getSelectedIndex()));
                    display.setCurrent(appForm);
            }
            else if(c==backCommand) {
                display.setCurrent(menu);
            }
        }
    }
}
```

In the preceding chapters, you developed functionality for adding, modifying, and deleting appointments. With the synchronization issue in mind, deleting an appointment on the MIDP device will only mark the record for deletion. The record will not be physically removed from data storage until a synchronization completes successfully. In addition, new methods are provided to collect appointments to be synchronized and to search appointments by data identification on a sync server. The updated version of CalendarDB.java is shown in Listing 12.11.

LISTING 12.11   CalendarDB.java

```java
/*
 * CalendarDB.java
 *
 */

import java.io.*;
import java.util.*;
import javax.microedition.rms.*;


public class CalendarDB  {
    RecordStore rs=null;
    public CalendarDB () {
        //the file to store the db is "calendarDB"
        String file="calendarDB";
        try {
            // open a record store named file
            rs = RecordStore.openRecordStore(file,true);
        }catch(Exception e) {
            System.out.println("Error: "+e.getMessage());
        }
    }

    //add new record
    public  synchronized boolean add(Appointment app) {
        if(rs==null) return false;
        boolean success=false;
        try {
            byte data[]=app.toBytes();
            rs.addRecord(data,0,data.length);
            success=true;
        }catch(Exception e) {
            System.out.println("Error: "+e.getMessage());
        }
        return success;
    }

    //close the record store
    public void close() {
        if(rs!=null) {
            try {
                rs.closeRecordStore();
            }catch (Exception e){}
```

LISTING 12.11   Continued

```
        }
    }

    //delete a record
    public synchronized boolean delete(Appointment app) {
        boolean success=false;
        int id=app.getId();
        if(id==0) return false;

        try {
            rs.deleteRecord(id);
            success=true;
        }catch(Exception e) {}

        return success;
    }

    //find the id of record whose remoteId match input's remoteId
    public int findIdByRemoteId(Appointment app) {
        if(rs==null) return 0;

        RecordEnumeration re=null ;
        int id=0;
        String remoteId= app.getRemoteId();
        try {
            if(rs.getNumRecords()==0) return 0;
            //try to find out the record id
            re= rs.enumerateRecords((RecordFilter)null,
                                    (RecordComparator)null, false);
            while(re.hasNextElement() &&id==0) {
                int i= re.nextRecordId();
                Appointment a = new Appointment(i, rs.getRecord(i));
                if(remoteId.equals(a.getRemoteId())) {
                    id=i;
                }
            }
        }catch(Exception e) {}
        finally{
            //clear
            try {
                if(re!=null) re.destroy();
            }catch(Exception e) {}
        }
```

12

DATA
SYNCHRONIZATION
FOR WIRELESS

LISTING 12.11   Continued

```
        return id;
    }

    public Appointment getAppointmentById(int id) {
        Appointment app=null;
        try {
            byte data[]=rs.getRecord(id);
            app= new Appointment (id, data);
        }catch(Exception e) {}
        return app;
    }

    /* Mark for delete. If there is a remote copy, the record
     *will not be physically removed until synchronization completes.
     */
    public boolean mark4Delete(Appointment app) {
        if(app.getRemoteId().length()==0) {//there is only local copy
            return delete(app);
        }
        app.setAttribute("delete");
        return update(app);
    }

    //set attribute to dirty.  Mark for Synchronization
    public boolean mark4Synch(Appointment app) {
        app.setAttribute("dirty");
        if(app.getId()>0) return update(app);
        else return add(app);
    }

    public Vector retrieveAll() {
        RecordEnumeration re=null;
        Vector apps= new Vector();
        try {
            //cutoff is 90 days old
            long cutoff=System.currentTimeMillis()-
                    new Integer(90).longValue()*24*60*60000;
            RecordFilter rf = new AppointmentFilter(cutoff);
            RecordComparator rc = new AppointmentComparator();
            re = rs.enumerateRecords(rf,rc,false);
            while(re.hasNextElement()) {
                int rec_id=re.nextRecordId();
                apps.addElement(
                    new Appointment(rec_id,rs.getRecord(rec_id)));
            }
```

LISTING 12.11   Continued

```
    }catch(Exception e) {}
    finally{
        //close the record store
        if(re!=null) re.destroy();
    }
    return apps;
}

public SyncOperations  getToSync(int startCmdId) {
    SynchOption so = new SynchOption();
    SyncOperations synOps= new SyncOperations();
    synOps.setCommandId(Integer.toString(startCmdId));
    int cmdId=startCmdId;
    RecordEnumeration re=null;
    try {
        re = rs.enumerateRecords(null, null, false);
        while(re.hasNextElement()) {
            int rec_id=re.nextRecordId();
            Appointment app= new
                    Appointment(rec_id,rs.getRecord(rec_id));
            if(app.getAttribute().equals("dirty") ||
               app.getAttribute().equals("delete")) {
                SyncOperation synOp=null;
                 cmdId++;
                 if(app.getAttribute().equals("dirty")) {
                     if(app.getRemoteId().length()>0) {//for update
                         synOp = new SyncOperation("Update");
                     }
                     else {
                         synOp = new SyncOperation("Add");
                     }
                 }
                 else if(app.getAttribute().equals("delete")) {
                     synOp = new SyncOperation("Delete");
                 }
                 synOp.addItem(new CalendarItem(app, so));
                 synOp.setCommandId(Integer.toString(cmdId));
                 synOps.addElement(synOp);
            }
        }
    }catch(Exception e) {}
    finally{
        //close the record store
        if(re!=null) re.destroy();
    }
```

LISTING 12.11 Continued

```
        return synOps;
    }


    public synchronized boolean update(Appointment app) {
        if(rs==null) return false;
        int id= app.getId();
        if(id==0) return false;

        boolean success=false;
        try {
            byte[] data= app.toBytes();
            rs.setRecord(id, data, 0, data.length);
            success=true;
        }catch(Exception e){}
        return success;
    }
}
```

Other classes used in the MobileScheduler applications are defined in
AppointmentComparator.java, AppointmentFilter.java, SynchOption.java, and
SynchOptionForm.java. These files are the same as the ones used in previous chapters, so they
are not listed here.

The XML parser class is included in the xml.jar file. To compile and execute the application,
you should include xml.jar in your classpath.

Sun's emulator contains bugs relating to RecordStore. These bugs will affect the execution of
this application. Thus, the examples are shown using Motorola's emulator.

NOTE

As the internal data format is changed to include synchronization information, the
old appointment data you stored in the record store needs to be deleted before you
save new appointments.

For example, suppose you start the scheduler and insert two appointments. You can retrieve them as shown in Figure 12.4. There is an asterisk in front of each appointment that indicates the appointment needs to be synchronized with the sync server. You can retrieve one appointment and delete it. The appointment will be physically removed from local storage because no entry on the sync server needs to be synchronized.

FIGURE 12.4

Retrieving appointments from the scheduler.

Now you want to sync appointments with a sync server. A test sync server is set up for this book. You can use the Synch Setting operation to set the SynchOption's URL as follows

```
http://64.28.105.108/servlets/webyu/SamsbookSyncAgent
```

which is served by www.webyu.com. After the URL has been set, you can start synchronization. If everything goes well, you will see a screen showing a successful message. After dismissing the screen, you can retrieve all appointments. You will see a screen like Figure 12.5. An appointment is added by the sync server. Because this appointment needs to be synced with the server again to update its local id to the server, it is marked with an asterisk.

You have now completed the MobileScheduler application, which contains four components: the GUI in which the user can modify and view appointments; persistent storage to hold all appointments; a calendar view for displaying monthly appointments; and a sync agent for data synchronization.

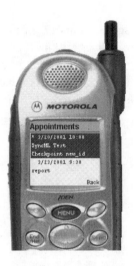

FIGURE 12.5

Retrieving all appointments after synchronization.

Summary

This chapter discussed the need for universal data synchronization. We talked about the SyncML open standard for data synchronization, and we implemented a subset of the SyncML protocol in the MobileScheduler example.

Appendixes

IN THIS PART

CLDC Class Libraries

IN THIS APPENDIX

java.lang

The class hierarchy of the java.lang package is shown in Figure A.1.

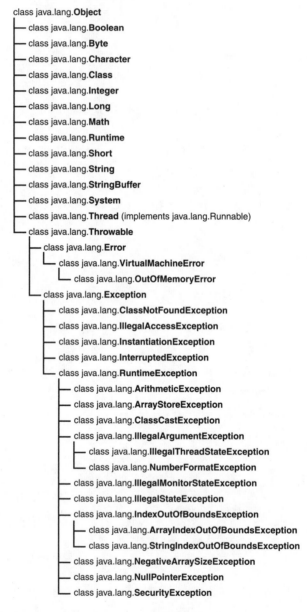

FIGURE A.1

The java.lang class hierarchy.

The interface hierarchy of the java.lang package is as follows:

```
interface java.lang.Runnable
```

java.io

The class hierarchy of the `java.io` package is shown in Figure A.2.

FIGURE A.2

The java.io *class hierarchy.*

The interface hierarchy of the `java.io` package is as follows:

```
interface java.io.DataInput
interface java.io.DataOutput
```

java.util

The class hierarchy of the `java.util` package is shown in Figure A.3.

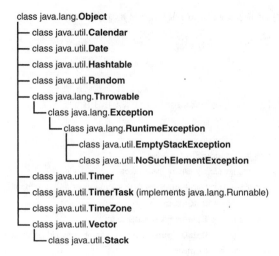

FIGURE A.3
The `java.util` *class hierarchy.*

The interface hierarchy of the `java.util` package is as follows:

```
interface java.util.Enumeration
```

javax.microedition.io

The class hierarchy of the `javax.microedition.io` package is shown in Figure A.4.

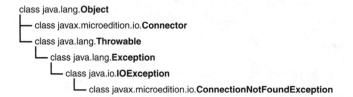

FIGURE A.4
The `javax.microedition.io` *class hierarchy.*

The interface hierarchy of the `javax.microedition.io` package is shown in Figure A.5.

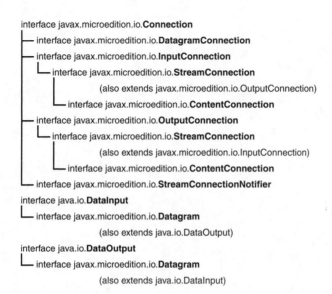

interface javax.microedition.io.**Connection**
├─ interface javax.microedition.io.**DatagramConnection**
├─ interface javax.microedition.io.**InputConnection**
│   └─ interface javax.microedition.io.**StreamConnection**
│   (also extends javax.microedition.io.OutputConnection)
│   └─ interface javax.microedition.io.**ContentConnection**
├─ interface javax.microedition.io.**OutputConnection**
│   └─ interface javax.microedition.io.**StreamConnection**
│   (also extends javax.microedition.io.InputConnection)
│   └─ interface javax.microedition.io.**ContentConnection**
└─ interface javax.microedition.io.**StreamConnectionNotifier**
interface java.io.**DataInput**
  └─ interface javax.microedition.io.**Datagram**
              (also extends java.io.DataOutput)
interface java.io.**DataOutput**
  └─ interface javax.microedition.io.**Datagram**
              (also extends java.io.DataInput)

FIGURE A.5

The javax.microedition.io *interface hierarchy.*

A

CLDC CLASS
LIBRARIES

MIDP Class Libraries

IN THIS APPENDIX

javax.microedition.midlet

The class hierarchy of the `javax.microedition.midlet` package is shown in Figure B.1.

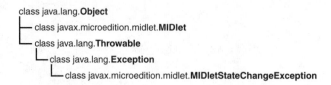

FIGURE B.1

The `javax.microedition.midlet` *class hierarchy.*

javax.microedition.lcdui

The class hierarchy of the `javax.microedition.lcdui` package is shown in Figure B.2.

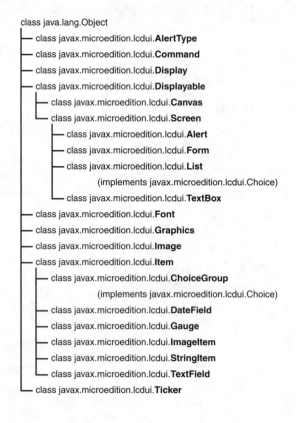

FIGURE B.2

The `javax.microedition.lcdui` *class hierarchy.*

The interface hierarchy of the `javax.microedition.lcdui` package is as follows:

```
interface javax.microedition.lcdui.Choice
interface javax.microedition.lcdui.CommandListener
interface javax.microedition.lcdui.ItemStateListener
```

javax.microedition.rms

The class hierarchy of the `javax.microedition.rms` package is shown in Figure B.3.

FIGURE B.3

The `javax.microedition.rms` *class hierarchy.*

The interface hierarchy of the `javax.microedition.rms` package is as follows:

```
interface javax.microedition.rms.RecordComparator
interface javax.microedition.rms.RecordEnumeration
interface javax.microedition.rms.RecordFilter
interface javax.microedition.rms.RecordListener
```

B

Resource Links

IN THIS APPENDIX

Documentation Resources

Java Community Process program:

`http://java.sun.com/aboutJava/communityprocess/`

Java 2 Platform, Micro Edition:

`http://java.sun.com/j2me/`

J2ME specification (JSR-068):

`http://java.sun.com/aboutJava/communityprocess/jsr/jsr_068_j2me.html`

CLDC and KVM:

`http://java.sun.com/products/cldc/`

KVM White Paper:

`http://java.sun.com/products/cldc/wp/`

CLDC specifications (JSR-030):

`http://java.sun.com/aboutJava/communityprocess/final/jsr030/index.html`

MIDP specifications (JSR-037):

`http://java.sun.com/aboutJava/communityprocess/final/jsr037/index.html`

PDA Profile specifications (JSR-075):

`http://java.sun.com/aboutJava/communityprocess/jsr/jsr_075_pda.html`

CDC and CVM:

`http://java.sun.com/products/cdc/`

CDC specifications (JSR-036):

`http://java.sun.com/aboutJava/communityprocess/first/jsr036/index.html`

Foundation Profile specifications (JSR-046):

`http://java.sun.com/aboutJava/communityprocess/first/jsr046/index.html`

Personal Profile specifications (JSR-062):

`http://java.sun.com/aboutJava/communityprocess/jsr/jsr_062_pprof.html`

RMI Profile specification (JSR-066):

`http://java.sun.com/aboutJava/communityprocess/jsr/jsr_066_rmime.html`

JavaPhone API:

`http://java.sun.com/products/javaphone/`

SyncML:

`http://www.syncml.org/`

WAP Forum:

`http://www.wapforum.org/`

Compact HTML (used by i-Mode):

`http://www.w3.org/TR/1998/NOTE-compactHTML-19980209/`

i-Mode:

`http://www.nttdocomo.com/i/`

Development Resources

Forte for Java:

`http://www.sun.com/forte/ffj/`

J2ME Wireless Toolkit:

`http://java.sun.com/products/j2mewtoolkit/`

JBuilder Foundation:

`http://www.borland.com/jbuilder/foundation/download/`

JBuilder Handheld Express:

`http://www.borland.com/jbuilder/hhe/`

CodeWarrior for J2ME:

`http://www.metrowerks.com/desktop/java/`

Sun's J2ME CLDC reference implementation:

`http://java.sun.com/products/cldc/`

Sun's J2ME MIDP reference implementation:

`http://java.sun.com/products/midp/`

LG Telecom ez-Java emulator:

`http://java.ez-i.co.kr/wire`

RIM BlackBerry Java IDE:

http://developers.rim.net/handhelds/software/jde/index.shtml

Motorola's MotoSDK:

https://commerce.motorola.com/idenonline/ideveloper/

IBM VisualAge Micro Edition and J9 VM:

http://www.embedded.oti.com/

Zucotto WHITEboard Software Development Kit:

http://www.zucotto.com/whiteboard/index.html

KVM-Interest Mailing List archives:

http://archives.java.sun.com/archives/kvm-interest.html

Wireless Developer Network:

http://www.wirelessdevnet.com

KVM World:

http://www.kvmworld.com

JScience Technologies (MathFP package floating-point support for KVM):

http://www.jscience.net/

Abstract Window Toolkit for J2ME CLDC KVM:

http://www.kawt.de/

SAX 1.0 Java API:

http://www.megginson.com/SAX/SAX1/index.html

TinyXML parser:

http://gibaradunn.srac.org/tiny/index.shtml

NanoXML parser:

http://nanoxml.sourceforge.net/index.html

Ælfred parser:

http://www.microstar.com/aelfred.html

NTT DoCoMo's Java for i-Mode

IN THIS APPENDIX

NTT DoCoMo

NTT DoCoMo is a formidable player in the wireless industry. After its huge success in deploying its i-Mode in Japan, the company recently released two Java-enabled i-Mode phones. The company is among the first few wireless vendors that endorse J2ME technologies on their wireless devices. In Chapter 2 you saw two i-Mode models that support J2ME: the F503i by Fujitsu and the P503i by Panasonic.

NTT DoCoMo also recently announced plans to expand into the U.S. market by investing in AT&T Wireless. Because most of the documentation on NTT DoCoMo's J2ME implementation is in Japanese, we feel that it is worthwhile to give you a quick overview of NTT DoCoMo's J2ME implementation in this appendix.

iApplis Versus MIDlets

NTT DoCoMo's J2ME implementation is not standard; in other words, it is compliant with CLDC but not with the MIDP 1.0 specification. J2ME applications developed using MIDP classes will not run on NTT DoCoMo J2ME phones.

NTT DoCoMo built its own proprietary class libraries to handle networking, graphical user interfaces, and so on, on top of KVM and CLDC. The last section of this appendix shows the class hierarchy of NTT DoCoMo's MIDP-equivalent class libraries. NTT DoCoMo says that the proprietary class libraries are optimized for DoCoMo's phones rather than the MIDP specifications. If you can read Japanese, you can find more information about NTT DoCoMo's Java platform at `http://www.nttdocomo.co.jp/i/java.html`.

Here are some of the main differences between the standard J2ME MIDP implementation and NTT DoCoMo's J2ME:

- NTT DoCoMo's class libraries are incompatible with MIDP 1.0 specifications. The MIDP classes are defined in the following four packages: `javax.microedition.midlet`, `javax.microedition.lcdui`, `javax.microedition.rms`, and `javax.microedition.io`. NTT DoCoMo's classes are defined in the following five packages: `com.nttdocomo.io`, `com.nttdocomo.util`, `com.nttdocomo.ui`, `com.nttdocomo.net`, and `javax.microedition.io`.

- An NTT DoCoMo J2ME application is called an iAppli instead of a MIDlet. A MIDlet is an MIDP application that extends the `javax.microedition.midlet.MIDlet` class and implements the following three methods: `startApp()`, `pauseApp()`, and `destroyApp()`. An iAppli must extend the `com.nttdocomo.ui.IApplication` class and implement the method `start()`. It also can optionally overwrite two other methods, `resume()` and `terminate()`, which are comparable to the `pauseApp()` and `destroyApp()` in a MIDlet.

- NTT DoCoMo offers similar Over-The-Air application deployment (discussed in Chapter 4). But the application descriptor used by DoCoMo is different from MIDP. First, the file extension is .jam instead of .jad. Second, the predefined fields are different. The following is a sample application descriptor file used by iAppli:

```
AppName = iAppliSample
AppVer = 1.0
PackageURL = iAppliSample.jar
AppSize = 811
KvmVer = 1.0
SPsize = 0
AppClass = iAppliSample
AppParam = arg1 arg2 arg3
LastModified = Wed, 07 March 2001 12:00:00
```

- Currently, the maximum size of an iAppli's JAR file is 10KB.

A Sample iAppli

Listing D.1 shows a sample iAppli program. All it does is display a textbox on the phone panel containing the message "Hello World".

LISTING D.1   iAppliSample.java

```java
import com.nttdocomo.ui.*;
import com.nttdocomo.util.*;

public class iAppliSample extends IApplication {

    Panel panel;
    TextBox textBox;

    public iAppliSample() {
        panel = new Panel();
        textBox = new TextBox("Hello World", 10, 5,
                              TextBox.DISPLAY_ANY);
    }

    public void start() {
        panel.add(textBox);
        Display.setCurrent(panel);
    }
}
```

You need to follow these steps to execute the Hello World iAppli:

1. Download and install NTT DoCoMo's emulator.

   The emulator's installation package I-JADEsetup.exe can be found at
   http://www.zentek.com/i-JADE/index.html. This emulator is called i-jade, which is
   provided by Zentek. Once you download it, execute the package and follow its instructions to install it.

2. Compile iAppliSample.java.

   We assume you already have JDK1.3 installed on your computer. In this case, JDK1.3 is
   installed on the C drive under the root directory. You can use the following command to
   compile the java file:

   ```
   C:\>c:\jdk1.3\bin\javac
       -classpath c:\i-jade\i-jade-p.jar iAppliSample.java
   ```

3. Preverify iAppliSample.class.

   We assume you already have the J2ME Wireless Toolkit installed on your computer. If
   you don't, please refer to Chapter 2 for installation instructions. You will need the preverifier and CLDC class library that come with J2MEWTK. In this case, the J2MEWTK is
   installed on the C drive under the root directory. Just like MIDlet applications, all iAppli
   class files have to be preverified before they are loaded by the class loader. You can use
   the following command to preverify the class file:

   ```
   C:\>c:\J2MEWTK\bin\preverify.exe -classpath
       c:\J2MEWTK\lib\midpapi.zip;c:\i-jade\i-jade-f.jar
       -d c:\appendix4\src  c:\appendix4\src
   ```

   The directory c:\appendix4\src is where iAppliSample.java and its class file are
   stored.

4. Package iAppliSample.class into a JAR file.

   You can use the following command to package the preverified iAppliSample.class
   into a JAR file:

   ```
   C:\>c:\jdk1.3\bin\jar cvf iAppliSample.jar iAppliSample.class
   ```

5. Create a JAM file.

   You need to create an application descriptor file as shown in the previous section and
   name it iAppliSample.jam.

6. Execute the iAppliSample program.

You can start i-jade's emulator using the following command:

```
C:>c:\jdk1.3\bin\java -jar c:\i-jade\i-jade-f.jar
```

You should be able to see the emulator's control panel, as shown in Figure D.1. At the prompt on the control panel, you can enter either the full path of the JAM file (such as **c:\appendixD\iAppliSample.jam**) or the full path of the class file (such as **c:\appendix4\iAppliSample.class**).

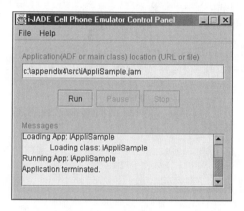

FIGURE D.1

Control panel of the i-jade emulator.

Figure D.2 shows the iAppliSample's execution result.

FIGURE D.2

The iAppliSample *result.*

Class Hierarchy

NTT DoCoMo's MIDP-equivalent APIs are contained in five packages: `com.nttdocomo.io`, `com.nttdocomo.util`, `com.nttdocomo.ui`, `com.nttdocomo.net`, and `javax.microedition.io`.

The class hierarchy of the `com.nttdocomo.io` package is shown in Figure D.3. The interface hierarchy of the `com.nttdocomo.io` package appears in Figure D.4.

```
class java.lang.Object
  └ class java.lang.Throwable (implements java.io.Serializable)
      └ class java.lang.Exception
          └ class java.io.IOException
              └ class com.nttdocomo.io.ConnectionException
```

FIGURE D.3

The `com.nttdocomo.io` *class hierarchy.*

```
interface javax.microedition.io.Connection
  └ interface javax.microedition.io.InputConnection
      └ interface javax.microedition.io.StreamConnection
            (also extends javax.microedition.io.OutputConnection)
          └ interface javax.microedition.io.ContentConnection
              └ interface com.nttdocomo.io.HttpConnection
interface javax.microedition.io.OutputConnection
  └ interface javax.microedition.io.StreamConnection
        (also extends javax.microedition.io.InputConnection)
      └ interface javax.microedition.io.ContentConnection
          └ interface com.nttdocomo.io.HttpConnection
```

FIGURE D.4

The `com.nttdocomo.io` *interface hierarchy.*

The class hierarchy of the `com.nttdocomo.net` package is shown in Figure D.5.

```
class java.lang.Object
  ├ class com.nttdocomo.net.URLDecoder
  └ class com.nttdocomo.net.URLEncoder
```

FIGURE D.5

The `com.nttdocomo.net` *class hierarchy.*

The class hierarchy of the `com.nttdocomo.ui` package is shown in Figure D.6. The interface hierarchy of the package `com.nttdocomo.ui` appears in Figure D.7.

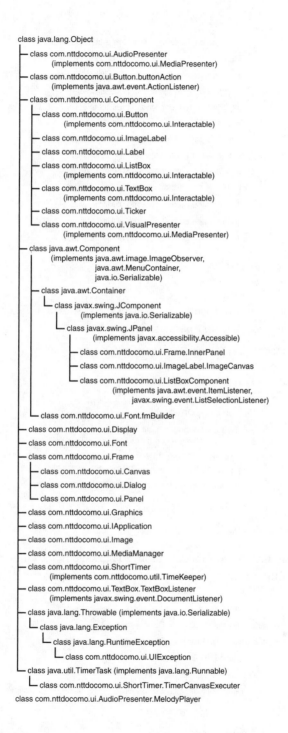

FIGURE D.6

The `com.nttdocomo.ui` *class hierarchy.*

interface com.nttdocomo.ui.ComponentListener

interface com.nttdocomo.util.EventListener
  └─ interface com.nttdocomo.ui.SoftKeyListener

interface com.nttdocomo.ui.FocusManager

interface com.nttdocomo.ui.Interactable

interface com.nttdocomo.ui.KeyListener

interface com.nttdocomo.ui.LayoutManager

interface com.nttdocomo.ui.MediaListener

interface com.nttdocomo.ui.MediaPresenter

interface com.nttdocomo.ui.MediaResource
  ├─ interface com.nttdocomo.ui.MediaData
  ├─ interface com.nttdocomo.ui.MediaImage
  └─ interface com.nttdocomo.ui.MediaSound

FIGURE D.7

The com.nttdocomo.ui *interface hierarchy.*

The class hierarchy of the com.nttdocomo.util package is shown in Figure D.8. The interface hierarchy of the com.nttdocomo.util package is as follows:

```
interface com.nttdocomo.util.EventListener
interface com.nttdocomo.util.TimeKeeper
interface com.nttdocomo.util.TimerListener
```

class java.lang.Object
  ├─ class com.nttdocomo.util.Timer
  │   (implements com.nttdocomo.util.TimeKeeper)
  └─ class java.util.TimerTask
         (implements java.lang.Runnable)
       └─ class com.nttdocomo.util.Timer.TimerExecuter

FIGURE D.8

The com.nttdocomo.util *class hierarchy.*

The class hierarchy of the javax.microedition.io package is shown in Figure D.9. The interface hierarchy of the javax.microedition.io package appears in Figure D.10.

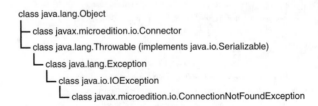

class java.lang.Object
  ├─ class javax.microedition.io.Connector
  └─ class java.lang.Throwable (implements java.io.Serializable)
       └─ class java.lang.Exception
            └─ class java.io.IOException
                 └─ class javax.microedition.io.ConnectionNotFoundException

FIGURE D.9

The javax.microedition.io *class hierarchy.*

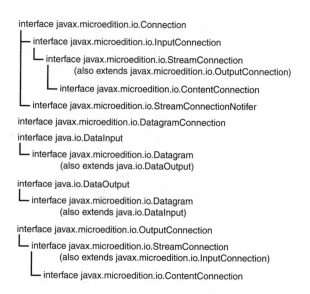

interface javax.microedition.io.Connection

    interface javax.microedition.io.InputConnection

      interface javax.microedition.io.StreamConnection
        (also extends javax.microedition.io.OutputConnection)

        interface javax.microedition.io.ContentConnection

    interface javax.microedition.io.StreamConnectionNotifer

interface javax.microedition.io.DatagramConnection

interface java.io.DataInput

    interface javax.microedition.io.Datagram
    (also extends java.io.DataOutput)

interface java.io.DataOutput

    interface javax.microedition.io.Datagram
    (also extends java.io.DataInput)

interface javax.microedition.io.OutputConnection

    interface javax.microedition.io.StreamConnection
    (also extends javax.microedition.io.InputConnection)

      interface javax.microedition.io.ContentConnection

Figure D.10

The `javax.microedition.io` *interface hierarchy.*

INDEX

Hey, you've got enough worries.

Don't let IT training be one of them.

Get on the fast track to IT training at InformIT,
your total Information Technology training network.

 | **www.informit.com** | **SAMS**

- Hundreds of timely articles on dozens of topics ■ Discounts on IT books from all our publishing partners, including Sams Publishing ■ Free, unabridged books from the InformIT Free Library ■ "Expert Q&A"—our live, online chat with IT experts ■ Faster, easier certification and training from our Web- or classroom-based training programs ■ Current IT news ■ Software downloads
- Career-enhancing resources

Other Related Titles

Java Thread Programming
Paul Hyde
0-672-31585-8
$34.99 US/$52.95 CAN

XML Development with Java 2
Michael Daconta and Al Saganich
0-672-31653-6
$49.99 US/$74.95 CAN

Java Security Handbook
Jamie Jaworski and Paul Perrone
0-672-31602-1
$49.99 US/$74.95 CAN

Developing Java Servlets, Second Edition
Jim Goodwill and Bryan Morgan
0-672-32107-6
$39.99 US/$59.95 CAN

Java 2 Micro Edition (J2ME) Application Development
Michael Kroll and Stefan Haustein
0-672-32095-9
$49.99 US/$74.95 CAN

Java GUI Development
Vartan Piroumian
0-672-31546-7
$34.99 US/$52.95 CAN

SAMS

www.samspublishing.com

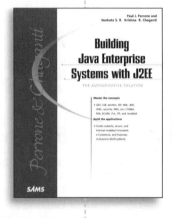

Building Java Enterprise Systems with J2EE
Paul Perrone and Krishna Chaganti
0-672-31795-8
$59.99 US/$89.95 CAN

Pure JSP: Java Server Pages
James Goodwill
0-672-31902-0
$34.99 US/$52.95 CAN

All prices are subject to change.